Mastering
Microsoft® Azure™
Infrastructure Services

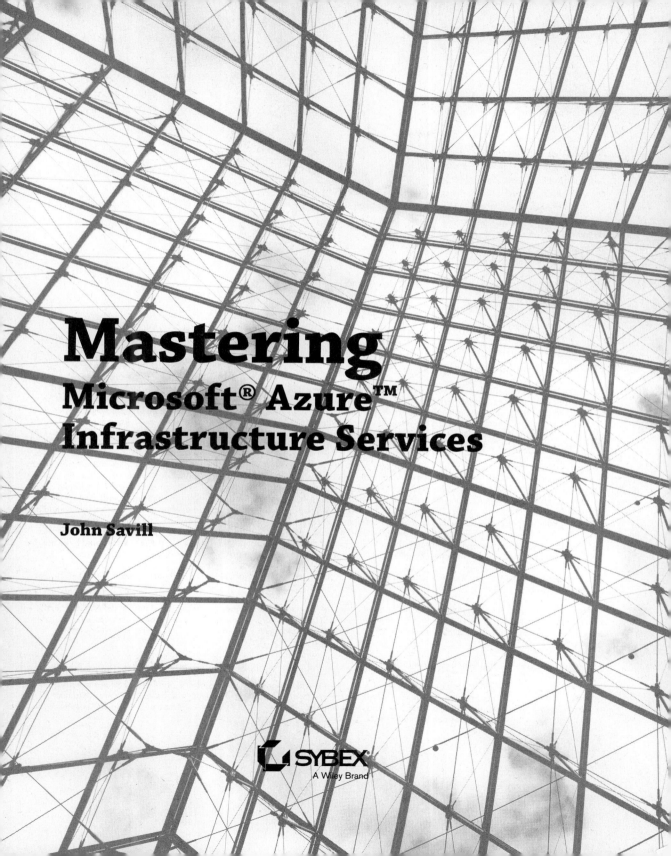

Mastering
Microsoft® Azure™
Infrastructure Services

John Savill

SYBEX
A Wiley Brand

Acquisitions Editor: Mariann Barsolo
Development Editor: Mary Ellen Schutz
Production Editor: Dassi Zeidel
Copy Editor: Liz Welch
Editorial Manager: Pete Gaughan
Production Manager: Kathleen Wisor
Associate Publisher: Jim Minatel
Book Designers: Maureen Forys, Happenstance Type-O-Rama; Judy Fung
Proofreader: Kathy Pope, Word One New York
Indexer: Ted Laux
Project Coordinator, Cover: Brent Savage
Cover Designer: Wiley
Cover Image: ©Getty Images, Inc./ColorBlind Images

For my wife Julie and my children Abby, Ben, and Kevin.

Acknowledgments

I could not have written this book without the help and support of many people. First, I need to thank my wife Julie for putting up with me being busier than usual for the last 6 months and for picking up the slack as always, and for always supporting the crazy things I want to do! My children, Abby, Ben, and Kevin, make all the work worthwhile and can always make me see what is truly important with a smile. Thanks to my parents for raising me to have the mind-set and work ethic that enables me to accomplish the many things I do while maintaining some sense of humor.

Of course, the book wouldn't be possible at all without the Wiley team: acquisitions editor Mariann Barsolo, developmental editor Mary Ellen Schutz, production editor Dassi Zeidel, copy editor Liz Welch, proofreader Kathy Pope, and indexer Ted Laux.

Many people have helped me over the years with encouragement and technical knowledge, and this book is the sum. The following people helped with specific aspects of this book, and I wanted to mention them for helping make this book as good as possible—if I've missed anyone, I'm truly sorry: Scott Guthrie, Mark Russinovich, Corey Sanders, Kenaz Kwa, Mahesh Thiagarajan, Michael Leworthy, David Powell, Paul Kimbel, Aashish Ramdas, Manoj K Jain, Praveen Vijayaraghavan, Andrew Zeller, Girija Sathyamurthy, Steve Cole, Eric Orman, Sirius Kuttiyan, Gautam Thapar, Karandeep Anand, Yochay Kiriaty, Justin Hall, Nasos Kladakis, Shreesh Dubey, Ganesh Srinivasan, Narayan Annamalai, Dean Wells, Leonidas Rigas, Ziv Rafalovich, Yousef Khalidi, Eamon O'Reilly, Beth Cooper, Rob Davidson, Brannan Matherson, Chris Van Wesep, Mark Sorenson, David Browne, Drew McDaniel, Pat Filoteo, Yu-Shun Wang, and Marie Honoré-Grant at Gartner.

About the Author

 John Savill is a technical specialist who focuses on Microsoft core infrastructure technologies, including Microsoft Azure, Windows, Hyper-V, System Center, and anything that does something cool. He has been working with Microsoft technologies for 20 years and is the creator of the highly popular NTFAQ.com website and a senior contributing editor for *Windows IT Pro* magazine. He has written six previous books covering Hyper-V, Windows, and advanced Active Directory architecture. When he is not writing books, he regularly writes magazine articles and white papers. He also creates a large number of technology videos, which are available on his YouTube channel, www.youtube.com/ntfaqguy, and regularly presents online and at industry-leading events, including TechEd and Windows Connections. As of this writing, he had just completed running his annual online John Savill Master Class—it was even bigger than last year. He also hosts annual Hyper-V, Azure, and PowerShell Master Classes that provide technical goodness.

Outside of technology, John enjoys teaching and training in martial arts including Krav Maga and Jiu-Jitsu; spending time with his family; and participating in any kind of event that involves running in mud, crawling under electrified barbed wire, running from zombies, and generally pushing limits. While writing this book, John was training for his first (and only) IRONMAN Triathlon.

John updates his blog at www.savilltech.com/blog with the latest news of what he is working on.

Contents at a Glance

Contents

Introduction

The book you are holding is the result of 20 years of experience in the IT world; over 15 years of virtualization experience that started with VMware, Virtual PC, and now Hyper-V; and many years focusing on public cloud solutions, especially Microsoft Azure. My goal for this book is simple: to make you knowledgeable and effective in architecting and managing an Azure-based public cloud environment. If you were to look at the scope of Azure functionality in a single book, that book would be the size of the *Encyclopedia Britannica*. My focus for this book is the infrastructure-related services, including virtual machines in Azure, storage, networking, and some complementary technologies. I will also show you how to automate processes using technologies such as PowerShell, how to integrate Azure with your on-premises infrastructure to create a hybrid solution, and how to use Azure as a disaster recovery solution. Although public cloud infrastructure services are relatively new, Microsoft is one of only two vendors that qualifies as a leader for a solution in the public cloud Infrastructure as a Service (IaaS) Gartner Magic Quadrant. In addition, Azure is being used by many of the largest companies in the world.

I am a strong believer that doing is the best way to learn something. I therefore highly encourage you to try out all the technologies and principles I cover in this book. Because Azure is a public cloud solution, you don't need any local resources except for a machine to connect to Azure and use PowerShell. Ideally, you will also have a small on-premises lab environment to test the networking to Azure and hybrid scenarios, but you don't need a huge lab environment. For most of the items, you can use a single Windows Server machine with 8 GB of memory to enable a few virtual machines to run concurrently. In this book, sometimes I provide step-by-step instructions to guide you through a process, sometimes I provide a link to an external source that already has a good step-by-step guide, and sometimes I provide a link to my videos to ensure maximum understanding.

This book was one of the most challenging I've written. Azure is updated so frequently that it was necessary to update the book while writing as capabilities changed. The Microsoft product group teams helped greatly, giving me early access to information and even environments to enable the book to be as current as possible. To keep the content relevant, I will be updating the digital version regularly, and I have created an application, Mastering Azure IaaS, available in the Windows Store, that provides easy access to the external links, videos, and code samples I use in this book (which I will also update with new information). You can download the application from www.savillte.ch/mstrazureapp and from the Windows Store (see the following figure). You must download this application and use it as a companion to the book. As you read each chapter, look at the application for videos and other information that will help your understanding. I do not specifically call these references out in the text of the book.

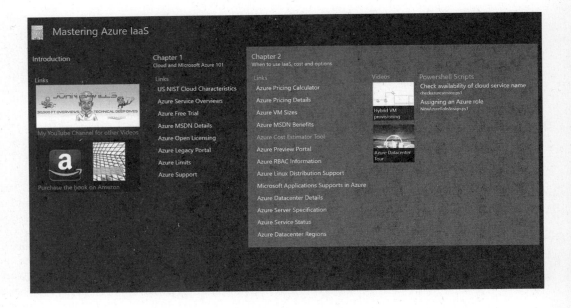

Who Should Read This Book

This book is intended for anyone who wants to learn Azure Infrastructure Services. If you have a basic knowledge, that will help but it's not a requirement. I start off with a foundational understanding of each technology and then build on that to cover more advanced topics and configurations. If you are an architect, a consultant, an administrator, or really anyone who just wants a better knowledge of Azure Infrastructure, this book is for you.

I make certain assumptions regarding the reader here:

◆ You have a basic Windows Server knowledge and can install Windows Server.

◆ You have a basic knowledge of PowerShell.

◆ You have access to the Internet and can sign up for a trial Azure subscription.

At times, I go into advanced topics that might seem over your head—don't worry. Focus on the elements that you do understand, implement and test them, and solidify your understanding. Then when you feel comfortable, come back to the more advanced topics. They will seem far simpler once you have a solid grasp of the foundational principles.

There are various Azure exams; the most relevant to this book is 70-533, Implementing Microsoft Azure Infrastructure Solutions. More information on that exam is available here:

```
https://www.microsoft.com/learning/en-us/exam-70-533.aspx
```

Will this book help you pass the exam? Yes, it will help. I took 70-533 cold without knowing what was in the exam and without any study and passed. Since most of my Azure brain is in this book, it will help. I advise you to look at the areas covered in the exam and use this book as one resource, but also use other resources that Microsoft references on the exam site. There were questions on the exam related to Azure Web Sites and Azure SQL Database, which I only cover at a very high level in this book. These included knowing the differences in the various SKUs of those services, so be sure that you know those details.

Another exam, 70-534, Architecting Microsoft Azure Solutions, is related to architecting Azure solutions. Infrastructure is only a small part of those solutions, and knowledge of development technologies is also required. This book does not contain enough information to pass 70-534, but it will help with the infrastructure-related elements.

What's Inside

Here is a glance at what's in each chapter.

Chapter 1: The Cloud and Microsoft Azure 101 provides an introduction to all types of cloud service and then dives into specifics about Microsoft's Azure-based offerings. After an overview of how Azure is acquired and used, Infrastructure as a Service (IaaS) is introduced with a focus on the difference between a best effort and a reliable service and why best effort may be better.

Chapter 2: When to Use IaaS: Cost and Options answers the first question posed by most organizations that have plenty of on-premises infrastructure: why would I use public cloud solutions? Key IaaS scenarios are explored to help you identify ways in which public cloud and IaaS solve problems that can't be easily replicated on-premises and how public cloud pricing can be compared to on-premises. The easiest way to understand the simplicity of IaaS is by creating a new VM and seeing the core options available. The sizes of virtual machines are explained and the cost and feature implications explored, including licensing of Windows and other applications such as SQL Server.

Chapter 3: Customizing VM Storage looks beyond creating a VM and explores customizing virtual machines with a focus on storage. Here you will learn about adding storage and the types of cache configuration, combining storage within virtual machines to make large volumes, how storage works and is replicated inside Azure and between datacenters, and more.

Chapter 4: Enabling External Connectivity explores offering services running from within Azure out to Internet-based consumers. Key concepts, such as endpoints for offering services and load-balanced services for greater service availability, are presented. Core Dynamic IP and Virtual IP concepts are introduced. You will see how they are used in Azure and under what circumstances they may change. The focus is on the difference between stopped and deprovisioned and the cost implications of those states. Local DNS will be explored, along with limitations for communication and name resolution between various cloud services in a subscription.

Chapter 5: Using Virtual Networks builds on the basic communication between VMs in a cloud service. Virtual networks provide a construct to enable customizable IP space configurations that are used by multiple cloud services, thus enabling cloud service–to–cloud service communication and on-premises communication. This chapter dives into architecting, configuring, and managing virtual networks and includes features such as reserving IP addresses for specific virtual machines via PowerShell. Availability sets and affinity groups are explained to help make multi-instance services as highly available as possible. Affinity groups form the foundation for virtual networks.

Chapter 6: Enabling On-Premises Connectivity builds on virtual networks and enables secure IP connectivity between services in Azure and those on-premises. This chapter starts by using site-to-site VPN gateway functionality, including basic configuration using software and hardware on-premises gateways, and then explores the point-to-site VPN options. The new ExpressRoute connectivity option is presented for organizations that do not want communication over the Internet and have connectivity and performance requirements that are not possible with the basic site-to-site VPN offering.

Chapter 7: Extending AD to Azure and Azure AD describes your next step once you've enabled IP connectivity between Azure and your on-premises infrastructure: joining VMs in Azure to the corporate Active Directory (AD). This can be done by accessing domain controllers on-premises once the appropriate DNS changes are configured in Azure virtual networks. Ultimately, you may want domain controllers in Azure, and this chapter looks at those options and best practices for offering your Active Directory in Azure. The Azure Active Directory is explained: how it compares to Active Directory Domain Services, how they can be connected, and some of the benefits of Azure Active Directory Premium.

Chapter 8: Setting Up Replication, Backup, and Disaster Recovery looks at a common scenario for using Azure for disaster recovery purposes. You should understand that this use case requires services and data to be replicated to Azure. This chapter looks at best practices and technologies for replicating various types of service, such as SQL Server, SharePoint, file services, and entire operating systems, to Azure. You will see what a failover would look like, and you'll learn about the possible implications. Using Azure as a backup target will also be explored, along with how to back up VMs running in Azure.

Chapter 9: Customizing Azure Templates and PowerShell Management dives into how to create your own Azure templates and key considerations that must be given focus if you want custom templates and existing VHDs to work in Azure. Capabilities for capturing existing Azure VMs and turning them into images are covered. PowerShell management is explored, along with the first steps to automation. The Azure VM Agent and its various capabilities are explained.

Chapter 10: Managing Hybrid Environments with System Center looks at architecting a hybrid environment. Here you will learn how to manage and monitor a true hybrid solution. The ability to move resources between on-premises and public cloud with custom code and with System Center is examined. How to perform bulk import and export operations for large-scale migrations is also covered. Advanced scenarios, such as a single provisioning service that automatically creates services on-premises or Azure based on the requirements of the VM request, are presented with a focus on a single experience for the end user.

Chapter 11: Completing Your Azure Environment dives into Azure services that, while not strictly Azure IaaS, provide benefits to a complete solution. You will be introduced to Azure Traffic Manager, Azure Web Sites, Azure Automation, Azure Scheduler, and more. Although IaaS is very powerful, the additional Azure capabilities covered in this chapter enable full-featured environments with the ultimate efficiency.

Chapter 12: What to Do Next brings everything together and looks at how to get started with Azure, how to plan your next steps, how to stay up-to-date in the rapidly changing world of Azure, and the importance of overall integration.

TIP Don't forget to download the companion Windows Store application, Mastering Azure IaaS, from www.savillte.ch/mstrazureapp.

The Mastering Series

The *Mastering* series from Sybex provides outstanding instruction for readers with intermediate and advanced skills, in the form of top-notch training and development for those already working in their field and clear, serious education for those aspiring to become pros. Every *Mastering* book includes:

- Real-World Scenarios, ranging from case studies to interviews, that show how the tool, technique, or knowledge presented is applied in actual practice.

- Skill-based instruction, with chapters organized around real tasks rather than abstract concepts or subjects.

- Self-review test questions, so you can be certain you're equipped to do the job right.

How to Contact the Author

I welcome feedback from you about this book or about books you'd like to see from me in the future. You can reach me by writing to john@savilltech.com. For more information about my work, visit my website at www.savilltech.com.

Sybex strives to keep you supplied with the latest tools and information you need for your work. Please check their website at www.sybex.com/go/masteringazure, where we'll post additional content and updates that supplement this book should the need arise.

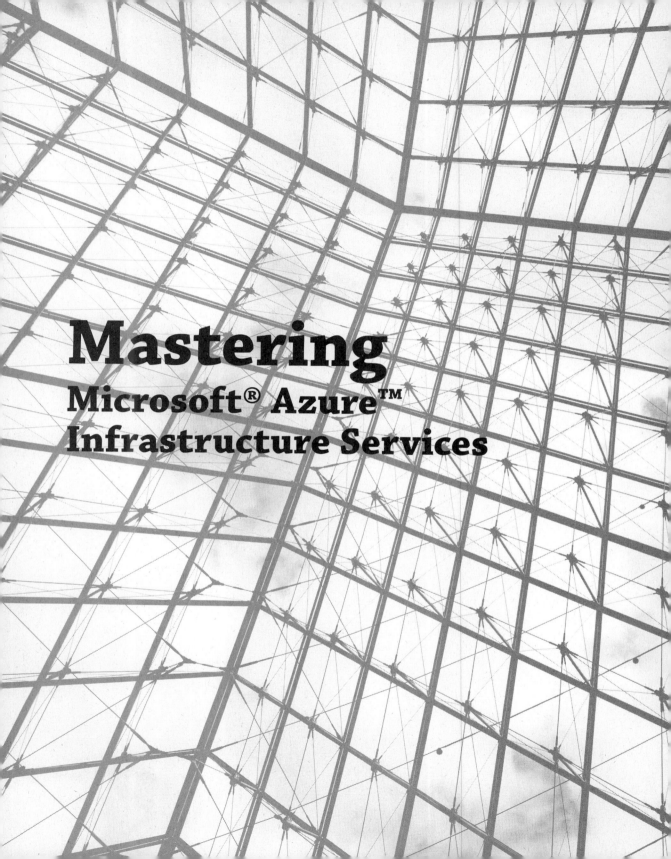

Mastering
Microsoft® Azure™
Infrastructure Services

## Chapter 1

The Cloud and Microsoft Azure 101

This chapter focuses on changes that are impacting every organization's thinking regarding infrastructure, datacenters, and ways to offer services. "As-a-Service" offerings—both on-premises and hosted by partners, and accessed over the Internet in the form of the public cloud—present new opportunities for organizations to operate.

Microsoft's solution for many public cloud services is its Azure service, which offers hundreds of capabilities that are constantly being updated. This chapter will provide an overview of the Microsoft Azure solution stack before examining various types of Infrastructure as a Service (IaaS) and how Azure services can be procured.

In this chapter, you will learn to

- ◆ Articulate the different types of "as-a-Service"

- ◆ Identify key scenarios where the public cloud provides the most optimal service

- ◆ Understand how to get started consuming Microsoft Azure services

Understanding the Cloud (or Why Everyone Should Play *Titanfall*)

When I talk to people about Azure or even the public cloud in general, where possible I start the conversation by playing *Titanfall* (www.titanfall.com), a game published by Electronic Arts. The game is primarily a first-person shooter, but in addition to running around as a normal person, you get to pilot these massive robots, known as Titans, that are great fun to fight in. Unlike many other games, it is exclusively online and requires a large infrastructure to support the many players. There are many reasons I try to play *Titanfall* when starting my cloud conversations:

- ◆ I need the practice, as my teenage son will attest.

- ◆ I can write off the console and game because I use it in a business scenario.

- ◆ I can present a perfect example of a use case for the public cloud.

Why is *Titanfall* a perfect example of a use case for the public cloud? That is something that will become clear later in this chapter, but in the meantime, I definitely recommend supporting the public cloud and specifically Azure by playing lots of *Titanfall*.

Introducing the Cloud

Every organization has some kind of IT infrastructure. It could be a server sitting under someone's desk, geographically distributed datacenters the size of multiple football fields, or something in between. Within that infrastructure are a number of key fabric (physical infrastructure) elements:

Compute Capacity   Compute capacity can be thought of in terms of the various servers in the datacenter, which consist of processors, memory, and other hardware (such as the motherboard, power supply, and so on). I will use the term *compute* throughout this book when referring to server capacity.

Storage   A persistent method of storage for data—from the operating system (OS) and applications to pure data such as files and databases—must be provided. Storage can exist within a server or in external devices, such as a storage area network (SAN). SANs provide enterprise-level performance and capabilities, although newer storage architectures that leverage local storage, which in turn replicate data, are becoming more prevalent in datacenters.

Network   These components connect the various elements of the datacenter and enable client devices to communicate with hosted services. Connectivity to other datacenters may also be part of the network design. Options such as dedicated fibre connections, Multiprotocol Label Switching (MPLS), and Internet connectivity via a DMZ are typical.

Datacenter Infrastructure   An often overlooked but critical component of datacenters is the supporting infrastructure. Items such as uninterruptable power supplies (UPSs), air conditioning, the physical building, and even generators all have to be considered. Each consumes energy and impacts the efficiency of the datacenter as well as its power usage effectiveness (PUE), which provides a measure of how much energy a datacenter uses for computer equipment compared to the other aspects. The lower the PUE, the more efficient the datacenter—or at least the more power going to the actual computing.

Once you have the physical infrastructure in place, you then add the actual software elements (the OS, applications, and services), and finally the management infrastructure, which enables deployment, patching, backup, automation, and monitoring. The IT team for an organization is responsible for all of these datacenter elements. The rise in the size and complexity of IT infrastructure is a huge challenge for nearly every organization. Despite the fact that most IT departments see budget cuts year after year, they are expected to deliver more and more as IT becomes increasingly critical.

Not only is the amount of IT infrastructure increasing, but that infrastructure needs to be resilient. This typically means implementing disaster recovery (DR) solutions to provide protection from a complete site failure, such as one caused by a large-scale natural disaster. If you ignore the public cloud, your organization will need to lease space from a co-location facility or set up a new datacenter. When I talk to CIOs, one of the things at the top of the *don't-want-to-do* list is write out more checks for datacenters—in fact, write out *any* checks for datacenters is on that list.

In the face of increased cost pressure and the desire to be more energy responsible (green), datacenter design becomes ever more complex, especially in a world with virtualization. If the three critical axes of a datacenter (shown in Figure 1.1) are not properly thought out, your organization's datacenters will never be efficient. You must consider the square footage of the actual datacenter, the kilowatts that can be consumed per square foot, and the amount of heat that can be dissipated expressed in BTU per hour.

FIGURE 1.1
The three axes of datacenter planning

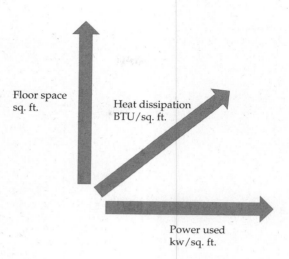

Floor space
sq. ft.

Heat dissipation
BTU/sq. ft.

Power used
kw/sq. ft.

If you get any of these calculations wrong, you end up with a datacenter you cannot fully utilize because you can't get enough power to it, can't keep it cool enough, or simply can't fit enough equipment in it. As the compute resources become denser and consume more power, it's critical that datacenters supply enough power and have enough cooling to keep servers operating within their environmental limits. I know of a number of datacenters that are only 50 percent full because they cannot provide enough power to fully utilize available space.

THE PRIVATE CLOUD AND VIRTUALIZATION

In the early 2000s as organizations looked to better use their available servers and enjoy other benefits, such as faster provisioning, virtualization became a key technology in every datacenter. When I look back to my early days as a consultant, I remember going through sizing exercises for a new Microsoft Exchange server deployment. When sizing the servers required that I consider the busiest possible time and also the expected increase in utilization of the lifetime of the server (for example, five years), the server was heavily over-provisioned, which meant it was also highly underutilized. Underutilization was a common situation for most servers in a datacenter, and it was typical to see servers running at 5 percent. It was also common to see provisioning times of up to six weeks for a new server, which made it hard for IT to react dynamically to changes in business requirements.

Virtualization enables a single physical server to be divided into one or more virtual machines through the use of a *hypervisor*. The virtual machines are completely abstracted from the physical hardware; each virtual machine is allocated resources such as memory and processor in addition to virtualized storage and networking. Each of the virtual machines then can have an operating system installed, which enables multiple operating systems to run on a single piece of hardware. The operating systems may be completely unaware of the virtual nature of the environment they are running on. However, most modern operating systems are enlightened; they are aware of the virtual environment and actually optimize operations based on the presence of a hypervisor. Figure 1.2 shows a Hyper-V example leveraging the VHDX virtual hard disk format.

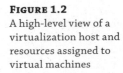

FIGURE 1.2
A high-level view of a
virtualization host and
resources assigned to
virtual machines

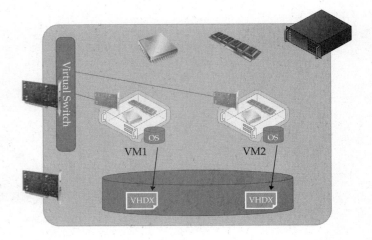

Virtualization has revolutionized the way datacenters operate and brought huge benefits, including the following:

High Utilization of Resources   Complementary workloads are hosted on a single physical environment.

Mobility of OS Instances between Completely Different Hardware   A single hypervisor allows abstraction of the physical hardware from the OS.

Potentially Faster Provisioning   Faster provisioning is dependent on processes in place.

High Availability through the Virtualization Solution   This ability is most useful when high availability is not natively available to the application.

Simplicity of Licensing for Some Products and OSs   For some products and OSs, the physical hardware is allowed to be licensed based on the number of processor sockets, and then an unlimited number of virtual machines on that hardware can use the OS/application. Windows Server Datacenter is an example of this kind of product. There is also an opposite situation for some products that are based on physical core licensing, which do not equate well in most virtualized environments.

There are other benefits. At a high level, if it were to be summed up in five words, I think "more bang for the buck" would work.

The potential of the datacenter capabilities can be better realized. The huge benefits of virtualization on their own do not completely revolutionize the datacenter. Many organizations have adopted virtualization, but have then operated the datacenter as if each OS is still on dedicated hardware. New OS instances are provisioned with dedicated virtualization hosts and even dedicated storage for different projects, which has resulted in isolated islands of resources within the datacenter. Once again, resources were wasted and more complex to manage.

In this book, I'm going to talk a lot about "the cloud." But, for on-premises environments, I would be remiss if I didn't also talk about another big change—the private cloud. Some people will tell you that the private cloud was made up by hypervisor vendors to compete against and stay relevant in the face of the public cloud. Others say it's a revolutionary concept. I think

I fall somewhere in the middle. The important point is that a private cloud solution has key characteristics and, when those are implemented, benefits are gained.

A customer once told me, "Ask five people what the private cloud is, and you will get seven different answers." While I think that is a very true statement, the US National Institute of Standards and Technology (NIST) lists what it considers to be the five critical characteristics that must be present to be a cloud. This applies to both private clouds and public clouds.

On-Demand Self-Service   The ability to provision services, such as a virtual machine, as needed without human interaction must be provided. Some organizations may add approval workflow for certain conditions.

Broad Network Access   Access to services over many types of networks, mobile phones, desktops, and so on must be provided.

Resource Pooling   Resources are organized in a multitenant model with isolation provided via software. This removes the islands of resources that are common when each business group has its own resources. Resource islands lead to inefficiency in utilization.

Rapid Elasticity   Rapid elasticity is the ability to scale rapidly outward and inward as demands on services change. The ability to achieve large-scale elasticity is tied to pooling all resources together to achieve a larger potential pool.

Measured Service   Clouds provide resources based on defined quotas, but they also enable reporting based on usage and potentially even billing.

The full document can be found here:

http://csrc.nist.gov/publications/nistpubs/800-145/SP800-145.pdf

People often say there is no difference between virtualization and private cloud. That is not true. The difference is the management infrastructure for a private cloud enables the characteristics listed here. To implement a private cloud, you don't need to change your hardware, storage, or networking. The private cloud is enabled through software, which in turn enables processes. You may decide that you don't want to enable all capabilities initially. For example, many organizations are afraid of end-user self-service; they have visions of users running amok and creating thousands of virtual machines. Once they understand quotas and workflows, and approvals, they understand that they have far more control and accountability than manual provisioning provided.

ENTER THE PUBLIC CLOUD

The private cloud, through enhanced management processes and virtualization, brings a highly optimized on-premises solution. Ultimately, it still consists of resources that the organization owns and has to house year-round. As I mentioned earlier, CIOs don't like writing checks for datacenters, no matter how optimal. All the optimization in the world cannot counter the fact that there are some scenarios where hosting on-premises is not efficient or even logical.

The public cloud represents services offered by an external party that can be accessed over the Internet. The services are not limited and can be purchased as you consume the service. This is a key difference from an on-premises infrastructure. With the public cloud, you only pay for the amount of service you consume when you use it. For example, I only pay for the amount of storage I am using at any moment in time; the charge does not include the potential amount of storage I may need in a few years' time. I only pay for the virtual machines I need turned on right now; I can increase the number of virtual machines when I need them and only pay for those extra virtual machines while they are running.

TURN IT OFF!

In Azure, virtual machines are billed on a per-minute basis. If I run an 8-vCPU virtual machine for 12 hours each month, then I only pay the cost for 12 hours of runtime. Note that it does not matter how busy the VM is. You pay the same price whether the vCPUs in the VM are running at 100 percent or 1 percent processor utilization. It's important to shut down and deprovision from the Azure fabric any virtual machines that are not required to avoid paying for resources you don't need. (*Deprovision* just means the virtual machine no longer has resources reserved in the Azure fabric.) The virtual machine can be restarted when you need it again. At that point, resources are allocated in the fabric automatically; the VM will start as expected.

In addition to the essentially limitless capacity, this pay-as-you-go model is what sets the public cloud apart from on-premises solutions. Think back to organizations needing DR services. Using the public cloud ensures there are minimal costs for providing disaster recovery. During normal running, you only pay for the storage used for the replicated data and virtual environments. Only in the case of an actual disaster would you start the virtual machines in the public cloud. You stop paying for them when you can fail back to on-premises.

There are other types of charges associated with the public cloud. For example, Azure does not charge for ingress bandwidth (data sent into Azure—Microsoft is fully invested in letting you get as much data into Azure as possible), but there are charges for egress (outbound) data. There are different tiers of storage, some of which are geo-replicated, so your data in Azure is stored at two datacenters that may be hundreds of miles apart. I will cover the pricing in more detail later in the book, but the common theme is you pay only for what you use.

If most organizations' IT requirements were analyzed, you would find many instances where resource requirements for a particular service are not flat. In fact, they vary greatly at different times of the day, week, month, or year. There are systems that perform end-of-month batch processing. These are idle all month, and then consume huge amounts of resources for one day at the end of the month. There are companies (think tax accountants) that are idle for most of the year but that are very busy for two months. There may be services that need huge amounts of resources for a few weeks every four years, like those that stream the Olympics. The list of possible examples is endless.

 Real World Scenario

SUPER BOWL SUNDAY AND THE AMERICAN LOVE OF PIZZA

I'll be up front; I'm English and I don't understand the American football game. I watched the 2006 Super Bowl. After five hours of two minutes of action, a five-minute advertising break, and a different set of players moving a couple of yards, it'll be hard to get me to watch it again. Nonetheless, it's popular in America. As Americans watch the Super Bowl, they like to eat pizza, and what's interesting is the Super Bowl represents a perfect storm for pizza ordering peaks. During the Super Bowl halftime and quarter breaks, across the entire United States, with all four time zones in sync, people order pizza. These three spikes require 50 percent more compute power for ordering and processing than a typical Friday dinnertime, the normal high point for pizza ordering.

Most systems are built to handle the busiest time, so our pizza company would have to provision compute capacity of 50 percent more than would ever normally be needed just for Super Bowl Sunday. Remember that this is 50 percent more than the Friday dinnertime requirement, which itself is much higher than is needed any other time of the week. This would be a hugely expensive and wasteful exercise. Instead Azure is used.

During normal times, there could be 10 web instances and 10 application instances handling the website and processing. On Friday nights between 2 p.m. and midnight, this increases to 20 instances of each role. On Super Bowl Sunday between noon and 5 p.m., this increases to 30 instances of each role. Granted, I'm making up the numbers, but the key here is the additional instances only exist when needed, and therefore the customer is charged extra only when the additional resources are needed. This elasticity is key to public cloud services.

To be clear, I totally understand the eating pizza part!

The pizza scenario is a case of predictable bursting, where there is a known period of increased utilization. It is one of the scenarios that is perfect for cloud computing. Figure 1.3 shows the four main scenarios in which cloud computing is the clear right choice. Many other scenarios work great in the cloud, but these four are uniquely solved in an efficient way through the cloud. I know many companies that have moved or are moving many of their services to the public cloud. It's cheaper than other solutions and offers great resiliency.

FIGURE 1.3
The key types of highly variable workloads that are a great fit for consumption-based pricing

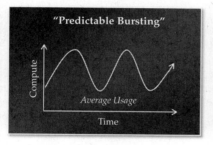

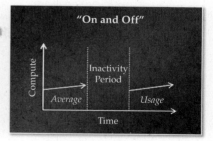

In a fast-growing scenario, a particular service's utilization is increasing rapidly. In this scenario, a traditional on-premises infrastructure may not be able to scale fast enough to keep up with demand. Leveraging the "infinite" scale of the public cloud removes the danger of not being able to keep up with demand.

Unpredictable bursting occurs when the exact timing of high usage cannot be planned. "On and Off" scenarios describe services that are needed at certain times but that are completely turned off at other times. This could be in the form of monthly batch processes where the processing runs for only 8 hours a month, or this could be a company such as a tax return accounting service that runs for 3 months out of the year.

Although these four scenarios are great for the public cloud, some are also a good fit for hybrid scenarios where the complete solution has a mix of on-premises and the public cloud. The baseline requirements could be handled on-premises, but the bursts expand out to use the public cloud capacity.

For startup organizations, there is a saying: "fail fast." It's not that the goal of the startup is to fail, but rather, if it is going to fail, then it's better to fail fast. Less money is wasted when compared to a long, drawn-out failure. The public cloud is a great option for startups because it means very little up-front capital spent buying servers and datacenter space. Instead, the startup just has operating expenditures for services it actually uses. This is why startups like services such as Microsoft Office 365 for their messaging and collaboration. Not only do they not need infrastructure, they don't need messaging administrators to maintain it. Public cloud IaaS is a great solution for virtual machines. Once again, no up-front infrastructure is required, and companies pay only for what they use. As the company grows and its utilization goes up, so does its operating expenditure, but the expenditure is proportional to the business. This type of pay-as-you-go solution is also attractive to potential financers, because there is less initial outlay and thus reduced risk.

At the start of this chapter, I said that everyone should play *Titanfall*, and this is where it fits in. *Titanfall* has a large number of artificial intelligence (AI) players, which would be burdensome if their computations had to be performed on a player's console. So, *Titanfall* leverages Azure to provide the services and processing needed. When lots of players are online, an increased number of environments are started in Azure. When fewer players are online, a decreased number of environments are required. Only the environments needed run, thus optimizing costs. The amount of infrastructure that would be required to host something like *Titanfall* would be immense, and leveraging the public cloud presents a perfect-use case, especially when the demand for the service will diminish after a few months as new games are released.

I see the public cloud used in many different ways today, and that adoption will continue to grow as organizations become more comfortable with using the public cloud and, ultimately, trust it. Key use cases today include but are not limited to the following:

Test and Development Test and development is seen by many companies as "low-hanging fruit." It is less risky than production workloads and typically has a high amount of churn, meaning environments are created and deleted frequently. This translates to a lot of work for the IT teams unless the private cloud has been implemented.

Disaster Recovery As discussed, for most companies a DR action should never be required. However, DR capability is required in that extremely rare event when it's needed. By using the public cloud, the cost to implement DR is minimal, especially when compared to costs of a second datacenter.

International DMZ I have a number of companies that would like to offer services globally. This can be challenging—having datacenters in many countries is hugely expensive and can even be politically difficult. By using a public cloud that is geographically distributed, it's easy to offer services around the world with minimal latencies for the end users.

Special Projects Imagine I have a campaign or special analytics project that requires large amounts of infrastructure for a short period of time. The public cloud is perfect for this, especially when certain types of licensing (for example, SQL Server licensing) can be purchased as consumed and other resources are paid for only as required.

A Desire to Get Out of the Datacenter Business I'm seeing more companies that just don't want to maintain datacenters anymore. These organizations will move as much as possible to the public cloud and maintain minimal on-premises infrastructure needed for certain services, such as domain controllers and file and print servers.

TYPES OF SERVICE IN THE CLOUD

Throughout this chapter, I have talked about making services available on-premises with a private cloud and off-premises in the public cloud, but what exactly are these services? There are three primary types of service: Infrastructure as a Service (IaaS), Platform as a Service (PaaS), and Software as a Service (SaaS). For each type, the responsibilities of the nine major layers of management vary between the vendor of the service and the client (you). Figure 1.4 shows the three types of service and also a complete on-premises solution. There are many other types of as-a-Service, but most of the other types of services use one of these three primary types. For example, Desktop-as-a-Service really has IaaS as a foundation.

FIGURE 1.4
The key types of highly variable workloads that are a great fit for consumption-based pricing

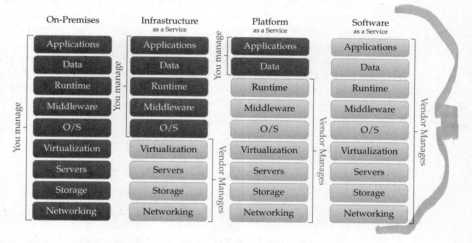

IaaS can be thought of as a virtual machine in the cloud. The provider has a virtual environment, and you purchase virtual machine instances. You then manage the operating system, the patching, the data, and the applications within. Examples of IaaS include Amazon's Elastic Computing 2 (EC2) and Azure IaaS, which offer organizations the ability to run operating systems inside cloud-based virtual environments.

PaaS provides a framework where custom applications can be run. Organizations only need to focus on writing the very best application within the guidelines of the platform capabilities, and everything else is taken care of. There are no worries about patching operating systems, updating frameworks, backing up SQL databases, or configuring high availability. The organization just writes the application and pays for the resource used. Azure is the classic example of a PaaS.

SaaS is the ultimate in low maintenance. The complete solution is provided by the vendor. The organization has nothing to write or maintain other than configuring who should be allowed to use the software. Hotmail, a messaging service, is an example of commercial SaaS. Office 365, which provides cloud-hosted Exchange, SharePoint, and Lync services accessed over the Internet with no application or operating system management for the organization, is an enterprise example.

Ideally, for the lowest management overhead, SaaS should be used, and then PaaS where SaaS is not available. IaaS would be used only if PaaS is not an option. SaaS is gaining a great deal of traction with services such as Office 365. PaaS adoption, however, is fairly slow. The primary obstacle for PaaS is that applications have to be written within very specific guidelines in order to operate in PaaS environments. Many organizations have custom applications that cannot be modified. Others don't have the budget to change their applications, which is why IaaS is so popular. With IaaS, an existing virtual machine on-premises can be moved to the IaaS solution fairly painlessly. In the long term, I think PaaS will become the standard for custom applications, but it will take a long time.

IaaS can help serve as the ramp to adopting PaaS. Consider a multitiered service that includes a web tier, an application tier, and a SQL database tier. Initially, all these tiers could run as IaaS virtual machines. The organization may then be able to convert the web tier from Internet Information Services (IIS) running in an IaaS VM and use the Azure web role, which is part of PaaS. Next, the organization may be able to move from SQL running in an IaaS VM to using SQL Azure. Finally, the organization could rewrite the application tier to directly leverage Azure PaaS. It's a gradual process, but the reduced overhead and increased functionality and resiliency at the end state is worth it.

I saw an interesting analogy using the various types of service put in the context of pizza services. (Yes, it's a second pizza example in one chapter; I like pizza.) Take a look at Figure 1.5. No matter where you plan to eat the pizza or how you plan to have it prepared, the actual pizza ingredients are the foundation. Other services and facilities, such as assembling the pizza, having an oven, cooking the pizza, having a table, and serving drinks, are also required. But as we move up the levels of service, we do less and less. At the highest level of service, pizza at a restaurant, we just eat and don't even have to wash up.

FIGURE 1.5

Various types of Pizza-as-a-Service

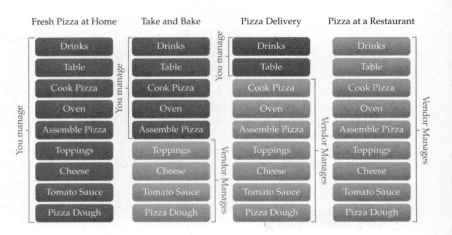

The analogy is not perfect. Ideally, I would have had the oven and power as the core fabric. Then, with IaaS, the oven and power would be provided, and I would supply the ingredients, and assemble and cook the pizza (maybe in a pizza cooking class). For PaaS, the dough, sauce, and cheese are provided as a base, and I just add the toppings I want. For SaaS, I eat what I'm given, but only the poshest restaurants can get away with serving whatever they want. I doubt that a pizza restaurant would do well with that model, but you get the idea of the types of service. As you progress through the types of as-a-Service, you are responsible for fewer and fewer elements and can focus on what you care about: the end service/application.

There is another key area in which the pizza analogy is not perfect. In the pizza world, as you progress up the service levels, the service gets better but the total cost increases. When I make a pizza from scratch at home, it's cheaper than eating out at a restaurant. In the IT service space, this is likely not the case. From a total cost of ownership (TCO) for the solution, if I can buy a service like Office 365 as SaaS, that solution is likely cheaper than operating my own Exchange, SharePoint, and Lync solution on-premises when you consider the server infrastructure, licenses, IT admin, and so on.

Microsoft Azure 101

Microsoft has many solutions in the public cloud. The IaaS and PaaS services focus on Azure services, formerly known as Windows Azure, but rightly renamed, as many services are not Windows-centric. Although the focus of this book is on services related to infrastructure, primarily IaaS, this section will provide a high-level overview of all the key Azure services. It's important to fully understand the capabilities that are available.

Figure 1.6 shows the three main building blocks of the Azure platform along with the networking and traffic management services that enable various types of connectivity. Azure Compute provides the primary compute capabilities, including virtual machines, cloud services, websites, plus the fabric controller, which manages all the virtual machines and hosts that provide the Azure platform. Azure Data Services, as the name suggests, provides storage, backup, and the SQL Server capabilities in the cloud, including relational databases (which are not available in the core Microsoft Azure component). Finally, the Azure App Services provide services such as access control, caching, directory services, and a service bus for communication between components within and outside of Azure. An Azure Marketplace facilitates the buying and selling of Azure applications, components, and datasets.

FIGURE 1.6
The three main building blocks of the Azure Platform: Azure, App Services, and Data Services

Once you decide what servers, storage, load balancing, and other goodness is needed to run your applications, you need to decide where you want those capabilities hosted. Microsoft has many datacenters distributed throughout the world; Azure applications can run from any of them. There are currently four datacenters in the United States, and two each in Europe and

Asia regions. When an application is deployed to Azure, the customer can select where the application should be deployed. All Azure datacenters are paired to provide protection from site failure and data is replicated.

In the next sections, I will introduce you to many of the services available in Azure. Understand that it is a constantly changing service, and my focus is to simply provide you with an idea of the scope of services. For the most up-to-date list of available services and to get more details, visit http://azure.microsoft.com/en-us/services/. Those services I will be covering in detail throughout the book, such as Azure Active Directory, Azure Automation, Azure Traffic Manager, and of course the networking, won't be covered in this chapter. (I have another 400 or so pages to tell you about those.) Microsoft often releases new services in a preview mode. You need to apply for preview services before you can use them. To check to see the previews that are available and to sign up, use the Preview website here:

```
http://azure.microsoft.com/en-us/services/preview/
```

Microsoft Azure Compute

The main building block of the Azure platform is Microsoft Azure itself. Here you'll find the key capabilities that enable the cloud-based hosting of applications and data. As Azure has evolved, so too has the naming and hierarchy of services. If you were able to look at what Azure was a year ago, the components would seem different from those I'm describing today.

The virtual machine, as shown in Figure 1.7, is the part that actually runs the applications, which could be a website, some custom middleware code, or some legacy application. All of the compute capabilities are enabled through virtual machines, which vary in size. Although virtual machines are directly accessible and used with Azure IaaS, other services, such as PaaS, websites, networking, and so on, are built using virtual machines; they simply may not be visible to you. I will focus on the IaaS virtual machines in this chapter.

FIGURE 1.7
The main components that make up Microsoft Azure Compute

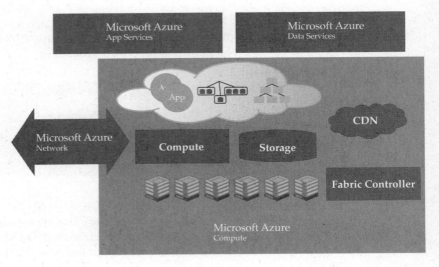

A web role acts as the web server for your web applications, such as ASP.NET, Classic ASP, PHP, Python, and Node.js. The web role leverages IIS to run the web applications. If you request five instances of a website role for your web application, then behind the scenes, five virtual machines running IIS are created and load balanced, and all run your web code. If in the future you want additional instances, you just request additional instances, and Azure automatically creates new instances of the web role, deploys your custom code, and adds those new instances to the load balancing. Azure websites, which are separate from the web roles, provide a very fast way to deploy a web application.

A worker role is used to run tasks for backend applications that are not IIS web applications but leverage PaaS. As with the web role, when you deploy your application, you tell Azure how many instances of the role you want, and Azure distributes your application to all instances and balances load. Using worker roles, you can run applications such as Java Virtual Machines or Apache Tomcat. This is where the Azure flexibility shines.

You can use any combination of web roles, worker roles, and VMs to support your application. Some applications may only require web roles, some may need web and worker roles, and some can be deployed using just VMs. The point is the flexibility is there to create roles that meet the needs of the application you are deploying.

Azure Compute also features a Mobile Services set. These services are designed to provide the backend for mobile applications running on Windows, iOS, and Android platforms. Numerous services are available; some of the most useful allow integration into authentication services, such as Microsoft and Facebook accounts, and provide the ability to push notifications to devices.

An auto-scale capability allows multiple Azure virtual machines to be grouped together using a construct known as an *availability set*. Through configuration, you can specify the minimum and maximum number of virtual machines that should run and how scaling should be performed. For example, if CPU requirements in each VM exceed a certain amount, scaling should occur. To accomplish this, you must precreate all the possible virtual machines in the set. The Azure auto-scale then simply stops (deprovisions) and starts them as needed and optimizes your charges so that only the VMs needed are running. As of this writing, auto-scale will not automatically create new instances of virtual machines from a template. Azure does make it easy to request and instantly deploy additional instances of a role. Auto-scale also allows you to leverage the System Center App Controller, and you can programmatically request new instances by writing your own auto-scaling functionality.

The Azure fabric controller itself seems to work magic. As a customer, you can deploy your application, and Azure just spins up as many instances as you say. You can scale up or down at any time. Your service is always available per the Azure "99.95%" monthly service level agreement (SLA). The operating systems and dependent services are constantly patched and tuned. The magic is enabled by the Azure fabric controller, which itself is a distributed application running on Azure that has a fabric agent that runs on all the virtual machines (except IaaS VMs) and hosts that make up the Azure compute fabric. The fabric controller constantly monitors, and if it sees a problem, it can spin up new instances of a role. If a request is made for more instances of a role, the fabric controller creates the new instances and adds them to the load balancer configuration. The fabric controller handles all patching and updates (again, except those VMs that are IaaS). Patching and updating is a key reason that Azure applications can be covered by the "99.95%" SLA. You must deploy at least two instances of any role to take advantage of this capability, as the fabric controller will take down one instance, patch it, and then once that instance is running again, take down the other. As you have more and more instances, more instances can be patched simultaneously by grouping role instances in upgrade domains. When patching occurs, all instances within an upgrade domain are brought down and updated at the same time. Then, once complete, the next upgrade domain is updated, and so on.

Microsoft Azure Data Services

The ability to store data is critical to any service. Azure data services provide several types of storage and make them available to both Azure-based services and on-premises solutions.

Four primary types of storage are available:

Binary Large Object (BLOB) Azure offers an unstructured collection of bytes that can be used to store basically anything, including large media files. Currently BLOBs can scale up to 200 TB.

Tables Table storage can be confusing because these are not tables in the relational table sense. For relational database needs, Azure uses a SQL database. Tables are a structured store based on key-values. They are designed to store large amounts of data for massive scale where some basic structure is required, but relationships between data don't need to be maintained. Azure tables can be thought of as a NoSQL implementation. These constitute a growing class of database management systems that don't use SQL as their language or implement relational table capabilities.

Queues Queues primarily provide reliable and persistent messaging between applications within Azure. A particularly common use for queues is for the communication between web roles and worker roles. Queues have a basic functionality, which makes them fast. They don't have familiar characteristics, such as first in, first out (FIFO). Instead, developers implement their own features on top of the Azure queue feature.

Files This is an SMB 2.1 implementation that provides an easy method to share storage within an Azure region. Using the standard SMB protocol, files can be created and read. The reads and writes are being implemented by Azure Storage.

Azure Drive is a feature that allows a BLOB to be used as a virtual hard disk (VHD) and formatted as a NTFS volume. Although it allows applications to interact with the BLOB as a volume, it is not actually a different type of storage.

Any data stored in Azure is replicated three times within the same datacenter, and any Azure BLOB, table, and file content are also geo-replicated to another datacenter hundreds of miles away to provide resiliency against site-level disasters. The geo-replication is not synchronous, but it is performed very quickly. There should not be much lag between the data content at the primary location and the geo-replicated location. Read-access is available to the geographically replicated copy of the storage if required. Applications interact with storage using HTTP or HTTPS. For the tables, the OData (Open Data Protocol) is used. OData builds on web technologies to provide flexible ways to interact with data.

Microsoft also features an import/export capability that provides a clean way to transport large amounts of data where transportation over the network is not practical. The import/export service copies data to a 3.5-inch SATA HDD that is encrypted with Bitlocker. The drive is then shipped to the Microsoft datacenter, where the data is imported and made available in your Azure account.

Where a relational database capability is required, Azure SQL databases, which provide relational data through a subset of SQL Server capability in the cloud, should be used. This gives the Azure application full access to a relational database where needed. SQL Azure is a pricing model separate from the Computer and Storage components of Azure, because you are paying for the SQL service rather than raw storage. Two types of database are available: Web Edition (10 GB maximum database size) and Business Edition (150 GB maximum database size). Billing is based on database size in gigabyte increments. SQL Reporting is also available.

Other types of service are available as well. For your Big Data Azure features, HDInsight is a Hadoop-based service that brings great insight into structured and unstructured data. A shared cache service is available to provide improved storage performance. Another service that is gaining traction is Azure Backup, which provides a vault hosted in Azure to act as the target for backup data. Data is encrypted during transmission and encrypted again when stored in Azure. This provides an easy-to-implement, cloud-based backup solution. Currently, Windows Server Backup and System Center Data Protection Manager can use Azure Backup as a target. Azure Site Recovery, which allows various types of replication to Azure, also falls within the Data Services family of services.

Microsoft Azure App Services

Azure App Services encompass various technologies that can be used to augment Azure applications. As of this writing, a number of technologies make up the Azure App Services, including the following:

Content Delivery Network (CDN) Azure datacenters are located all around the globe, as we've already discussed, but there are certain types of data you may want to make available even closer to the consumer for the very best performance of high-bandwidth content. The CDN allows BLOB data within Azure Storage to be cached at points of presence (PoPs). PoPs are managed by Microsoft and are far greater in number than the Azure datacenters themselves. Here's how the CDN works. The first person in a region to download content would pull the data from the CDN, which originates from the Azure Storage BLOB at one of the major datacenters. The content is then stored at that CDN PoP, and from there, the data is sent to the first user. The second person to view the data in that location would then pull the data directly from the PoP cache, thus getting a fast response. Use of the CDN is optional and has its own SLA with a pay-as-you-go pricing structure based on transactions and the amount of data. Many organizations leverage the CDN for delivering their high-bandwidth data, even if it's separate from an actual Azure application. CDN is easy to enable.

Microsoft Azure Active Directory Active Directory (AD) provides an identity and access management solution that integrates with on-premises (where required) and is leveraged by many Microsoft solutions, such as Office 365, in addition to your own custom solutions. Multifactor authentication is available and can enable your mobile phone to act as part of the authentication process; a code required to complete the logon can be sent in a text.

Service Bus Service Bus supports multiple messaging protocols and provides reliable message delivery between on-premises and cloud systems. Typically, problems occur when on-premises, mobile, and other solutions attempt to communicate with services on the Internet because of firewall and IP address translation. With Azure Service Bus, the communication is enabled through the Service Bus component.

Media Services Providing high-quality media experiences, such as streaming of HD live video, is the focus of media services. Various types of encoding and content protection are supported.

Scheduler As the name suggests, the scheduler queues jobs to run on a defined schedule.

Reliable vs. Best-Effort IaaS

I want to cover how a service is made highly available early on in this book; it's a shift in thinking for many people, but it's a necessary shift when adopting public cloud services.

For most datacenter virtual environments, on-premises means that the infrastructure is implemented as a reliable infrastructure, as shown in Figure 1.8. Virtualization hosts are grouped into clusters, and storage is provided by enterprise-level SANs. A stand-alone virtual machine is made reliable through the use of clustering. For planned maintenance operations such as patching, virtual machines move between nodes with no downtime through the use of technologies like Live Migration. The result is minimal downtime to a virtual machine.

FIGURE 1.8

A reliable on-premises virtual environment

Compute Cluster

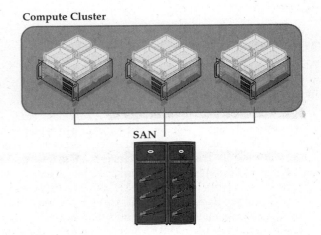

SAN

This type of reliable infrastructure makes sense for on-premises, but it does not work for public cloud solutions that have to operate at mega-scale. Instead, the public cloud operates in a best-effort model. Despite the name, best effort does not mean it's worse—in reality, it often is better. Instead of relying on the infrastructure to provide reliability, the emphasis is on the application. This means always having at least two instances of a service and organizing those services in such a way as to assure that those two instances do not run on the same rack of servers (fault domain). Further, the two instances can never be taken down at the same time during maintenance operations. The application needs to be written in such a way that multiple instances are supported. Ideally, the application is aware there are multiple instances and can perform certain types of recovery action where required. (See Figure 1.9.) Some kind of load-balancing technology is also needed so that incoming connections are sent to an active instance.

The reality is with a multiple-application instances model, the level of application availability is higher than when using a reliable infrastructure model. Although the reliable infrastructure provides zero downtime from planned maintenance operations (as does the best-effort infrastructure with multiple instances of the application on different fault domains), a reliable infrastructure cannot protect from downtime in an unplanned failure. If a host fails, the cluster

FIGURE 1.9
An example of design
in a best-effort
infrastructure

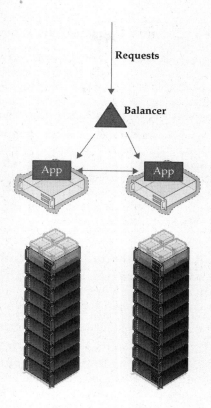

infrastructure in the reliable model will restart the VM on another node. That restart takes time, and the OS and/or application may need integrity checks and possibly recovery actions because essentially the OS inside the VM was just powered off. In the best-effort infrastructure using multiple instances of the application, unplanned failure is covered without risk of corruption, as the other instance would still be running. Additionally, though the reliable infrastructure protects against host failure, it cannot provide protection if the OS inside a VM hangs or errors in some way that is not seen as a problem for the host environment. In such a case, no corrective action is taken, and the service is left unavailable. Using an application-aware approach, any issues in the application could be detected, and clients would be sent to the other instance until any problems were resolved.

Getting Access to Microsoft Azure

For a typical on-premises solution, there are many hurdles to the access and adoption of a new technology. You need hardware to run the solution and somewhere to store that hardware, and you have to obtain and deploy the various operating system requirements and applications. With public cloud solutions, the services are sitting out there, just waiting for you to start using them. Primarily, that means a way to pay for the services. If, however, you want to just try Azure, you don't even need that.

IMPORTANCE OF PLANNING FOR SERVICES

Azure services (like most public cloud services) are easy to access and can be used with almost no barriers. This does not mean an organization should instigate the use of public cloud services with any less consideration and planning than would be given to solutions implemented on-premises. In fact, because the services are hosted externally, additional planning is likely required to ensure integration with on-premises solutions and adherence with security and compliance requirements.

Many organizations (or more specifically parts of organizations) have not done this planning and adopted public cloud services without central governance or planning, which causes problems in the long run. It is common to hear about a particular business unit in a company using the public cloud because their own internal IT department takes too long to deliver a service. Essentially, that business unit makes a decision to host the solution themselves without the required skill sets to ensure the solution is secure and adheres to requirements. The public cloud offers huge benefits, but ensure that its adoption is well thought out.

Free Azure Trials and Pay-as-You-Go

The first way to gain access to Azure (and the best way for most people who want to get an idea of what it's like to use Azure) is to sign up for a one-month free trial. The trial includes a $200 Azure credit that can be used for any Azure services. The free trial offer is available here:

```
http://azure.microsoft.com/en-us/pricing/free-trial/
```

To sign up, you will need a Microsoft Account (formerly known as a Windows Live ID), a phone number, and a credit card. Nothing is charged to the credit card, nor will anything be charged to the credit card—by default, once you hit the $200 Azure spend, the account is suspended. You have to agree to pay for services beyond the included $200 and change the default configuration to a Pay-as-You-Go subscription before any expense is incurred. A credit card is required for identity verification only. Once the 30 days has expired, again by default, the account is deactivated and all services removed unless you have converted the account to Pay-as-You-Go. Of course, you can always simply buy Azure services on a Pay-as-You-Go basis and be billed for the service used at the end of each billing cycle.

As you can imagine, any kind of public cloud service where VMs can be run for free is attractive to people with dubious intentions, such as running botnet services and even mining crypto currencies. Microsoft, like all public cloud services, tries to ensure trial services are used in the spirit they are intended: to try out Azure.

A BUCKET OF AZURE MONEY

Unlike many other types of purchasing in the IT world, with Azure you essentially have a bucket of money to use for Azure services. You can use that bucket for any of the types of service, virtual machines, storage, media services, backup, databases—it doesn't matter. You don't purchase $10,000 of VM quota and $5,000 of storage. You purchase $15,000 of Azure service and then spend it however you want. This is a much better option for organizations that, over time, may change the type of Azure service they want. You may begin by running SQL Server in Azure IaaS VMs with lots of storage but eventually move to using Azure SQL Database. You can make that change easily, since Azure money is not service specific.

Azure Benefits from MSDN Subscriptions

Another great way to experiment with Azure (and even use it on an ongoing basis as part of development and testing) is to leverage the Azure benefits that are part of Microsoft Developer Network (MSDN) subscriptions. MSDN subscriptions are a paid service that enables access to pretty much all Microsoft software. It is intended to be used as part of development and testing efforts. Also included with MSDN subscriptions is a monthly Azure credit, which varies depending on the level of the MSDN subscription, as shown in Table 1.1. (The credits are accurate as of this writing, but they could change over time.) Additionally, the MSDN Azure credits go further than regular Azure spending since the OS licenses are part of the MSDN subscription. Windows virtual machines are 33 percent discounted, as are some other services. Benefits for MSDN Ultimate subscriptions are documented on the MSDN Azure benefits details page:

```
http://azure.microsoft.com/en-us/offers/ms-azr-0063p/
```

TABLE 1.1:   MSDN Azure benefits

SUBSCRIPTION LEVEL	VISUAL STUDIO PROFESSIONAL WITH MSDN	VIRTUAL STUDIO TEST PROFESSIONAL WITH MSDN	MSDN PLATFORMS	VISUAL STUDIO PREMIUM WITH MSDN	VISUAL STUDIO ULTIMATE WITH MSDN
Azure Credits per month	$50	$50	$100	$100	$150

http://azure.microsoft.com/en-us/pricing/member-offers/msdn-benefits-details/

Like the Azure trial accounts, by default the MSDN Azure benefit accounts will not allow you to exceed the Azure credits associated with your MSDN subscription. When your monthly limit is reached, your services will be stopped until the start of the next billing month. You need to manually disable the spending limit and specify a credit card if you wish to use more than the Azure benefit credits each month. With the highest-level MSDN subscription (Ultimate), it's possible to run three standard-service single-core virtual machines with just under 2 GB of memory all month, which is a pretty nice testing environment. It is important to note that the MSDN Azure benefit is for development and testing only and cannot be used to run production services. Microsoft can shut down your services if it finds they are being used for production purposes.

Most Microsoft-focused developers already have MSDN subscriptions, so this is a great way to get Azure services to continue that development into the cloud. When I talk to customers about the MSDN benefit, a common question I hear is: "We have lots of MSDN subscriptions—can we pool all the Azure credits together to use as an organizational credit pool?" The answer is no, there is no way to pool MSDN Azure credits together—they are designed to be used by the individual MSDN subscriber for their test and development efforts.

As Figure 1.10 shows, it's easy to check on the current credit status of your subscription; by default, it is pinned to the Azure Startboard. If you select the pinned tile, more details related to the billing (for example, the number of days left) appear. Detailed information is also available on the older portal available at `https://manage.windowsazure.com`.

FIGURE 1.10
Viewing billing
information for Azure
subscription

If you wish to remove the spending limit and pay for Azure services beyond the MSDN subscription, perform the following steps:

1. Navigate in a browser to https://account.windowsazure.com/Subscriptions/.

2. Select the MSDN Azure subscription that has a spending limit enabled. Click the subscription name.

3. In the Subscription Status section, click the Remote Spending Limit link, shown in Figure 1.11.

4. When the Remote Spending Limit dialog box opens, change the selection to Yes, remote the spending limit, and then click the check mark.

FIGURE 1.11
Removing the
spending limit for
Azure subscription

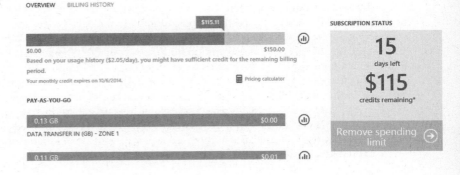

It's important you understand the ramifications of removing the spending limit. If you accidentally start a lot of virtual machines and leave them running, you may end up with a large bill at the end of the month. So, if you do remove the spending limit, ensure that you keep a close eye on your Azure spend.

Azure Open Licensing

Another option for organizations that don't want to use the Pay-as-You-Go via a credit card but are not ready for an Enterprise Agreement Azure commitment is to purchase Azure Open Licensing credits from a distributor or reseller. The Azure Open Licensing credits model is similar to that of a prepaid phone. You buy credits and add minutes or services to your phone. Then, you add more credits when you get low. Azure Open Licensing has the same credit model. Units of Azure credits are purchased in blocks equivalent to $100 USD. At purchase, an Online Service Activation (OSA) key is provided; the code is valid for up to 12 months. This means that the $100 of Azure credit associated with the OSA must be used within 12 months. By default, when the amount of credit left reaches 30 percent of the initial purchase, you will be alerted via an email and through the Azure Management Portal. Additional credits can be purchased and applied to the account when you receive a notification—or at any other time you wish. It works a lot like my son's school lunch card. I deposit funds in a lunch account, and he buys lunches using his lunch card. I get reminders from the school when the account runs low, but I can add additional credit at any time. Details on the Azure Open Licensing can be found here:

```
http://azure.microsoft.com/en-us/offers/ms-azr-0111p/
```

Note that if a customer using Azure Open Licensing chooses to move to an Enterprise Agreement (EA), it is possible to move the unused Azure credit associated with Open Licensing to the EA by making a support request.

Enterprise Enrollments for Azure

For larger organizations wanting to adopt Azure, the idea of using a credit card to pay for monthly services is not ideal. Although it is possible to be invoiced by Microsoft, enterprises typically want more granular control of their expenditures. For example, they may wish to have high-level enterprise administrators who administer the entire Azure service for the organization. Those enterprise administrators can then create separate accounts and delegate account owners, who can group like services or groups together into subscriptions. The subscriptions can be used by service administrators and co-administrators. Azure Enterprise Enrollment allows exactly that. Organizations can add Azure services as part of their Microsoft Enterprise Agreements based on a certain amount of Azure spend. For example, an organization might make a commitment to spend $50,000 a year and with that agreement comes special pricing and possibly other benefits. There have been offers from Microsoft that a certain Azure commitment spend enables the organization to receive a free StorSimple storage appliance.

Beyond just the purchasing options, a key benefit for enterprise enrollment is the account and subscription flexibility and control. Typically, when an individual or small organization purchases Azure services, that user receives an individual Azure subscription with a specific subscription ID. That user is the service administrator for that subscription. Additional people can be made co-administrators. As of this writing, there is a limit of 200 or fewer co-administrators depending on the subscription type. Co-administrators can use the services within the subscription.

An enterprise enrollment via an Enterprise Agreement enables more flexibility in the administration and separation of services by providing three layers, as shown in Figure 1.12. Within the enterprise's enrollment, one or more accounts and subscriptions can be authorized.

FIGURE 1.12
Hierarchy when using an enterprise enrollment

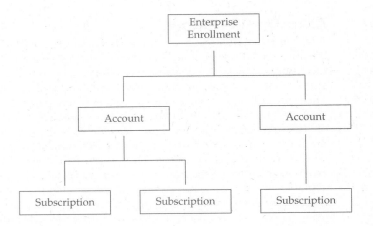

At the top of the enterprise enrollment is the enterprise administrator for the entire enterprise Azure enrollment. Nominate someone from your organization to receive an email and hold a Microsoft account. The work email address associated with the Microsoft account must be someone who will be able to activate the service. Once the service is activated, additional people from the organization can be made enterprise administrators. The enterprise administrators can in turn create separate accounts within the enrollment. Each account can have one or more account administrators assigned. Once again, each administrator needs a Microsoft account unless integration with your organization's AD has been implemented through the use of synchronization to Azure AD. If your AD and Azure AD are synched, organizational accounts in Azure can be used. (Active Directory is covered in detail in Chapter 7, "Extending AD to Azure and Azure AD.") The organizational account owners can create one or more subscriptions within the account. Each subscription has a single service administrator who manages the subscription and can add additional co-administrators who can use the services.

A key benefit is that the enterprise administrators at the top of the hierarchy have visibility into Azure usage across all accounts, whereas account owners have visibility into Azure usage for all subscriptions within the account. Billing reports are broken down at a subscription and account level for easy accounting. The hierarchical nature of an enterprise enrollment opens up a number of methodologies for setting up accounts and subscriptions, some of which are shown in Figure 1.13. Notice that in a functional methodology, the accounts are based on the functions of different groups. When using a geographical methodology, the accounts are based on physical locations. Business group methodologies often give each group their own account. Your organization may need a hybrid methodology. Ultimately, the right methodology depends on how you want to delegate the creation of subscriptions and how billing information and even chargebacks will be used within the organization. Once the account methodology is decided, how subscriptions are used must also be decided. This can be broken down by group,

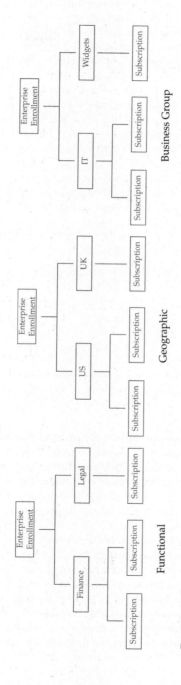

FIGURE 1.13

Possible methodologies for enterprise enrollment account setup

task, location, deployment life-cycle stage (such as a subscription for development and one for testing), and so on, ideally complementing the methodology picked for the accounts.

With the introduction of role-based access control (RBAC) and resource groups, some of the reasons for separate subscriptions and accounts no longer apply, since granular permissions, and even spend reporting, are now possible based on specific resources. But the concept of separating accounts and subscriptions can still be very useful.

Note that when paying by credit card or via invoice, you pay the list price for Azure services. However, when you purchase via an Enterprise Agreement, you can get substantial discounts depending on the level of the agreement. Based on the November 2013 Enterprise Spotlight report, the discount for EA agreements is based on the EA level, as shown in Table 1.2. The discount applies to the amount prepurchased under the agreement and to any overage charges beyond the amount in the agreement. This means no penalty for going over your prepurchase, and not surprisingly, Microsoft makes it pleasant to use more Azure! Depending on the amount of overage, you may be billed at the end of the year or potentially earlier; that is something you'd have to discuss with your Microsoft account representative.

TABLE 1.2:   Enterprise-level Azure discounts

EA LEVEL	AZURE DISCOUNT
A	27%
B	30%
C	33%
D	36%

http://download.microsoft.com/documents/uk/licensing/resources/Spotlight_November_2013_to_Customer_-_AZURE.pdf

The discount available when purchasing Azure as part of an Enterprise Agreement is potentially huge, but it is important to realize the Azure purchase on an EA is prepurchased on an annual basis and is "use it or lose it." Suppose that as part of an EA you purchase $100,000 of Azure for Year 1. This gets you a certain level of discount. However, if at the end of the year you have only used $20,000 worth of Azure service, that other $80,000 is lost. It does not carry over to the next year. Customers can change the annual Azure amount each year, up or down, but they cannot reclaim any lost spend.

The risk of losing Azure dollars may encourage customers to commit to a lower up-front Azure spend, since any overage receives the same discount. That has to be balanced against the fact that the more Azure spend you commit to and pay, the greater the discount. Numerous calculators and tools are available to help you estimate the Azure spend and reach to as accurate a number as possible for the coming year. In general, I would err a little on the low side, since you get the same discount for overage anyway. Be aware that erring on the low side could place you in a different EA level band and therefore a lower discount. Also, remember that there are many services available in Azure that can be used to consume your bucket of Azure money. If you are not using as much IaaS as you planned, maybe you can use more storage or media services.

To summarize, Azure can be obtained in a number of ways, including:

◆ Trial subscription

◆ Pay-as-You-Go subscription

◆ MSDN Azure benefits

◆ Azure Open Licensing

◆ Enterprise Azure enrollment

Increasing Azure Limits

By default new Azure subscriptions are initially configured with very low limits. The default limits are in place to stop new Azure customers from initially over-consuming services. The limits can (and will need to be) increased for serious Azure usage. For most limits, there is a default value and a maximum value. Although it may be tempting to try to raise limits to the maximum, remember that the limits are there to help protect your own usage. I advise increasing to a realistic value that meets your needs. It's also critical to have proper processes in place to ensure that services are running only as needed and monitoring is in place to ensure that you have the required levels of insight to your environment. (I will cover those throughout this book.)

The Azure default limits and maximums are outlined here:

```
http://azure.microsoft.com/en-us/documentation/articles/azure-subscription-service-limits/
```

The key limits you will want to change include the following:

Cores per Subscription Twenty cores per subscription is the default, which is a very low number and should be increased. Note that when using the A0 shared core instance size, the shared core counts as a whole core from a cores-per-subscription limit measurement.

DNS Servers per Subscription Nine DNS servers per subscription is the default. Many customers find this too low, especially when using Azure for testing and development and multiple virtual networks representing different environments.

Cloud Services and Storage Accounts per Subscription Both of these limits are set to 20 by default, but you may need to increase them based on how you build your Azure services.

To raise a limit, contact Azure support on the phone or via the Azure Management Portal. You'll find full details on how to get Azure support here:

```
http://azure.microsoft.com/en-us/support/faq/
```

The steps to complete an online quota request are as follows:

1. From the Azure portal, select your name from the top corner to display the hidden menu, and select the contact support option. (The exact text will vary depending on whether you are using the new or the old portal.)

2. For Support Type, select Billing and then click Create Ticket.

3. For Problem Type, select Quota or Core Increase Request.

4. For Category, select the quota you wish to increase, as shown in Figure 1.14.

5. Complete the required details, such as the desired new value, and then click Submit.

FIGURE 1.14
Selecting the type of quota to increase

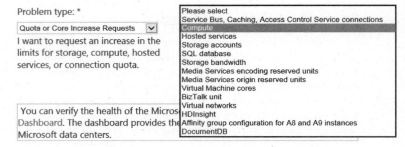

The Bottom Line

Articulate the different types of "as-a-Service."   Three core types of service are offered within clouds. Infrastructure as a Service (IaaS) provides a virtual machine with all the underlying compute, network, and storage fabric provided by the service vendor. The customer has full control of the operating system and services running within the virtual machine. Platform as a Service (PaaS) provides an environment where applications can be deployed without the customer having to consider the management or maintenance of operating systems or middleware services. Applications may be required to follow certain guidelines to run in a PaaS environment. Finally, Software as a Service (SaaS) provides a complete solution that requires customers to perform only basic administration. Good examples of SaaS are services such as Office 365.

> **Master It**   Why do many organizations initially use IaaS but ultimately move to PaaS and SaaS?

Identify key scenarios where the public cloud provides the most optimal service.   A key attribute of the public cloud is that customers pay only for what they consume. This means any type of scenario where the usage is not flat over time is a great fit for the public cloud; when there is a lull in activity, the customer can scale back the service and pay less. The public cloud can also be useful for start-ups that wish to avoid the initial outlay for hardware and software. Again, in the public cloud you pay only for what is needed.

> **Master It**   How is the public cloud used in hybrid scenarios while still gaining the benefits of public cloud pay for consumption only?

Understand how to get started consuming Microsoft Azure services.   For individuals who want to try Azure, the best way to gain access is to sign up for a free one-month trial. If you have an MSDN subscription, you can activate the Azure benefits for monthly Azure credits to be used for test and development purposes. For organizations wishing to leverage Azure for production purposes, numerous options exist, including Pay-as-You-Go via credit card or invoice, Open Licensing, or adding Azure services to your Enterprise Agreement. A key point is to have a clear project that you wish to implement in Azure that will help you start leveraging Azure quickly.

Master It How can I avoid going over my MSDN monthly quota each month?

## Chapter 2

When to Use IaaS: Cost and Options

Now that you're familiar with the concepts of the public cloud and the various types of "as-a-Service," this chapter will focus on helping you understand the true value of leveraging the public cloud. Here you will learn how to evaluate the associated costs and the types of workloads supported in Azure.

The details of how Azure provides its services also will be covered in order to help you make architectural decisions when designing services and planning for disaster recovery.

In this chapter, you will learn to

- ◆ Understand all the cost elements related to hosting services
- ◆ Identify workloads that can run in Azure IaaS
- ◆ Describe how Microsoft Azure infrastructure provides services

Understanding Why an Organization Wants IaaS in the Public Cloud

In the previous chapter, I discussed key scenarios where leveraging the public cloud makes sense. Typically, the decision pivots on the fact that with the public cloud you only pay for the service you consume. This is key in many scenarios, including those where

- ◆ A service is only needed for a short term.
- ◆ The amount of service varies over time.
- ◆ It's not clear what the service need will be.

Although the public cloud is uniquely positioned for many of these fluctuating resource requirement scenarios, it may also be the case that the public cloud can deliver any service less expensively than you can offer it in your own datacenter. This can be a sobering thought for many datacenter administrators—who almost certainly will push back. "How can a company possibly offer a service cheaper than I can and still make a profit?" is a common response. But that argument does not consider the economies of scale achieved by mega-cloud providers like Microsoft and Amazon. Neither does it consider the various ways to provide service and resiliency. As I discussed in the first chapter, on-premises' high availability of services is accomplished through expensive storage arrays and clusters of servers. Instead, through software, Azure ensures that all data is replicated both within the datacenter and to another datacenter hundreds of miles away to ensure the protection of the data, including the actual OS virtual hard disks (which are just data to Azure), thus allowing the actual workloads to be protected. This enables Azure to use commodity storage.

What constitutes the right mix of public cloud and on-premises will differ for every organization. Some won't want to be in the business of running datacenters at all; they want to move everything to the cloud. Others, like the computer company that used Azure for Black Friday sales web hosting, will focus on hybrid scenarios and supplement their on-premises resources with the public cloud when required. (That organization, in total, paid only a few hundred dollars for services to handle the entire day's sales traffic.) Still other organizations will use the public cloud in regions where they have no local datacenter but want to offer low latency services. Some will use Azure to enable disaster recovery for services.

When thinking about the costs of hosting on-premises compared to those in the public cloud, it can help to think about some of those key costs and how they vary. Figure 2.1 was a small picture that I originally created on a whiteboard while talking to a customer who was convinced they could host anything less expensively than was possible in Azure. I wanted to be sure they were thinking about all the various aspects.

FIGURE 2.1

Key cost considerations for on-premises and Azure

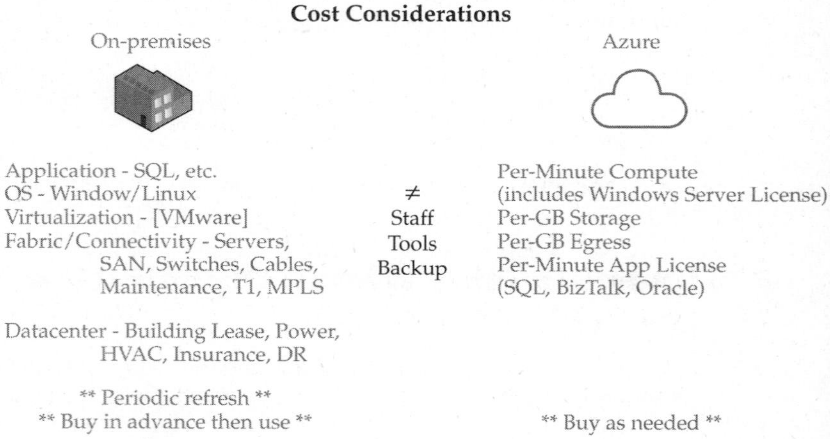

Cost Considerations

On-premises

Azure

Application - SQL, etc.
OS - Window/Linux
Virtualization - [VMware]
Fabric/Connectivity - Servers,
    SAN, Switches, Cables,
    Maintenance, T1, MPLS

≠
Staff
Tools
Backup

Per-Minute Compute
(includes Windows Server License)
Per-GB Storage
Per-GB Egress
Per-Minute App License
(SQL, BizTalk, Oracle)

Datacenter - Building Lease, Power,
    HVAC, Insurance, DR

** Periodic refresh **
** Buy in advance then use **

** Buy as needed **

Ultimately, you should use the right solution for your organization. That could be on-premises, hybrid, or the public cloud. Of course, price is not necessarily the deciding factor. Maybe you can host a service on-premises less expensively, but will you have the same disaster recovery capabilities as available in Azure? Maybe you can host in the public cloud less expensively, but can Azure meet the regulatory requirement challenges you face?

On-premises Costs

On-premises costs will be well understood by most organizations, but it's easy to overlook some aspects of hosting resources on-premises or even in a co-location facility, including the following:

Physical Plant Costs An on-premises datacenter requires a physical location. The building could be bought or leased (a significant cost). Now, add taxes and insurance. Next, consider the specific facility requirements for a datacenter, which may include raised flooring, fire suppression, hot and cold aisle containment, cooling systems, backup power generators, protection from unauthorized access, and more. All of this is very expensive. Utility bills for the datacenter, such as electricity and water, can amount to a significant cost. What about disaster recovery? Will you need additional datacenters and all the various components duplicated there? You may also service customers globally. Will you need datacenters in different geographical regions and, again, need to fill them with all the components needed to deliver services?

Fabric Costs Within the datacenter are the actual fabric resources: the storage, the networking, the servers, the cabling, and connectivity to the outside world via means such as MPLS and dedicated connections. The fabric is not just an initial significant cost, but it requires periodic refreshing, such as replacing the servers, networking equipment, and storage every five years.

Virtual Environment Costs Most organizations operate on a virtual first directive. When you look at the capabilities of the current generation of hypervisors such as Microsoft Hyper-V and VMware ESXi, there are very few workloads that cannot be run in a virtual machine. This means that the IT department has to manage and potentially pay for the hypervisor. I say potentially, since for some hypervisors (such as ESXi), you pay for the capabilities of the hypervisor, whereas for a hypervisor like Hyper-V, there is no cost. Hyper-V is included as a role within Windows Server—which means you'll be paying to run Windows Server in the virtual machines. Or if you are running Linux or Virtual Desktop Infrastructure (VDI) workloads, you can use the Microsoft Hyper-V Server, which is a free download. The Microsoft Hyper-V Server has all the same capabilities as the Hyper-V role inside Windows Server. However, even if the hypervisor is cost-free, it still needs to be managed. For something like Hyper-V, the built-in administration tools (Hyper-V Manager and Failover Cluster Manager) are not designed to be used as the central tool for enterprise management. Microsoft's System Center, which is not free, is the tool of choice. A license is required for all the OS instances managed by System Center. There are benefits to virtualization, because the physical hosts can be licensed for System Center. Licensing the physical hosts allows all virtual machines to be managed by System Center without additional cost, but there is still a cost associated with the initial purchase and the training of your staff, and with maintaining enterprise agreements to ensure access to latest versions. Even if you leverage a public cloud IaaS solution, you will still need solutions for monitoring within the OS, backup, patching, automation, and so on—which means you likely will still need System Center.

SYSTEM CENTER IN AZURE IAAS

In an on-premises environment, System Center is licensed in two physical processor (or socket) increments, and all processors in the server must be licensed. The number of cores on each processor does not affect the licensing. For example, if I had a server with four processors, I would need two licenses of System Center. System Center can be purchased as a Standard or Datacenter edition. The two are identical from a feature perspective—the difference is in the number of virtual instance rights included. A Standard license includes support for up to two virtual instance rights (two virtual machines that are being managed by some aspect of System Center). Standard licenses are typically used for physical OS deployments, where virtualization is used very lightly or not at all, such as a branch office with only 1 or 2 virtual machines. A Datacenter license covers an unlimited number of virtual machines, which makes this license the best fit for virtualization hosts that are running a large number of virtual machines managed by System Center.

Now, consider Microsoft Azure IaaS. Here, the physical servers are completely hidden from you as a consumer, and your only insight is into the number of virtual CPUs that are assigned to your virtual machine. You do not see the number of physical processors that are being used, or even which physical hosts your virtual machines are running on, but you still want to use System Center for aspects of the OS instances running in Azure IaaS. On-premises licensing does not work in a public cloud scenario. Microsoft has separate licensing information for using System Center in Azure (which is covered in detail at http://azure.microsoft.com/en-us/pricing/licensing-faq/). For Azure, a System Center Standard license covers managing two Azure VM instances, and the System Center Datacenter license covers managing eight Azure VM instances. As of this writing, the list Datacenter license cost is less than three times the cost of a Standard license and gives four times the number of VM instances. For many organizations, this makes the Datacenter choice the optimal way to license VMs in Azure for System Center. So, if you want to manage 40 VM instances running in Azure with System Center, you will need to buy five licenses for System Center Datacenter edition.

Operating System Costs   Once the virtual environment is in place, the operating systems are installed into the virtual machines. For VMs running Windows Server, typically the physical hosts are licensed for Windows Server Datacenter edition. This enables an unlimited number of VMs running on the hosts to run the Windows Server OS. (Like System Center, Windows Server is licensed in two processor increments, and all processors must be licensed.) If you are running a Windows client OS in the VMs, such as a VDI environment, you need to license each client OS appropriately. And if you're running Linux, you need to license those instances as well. As you would expect for environments running on-premises, you are responsible for the licensing of all the various OS instances you are running.

Application Costs   Finally, there are the actual workloads, such as Exchange, SQL Server, and various other applications, running on the OS instances. There may also be other frameworks, middleware components, and other support software installed. Some of the applications may be licensed solutions, whereas others may be in-house software. In any case, there are likely to be licenses associated with some of the applications running in the environment.

As you can see, many layers of cost and complexity are associated with on-premises solutions. The scenarios are simplified greatly in a public cloud IaaS solution and, more specifically, with an Azure IaaS solution.

Azure Costs

In an Azure IaaS solution, there are no separate costs for the datacenter, power, HVAC, insurance, servers, network equipment, storage services, cables, virtualization software, or the management fabric needed to keep everything running. As a customer, you see various menu items for the services you wish to use, such as:

◆ Per-minute compute resources based on the size of the VM

◆ Per-minute Windows Server license (included in the price of Windows VMs in Azure)

◆ Per GB of data storage used (different tiers of storage and different types of storage are available)

◆ Per GB of egress data (data sent from Azure—there is no cost for ingress data to Azure)

◆ Per-minute application license when applications such as SQL Server, BizTalk, or Oracle are used

The key point is that you pay only for the services you need. None of the physical plant or fabric costs associated with providing the service are exposed to you. They are baked into the costs for the services you buy. Remember that with an Azure IaaS solution, you are purchasing a VM and optionally certain applications. For the majority of instances, you will need to bring your own license for the applications you want to run on those VMs. You may also need to bring licenses for any Linux distributions you want to run in Azure. Finally, you will need to bring licenses for the software you want to use to manage the Azure VMs.

Comparing the Costs and Evaluating Solutions

Whether you use an on-premises solution or a public cloud solution, there are some similar requirements, although the actual resources and costs may not be equal.

Tools   Consider the tools used to maintain the environment—monitoring, deploying, and maintenance of the environment. Potentially, exactly the same tools would be used for on-premises and public cloud–based services. System Center can be used across a heterogeneous environment, which means the actual toolset may be the same. This is an important point for any organization looking to use the public cloud. Just using the public cloud is a huge change for any organization, and if that change also means using a completely separate toolset than is used on-premises, the implementation is likely to be difficult. If an existing, well-known toolset that the team is familiar with can be used, this will make adoption far simpler and less prone to problems. Using a single toolset can also be beneficial for end users, since a single interface can be enabled and services can be provisioned running on-premises or in the public cloud. Alternatively, the move to the public cloud may involve completely new tools if the current toolset does not support public cloud services. Perhaps there is no solution used on-premises, but the shift to the public cloud is the catalyst for improving operational processes. The key point is, when you leverage IaaS, you still need tools. Although the fabric is managed by the provider, the organization's IT team is still responsible for the OS, everything installed in the OS, and as many automated actions as possible.

Backup   Backup, a key aspect of any IT operation, is another interesting consideration. The need for backups does not go away when you move to the public cloud. On-premises backups often involve off-site storage. Since the public cloud is already off-site, there are a couple of common misconceptions about backing up the public cloud and Azure:

◆ I don't need backups—my Azure Storage is replicated several times in the datacenter and is also geo-replicated to another Azure datacenter hundreds of miles away. My data is safe.

◆ If I need my data restored, I can call up Azure support and ask them to restore a backup from a week last Tuesday.

Both of these misconceptions are serious ones. First, replication of data is useful for disaster recovery, but it is not a replacement for backups. If there were some kind of deletion or logical corruption, that deletion or logical corruption would replicate. Backups provide point-in-time saved data, which are critical in the event of corruption, data loss, or simply for regulatory purposes. When using IaaS in the public cloud, you still need to ensure you are performing backups. This leads to the second misconception: the public cloud provider, in this case Microsoft, is doing routine backups and, in a worst-case scenario, can restore the data for you from some point in the past. This does not happen. Microsoft replicates the data, but Azure Storage data is not backed up. The data is replicated multiple times, and even replicated to another datacenter to ensure data is not lost because of hardware or even datacenter failure—but the Azure fabric does not perform actual backups and cannot get old data back for you. For those services that do have the ability to restore data, it is because that service has specifically implemented its own backup/checkpoint functionality. (Azure SQL Database offers self-service point-in-time restoration.) Once again, the main point is that you need backup software when using IaaS in the public cloud.

Staffing   The final consideration often involves very sensitive conversations. The staff needed to run the infrastructure on-premises must be compared to the staff needed in the public cloud, and potentially the staff needed to run services, if you move beyond IaaS. Services such as Office 365 and Azure SQL Database remove most management tasks related to the service, and organizations only perform basic administration once the architecture and implementation/migration is complete. Office 365 is a perfect example. Prior to Office 365, organizations would have Exchange, SharePoint, and Lync administrators who would deploy the products, upgrade them every couple of years, keep them patched, back them up, provide for disaster recovery, and troubleshoot when problems arose. Once a move to Office 365 is performed, all of those tasks are gone, and the organization now has a service provided that gets updated more frequently than could ever be achieved on-premises. Features are added to Office 365 long before being added to the on-premises equivalents. Organizations with large teams of people looking after those products likely would need to retool staff for other tasks.

Team members who look after the physical servers, the datacenter, and the storage fabric are likely going to have far less work to do—possibly none in the event of a complete migration to the public cloud. This would apply to staff who manage the on-premises hypervisor as well. As the amount of on-premises infrastructure declines, there will be fewer instances to manage. As more of the forward thinking is based in public cloud services, there is less focus on the on-premises virtualization. Compatibility between on-premises and public cloud deployments and processes will become a new consideration for the hypervisor team.

There is a downside, though. More people may be needed for some roles, or at least the roles may become more involved. Consider the network architects and engineers. In a hybrid environment, additional design elements are related to the connections between on-premises and the public cloud. Those connections must ensure the right levels of communication and performance. This would also extend to those who focus on security. Corporate resources in the public cloud potentially are exposed to the Internet. It takes a great deal of planning and ongoing governance to ensure adherence to corporate and regulatory requirements.

The way in which IT time is spent is the most common change I find when adopting public cloud services. It is likely far more time will be spent on designing architecture, automating services, performing monitoring/reporting, understanding the capabilities to best ascertain services to be placed in the public cloud, keeping up to speed on rapidly changing capabilities, and reassessing how services are architected and deployed to match those capabilities. Realistically, you should expect to need fewer people as you move to the public cloud, but ideally there are processes and initiatives in place focused on the retooling of people with skillsets applicable to the new environment. Retasking does not just maintain an equilibrium of service, but also brings enhanced services and makes IT a value to the business through enabling new options.

Upfront Investment   For all on-premises solutions, resources are purchased in advance and then used over time. Initially, a new petabyte SAN might not be highly used (it will be over time), but the monetary outlay happens in advance. This is a huge difference from the cloud, where your costs are proportional to your actual resource requirements. Purchasing is not always a bad thing. There are ways to purchase resources to minimize the up-front cost, and organizational accountants can work miracles with expenses, but the point remains, with the cloud you pay for exactly what you use and only when you are using it. I also never have to periodically upgrade my public cloud investment; that is the responsibility of the service provider.

Disaster Recovery and High Availability   Azure data is replicated to a paired datacenter, so disaster recovery is provided. Additionally, there are Azure datacenters all over the world, so you can provide services in the major regions and give an optimal end-user experience without the expense of standing up entire datacenters. You could literally run a web server in all the major locations in the world for a few hundred dollars a month.

As I previously mentioned, cost is not the deciding factor, but it can certainly be a big factor. The differences in the flexibility for procuring the various services all over the world may be a huge factor for a company that operates internationally and whose country-specific data may have to stay in that country. As an organization, you may be able to run one on-premises datacenter for the same cost as running VMs in Azure, but if you need disaster recovery and some VMs in Europe, some in Asia, and some in North America, suddenly hosting in your own datacenters becomes far less plausible.

Understanding Costs, Options, and Licensing

So far in this book I've been focusing on the public cloud more than Azure. The reason is that many of the public cloud considerations are not unique to Azure but are available from Microsoft and other providers. Now, I want to look at the specifics of how services in Azure are purchased and licensed.

The fundamental principle of Azure pricing is that you pay based on what you use, be that compute hours, storage, egress bandwidth, or another factor. Each type of service offers sizes, tiers, options, and capabilities to choose from—and those choices affect the price of the service. The best way to start understanding how Azure is licensed is by using the Azure Pricing Calculator, which is available at http://azure.microsoft.com/en-us/pricing/calculator/. Because pricing changes, there is little benefit to documenting current prices here. I use the Azure Pricing Calculator as my guide, but keep in mind that the calculator shows retail pricing. Your organization could have substantial discounts if you have an Azure commitment in your Enterprise Agreement. (You might want to take another look at Table 1.2 in Chapter 1, "The Cloud and Microsoft Azure 101.") Additionally, the calculator is based on prices in the US region, and prices can vary by region. You can find region-specific pricing at http://azure .microsoft.com/en-us/pricing/overview/.

Start your web browser, and walk through the following exercise to get a look at the various pricing options and some of the licensing options for running workloads in Azure:

1. Open http://azure.microsoft.com/en-us/pricing/calculator/ in your browser.

2. Notice that in the main view (shown in Figure 2.2) the Azure services are grouped into categories. You can select a category to see the services included. There is also a full

calculator option, which shows all the services in a single view. Prices are displayed in dollars, but you have the option to change the currency.

FIGURE 2.2
Main Azure Pricing
Calculator interface

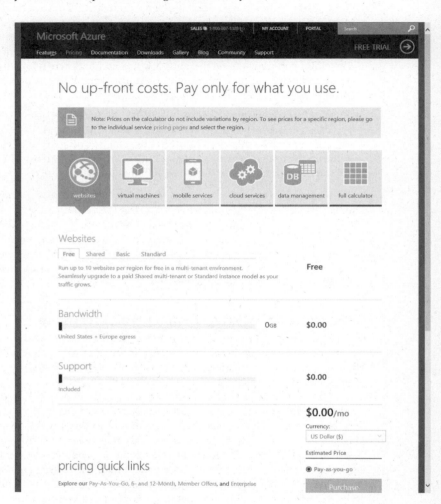

3. This book focuses on infrastructure services in Azure, which means virtual machines are a primary focus. These compute services are accessed via the virtual machines category, so select that category. As shown in Figure 2.3, the various virtual machine services are grouped by Windows and Linux, and then by certain specific application workloads, such as SQL Server, BizTalk, and Oracle.

4. In each section, you can select either a standard or a basic service tier. As the name suggests, the basic tier lacks features available in the standard tier. It also has differences in terms of storage and network performance. As expected, the basic tier is cheaper, which means you should use the basic tier unless you need a capability that is specific

FIGURE 2.3
Virtual machine pricing options

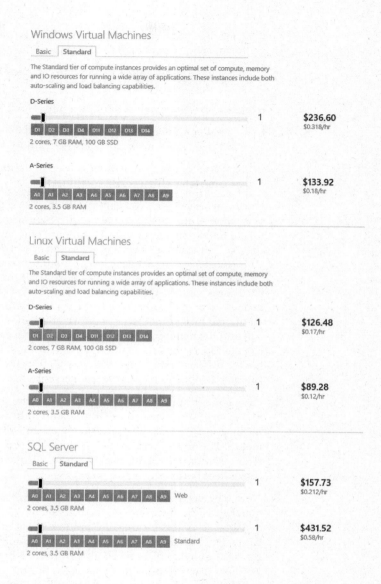

to the standard tier. If you need to change the tier of a virtual machine, you can. It does require a shutdown and restart of the virtual machine, because the VM has to be reprovisioned on the Azure fabric. Here are some of the differences you'll find at the basic tier:

◆ There are no load-balancing features.

◆ There is no auto-scaling support.

◆ CPU performance is reduced compared to the standard tier.

◆ Each disk has a 300 IOPS limit; 500 IOPs is available for standard-tier VMs. (See `http://msdn.microsoft.com/en-us/library/azure/dn197896.aspx`.)

◆ Basic has a lower egress bandwidth cap; the Mbps output capability is low compared to the equivalent standard-tier VM.

◆ Basic does not support multiple vmnics for a VM.

◆ A smaller number of VM sizes are available on the basic tier compared to the standard tier—specifically, there are no memory-intensive sizes.

Most commonly, the basic tier is used in development scenarios, where the lower cost is more important than certain features.

5. Once you select a tier, you can specify the VM size you're interested in. As of this writing, your choices are A-Series, D-Series, DS-Series, and G-Series. You cannot customize the mix of the number of processors, amount of memory, maximum number of disks, and the like, but you must pick a specific size of VM. Many options are available, including VMs (sizes A5–A7) that have large amounts of memory for memory-intensive workloads. Once you select a VM size, the calculator will show you the amount of memory and CPU cores associated with the size. The full list of all VM sizes is shown at `http://msdn.microsoft.com/en-us/library/azure/dn197896.aspx`. The listing shows two additional important pieces of information: the size of the temporary disk added to each VM and the maximum number of data disks that can be added to a VM. (I will cover the storage aspects in detail in Chapter 3, "Customizing VM Storage.") What is not shown are the differences in network egress QoS for the various VM sizes; I will cover that in Chapter 4, "Enabling External Connectivity."

6. Once you select the VM size, you can move the slider to select the number of instances of that size. (You can also use the left and right arrow keys to change the number of instances.) The dollar amounts shown assume that each VM is running 24/7 for the month. The hourly price is shown as well. If you select several types of VMs, a grand total is shown at the bottom of the price calculator web page. And, of course, there is a convenient button so you can purchase the Azure services.

7. Now, try selecting a Linux VM or a SQL Server instance using the same VM size and quantity. Notice that the price is different.

Why? As of this writing, a Windows VM is 50 percent more expensive than the equivalent Linux VM. This is because the Windows license is included as part of the consumption-based charge. You don't need to bring your own Windows license—the Windows license cost is included in the hourly cost. There is no mechanism to bring your own Windows Server license to Azure. For Linux VMs, Microsoft does not provide the license—you need to bring your own.

Now, look at the cost of a SQL Server Standard VM of the same size: 58 cents an hour instead of 18 cents an hour for the Windows Server VM when you look at standard-tier A2 size. Notice the steep difference in price? Once again, Microsoft provides the license for SQL Server on a consumption basis. This is also available for BizTalk, and even Oracle products can be licensed on a consumption basis. The increased price covers the application license as it's used, and this ability to pay on consumption is a huge benefit for organizations that need the application only for certain periods of time. If you want to use SQL Server, BizTalk, or Oracle but don't want to lease the license from Microsoft and instead have your own, simply create regular Windows VMs, install the applications in them postcreation, and then specify your license. It's only when you select one of the application images from the Azure gallery that you lease an application license from Microsoft as it's consumed.

8. Scroll down to the bottom of the Virtual Machines tab and notice there are two other items: bandwidth and support.

   There are two types of network traffic: ingress (data into Azure) and egress (data out of an Azure region). You only pay for egress traffic; Microsoft picks up upload data costs, since that's what they want you to upload to Azure. Traffic flowing out of Azure does incur a cost, and the slider allows you to see the cost per gigabyte. Although you pay for data flowing out of Azure, there is no cost for data traffic flowing between services hosted in the same Azure region, such as VM-to-VM traffic.

   The Support slider enables different levels of support that can be purchased and includes options for third-party support, such as SuSE Linux Enterprise Server (SLES).

9. You'll see tabs for other types of service, and you should take time to scroll through to get an idea of how pricing works for various services. It will take time to look at the Data Management tab, because it outlines the costs of various types of storage. Storage costs will apply to those using Azure IaaS VMs, since the compute costs do not cover the cost of storage. When calculating your estimated costs, it's important to also include the cost of storage you are using. The various types of storage redundancy give different levels of protection and access from an Azure region failure. When calculating costs for Azure IaaS VM storage, you need to select the Page Blobs and Disks options. (Azure Disks are stored in Page Blobs.)

WHETHER TO BRING YOUR OWN APPLICATION LICENSE

The ability to lease application licenses in Azure opens up new options for organizations. It can, initially, be unclear if it is better to bring your own license for the applications or pay for the license through Azure as it's used. There is no clear right or wrong answer, but some scenarios will heavily favor leasing the licenses as part of the VM consumption. Consider a short-term project that will run for only two weeks and requires four SQL Service instances. A monthly job that runs for one day but needs a lot of SQL Server on that day is another candidate. In these scenarios, the option to pay for the SQL Server license for the limited time it is used is far more cost-efficient than buying SQL Server licenses that sit idle most of the time. If you will be running the VM in Azure 24/7, you have to work out the price of leasing the license in Azure, and compare that with the cost of purchasing and maintaining support on your own SQL Server license for use in Azure. I suspect it will be very close, but every company has different pricing and different levels of discount in Azure, so the exact delta may vary.

One question I often hear when looking at the Azure cost calculator related to the included Windows Server license is which version of Windows Server is included—the Standard or the Datacenter SKU? The reality is, in Azure, there is no difference. Since Azure licenses are virtual, the use of Standard or Datacenter makes no difference—they are functionally identical. As a point of reference, the Azure images are based on the Datacenter SKU of Windows Server.

Also, note that no Windows client image (such as Windows 10) is available through Azure. Currently, there is no way to legally license Windows client operating systems in a public cloud environment. The only time you will ever see a Windows client in Azure is for MSDN subscriptions, since they are designed for testing and development and include licensing. When you look at the gallery while logged in with an MSDN subscription, you will see client images that are not visible under a normal Azure subscription. Figure 2.4 shows a client image in an MSDN Azure subscription. The client images are only to be used as part of testing.

FIGURE 2.4
Client images are available only when you have an MSDN Azure subscription.

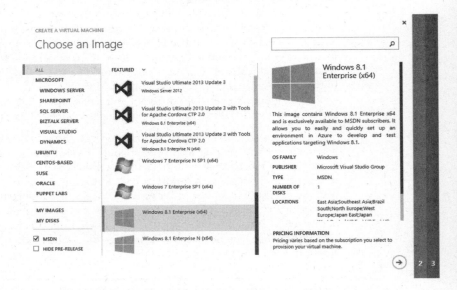

If you are first getting started with Azure, you may very well be using your MSDN Azure benefit. In addition to the Azure credit you receive each month, your MSDN subscription has a benefit detailed at http://azure.microsoft.com/en-us/pricing/member-offers/msdn-benefits-details/. You will remember that under a typical Azure subscription, Windows VMs are 50 percent more expensive than an equivalent Linux VM because the Windows Server license is included. For MSDN subscriptions, the licenses are provided as part of the MSDN subscription, which means you should not have to pay extra for a Windows license when running an Azure IaaS VM. This is the additional MSDN Azure benefit. Windows VMs are priced at a 33 percent discount for MSDN Azure subscriptions, which brings the VM to the same price as the equivalent Linux VM. There are discounts for some additional types of services as well. You may notice I used 50 percent more expensive, but only a 33 percent discount. Consider that 18 cents is 50 percent more expensive than 12 cents, but a 33 percent discount on 18 cents brings you back to 12 cents—it just depends how you perform the comparison.

The pricing calculator is a great tool, but remember that it uses the basic retail pricing. Your organization may have additional discounts. For most organizations, the best way to get accurate pricing is to work with your Microsoft account team.

Although the calculator is powerful, you still need to know how many VMs, what size VMs, and how much storage will be required for your operations. Tools such as the Microsoft Assessment and Planning Toolkit (MAP) can help you perform discovery, but Microsoft has created a tool that specifically looks at existing on-premises infrastructure and provides output on which on-premises could run in Azure. You can learn what size infrastructure is needed based on actual resource utilization and will receive an estimated 30-day cost of running that infrastructure in Azure. The tool, the Microsoft Azure (IaaS) Cost Estimator Tool, is available at `http://aka.ms/AzureCostTool`. The tool hooks into the following environments:

◆ Microsoft Hyper-V environments (including System Center Virtual Machine Manager [SCVMM])

◆ ESXi environments (including vCenter)

◆ Physical Windows and Linux environments

Once deployed, the tool connects to the target environments, finds all the OS instances, evaluates resource usage over a period of time, and then reports on Azure compatibility and cost.

Creating VMs in Azure

You're well into Chapter 2, and you're probably eager to create VMs in Azure. In this section, I will walk through some of the interfaces that can be used to provision VMs in Azure. I will introduce the various interfaces and other Azure VM concepts, but I urge you to refrain from creating any production VMs yet because you must first understand concepts such as storage and networking. Some of these items cannot be changed once you create a VM. I recommend going through the steps in this section with a test VM in Azure to help cement the concepts.

As of this writing, there are two web-based portals that you can use to manage Azure services:

◆ The legacy portal (which is actually the second-generation Azure portal that moved away from Silverlight in favor of HTML5) is available at `https://manage.windowsazure.com`.

◆ The preview portal (which is based on the latest web technologies, features a very modern look and feel, and maintains the tile-and-journey-based approach of Windows 8 and later) is available at `https://portal.azure.com/`.

Ideally, I would only cover the newest-generation portal, but not all functionality has been migrated from the legacy portal to the preview portal yet. This is true especially for infrastructure Azure services. Currently, there are many tasks that can only be done in the legacy portal (or through PowerShell or REST APIs, but more on that later). I'll focus on the legacy portal here, but over time all functionality will be migrated to the preview portal. At that point, the preview portal will become the primary portal. Even today, features are being added that are available only through the preview portal, so it is important to be able to navigate and use both portals.

Using the Legacy Azure Portal

Looking at Figure 2.5, it quickly becomes clear why the Azure portal needed to be redesigned. Notice the Navigation pane on the left-hand side—and its scroll bar. When Azure had only a few different services, the Navigation pane was fine. But when you have 20 different categories of services, it becomes cumbersome to find the category. Additionally, to quickly move between different areas, users must continually re-navigate to the correct place.

Let's look at the elements of the Azure portal. The Navigation pane on the far left enables access to the various services available in Azure. Once a category is selected, the details

FIGURE 2.5
The legacy Azure
portal main screen

appear in the main window. As shown in Figure 2.5, the Virtual Machines navigation node displays a list of virtual machines. When you select a virtual machine, the details area displays information about it.

The title bar at the top of the window shows the currently logged-on user. When you select that user, the portal displays options for signing out, changing your password, viewing billing and support options, and switching to the new Preview Azure portal. Click the globe icon to change the localization of the portal. Click the subscriptions icon to open a window where you can change the subscriptions you're managing (providing your logged-on account has access to more than one subscription). You'll also see links to common actions related to account and subscription management.

At the bottom of the window is the context-sensitive command bar. The commands displayed there change depending on the focus of the main display area. For example, if a VM is selected, the actions in the command bar, such as Start and Stop, are relevant to a VM. If you select an action that is confirmed, the confirmation will display as a bar above the command bar, as shown in Figure 2.6. To the right of the commands is a help icon, which you can click to access various help topics.

FIGURE 2.6
Azure portal
confirmation display

Other icons may be displayed to the left of the help icon. If an activity is currently running, an icon that shows moving bars representing activity is displayed with a number that indicates the number of running activities. If you click that icon, the details of the activities appear, as shown in Figure 2.7. Completed activities also appear and need to be acknowledged to be cleared. You might also see a notification icon, which you can click to display details about notifications.

FIGURE 2.7
Azure portal running
activity display

To the far left of the command bar is the New icon. As the name suggests, the New icon brings up a cascading menu of services that can be created in Azure, as shown in Figure 2.8. The menu is intelligent and automatically selects the type of object as a creation type based on the navigation area of the portal currently selected. For example, if you are currently in the Virtual Machine area when the New icon is selected, the menu will automatically navigate to the Virtual Machine new service options, as shown in Figure 2.8. All the other service types can still be created; simply select different menu items.

FIGURE 2.8
Creating a new Azure
service

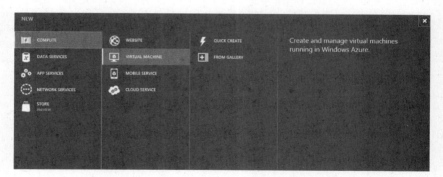

Now that the portal elements are familiar to you, let's create a VM in Azure:

1. After logging in to the portal, click the New icon on the command bar and navigate to Compute ➤ Virtual Machine.

2. Select the From Gallery option, which lets you create a VM based on an existing template.

3. When the Create A Virtual Machine wizard (which consists of four pages of configuration) opens, select an image for the new VM. Figure 2.9 shows the first page of the wizard. Once you create your own images and disks, those images will be available from the wizard as well. For this exercise, select the Windows Server 2012 R2 Datacenter image and click the Next icon.

FIGURE 2.9
Page 1 of the Create
A Virtual Machine
wizard

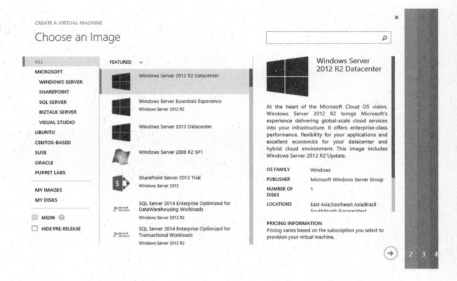

4. The next page, shown in Figure 2.10, allows you to enter details about the virtual machine to be configured. Most images have a version release date option, which enables you to select different versions of the image. For example, most commonly this will be a certain patch level. Choosing the latest date will give you the most recent patch level of the image. You will need to enter a name for the virtual machine. You can use between 3 and 15 characters consisting of letters, numbers, and hyphens. Next, select a tier and size for the virtual machine. Finally, enter a username for the local administrator of the machine.

FIGURE 2.10
Page 2 of the Create
A Virtual Machine
wizard

FIGURE 2.11
Page 3 of the Create
A Virtual Machine
wizard

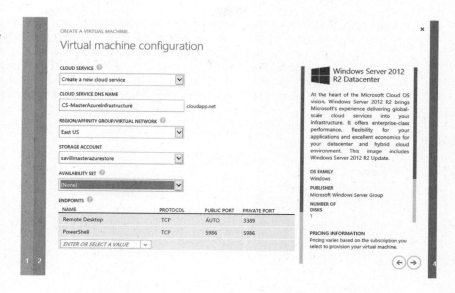

(For Windows, you cannot use Administrator, and for Linux, you cannot use root.) Now set a complex password for Windows. For Linux, an SSH key can be uploaded and/or a password can be configured. When you've finished, click the Next icon.

5. As shown in Figure 2.11, the next page is the most complex of the wizard. Not all of the concepts will make sense at this point, but you'll learn more in Chapter 4. When VMs are created in Azure, they are created in a construct called a *cloud service*. Multiple virtual machines can exist in the same cloud service. The cloud service has a DNS name with a suffix of *cloudapp.net*. Each cloud service DNS name must be globally unique across all Azure subscriptions. By default, a new cloud service is created for each new VM. You can, however, select an existing cloud service from the Cloud Service drop-down menu and add the new VM there. When you enter a name for a new cloud service, the name is validated to ensure that it meets naming requirements and is not already in use. Next, select an Azure region. To minimize latencies, regions typically are selected based on closeness to the service user base. Every Azure virtual machine has at least one virtual disk, which is stored in a storage account. In a production environment, you will pre-create storage accounts. For this test walk-through, you can select the option to automatically generate a storage account. Leave Availability Set as None, but take note of the two endpoints automatically created for a Windows VM and the single endpoint for a Linux VM, as shown in Figure 2.12. Leave the default endpoints in place. Very simply, the cloud service the VM resides in has an Internet addressable IP address, called the Virtual

FIGURE 2.12
Default endpoints for
a Linux VM

ENDPOINTS			
NAME	PROTOCOL	PUBLIC PORT	PRIVATE PORT
SSH	TCP	22	22
ENTER OR SELECT A VALUE			

IP (VIP). Actual VMs do not; the VMs only have internal IP addresses. The endpoints are mappings from the cloud service IP to specific ports on VMs within the cloud service, which is why the public port may not match the private port. Multiple VMs cannot share the same port on the shared cloud service public IP. If you wanted to use Remote Desktop Protocol (RDP) to access your Windows VM from the Internet, you would connect via the cloud service DNS name and the public port of the Remote Desktop endpoint for the VM. I show this in Figure 2.13 to make this clearer. Click Next to proceed to the final page of the wizard.

FIGURE 2.13
Cloud service
endpoints in action

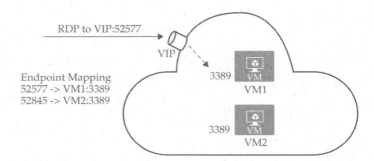

CHECKING CLOUD SERVICE NAME AVAILABILITY

There will be times when you want to check if an Azure cloud service name is available before creating your cloud service. This is especially true when you are creating the service through scripts (which is possible using the Azure PowerShell module). To test if a name is available, use the following:

```
Test-AzureName -Service 'CloudServiceNameToTestFor'
```

If the result is False, the name is available.

6. The final page of the wizard, shown in Figure 2.14, allows you to install the Azure VM Agent. The option is enabled by default. If you decide to install the VM Agent, you can add a number of optional extensions, such as automation and security. The particular extensions vary based on the OS (Windows or Linux) running inside your VM. The VM Agent is a recent addition to Azure IaaS, and though not required, it offers additional services and capabilities, including the ability to reset a forgotten local password or resolve networking problems from PowerShell. I advise you to install the VM Agent unless you have a specific reason not to. Click the check mark icon to complete the wizard and start the provisioning of the virtual machine.

VM creation in Azure typically takes around 6 minutes, although the exact time may vary based on the template and the tier/size selected. The Activity icon in the command bar will

FIGURE 2.14

Page 4 of the Create
A Virtual Machine
wizard

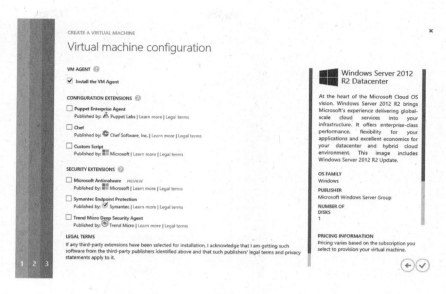

FIGURE 2.14

Page 4 of the Create
A Virtual Machine
wizard

show the VM provisioning activity, and in the main Virtual Machines view, the new VM will appear as being Provisioned, then Starting, and finally Running. Running is the point at which users can connect to the VM. Once the VM is running, select the VM in the Virtual Machines view and notice the actions available on the command bar. One of the options is Connect for Windows VMs (this is grayed out for Linux VMs). Connect generates and opens an RDP file that is automatically populated with the cloud service name and the RDP endpoint for the VM, and enables access to the VM over the Internet via RDP. When you select the VM, a dashboard will open. You can view details and statistics about the VM and use the various tabs to perform additional configurations. Take some time to look at all the options available. In this book, the various aspects of the portal will be explored, but this basic exercise has given you a good overview of the portal's structure and the mechanics to interact with it.

Using the Preview Azure Portal

The Preview Azure portal (code name Ibiza) is completely different from the previous version. It is designed to be more intuitive and less cluttered. You can more easily see and organize the information you care about.

The portal is available at https://portal.azure.com/. Figure 2.15 shows the Startboard for the new portal. The Startboard is focused on new constructs, primarily blades and journeys. It embodies DevOps, the idea of being able to manage the services and also understand the state of those services, billing, analytics, errors, and so on with flexibility.

On the left side of the portal is the hub menu, which contains the core hubs that are common across all the services available in Azure. The hub menu integrates information across the various services. The Notifications hub is a great example; it brings notifications from all the Azure services into one central location. The hub items are the starting point for accessing information in the portal. The resource parts, or tiles, are by default pinned to the Startboard. These include Azure service health, billing information, and access to the Azure gallery—the starting point for creating new services in Azure.

FIGURE 2.15
The Startboard for the preview Azure portal

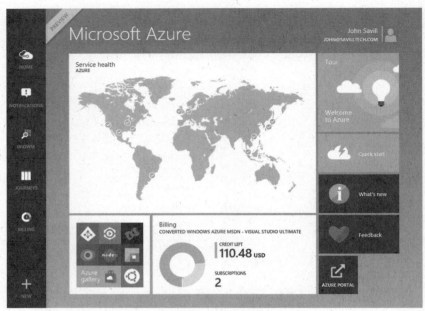

Clicking an item opens up a new *blade*, as shown in Figure 2.16. Selecting items in blades will likely open additional blades, which are added to the right of the current blade and can be scrolled left and right. The flow of created blades for a particular activity is known as a *journey*. Blades contain one or more *lenses* (groups of parts that have a common theme). For example, the blade for the test virtual machine shown in Figure 2.16 has a Summary lens, a Monitoring lens,

FIGURE 2.16
Multiple blades showing virtual machines and details for a specific virtual machine

a Usage lens, and more. Each lens contains parts that are relevant to that particular lens group. Notice that a command bar at the top of the test VM blade exposes actions (Connect, Restart, Shut Down, and Delete) that are relevant to the VM.

Each blade can be closed, minimized, maximized, and customized independently. Click the ellipsis (shown in Figure 2.17) at the top-right corner to customize the blade. Choose the Customize option, and you can customize each part by clicking on it.

FIGURE 2.17
Viewing the blade options

Three icons, as shown in Figure 2.18, will be displayed. The green pin icon pins the part to the Startboard; the orange pin removes it. You can also remove a part from the Startboard by right-clicking and selecting Unpin from the context menu.

FIGURE 2.18
Customizing an Azure portal part

The Customize icon provides options related to the size of a part within a lens on the dashboard and the ability to clone that part to create a new part. Cloning a chart part, such as the CPU percentage chart, can be very useful. Right-clicking on a part displays an Edit Chart context menu, which lets you modify the data shown on the chart. You can modify the date range and even the type of data displayed. You can clone the CPU percentage chart and edit it to display disk reads, as shown in Figure 2.19.

FIGURE 2.19
Editing the properties of a chart part

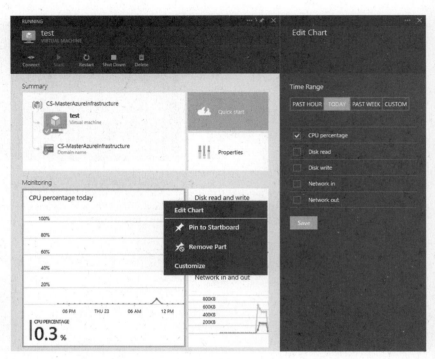

The primary driver behind these capabilities is to enable you to customize the entire dashboard to provide you with the information you care about. You can remove default parts from the blades, move parts around in a blade and even between blades, remove default parts from the Startboard, and restore removed parts if necessary. While in customize mode, if you double-click on an area of the portal that does not contain a part, the display will cycle between the three color themes: blue, white, and black. You can set the theme color by selecting your name in the top-right corner of the Startboard. Midway down the menu, you will find the theme choices.

Consider the scenario where you embark on a journey in the Azure portal that opens a sequence of blades, but now you want to look at another set of blades related to a complementary area. You simply scroll to the left of your dashboard and select a new hub from the hub menu. Perhaps a part on your Startboard opens a new blade, and your old set of blades disappears from view and makes it very hard to go back to where you were last. Getting back to where you were last was a big pain in the legacy version of the portal. This is not the case in the new portal. When you select a new part, a new set of blades opens a new journey. But in the new portal, your old journey is saved and can easily be opened by selecting the Journey hub menu (Figure 2.20), which will display all open journeys. Any open journey can be selected to restore that specific journey in the dashboard. Even if you sign out of the Azure portal and then connect again, your open journeys are saved and rehydrated on connection. I think of journeys as pressing Alt+Tab (which switches applications in Windows) for Azure, which enables simple switching between the open journeys. To close a journey, simply click the Close button at the top-right corner of the journey in the Journey hub or manually close all the blades that are part of the journey.

FIGURE 2.20
Viewing the open journeys

Another huge benefit of the new Azure portal is that it embraces the ways people work today—primarily on touch and mobile devices. The portal is very touch friendly, with large parts and buttons; the scrolling motion that moves horizontally along the dashboard as blades are opened is very natural. The blade and lens architecture also lends itself well to mobile devices, such as a phone, that have very small form factors, since only the current blade and lens have focus.

Performing a familiar action highlights the changes in the new portal. So let's look at creating a virtual machine in Azure:

1. Click the New button on the hub menu, and by default the most commonly created services, such as Windows Server 2012 R2 Datacenter and SQL Server Always On deployment (a feature of the new portal that enables deployment of multi-instance templates), will be displayed.

2. If the service or template you want to use does not appear, click the Everything button. When the Azure Gallery Home blade opens, you will have access to every type of available service and template.

3. Select the Windows Server 2012 R2 Datacenter VM template from the New menu.

4. When the Create VM blade (shown in Figure 2.21) opens, the interface is very simple and requires entering only a hostname, a username, and a password.

5. When you're finished, if you wish to create a default VM, click the Create button. Your newly created VM will be added to the Startboard. It will contain all the default options, such as tier and size, location, and storage group, for all the other configurations.

6. If you want new configurations for your options, you can change them. Notice that in Figure 2.21 the Pricing Tier has been selected. That opens up the Recommended pricing tiers blade and shows you the most common VM sizes: the Basic A1, the Standard A2, and the Standard A6. You can view more sizes by clicking the Browse All Pricing Tiers link. Likewise, advanced storage, network, and other options are available through various links. The new portal interface simplifies the experience and brings the most common options to the foreground. When all your option choices have been made, click the Create button.

FIGURE 2.21
The Create VM blade in action

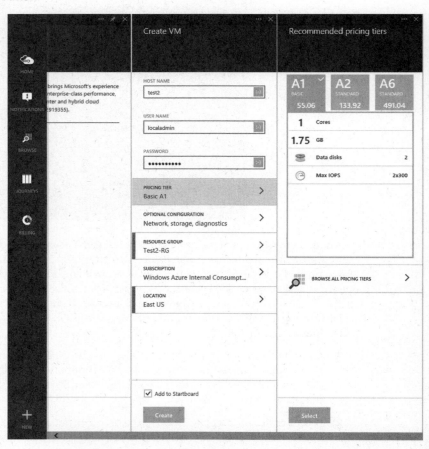

The newly created VM will be available on the Startboard, and you can browse all of your VMs by selecting the Browse hub and then selecting Virtual Machines. Clicking Virtual

Machines opens a blade containing all VMs in the subscription. From there you can select a VM and see its details, including the resource nap that shows the relationship between resources in the resource group (more on this later in this chapter).

Once again, the best way to learn the portal is to look around, investigate all the options, and try customizing the configuration of the environment. On the Startboard is a What's New part. I recommend looking at this frequently to keep up-to-date on changes.

RESOURCE GROUPS AND ROLE-BASED ACCESS CONTROL

Azure began as PaaS, which was focused on the deployment of cloud services. Over time, other roles, endpoints, and then virtual machines were added. However, the model remained focused on a cloud service and not the actual resources, which are more important in an IaaS environment. A large deployment of VMs in Azure is fairly complex today—everything is done imperatively in scripts. You have to code all the error handling, look for links between different VMs and substitute variables, check if resources already exist, and so forth. I've seen Microsoft scripts that deploy a SharePoint farm in Azure; this approach is very complex, and most people want to avoid it. The goal is to be able to deploy a service that is made up of many resources, and those resources should live in an application life cycle container so that they share a common life cycle. Access control should be governed on that container and billing information available for the resources in that container. Resources within that container should be able to communicate with and access each other using their own identity instead of the complex methods used today. This container is called the resource group, and going forward every resource created lives inside a resource group. Key capabilities, such as access control, management, and billing, will be aggregated to the resource group level.

A resource can exist only in a single resource group, and you cannot nest resource groups. You can, however, link resources from one resource group to another resource group. For example, you can link a SQL database from one resource group to another resource group if you use that SQL database to make it easier to see the resources used by your service. There are currently no limits to the number of resources in a resource group, but you cannot rename a resource group. Given that a rename operation can be highly destructive to mechanisms, such as role-based access control (RBAC) that use the name, I would not expect to see renaming available any time soon.

Here is an example view of a resource group in the Azure portal (https://portal.azure.com/). Note all the resources (domain names, virtual machines, and networks) can be seen. If any other resources were linked, they would also appear.

Resource groups are not available in the older portal, `https://manage.windowsazure.com/`; the new portal at `https://portal.azure.com/` must be used. To see all resource groups, click the Browse button and then select Resource Groups. A blade with all resource groups available will open. Selecting a resource group will reveals details about that group and expose its capabilities, such as configuring RBAC. Any new resource created is automatically created within a resource group. (You can choose to create a new resource group or add the new resource to an existing one.) When you deploy a template within the new portal, all resources from the template are placed together into a resource group. Alternatively, it is possible to create an empty resource group using the `New-AzureResourceGroup` PowerShell cmdlet, create resources, and then place them within the resource group.

The real power of resource groups is when they are combined with the new declarative template model that is exposed in the new Azure portal. This enables entire services to be deployed simply. You no longer have to write code to check for errors, see if resources exist, and so on.

The new portal also exposes granular RBAC. As of this writing, three roles are available, and this will expand in the future. Here are the roles and their capabilities:

Owner—Full control over the resources and access management

Contributor—Same as owner but without access management capabilities

Reader—View resources except resource secrets

Users and groups (which could be synced from on-premises Active Directory) can be assigned to the roles, and the roles are available at the subscription, resource group, and resource level. The access rights are inherited, which means if, for example, I have Contributor rights at the subscription level, I also have Contributor rights to all resource groups and resources within the subscription. Likewise, if I have Owner rights at a resource group level, I have Owner rights for all resources in the resource group.

To set the RBAC controls, navigate to the subscription, resource group, or resource within the new Azure portal by selecting Browse from the hub menu and then selecting Everything. (Everything will show all types, including Subscriptions.) Now, select the object (Subscription, Resource Group, or Resource). In the Access area, select the role you wish to grant users or groups and then click Add to add people. Note that this only works in the new portal; the old portal will not honor the RBAC settings.

Note that RBAC can also be assigned using PowerShell via the `New-AzureRoleAssignment` cmdlet. Here's an example:

```
New-AzureRoleAssignment -Mail kev@savilltech.net -RoleDefinitionName
Contributor -ResourceGroupName JohnGroup
```

Users and groups can be removed by selecting the role, selecting the user or group, and clicking Remove. Also, the `Remove-AzureRoleAssignment` cmdlet can be used via PowerShell.

Microsoft has a good page on RBAC at `http://azure.microsoft.com/en-us/documentation/articles/role-based-access-control-configure/`. I recommend taking a look.

Other Ways to Interact with Azure

Although the Azure portal (legacy or preview) is almost certain to be the first interface that newcomers to Azure will use, for most organizations it will not be the interface of choice on an ongoing, production basis. Organizations want the ability to have their own automations driving provisioning and actions. Organizations want to have workflows, including authorization. Organizations want to have a repeatable process to recreate environments in Azure in the event of disasters. Organizations want integration with existing services and service catalogs so that deployment to Azure is just one of a number of options, especially in hybrid environments.

Azure uses Representational State Transfer (REST) APIs for all of its communication and for the Azure portals. (Even PowerShell cmdlets use these REST interfaces behind the scenes.) This means it's possible for other services to integrate and manage Azure using standardized protocols. Although many solutions are available, I want to briefly cover the primary Microsoft-based solutions that are part of the System Center product.

System Center will be covered in detail in Chapter 10, "Managing Hybrid Environments with System Center." App Controller is a System Center component that provides direct integration for service provisioning, and another set of components, Orchestrator and Service Manager, can provide a more customized workflow for provisioning.

App Controller is a Silverlight-based web portal that runs on-premises and can connect to a number of cloud services:

◆ Private clouds managed using System Center Virtual Machine Manager, which itself can manage clouds using Hyper-V, ESXi, and XenServer

◆ Microsoft Azure

◆ Hosting service providers that leverage the Service Provider Foundation (SPF), which itself is part of System Center

Once clouds are connected, it is possible to view the overall status of the services running and details about VMs, as shown in Figure 2.22, including the ability to manage the VMs and provision and deprovision services. App Controller provides a true hybrid interface for customers using Microsoft cloud services. It can even deploy VMs to Azure from VMs stored in an on-premises library. The challenge with App Controller is that it's not possible to customize additional automation or workflows for processes, such as VM creation. However, it does provide a rich interface for ongoing management tasks, including starting, stopping, and even checkpointing (storing a point-in-time view of a VM that includes disk, memory, and device state).

The richer provisioning experience, which facilitates more complex automations and workflows, including authorizations, is enabled through a combination of Orchestrator and Service Manager. Orchestrator is the IT process automation toolbox of System Center. It can connect to almost any system and perform activities. Many activities are connected together with different paths to form a *runbook* based on the result or output of the activity. Orchestrator has many built-in activities, such as running a .NET script (PowerShell), running a SSH command, querying WMI, and much more. It's also possible to import integration packs (IPs), which are collections of activities related to a specific technology; examples include the VMware IP, the System Center Virtual Machine Manager IP, the FTP IP, and the Exchange IP. There is even a Windows Azure IP. Using the IPs is great, but Microsoft's forward direction is more focused on the Orchestrator Service Manager Automation (SMA), which is PowerShell workflow based. So, my suggestion is to use Orchestrator today but don't focus on the IPs. Instead, write most of the functionality using PowerShell and call using the Run .NET Script activity.

Orchestrator still provides value as a highly available engine to execute runbooks. It provides interfaces that enable those runbooks to be called from other services, such as

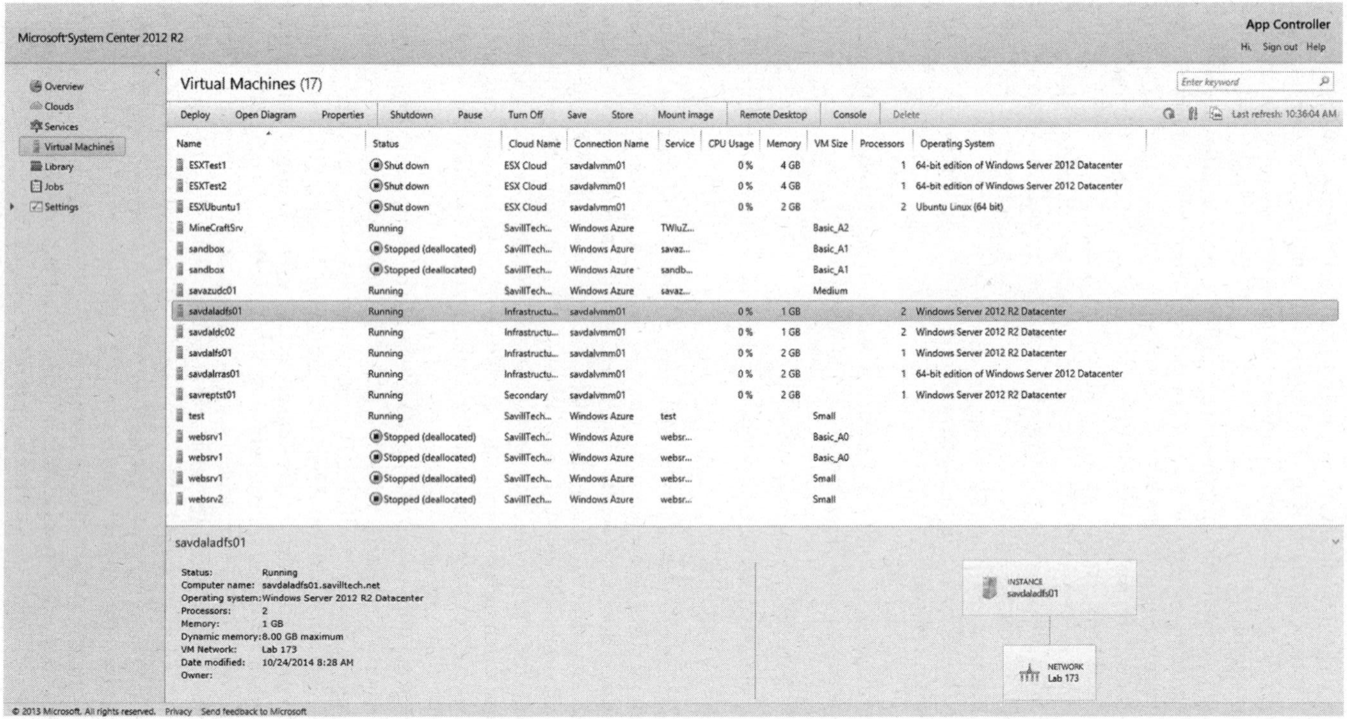
Microsoft System Center 2012 R2
App Controller
Hi, Sign out Help
Overview
Clouds
Services
Virtual Machines
Library
Jobs
Settings
Virtual Machines (17)
Enter keyword
Deploy Open Diagram Properties Shutdown Pause Turn Off Save Store Mount image Remote Desktop Console Delete
Last refresh: 10:36:04 AM
Name Status Cloud Name Connection Name Service CPU Usage Memory VM Size Processors Operating System
ESXTest1 Shut down ESX Cloud savdalvmm01 0 % 4 GB 1 64-bit edition of Windows Server 2012 Datacenter
ESXTest2 Shut down ESX Cloud savdalvmm01 0 % 4 GB 1 64-bit edition of Windows Server 2012 Datacenter
ESXUbuntu1 Shut down ESX Cloud savdalvmm01 0 % 2 GB 2 Ubuntu Linux (64 bit)
MineCraftSrv Running SavillTech... Windows Azure TWluZ... Basic_A2
sandbox Stopped (deallocated) SavillTech... Windows Azure savaz... Basic_A1
sandbox Stopped (deallocated) SavillTech... Windows Azure sandb... Basic_A1
savazudc01 Running SavillTech... Windows Azure savaz... Medium
savdaladfs01 Running Infrastructu... savdalvmm01 0 % 1 GB 2 Windows Server 2012 R2 Datacenter
savdaldc02 Running Infrastructu... savdalvmm01 0 % 1 GB 2 Windows Server 2012 R2 Datacenter
savdalfs01 Running Infrastructu... savdalvmm01 0 % 2 GB 1 Windows Server 2012 R2 Datacenter
savdalrras01 Running Infrastructu... savdalvmm01 0 % 2 GB 1 64-bit edition of Windows Server 2012 Datacenter
savreptst01 Running Secondary savdalvmm01 0 % 2 GB 1 Windows Server 2012 R2 Datacenter
test Running SavillTech... Windows Azure test Small
websrv1 Stopped (deallocated) SavillTech... Windows Azure websr... Basic_A0
websrv1 Stopped (deallocated) SavillTech... Windows Azure websr... Basic_A0
websrv1 Stopped (deallocated) SavillTech... Windows Azure websr... Small
websrv2 Stopped (deallocated) SavillTech... Windows Azure websr... Small
savdaladfs01
Status: Running
Computer name: savdaladfs01.savilltech.net
Operating system: Windows Server 2012 R2 Datacenter
Processors: 2
Memory: 1 GB
Dynamic memory: 8.00 GB maximum
VM Network: Lab 173
Date modified: 10/24/2014 8:28 AM
Owner:
INSTANCE savdaladfs01
NETWORK Lab 173
© 2013 Microsoft. All rights reserved. Privacy Send feedback to Microsoft

FIGURE 2.22
App Controller view of Virtual Machines showing VMs running on-premises and in Azure

Service Manager or any other service that can make a REST API call, including ServiceNow. In Figure 2.23 you can see a basic runbook, which I created, that deploys a VM in a hybrid scenario. (I used a mix of IP activities and PowerShell.) The runbook gets some starting data from whatever service calls it, and then checks the clouds available for the requesting user. Then, depending on whether fabric high availability requires it, it deploys the VM to a private cloud (SCVMM) or to the public cloud (Azure). Whichever path is taken, an RDP file is generated and emailed to the requesting user. Pretty neat! You will notice some other activities related to getting and closing service requests. This is because I wrote the runbook to integrate with Service Manager.

The Orchestrator runbook is very powerful, but to complete the solution, you need to make its functionality available to end users. You may also want the more advanced authorization workflow. Many organizations have a service catalog, which some portal users can use to request services. In System Center, it is Service Manager that provides a service catalog. Service Manager allows Orchestrator runbooks to be called as part of Request Offering workflows. These workflows can also include authorization steps, and the request offerings can be grouped into service offerings, which are made available through the Service Manager web portal or through the on-premises Azure Pack portal, as shown in Figure 2.24. (An Azure Pack portal is an on-premises experience built on System Center that mirrors the public cloud Azure experience.) When you're using an Azure Pack to communicate with Service Manager, the third-party GridPro solution is also used.

I walk through the complete solution here:

```
http://savilltech.com/blog/2014/07/15/new-demo-integrating-a-hybrid-vm-
deployment-with-windows-azure-pack/
```

The demo includes a video, an export of my runbook, and a template RDP file.

In this section, I've talked about App Controller, Orchestrator, and Service Manager. Of those components, end users see two different interfaces. The first interface is for the rich, workflow-based provisioning of services via the service catalog. Then, to stop, start, and connect to VMs, end users use App Controller, which is not an ideal experience. The good news is this will change with the next version of System Center. The new version will consolidate the user experiences with Azure Pack v2, and that will natively integrate with Azure. The new version enables you to control both Azure VMs and those on-premises, while maintaining integration with Service Manager for the rich provisioning workflows.

Azure IaaS-Supported Configurations

I've consistently talked about Azure IaaS as a VM in the cloud. Since Azure uses Hyper-V as the hypervisor, it may seem logical that any configuration that runs on Hyper-V should work in Azure—but that is not the case. Other factors come into play, such as how Azure is architected, especially for storage and networking; which version of Hyper-V is used; and the testing matrix that controls which versions of OS are supported.

It's important to validate your configuration; in the world of Azure, things change very quickly. For the operating system and VM, the following requirements exist as of this writing:

◆ Only 64-bit operating systems are supported. (Although 32-bit operating systems will work, they are not supported.)

◆ For Windows, the OS must be Windows Server 2008 R2 SP1 or later.

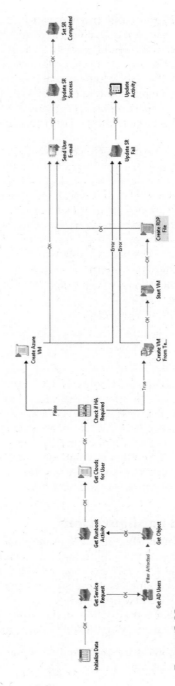

FIGURE 2.23
Orchestrator runbook that creates a VM in a hybrid environment

FIGURE 2.24
Calling a request
offering using Azure
Pack on-premises

- A large number of Linux distributions are supported. See the list at http://azure
.microsoft.com/en-us/documentation/articles/virtual-machines-linux-
endorsed-distributions/. (Once again, just because something is not listed does not
mean it would not work, but it would be unsupported.)

- The OS disk must be 127 GB or less.

- Data disks must be 1,023 GB or less, and the maximum number depends on the size of the VM.

- All virtual disks must be VHD and not VHDX.

- VHDs cannot be shared. (Shared VHDX was introduced in Windows Server 2012 R2.) Other
types of shared storage, even a virtual iSCSI appliance, are possible through Azure Files.

- Multiple vmnics, each with a single IP address, are supported. The exact number varies
depending on the size and tier of the VM. The current maximum number of vmnics is
four for the large VMs, such as A4, A7, D4, and D13. Basic-tier VMs do not support multiple
vmnics.

- IPv4 is supported (but not IPv6). Support is provided for TCP, UDP, and ICMP.

- No multicast or broadcast traffic is allowed.

- Only VM Generation 1 VMs are supported. (VM Generation 2 was introduced in Windows
Server 2012 R2 but is currently not supported in Azure.)

Providing your workload fits within the capabilities listed here, your workload should be a good fit.

The next step is to confirm the application vendor supports running in Azure. This must be confirmed with each vendor. For Microsoft applications, check `http://support.microsoft. com/kb/2721672/en-us` for a list of Microsoft applications supported in Azure. The article also lists which roles and features of Windows Server are supported for Azure.

Earlier, I talked about workloads, and I listed some scenarios where Azure might be a good fit. Another approach is to move everything to Azure except workloads that are not currently supported based on Azure's capability profiles.

TIP   Don't forget that the capability profiles are constantly changing and enhancing, so just because a workload does not fit in Azure today, does not mean it won't tomorrow. IOPS and large virtual machines were Azure limitations in the past, but with the introduction of Premium Storage and the G series virtual machines, even the largest, most I/O-intensive workloads can run in Azure. Considering how long it will take for organizations to start migrating workloads, it is highly likely that constraints that stopped you from moving a workload to Azure may no longer apply later in your project.

So, is there any situation where on-premises is better than Azure? As of this writing, there are technologies and scenarios when on-premises has a benefit. This is why embracing hybrid is so important. Here are a few thoughts:

◆ Where a service should be close to end users, such as file and print servers and domain controllers (in case Azure is disconnected), on-premises offers a benefit.

◆ As organizations leverage ExpressRoute, which gives very fast and low-latency connections to Azure, it may be possible to move file, print, and domain controller services to Azure without impacting end-user experience.

◆ On-premises deployments can scale up by adding extra cores to a VM, and limits can be used to modify the resources available at runtime while running. Scaling up without downtime is not possible in Azure; the focus is on scale-out.

◆ On-premises deployments can share cores to optimize resource utilization. However, the whole point of the public cloud is that you don't worry about how services are provided. In terms of pure efficiency, there is a benefit to sharing cores and tuning workloads.

◆ Client SKUs can run only on-premises; they cannot run in the public cloud.

◆ Resource allocation, such as memory amounts, can be customized independently of other resources. This type of customization is limited in Azure, but the number of different combinations is constantly growing and will continue to give more flexibility.

◆ Full control and insight of fabric is available only on-premises. Once again, if you don't want to be in the datacenter business, this is not a good thing necessarily.

◆ Azure cannot meet a need for high availability that can be provided through hypervisor for single-instance VMs. It is simply not possible. Instead, multiple instances of VMs are deployed in an availability set. This is actually a better solution, but if you have applications that can't have multiple instances that would be an issue.

Understanding Azure Architecture

Azure is a public cloud solution, and even with IaaS, as the customer we don't care about how the compute, storage, network, or even hypervisor are architected, implemented, or managed as long as our promised service is delivered. It is still useful to understand some of the core architecture of Azure and its datacenters that impacts delivering your services. Also, later on in the book, some of the concepts will make more sense when you already have a basic understanding of the Azure architecture.

Azure datacenters are architected and managed by the Microsoft Global Foundation Services. (Learn more at `www.globalfoundationservices.com`.) Microsoft is constantly re-architecting and re-evaluating the design of their datacenters based on research and lessons learned running some of the largest datacenters in the world. If you ever have the opportunity to tour a Microsoft datacenter, you will hear them talk about different generations of datacenters, which include datacenters based on warehouses full of racks, container-based approaches, and traditional datacenter type architectures. Microsoft published the blueprints for the datacenter servers they use here:

`http://blogs.microsoft.com/blog/2014/01/27/microsoft-contributes-cloud-server-designs-to-the-open-compute-project/`

And the actual specification is available here:

`http://www.globalfoundationservices.com/posts/2014/january/27/microsoft-contributes-cloud-server-specification-to-open-compute-project.aspx`

To get an idea about the operation of the datacenters, you'll find a great video tour here:

`http://cdn.globalfoundationservices.com/videos/Video_Data_Center_Long_Tour_8000k.wmv`

I recommend you watch.

Azure Regions

When moving services to the public cloud, you need to consider where the users who will be consuming those services are located in order to minimize latency and improve the end-user experience. There may also be data sovereignty and regulations that require your data and services to stay within a specific locale, which means your provider needs datacenters in a particular region.

Microsoft covers the largest number of regions of all the public cloud providers, and they are constantly adding locations. The best way to see the current locations for services is via the Azure status page at `http://azure.microsoft.com/en-us/status/`. Here you can see all of the service and health information for each region. A similar view is also available on the new Azure portal. There you will see overall service health, as shown in Figure 2.25. Azure has services in the United States, Japan, Brazil, and Australia, as well as in Europe and Asia. In China, however, Azure services are delivered with 21Vianet. Throughout the rest of the world, Microsoft owns and operates its own datacenters. For details of the locations, see `https://azure.microsoft.com/en-us/regions/`.

In most geographies, there are two Azure regions. For example, Europe has two, Asia has two, and the United States has several. These regions are spaced hundreds of miles apart but are paired for the purposes of asynchronous data replication and service protection. In each Azure region, there are one or more datacenters that provide the services, although the actual

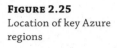

FIGURE 2.25
Location of key Azure
regions

individual datacenters are not surfaced to the customer, who selects only an Azure region, not a specific datacenter. Table 2.1 lists the Azure region pairings as of this writing. India and others will shortly be joining the list.

When a service is deployed to Azure, the user selects the region they want to deploy the service to. At that point, the Red Dog Front End (RDFE), which is the master brain of Azure, routes incoming service requests to a specific cluster based on resource availability and existing aggregations (such as affinity groups). Each cluster has a number of instances of a fabric controller running. The primary instance performs the more detailed actual deployment of VMs and other configurations. The name Red Dog was coined by Dave Cutler, one of the original architects, and was the original code name for Azure.

TABLE 2.1:   Azure region pairings

AZURE REGION 1	AZURE REGION 2
US West	US East
US North	US South
US Central	US East 2
Europe North	Europe West
Asia East	Asia Southeast
China North	China South
Japan East	Japan West
South Brazil	US South
Australia East	Australia Southeast

Server Structure in Azure

Throughout these early chapters, I use the term *cluster*. Clusters are key to understanding how Azure deploys and organizes the servers throughout its datacenters. Even though as the customer you really don't need to know, I promise that understanding the server structure will help you understand some of the Azure concepts and how they provide the various service levels. Figure 2.26 shows some core Azure server concepts.

FIGURE 2.26
Core Azure server internals

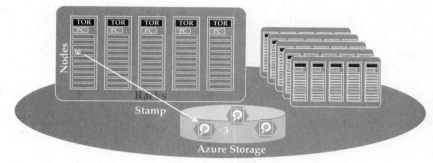

Behind the scenes are a huge number of servers or nodes, primarily the modular blade servers, that are divided into compute and storage roles. Somewhere between 40 and 50 blades are stored in a single rack. Each rack has a top-of-rack switch, which is connected to various levels of aggregation switches to enable connectivity between racks. These facilitate traffic between datacenters and out to the Internet. A number of racks also have an instance of the fabric controller (five as of this writing). The fabric controller can be thought of as the kernel of the Azure cloud operating system. It takes care not just of provisioning, but of the entire life cycle and health of the VMs and the nodes, including healing failed VMs and rehydrating.

Around 20 racks are grouped together to make up a stamp, which is the Azure scale-unit that is also called a cluster. When resources are added to an Azure datacenter, they are added in units of stamps. The stamp also provides a boundary of catastrophic failure, which is important when dealing with services the size of Azure. Critical failures on the fabric controller that do not fail to another instance affect only the services running in that stamp and not all of Azure. Each Azure datacenter contains many stamps that are centrally orchestrated by the RDFE.

All of the hardware within a stamp contains the same processor generation. Over time, Microsoft has used newer processors in Azure, but if all your resources are deployed in the same stamp, you are guaranteed to be running on the same generation of hardware. The stamp is surfaced to you as a customer through affinity groups. When creating resources, you can choose to deploy to an affinity group and bind those resources to a single stamp. This guarantees you are using homogenous hardware and therefore will see predictable performance across VMs in the same affinity group.

As a point of reference, even if you don't use an affinity group and deploy multiple VMs across different stamps that are running different generations of hardware, you will still see equivalent performance for the A0 through A7 series VMs. On newer hardware, the processor cores are throttled to match that of the previous hardware (around 1.5 GHz). This ensures that customers get predictable performance no matter where their A0 to A7 series VMs are deployed. Note that the new sizes, such as the A8, A9, D, and G series VMs, run at the full Xeon E5 clock speed of 2.2 GHz, a 60 percent performance improvement over the older AMD Opteron–based servers. There are some slight differences in the D, G, and A8/A9 performance, but they are minor. For example, the D series uses slightly slower hardware than the A8/A9. The G series uses the new Haswell processors, but the processors are clocked at 2.0 GHz. These VM sizes are not available on the older-generation stamps, and there is no need to throttle the performance.

The end result is that VMs are deployed to nodes in the stamp by the fabric controller. Behind the scenes, the persistent storage of the VM (its OS and data disks) are held in Azure Storage, which replicates all data three times within the datacenter and is optionally asynchronously paired to the datacenter for geo-redundancy.

The Azure datacenters have many other components, such as networking, storage, security, HVAC, and some of the other core components that will be covered in other sections later in this book.

The Bottom Line

Understand all the cost elements related to hosting services. When trying to compare costs between on-premises and the public cloud, it's easy to consider only the price of the VM in the public cloud, the cost of a license, and some server space on-premises. But the real costs are completely different; you need to factor in the entire datacenter, power, cooling, and labor. Take time to look at all the aspects to perform a true cost comparison.

Master It Why does the amount a service that is used heavily change when comparing on-premises to Azure?

Identify workloads that can run in Azure IaaS. Azure IaaS VMs can cater to a large number of workloads. The most successful are based on the capability profiles that, when exposed, are focused on VM series and sizes, network speeds, types of traffic, storage size, and performance. If your workload fits within the Azure capabilities, uses an Azure-supported OS, and runs an application that is supported by the vendor for Azure, then it can be evaluated more closely as a potential workload to run in Azure.

Master It What operating systems are supported in Azure?

Describe how Microsoft Azure infrastructure provides services. Azure consists of geographically distributed regions. Each region contains one or more datacenters. Within the datacenters are multiple Azure scale-units, or stamps, which consist of about 1,000 servers that are split among multiple racks. A central Red Dog Front End accepts service requests and distributes to fabric controllers running in each stamp for the actual deployment and life-cycle management.

Master It Do all Azure regions provide the same Azure services?

Chapter 3

Customizing VM Storage

Without durable, persistent storage, compute services have little value. Storage is key to enable full services to be delivered. In this chapter, we'll explore a number of options and configurations related to the storage delivered. Topics include customizing VM storage, configuring caching, optimizing virtual storage size and performance, and sharing storage. You'll learn how Azure is built to provide storage services.

In addition to native storage tools and services, I'll introduce you to third-party tools that help manage Azure Storage as well as hybrid storage and backup solutions that leverage Azure.

In this chapter, you will learn to

- ◆ Understand the types of storage exposed to a virtual machine
- ◆ Know when to use Azure Files
- ◆ Understand how StorSimple uses Azure Storage

Basic Virtual Machine Storage

In the previous chapter, I walked you through the processes that create a new virtual machine using the various Azure portals and experiences. The end result is that you created a virtual machine, and it is running in Azure. To help you understand what's happening with the storage assigned to that VM, we'll now connect to that virtual machine using the Remote Desktop Protocol (RDP). An endpoint was automatically created when you created the VM. If you created a Linux VM rather than Windows VM, then a Secure Shell (SSH) endpoint was automatically created. For this walk-through, I'll focus on a Windows VM.

Understanding Types of VM Storage

In the new Azure portal, if you navigate to your VM via Browse ➢ Virtual Machines ➢ *<Your VM>*, you'll see a Connect button at the top of the VM blade. If you are using the legacy Azure portal, navigate to Virtual Machines ➢ *<Your VM>* ➢ Dashboard, where you'll see a Connect button at the bottom of the screen. In both scenarios, the Connect button creates and downloads an RDP file that has been configured with a target of your cloud service name. The endpoint port number for your VM maps to RDP (3,389) for your VM. You can see the information via the Endpoints tab in the old portal and via the Configure lens in the new portal. You'll be prompted to open or save the generated RDP file. If you want to examine the RDP file, perhaps to customize the connection configuration, select Save. You can then edit the RDP file in mstsc.exe, which will show the target. Figure 3.1 shows an RDP file in mstsc.exe. If you just want to connect, select the Open option instead. Once you have connected, enter the username and password that you set when you created the VM.

FIGURE 3.1
The connection
string for an RDP file
connecting to Azure
VM

Once you're connected to the VM, launch Explorer. In a standard virtual machine, you'll see two drive letters:

C: C: identifies the OS disk for the virtual machine; it is 127 GB in size. The disk is a virtual hard disk (VHD) persistently stored on the Azure Storage fabric; it is durable. It doesn't matter if Azure hosts are rebooted or even lost. The VHD is safe and the content will not be lost. I'll cover Azure Storage in more detail later in this chapter.

D: D: identifies a temporary drive for the VM. The exact size varies depending on the size of the VM, as explained at http://msdn.microsoft.com/en-us/library/azure/dn197896. aspx. Temporary drives are anywhere from 20 GB to 800 GB as of this writing. Typically, the larger the VM, the larger the amount of temporary storage. As the name suggests, the temporary drive is not persistent or durable storage. It is local storage in the Hyper-V host that is running the virtual machine. In the event the VM moves to another host due to maintenance operations, failure, or for any other reason, the contents of the temporary drive are lost. It is therefore critical not to place any data you care about on the D: drive. By default, the only content that is stored on the D: drive is the Windows pagefile. If this content is lost due to a failure or maintenance operation, it is easily recreated.

The pagefile is not stored on regular Azure Storage to save space on the durable Azure Storage; to provide higher performance for the pagefile on the local storage; and because there's simply no benefit to placing the pagefile on Azure Storage. You can use the temporary drive if your application needs a scratch area that does not need persistent or even reliable storage. Think about TempDB on SQL; this is a great use for the D: drive, and it saves space on the Azure Storage that you must pay for. For regular A series virtual machines, the disks that host the temporary drives are regular hard disk drives (HDDs) that are in a RAID-type configuration. For D/DS series and G series virtual machines, the disks are solid-state drives (SSDs) in a RAID configuration, which give much higher performance. The only difference between the A series and the D series is that for the D series the temporary drive is hosted on SSDs. There are clearly many applications where a nonpersistent, but very fast, temporary storage is beneficial.

HANDLING THE NONPERSISTENT NATURE OF THE SCRATCH DRIVE

Many scenarios involve the scratch drive—for example, hosting TempDB on the scratch drive or allowing SQL Server 2014 to use it for the buffer pool extension. However, you must keep the following in mind: if you have to create a folder or even set permissions before an application can use the scratch drive, it may not work consistently. The scratch drive is not persistent and may be recreated at any time. You need to have a process that recreates any required folders and permissions before the application actually starts.

I recommend this approach:

1. Set the service to startup type Manual.

2. Create a PowerShell script that verifies that the required folder/permissions are in place. If they aren't, the script creates the folder/permissions and only then starts the services. For example:

```
$SQLService="SQL Server (MSSQLSERVER)"
$SQLAgentService="SQL Server Agent (MSSQLSERVER)"
$tempfolder="D:\SQLTEMP"
if (!(test-path -path $tempfolder)) {
    New-Item -ItemType directory -Path $tempfolder
}
Start-Service $SQLService
Start-Service $SQLAgentService
```

3. Set the PowerShell execution policy on the machine to allow locally unsigned scripts:

```
Set-ExecutionPolicy RemoteSigned
```

4. Call the script at machine startup. The easiest way is through the Task Scheduler. Use a Basic Task type that has an option to execute at computer startup, but ensure the task runs as an NT AUTHORITY\SYSTEM with the highest privileges. The program should be created in PowerShell and the argument is `-file "<location and name of the ps1 file>"`. Another option is to use a local policy to call the script as part of computer startup.

You can add data disks to a virtual machine. Typically, this storage is used for application data, so you don't want it on the OS drive. Also, you commonly need to control the level of caching, which is limited on the OS drive. The exact number of data disks that can be added to a virtual machine vary, once again, based on the size of the VM. Like the temporary drive, the larger the VM, the more data disks you can add. The number of data disks that can be added ranges from 1 to 32. Each data disk has the following characteristics:

◆ Standard-tier VMs are limited to 500 input/output operations per second (IOPS)— 300 IOPS for a basic-tier VM. If you are using Premium Storage accounts, then as of this writing, the IOPS is limited to 4,000 per disk.

◆ Each disk can be up to 1,023 GB in size. This is not a typo—although a TB is 1,024 GB, behind the scenes each VHD is stored in an Azure binary large object (BLOB), which has a 1 TB limit. There is some overhead, so the VHD can only be 1,023 GB.

◆ Each disk is a fixed-size VHD because all Azure VHDs are stored in paged Azure BLOBs.

SPARSE STORAGE IN AZURE

Azure uses fixed-size VHDs, which means all space is allocated at time of creation. This contrasts with the dynamic VHDs that grow as data is written. (You might know this as *thin provisioning*.) This may lead you to believe that you should create smaller sized VHDs, since space is allocated and paid for at creation time. Actually, this is not the case. Behind the scenes, Azure uses sparse storage. This means that no matter how large the VHD, you pay only for data that actually is written.

If you have a 100 GB VHD but have only 50 MB of data written to it, you only pay for 50 MB of data. This means you should always create your data disks as 1,023 GB, the maximum. It's difficult to resize a disk post-creation on regular Azure Storage. Additionally, Azure Storage supports TRIM. When data is deleted, that deletion flows through to the underlying Azure Storage. Almost like shrinking a VHD, you no longer pay for deleted space.

Because sparse storage is used, it is vital to perform a quick format when you need to format the data disks. When a full format is performed, 0s are written to the entire disk. Having written data to the entire disk, you would then be required to pay for the entire disk size. You should also avoid defragmentation in most scenarios. You want to minimize the movement of blocks and reduce the chance of increasing the physical disk footprint, which leads to greater costs.

To attach a disk to a VM via the portal, open the VM blade in the Azure portal. Under the Configure lens, select the Disks part. On the Disks blade, select the Attach New command. When the Attach A New Disk blade (shown in Figure 3.2) opens, configure a name and size for the new empty VHD. Notice the host caching options, which I'll cover shortly.

FIGURE 3.2

Attaching an empty VHD to a VM in the new Azure portal

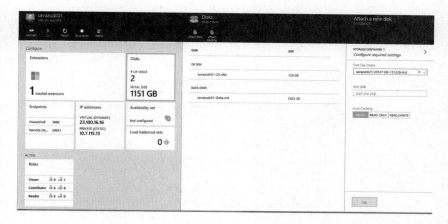

If you are using the old portal, the process is similar, except that you select the Attach button from the VM's dashboard view. This opens a menu that allows an empty or existing VHD to be attached to the VM. A dialog box with options for the new VHD, as shown in Figure 3.3, allows you to configure a name and size. Note that though in this example the attached disk is a new empty disk, if you have existing VHDs from previous VMs or perhaps that were uploaded from on-premises, they could also be attached.

Detailed coverage of using PowerShell to manage Azure will be presented in Chapter 9, "Customizing Azure Templates and PowerShell Management." However, now is a good time to point out that everything that can be done in the portal can be done in PowerShell (via the REST APIs), but PowerShell goes further. Azure functionality is enabled first through PowerShell and later finds its way to the Azure portal. (You can look ahead to Chapter 9 to understand how to enable Azure PowerShell for your system, if you want to try these cmdlets now. When you're finished, jump back to this section.)

The PowerShell code that follows retrieves the object for a VM, adds two empty VHDs to the VM, and then applies the updated configuration:

```
Get-AzureVM -Name $myVM -ServiceName $mySvc |
    Add-AzureDataDisk -CreateNew -DiskSizeInGB 1023 `
      -DiskLabel 'datadisk1' -LUN 0 |
    Add-AzureDataDisk -CreateNew -DiskSizeInGB 1023 `
      -DiskLabel 'datadisk2' -LUN 1 |
    Update-AzureVM
```

The new disks are added to the SCSI controller for the VM. This process enables hot-add, which means the VM does not have to be rebooted before the new disks can be used. Within

FIGURE 3.3
Attaching an empty
VHD to a VM in the
legacy Azure portal

Attach an empty disk to the virtual machine

VIRTUAL MACHINE NAME

savazudc01

STORAGE LOCATION

https://savtechstoreeastus.blob.core.windows.net/vhd

FILE NAME

savazudc01-savazudc01-1103-2

SIZE (GB)

HOST CACHE PREFERENCE

| NONE | READ ONLY | READ/WRITE |

the VM, the new empty disks must be initialized (use GPT) and then formatted before data can be written using normal methods, such as the Disk Management snap-in or in the File and Storage Services ➤ Volumes ➤ Disks area of Server Manager, as shown in Figure 3.4. When formatting, be sure to use the Fast Format option. Do not use Full Format, as previously mentioned.

FIGURE 3.4
Initializing the new disk through Server Manager

Note that the data disks added to an Azure VM are stored in the durable, persistent Azure Storage service, which means their content is safe even in the event of unplanned host failures. Figure 3.5 shows an overview of the storage architecture for a VM with its OS disk and one or more data disks. As shown in the figure, the VM is hosted on a node in an Azure compute cluster, and its temporary drive (D: by default) is hosted as a VHD on local storage to the node. The OS and data disks are hosted in Azure Storage in an Azure Storage cluster. Azure Storage provides three replicas of data, and depending on the type of storage replication configured, the data may also asynchronously replicate to a paired datacenter hundreds of miles away, where it is also stored three times.

FIGURE 3.5
Overview of the Azure Storage for a VM

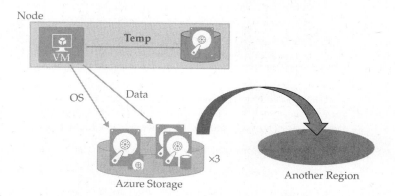

It is also possible to upload VHDs to Azure Storage for use as data or even OS disks. The PowerShell script that follows uploads a VHD file from your machine to your Azure Storage account. Then, the VHD is added as a disk in Azure and marked as containing a Windows operating system, thus enabling it to be used as the OS drive as part of a new VM creation.

```
$sourceVHD = "D:\Virtuals\Win2k3\Virtual Hard Disks\wintst.vhd"
$destinationVHD = "https://savtechstore.blob.core.windows.net/vhds/wintst.vhd"
Add-AzureVhd -LocalFilePath $sourceVHD -Destination $destinationVHD `
        -NumberOfUploaderThreads 5
Add-AzureDisk -DiskName 'wintst' -MediaLocation $destinationVHD `
        -Label 'wintst' -OS "Windows"
```

The example shows the creation of two variables. The first is the location of the source VHD on my local system and the second the target location in my Azure Storage account. The Add-AzureVhd cmdlet uploads the VHD, and the Add-AzureDisk adds the VHD as an Azure disk available as a Windows-type OS drive.

CHANGING THE TEMPORARY DRIVE FROM THE D: DRIVE

Some applications might want to use the D: drive for their own purposes. To change the drive letter that identifies the scratch drive:

1. Use RDP to create a remote session to the Azure virtual machine.

2. You need to temporarily move the pagefile from D: before you can change the drive letter. Open the Control Panel System applet and select Advanced System Settings.

3. On the Advanced tab, select Settings in the Performance area. Click the Advanced tab, and select Change in the Virtual Memory area. Set the pagefile size on D: to No Paging File, and select System Managed Size On C:. Make sure you click Set and then click OK.

4. Restart the virtual machine.

5. After the virtual machine restarts, the pagefile will be on the C: drive. Launch Disk Manager (diskmgmt.msc) and change the drive letter from D: to another letter, such as S:.

6. You now need to move the pagefile to the new drive letter for the scratch disk. Repeat the process that you initially used to move the pagefile, but this time set C: to No Paging File and select System Managed Size On S: (or whatever letter you used). Click Set and then OK.

7. After you reboot the virtual machine, you'll be able to add data disks to the virtual machine and assign one of them the D: drive letter.

It is possible to look inside the Azure Storage service to see the VHD files that are used by your virtual machine. I'll focus on the legacy Azure portal because, as of this writing, the full capabilities of storage management are not available in the new portal. This will change.

1. Navigate to the legacy portal at https://manage.windowsazure.com and log in.

2. Select the Storage navigation node.

3. Select the storage account that you used to create the VM. If the account was automatically created, it will likely have a name like portalvhds<*random string*>.

4. In the storage account view, select the Containers tab and then select the vhds container. As shown in Figure 3.6, all the contents of the vhds container in the storage account will be shown. Notice that the OS VHDs are 127 GB, whereas the data disks I added are all 1,023 GB.

The process previously described shows the contents of a container called vhds, but what it actually shows are page BLOBs, which happen to contain VHD files. If you tried to delete one of these, it would fail with the following error:

```
There is currently a lease on the blog and no lease ID was specified in the request.
```

FIGURE 3.6
Overview of the Azure
Storage for a VM

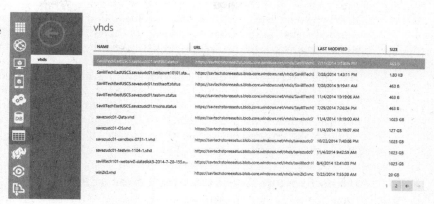

The VM that is using the VHD in the BLOB has an infinite lease on the BLOB. To delete the BLOB, you first need to delete the VM or detach the disk from the VM. To see the actual VM disks in a VM context, navigate to the Virtual Machines ➤ Disks view, as shown in Figure 3.7. The Virtual Machines ➤ Disks view shows just the VHDs. Through this view, you can delete VHDs, provided the VM using VHDS has been deleted or the disks have been detached from VMs. Note that the VM disk view also shows the OS running in the VHD for OS disks and, for all disks, the type of caching that will be used. You can also see which VM is using the disk, which you'll find useful when you want to identify how storage is actually being used.

FIGURE 3.7
Viewing VM disk view
in the v2 portal

virtual machines

INSTANCES   IMAGES   **DISKS**

NAME ↑	ATTACHED TO	CONTAINS OS	HOST CACHE	SUBSCRIPTION	LOCATION	
savazudc01-Data	savazudc01		None	Windows Azure Internal Co...	https://savtechstoreeastus.b
savazudc01-OS	savazudc01	Windows	Read/Write	Windows Azure Internal Co...	https://savtechstoreeastus.b
savazudc01-sandbox-0-20...	sandbox	Windows	Read/Write	Windows Azure Internal Co...	https://savtechstoreeastus.b
savazudc01-sandbox-0-20...	sandbox	-	None	Windows Azure Internal Co...	https://savtechstoreeastus.b
savazudc01-testvm-0-2014...	testvm	Windows	Read/Write	Windows Azure Internal Co...	https://savtechstoreeastus.b
savazudc01-testvm-0-2014...	testvm	-	None	Windows Azure Internal Co...	https://savtechstoreeastus.b
test-test-0-201410231532...	test	Windows	Read/Write	Windows Azure Internal Co...	https://savillmasterazuresto
websrv1-websrv1-0-20140...	websrv1	Windows	Read/Write	Windows Azure Internal Co...	https://savillmasterazuresto
websrv1-websrv1-0-20140...	websrv1	-	None	Windows Azure Internal Co...	https://savillmasterazuresto
websrv1-websrv1-0-20140...	websrv1	Windows	Read/Write	Windows Azure Internal Co...	https://savtechstorenortheu
websrv1-websrv1-0-20140...	websrv1	Windows	Read/Write	Windows Azure Internal Co...	https://portalvhdsl0xfqrcjp3
websrv1-websrv1-1-20140...	websrv1	-	None	Windows Azure Internal Co...	https://savillmasterazuresto
websrv1-websrv2-0-20140...	websrv2	Windows	Read/Write	Windows Azure Internal Co...	https://savtechstoreeastus.b
websrv1-websrv2-1-20140...	websrv2	-	None	Windows Azure Internal Co...	https://savtechstoreeastus.b
win2k3	-	Windows	-	Windows Azure Internal Co...	https://savtechstoreeastus.b

When you delete a VM, you are given the option to keep the attached disks. If you keep the attached disks, Azure will not delete any of the storage. If you delete the attached disks, Azure will automatically delete all attached VHDs and the associated BLOBs. If you are removing a VM but intend to use its disks for other VMs in the future, make sure you select the option Keep The Attached Disks. The disks will then stay in your storage account. If you delete data from Azure, there is no way to get it back through Microsoft. Microsoft does not perform backups of Azure Storage accounts; resiliency and protection from failure is provided through replication, but a deletion also would replicate. If you have important information in Azure Storage, you should make sure you have some process to back it up. I will cover backups in Chapter 8, "Setting Up Replication, Backup, and Disaster Recovery."

Using Storage Accounts and Types of Replication

Later in this chapter, I'll walk you through some of the internals of Azure Storage. However, I've already referred to storage accounts a number of times, so it's important to understand what a storage account is, how Azure limits storage accounts, and how to choose your storage account design. All data stored in Azure Storage is stored in a storage account. A storage account has a number of attributes:

◆ Each account must have a name that is unique across all of Azure Storage namespace. Azure Storage can be accessed using URLs, and the name you specify is a component of the URL.

◆ Each account must belong to a subscription.

◆ Each account must be created in a particular region. When VMs are created, the storage must reside in a storage account in the same region as the VM.

◆ Each account must specify the replication to be used for the content.

◆ Each account has a storage level, which by default is based on HDD/magnetic Azure Storage stamps. It is possible to specify Premium Storage clusters with predictable I/O for higher-performing storage.

◆ Each account has a maximum number of IOPS. A standard Azure Storage account supports up to 20,000 IOPS. If, for example, you have 40 disks, each with a 500 IOPS limit, the storage account would have reached its IOPS limit. Adding disks will affect the performance of all disks.

◆ Each premium storage account has a higher limit: approximately 500 MBs of traffic can be pushed per VM. An 8 KB I/O would be around 64,000 IOPS. This is current as of this writing.

◆ Each account also has size, ingress, and egress limits.

◆ Each account has a set of URL endpoints that are used to access the storage. The URL includes the name specified during creation. A different URL is used for each of the four types of storage service available: blogs, tables, queues, and files. The URLs use the following format:

```
https://<storage account name>.<storage service>.core.windows.net
```

For example, `https://savillstorage.blob.core.windows.net/` would be my BLOB endpoint. You can add custom URLs to access storage accounts. Custom URLs are documented at `http://azure.microsoft.com/en-us/documentation/articles/storage-custom-domain-name/`.

◆ Each account has storage keys that are used to securely access storage accounts.

Many of these elements can be seen in Figure 3.8, which shows the blades that relate to an example storage account in the new portal. Note that rich metrics related to the performance of the storage account, the amount of egress data, and the latencies experienced are displayed. Notice, too, that although I talked about different types of service supported by Azure Storage accounts—BLOBs, queues, tables, and files—file accounts are not shown in Figure 3.8. This is because, as of this writing, the Azure Files service is in preview and isn't enabled through the portal. This will change, likely by the time you are reading this.

FIGURE 3.8
An example Azure Storage account showing many of the key attributes

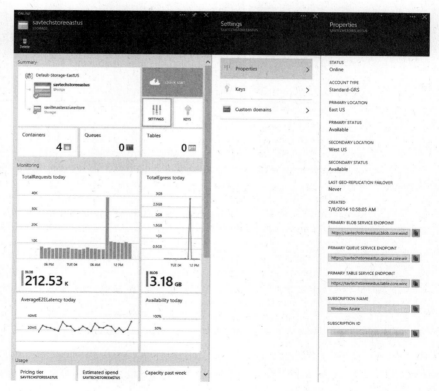

LIMITING IOPS THROTTLING RELATED TO STORAGE ACCOUNTS

Each storage account has a 20,000 IOPS limit, and each standard disk is throttled to 500 IOPS. If you have too many disks in a storage account, the storage account may cause further throttling on the IOPS of the contained disks. PowerShell provides an easy way to check a storage account for the number of disks that are attached to virtual machines:

```
Get-AzureDisk | Where-Object {$_.AttachedTo } |
    Group-Object {$_.Medialink.Host.Split('.')[0]} -NoElement
```

This code will output the number of disks attached to a virtual machine for each storage account. If you see a number greater than 40, you should scale out and use a new storage account—especially if you're seeing performance issues.

If you want to check whether throttling is affecting your storage, go to the v2 Azure portal:

1. Open the Azure portal.
2. Select the Storage workspace.
3. Select a storage account.
4. Select the Configure tab.
5. Change the monitoring of BLOBS to at least Minimal.
6. On the Monitoring tab, add metrics for Throttling Error and Throttling Error Percentage.

You'll now be able to see any throttling occurring on your account. You can also add a rule for the throttling metric to generate an alert and send you an email message in the event that a certain level of throttling is reached.

If you select the Keys option, two very long access keys are displayed: a primary and a secondary. These keys must be kept secure because, as the name suggests, they are the keys for entry to your storage account. Armed with the URL for the storage service and one of the keys, anyone has full access to the data. Two keys are displayed because over time you may wish to regenerate a key. Having two keys makes it possible to regenerate one key while allowing access to continue with the second key, thus avoiding any interruption to storage access and service. As Figure 3.9 shows, regenerating the keys is a simple process. Just click the Regenerate button. The new key can be placed into the tool or script that leverages the key. The clipboard icon next to the key makes it easy to paste the key into the script that needs to use it. (I regenerated the keys immediately after taking this screenshot.)

Keys are commonly used when performing storage actions using PowerShell or third-party tools. When creating a handle to an Azure Storage account, a context, a key must be passed along with the storage account name. For example, as shown here, I can connect to my storage account and then examine the basic information about it:

```
PS C:\> $storageaccount1 = new-azurestoragecontext -storageaccountname
    'savillmasterazurestore' -storageaccountkey '1WoVo…R6yw=='

PS C:\> $storageaccount1
```

```
StorageAccountName : savillmasterazurestore
BlobEndPoint       : https://savillmasterazurestore.blob.core.windows.net/
TableEndPoint      : https://savillmasterazurestore.table.core.windows.net/
QueueEndPoint      : https://savillmasterazurestore.queue.core.windows.net/
Context            : `
          Microsoft.WindowsAzure.Commands.Common.Storage.AzureStorageContext
Name               : `
EndPointSuffix     : core.windows.net/
```

FIGURE 3.9
Displaying the access keys for a storage account

The storage account replication choice is a major decision, and one that should be carefully considered because you cannot always change the replication type of a storage account post-creation. It is possible to change replication type between all types of replication except the Zone Redundant Storage (ZRS). ZRS organizes the copies of data differently. The types of replication available are as follows:

Locally Redundant Storage (LRS)   With LRS, the data is stored within a single Azure facility in a region. More specifically, all data is replicated three times within an Azure Storage stamp. Each copy of the data resides on a different disk, node, and rack. This offers the highest resiliency possible for the data. All copies of the data are written synchronously, and thus, any risk of data loss in the event of a failure of a disk, node, or rack is removed.

Zone Redundant Storage (ZRS)   When you create an Azure Storage account, you select a region for your storage. However, most Azure regions consist of many datacenters, since it's not possible to achieve the scale required by Azure within one datacenter. LRS stores all three copies of the data within a single Azure Storage stamp (cluster), which while providing great resiliency, cannot protect the data in the event of a large-scale problem such as fire, flood, or a lightning strike. All disks in the stamp could be destroyed, and in that case, the data is lost. With ZRS, there are still three copies of the data, but the data is spread over at least two datacenters. Ideally, the datacenters are located within the same region (where multiple datacenters are available), but data is replicated across regions when required. The copies of data are written synchronously within the datacenters in the region. If a copy must be sent to another region, then initially three copies of the data are synchronously written within the region. Following that, a copy of the data is asynchronously sent to another region to achieve the desired physical data distribution. ZRS is only available for block BLOBs as of this writing.

Geo-redundant Storage (GRS)   GRS takes LRS, asynchronously replicates the data to the paired region (which is hundreds of miles away), and then stores the data in that paired region three times. Under GRS, a total of six copies of your data are stored. If there is a failure in the primary region, the Azure Storage account is failed over to the secondary region. Because the replication between regions is asynchronous, there is a risk of data loss in the event of a disaster. Microsoft documentation states the Recovery Point Objective (RPO) is 15 minutes, which means that up to 15 minutes of data could be lost. (There is no SLA that commits to 15 minutes; 15 minutes is typical.) If this does not meet your requirements, you should look at other options to replicate data. For example, application-level replication could be AlwaysOn in a SQL Server scenario. This is spelled out in detail here:

```
http://blogs.msdn.com/b/windowsazurestorage/archive/2013/12/11/introducing-read-
access-geo-replicated-storage-ra-grs-for-windows-azure-storage.aspx
```

Read-Access Geo-redundant Storage (RA-GRS)   RA-GRS is much the same as GRS, except that the replica copy of the data is available only for read via a secondary endpoint. The secondary endpoint has `-secondary` appended to the storage account name, as in `savillstorage-secondary.<service>.core.windows.net`.

When choosing the type of replication, you should consider whether application-level replication is available. If so, you can natively replicate data instead of relying on the storage subsystem. Think about your RPO and the costs for different types of replication. The higher the level of durability, the greater the cost. In terms of durability, GRS is the best, then ZRS, and lastly LRS:

GRS > ZRS > LRS

The same applies to the cost. A storage account is required in each region where services will use the storage. Remember the IOPS limit for each storage account. You will likely need multiple storage accounts spread over the various Azure regions. You also may need multiple storage accounts within each region, since different workloads need different replication options. When creating your storage accounts, use a naming convention that makes obvious the purpose, region, and replication type of the storage account. For example, you might use a naming scheme with the following format:

```
<purpose/business area>-<region>-<replication type>
Project1-EastUS-GRS
```

The maximum length for the storage account name is 24 characters. Use some kind of descriptive naming scheme; when you look at reports, it will be easy to identify basic details about the account.

Storage accounts can be created through the Azure portals, which is a very intuitive process that asks for the various attributes I've just described. Note that when using the new Azure portal, after clicking the New button, you need to select the Everything link at the top corner to view the complete list of service options. From there, you can select the storage, cache, and backup group. That group allows the option to create a storage account.

As an alternative, you can use PowerShell to create a storage account with the `New-AzureStorageAccount` and `Set-AzureStorageAccount` cmdlets. The `New-AzureStorageAccount` cmdlet creates an LRS storage account. If you want to enable geo-replication, use the `Set-AzureStorageAccount` cmdlet with the `-GeoReplicationEnabled $true` parameter.

Within the storage accounts, various types of objects are created, such as containers for BLOBs, tables for entities, and queues for messages and file services. Other Azure services, such as an Azure SQL Database, use the storage differently.

Caching in Azure Storage

Earlier in this chapter you created an empty virtual disk and added that disk to a virtual machine. One of the configurable options for the disk was the caching option, which by default was set to No Caching. Caching is very common in all operating systems. Typically, memory in the host caches information previously read from a disk (read caching), which provides a higher level of performance if the same data is read again. (Memory provides far higher performance than physical disks.) Write caching is also possible. This works by leveraging a faster cache. That faster cache could be created in memory, although this introduces the risk of data loss in a failure, or on a faster disk. When writes are performed, the write is persisted to the cache, and then the write is acknowledged to the source process. Finally, in the background, the write is transferred from the cache to the target disk.

For storage, Azure uses the same concepts as caching, but with a slight twist. The VMs run on Azure compute nodes and, through the Azure Storage filter driver running on the compute nodes, the Azure Storage accessed for the storage of the VMs associated VHD files. Each of the compute nodes is assigned a portion of local disk and memory that can be used as a cache for the Azure Storage to improve performance. On A series VMs, this local disk is a traditional HDD, whereas on D and G series, the local disk is an SSD. The host cache is known as the Azure BLOB Cache or ABC.

Standard-tier VMs have a 500 IOPS limit per disk, but it is possible to configure one of three caching options to improve performance:

Read/Write Host Caching Both reads and writes leverage the local host cache. This is the default for OS disks.

Read Host Caching Only reads leverage the cache. Writes are always persisted directly to the Azure Storage.

No Host Caching No caching is used, and all reads and writes are serviced directly from Azure Storage. This is the default for data disks.

For OS disks, caching can be set for either the default Read/Write or Read-only caching, but OS disks cannot be configured for no caching. Data disks can use any of the three caching options. The caching configuration is set at the time of the disk creation and can be changed by editing the disk properties, as shown in Figure 3.10. Changing the cache configuration does not require the VM to be stopped; the change is at the host level only in relation to how it handles read and write for Azure Storage. The cache configuration can also be configured using PowerShell. Different cmdlets are used depending on whether the disk is an OS or data disk:

```
Set-AzureOSDisk -HostCaching ReadOnly|ReadWrite
Set-AzureDataDisk -HostCaching ReadOnly|ReadWrite|None
```

FIGURE 3.10
Modifying the cache configuration for a disk

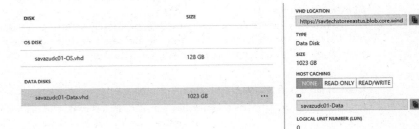

As of this writing, a maximum of four standard data disks per VM can be enabled for caching because the cache does consume host resources. For virtual disks created on premium storage (SSD), all disks can be enabled for caching.

The ability to turn off caching is critical for many types of workloads. Most databases require caching to be disabled on the storage subsystem, because this ensures any data is durably written. SQL Server databases and even Active Directory (AD) databases should use data disks that have had the caching configured as disabled. In the case of a domain controller, it is important that before promoting the server to a domain controller, you add a data disk with no caching configured. Then during the promotion process, specify the no caching data volume as the target for the AD database and logs.

Large and High-Performance Volumes

Each data disk stored in Azure Storage can be up to 1,023 GB in size (OS disks are limited to 127 GB) and is limited to 500 IOPS for standard tier. What if you need a volume larger than 1 TB or need performance greater than 500 IOPS? The solution is the same as the one that would be applied to a physical server. If more space is needed than provided by a single disk, you would add multiple disks and then create some kind of spanned/striped volume that aggregates the total available space into a single volume. If you need more IOPS, you combine multiple disks to acquire the aggregated performance.

In Azure, the solution is to add multiple data disks to a VM. If you need 4 TB of storage, you add four 1 TB data disks. If you need 8,000 IOPS, you add 16 1 TB data disks, since each disk gives you 500 IOPS. Remember that the maximum number of data disks depends on the size of the VM, which means you may need to increase the size of the VM to enable the number of data disks you require to be added. Refer to http://msdn.microsoft.com/en-us/library/azure/dn197896.aspx for the exact numbers.

Once you have added the multiple data disks, each of these disks will be available as separate disks. For Windows Server 2012 and later, the technology to combine them is known as Storage Spaces. Storage Spaces combines disks into a pool. Then virtual disks are created from the pool (not VHDs, the nomenclature is unfortunately confusing here). The virtual disks are exposed to the OS as normal disks, which can be formatted and have volumes. The virtual disks created support thin provisioning and different levels of resiliency, such as simple (no resiliency), mirroring, and parity. The term RAID is not used with Storage Spaces, since RAID defines very specific functionality. (RAID 1 means everything on one disk is replicated to another. Storage Spaces does not do this.) When mirroring is enabled, Storage Spaces guarantees that each bit of data is also written somewhere else, but the data and copies could be spread over many disks, not a single source and single target. Storage Spaces are available through Server Manager (and PowerShell). The basic process for using a Storage Space is demonstrated in the following example. In this example, I add four 1 TB disks to my VM. I then combine those disks into a single 4 TB NTFS volume, which delivers a maximum of 2,000 IOPS:

1. Log onto the VM.

2. Start Server Manager. It should automatically launch at logon. If not, you can manually launch by clicking the Server Manager shortcut that is next to the Start button on the taskbar.

3. Navigate to File and Storage Services ➤ Volumes ➤ Disks. The four 1,023 GB disks will be displayed.

4. On the Navigation menu, select the Storage Pools menu item.

5. A default storage pool named Primordial exists, as shown in Figure 3.11. It shows the four disks. The primordial pool contains disks not currently assigned to a pool.
   From the Storage Pools Tasks drop-down (located in the upper right), select New Storage Pool.

6. On the New Storage Pool Wizard starting page, click Next to move to the page that allows the Storage Pool to be named.

7. Enter a name for the new Storage Pool and click Next.

8. From the Physical Disks list, select the disks to be added to the new pool, as shown in Figure 3.12, and click Next.

9. Click the Create button. Once the pool creation is complete, check the Create A Virtual Disk When This Wizard Closes option, and click Close.

10. When the start page of the New Virtual Disk Wizard opens, click Next.

11. When the Select Storage Pool page opens, select the storage pool that you just created and click Next.

12. Enter a name for the new virtual disk and click Next.

13. For the storage layout, select Simple and click Next.

14. For the provisioning type, select Fixed and click Next.

15. For the size, select the Maximum size radio button and click Next.

FIGURE 3.11
Viewing the
data disks in the
primordial pool

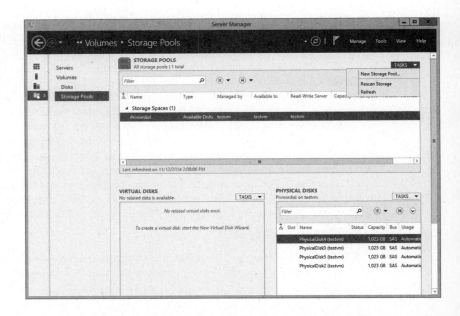

FIGURE 3.12
Adding disks to the
new storage pool

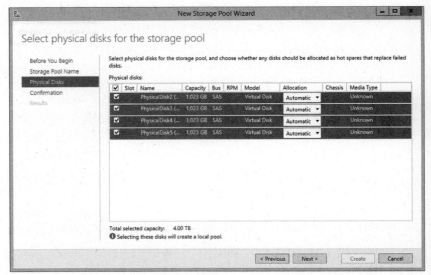

16. Click Create to create the new virtual disk.

17. You can now launch the Create A Volume Wizard or create the volume using other means and format the disk for NTFS. Use a quick format and not a full format. The VM will now have a single volume comprised of the space of all the data disks with aggregated performance.

USING MULTIPLE DISKS ON A NON-WINDOWS SERVER 2012 OS

If you are using Windows Server 2008 R2, you will need to convert the disks to dynamic and create a RAID 0 (stripped set). For Linux implementations, use the MD capability or LVM to create the stripped set within the OS.

Never use any kind of RAID/Storage Space resiliency option, such as mirroring, parity, RAID 1, RAID 5, and the like. The point of these resiliency options is to provide data protection in the event of a disk failure. They are not required in Azure; all data is replicated at least three times. The storage is already resilient. The RAID/Storage Space technology is being used to combine the separate disks into an aggregated volume, and there is no benefit to wasting space and compute resource with additional resiliency. Always choose simple/RAID 0 options when creating the virtual disk.

When an application like SQL Server has its own capability to use multiple disks, the best option for the highest level of performance is to use the native distribution feature. This feature will write the database over the multiple disks that are exposed to it. However, this approach has some trade-offs in terms of simplicity and flexibility. Let's look at SQL Server in greater detail.

SQL Server works by having a database that contains a file group (although it can contain multiple file groups); the file group contains one or more files, with each file possibly stored on different physical disks. Objects are written to the file group, which then uses a proportional fill algorithm to ensure all files in the group contain roughly the same amount of data. This distributes the load. You must manually add the files for each disk to the file group. If in the future you wanted to add another disk, you'd need to add a file stored on that new disk to the file group. However, because there's no automatic re-optimization of data to spread equally, a large amount of the new data would be written to the new disk, which might affect performance.

This situation contrasts with Storage Spaces, which lets you just add disks to the storage pool. Disks are then automatically used as needed based on the data. Background optimization occurs whenever necessary.

Although the SQL Server native distribution provides the best performance, Storage Spaces offers a simpler experience, albeit at the expense of some performance. The decision is up to you.

USING PREMIUM STORAGE

Standard storage is serviced by Azure compute stamps that are predominantly made up of HDDs. Each standard-tier VHD has an enforced IOPS limit. However, you should understand that this is a limit and not a guaranteed level of performance. You should expect to see around 500 IOPS, but there may be times you get less. It all depends on what other customers are doing and how they leverage the same pool of storage as your resource. Customers have had two issues:

500 IOPS was not enough, and even with multiple disks aggregated, the total amount of IOPS often did not meet requirements.

Customers wanted a more predictable level of performance.

With these requirements in mind, Microsoft introduced Premium Storage, formerly known as Provisioned IO. Premium Storage is serviced by a completely new set of storage stamps that leverage

SSDs instead of HDDs, thus enabling much higher IOPS per disk. Additionally, the architecture for Premium Storage is intended to deliver a predictable performance (up to 5,000 IOPS as of this writing). The limit matches the expected performance without significant variance.

Because of the predictable performance aspect of Premium Storage, it will be available only for the DS and GS series virtual machines that run on the newer compute stamps and have local SSDs available for local caching. VHDs created on Premium Storage have the same size and number limits as VHDs created on regular Azure Storage. As of this writing, Premium Storage supports only LRS and cannot be geographically replicated.

If you have workloads that require very high and predictable performance that is both durable and persistent, evaluating Premium Storage is a good next step.

Using Disks and Images

Throughout this chapter, I have referred to virtual hard disks, which are the predominant way storage is used in an IaaS world. There are also OS images, like those used as the template to create a virtual machine in Chapter 2, "When to Use IaaS: Cost and Options." A regular disk in Azure is an OS or data disk that can be written to. These disks can be created as part of VM provisioning or uploaded to Azure Storage and assigned to virtual machines.

An OS image is used as a template; it is used as the starting point for new virtual machines and is read-only in Azure. Azure provides a large number of built-in templates. Many of them are exposed during the VM creation process through the Azure portals, but they can also be viewed using the `Get-AzureVMImage` PowerShell cmdlet. The number of images changes over time, as do the image versions. Microsoft updates the images frequently with the most current updates, so I created a small piece of PowerShell to automatically find the latest Windows Server 2012 R2 Datacenter image. The code essentially stores all of the images in an array, searches for the 2012 R2 Datacenter text in the label, and if found, adds that image to a new array. The code then reorders the elements in the array in descending order, so the newest image is first.

```
$images = Get-AzureVMImage
$2012R2imgs = @() #Create array of objects
foreach ($image in $images)
{
    if ($image.Label.Contains("Windows Server 2012 R2 Datacenter"))
    {
        $2012R2imgs += $image
    }
}
$2012R2imgs = $2012R2imgs | Sort-Object PublishedDate -Descending #put the newest
# first which is the highest patched version
$2012R2imgs[0].ImageName # Newest image
```

In addition to the Microsoft images, you may wish to upload your own images to be used as templates for the creation of new virtual machines. I will cover the process for creating custom images in Chapter 9. That discussion will include the processes for creating both Windows and Linux images. For now, you only need to understand the distinction between disks and images.

Leveraging Azure Files

Azure IaaS VMs use the Azure Storage in one way—to store VHD files in page BLOBs. However, BLOBs are only one way in which Azure Storage is surfaced. Although queues and tables are typically of interest to developers, Azure Files is very useful and a type of service familiar to IT administrators.

Azure Files enables Azure Storage to be accessed via the Server Message Block (SMB) protocol. As of this writing, version 2.1 of SMB is supported. Version 3.0, which was introduced with Windows Server 2012, enables not only higher performance, but also enterprise levels of functionality. SMB 3.0 support is, we hope, on the future roadmap. SMB is a file-level protocol, and the same share can be accessed by many environments concurrently. Common uses for Azure Files include:

◆ Using a shared folder to store data and configuration between different virtual machines

◆ Providing a central location to save diagnostic and other log information

◆ Providing a central software storage location

◆ Emulating file services previously available only on-premises

◆ Using an Azure Files share as the cluster file share witness on Windows Server 10 systems

Any scenario where shared file-level services are needed applies. One important restriction is that the Azure Files shares are only available within the Azure region that contains the storage account that hosts the Azure Files instance. If you create an Azure Files storage share in a storage account in the Eastern United States, then only services running in the Eastern US Azure region will be able to access the share. The share would be unavailable in other regions and unavailable from your on-premises locations via SMB, but would be available via REST. As of this writing, the Azure Files service is in Preview, which means it must be activated via the Preview features site at http://azure.microsoft.com/en-us/services/preview/. However, hopefully by the time you read this, it should be generally available.

There is no portal management for Azure Files; instead PowerShell is used. In the next PowerShell script, I have added comments to show the various cmdlets that are used in Azure Files configuration. Note that you will need the storage account name and the access key to use the script, but this time I incorporated my shortcut to fetch the key via PowerShell. In this example, I create a share, copy a file to it, list the content, download the file, and then delete the file from the share:

```
#Create a variable to store the Storage Account name
$StorageAccount = 'savtechstoreeastus'

#Save the storage account key
$StorageKey = (Get-AzureStorageKey `
    -StorageAccountName $StorageAccount).Primary

#Create a context to the storage account
$storageaccount1 = new-azurestoragecontext `
    -storageaccountname $StorageAccount `
    -storageaccountkey $StorageKey
```

```
#Create a new share called images in the storage account
$s = New-AzureStorageShare images -Context $storageaccount1

#Create a directory in the test share just created
New-AzureStorageDirectory -Share $s -Path jpg

#Upload a local file to the testdir directory just created
Set-AzureStorageFileContent
    -Share $s -Source E:\testing\BatmanCVR612.jpg -Path jpg

#List the files and subdirectories in a directory
Get-AzureStorageFile -Share $s -Path jpg

#Download files from Azure storage file service
Get-AzureStorageFileContent -Share $s -Path jpg/BatmanCVR612.jpg `
-Destination E:\testing\Download

#Remove files from Azure storage file service
Remove-AzureStorageFile -Share $s -Path jpg/BatmanCVR612.jpg
```

In the preceding code, I accessed the SMB share via PowerShell using Azure-specific cmdlets, but that is not a requirement. I can connect to the share from an Azure service in the same region using normal SMB means, such as by mapping a share. The username (u:savtechstoreeastus) is the name of the storage account, and the password is the storage key. Here's an example:

```
Net use z: \\savtechstoreeastus.file.core.windows.net\images
    /u:savtechstoreeastus <storage key>
```

Notice that the path connects to the file service of my storage account, which follows the normal DNS scheme for Azure services—that is, <storage account>.<service>.core.windows.net ; file is the service type. Microsoft has a very good blog on Azure Files here:

```
http://blogs.msdn.com/b/windowsazurestorage/archive/2014/05/12/introducing-
microsoft-azure-file-service.aspx
```

Azure Storage 101

An in-depth knowledge of the internals of Azure Storage is not a requirement for leveraging the services. The whole point of cloud services is that, as the consumer of the service, you do not need to know or care how your services are being delivered. Providing the capabilities and performance that you signed up for are available and any SLAs are met, as the customer you should be happy.

I do believe, however, that it can be useful to understand how services are provided. That knowledge can enable a better understanding of why things behave the way they do and are used the way they are. This section provides a basic overview of the Azure Storage architecture. If you want a detailed explanation, I recommend you download and read the white paper from this site:

```
http://sigops.org/sosp/sosp11/current/2011-Cascais/11-calder-online.pdf
```

This white paper was written by the Azure Storage team to document their architecture.

Azure Storage Architecture

In most enterprise datacenters, you will find one or more storage area networks (SANs). These are very large, multirack systems that consist of hundreds, if not thousands, of enterprise disks. They are typically a mix of HDDs and SSDs. The SAN has a number of controllers, which are essentially scaled-down operating systems, that enable access to the storage services and management. The SANs then connect to hosts that leverage the storage through various media, typically Fiber Channel and iSCSI. This requires the hosts consuming the storage to have a specific type of host bus adapter (HBA)/network card in addition to the often expensive switching equipment in the datacenter.

SANs offer many benefits, including redundant connectivity, power, controllers and everything else, high levels of performance and functionality, and centralized shared storage. These benefits come at great financial cost. You will not find a SAN in an Azure datacenter. SANs are not economically viable at the mega-scale of any enterprise public cloud service. Instead, Azure leverages its own distributed, software-defined storage solution, which enables the use of more commodity hardware. By using software-based solutions, the level of customization and ability to respond to the needs of services is much higher.

Previously, I discussed Azure compute stamps, which are racks of compute nodes that run the actual VMs. Similarly, there are Azure Storage stamps, which consist of nodes of lots of disks that together offer the Azure Storage services.

Azure Storage is provided using a three-tier architecture, which is shown in Figure 3.13. On the Compute side, each host has some local disks. They are used as part of the local cache and for the temporary drive. The persistent storage of items such as the OS and data is serviced via the VHD Driver, which in turn accesses the Azure Storage service.

FIGURE 3.13
Azure Storage architecture and its interaction with Azure Compute services

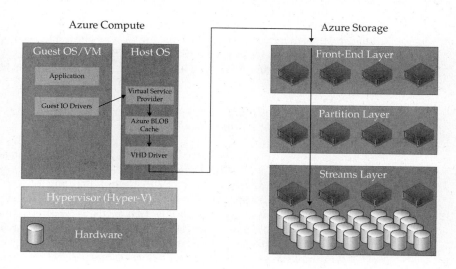

The front-end layer is a stateless system that provides REST authentication and interfaces, accepts requests, performs actions such as throttling performance, and then routes the requests to the partition layer. The partition layer understands higher-level data abstractions, such as BLOBs, tables, queues, and files, and provides the scalable namespace. Finally, the stream layer contains the disks, manages writing the actual bits to disk, and ensures data durability by taking responsibility for the distribution and replication of the data across servers in the stamp. Within the stream layer are file streams, which are ordered lists of large storage chunks (also called extents). These units of replication are themselves made up of blocks. If you are interested in more detail on these internals, refer to the white paper mentioned earlier.

There are two types of replication for Azure Storage, and both are critical to providing the various resiliency levels offered:

Intra-stamp Replication (Stream Layer) Intra-stamp replication provides synchronous replication. This keeps data durable within the stamps through replication across nodes in different fault domains.

Inter-stamp Replication (Partition Layer) When inter-stamp replication is employed, asynchronous replication of data is provided across stamps.

DNS is used for the Azure Storage namespace, which is why when talking about Azure Storage accounts and services, you will see this format:

```
http(s)://<account>.<service>.core.windows.net/<partition>/object
```

Interacting with Azure Storage

In an IaaS world, most of the Azure Storage interaction will be for the storage of Azure virtual machines. Very little direct interaction with the storage service takes place. There may be times you look at metrics for the storage for a VM, and you may need to delete VHDs, but typically the interaction is light. In this section, we'll explore tools that can help you manage Azure Storage. We will look at tasks like copying data between storage accounts, sharing storage between VMs, and gaining insight into the storage usage.

Many times, you will have multiple storage accounts and want to move data between them. One option is to download the VHD to your local machine and then upload it back into Azure. Earlier in this chapter, I showed you how to use PowerShell to copy a VHD into Azure. When you need to download a VHD, you use the Save-AzureVHD cmdlet. Here's some example code:

```
Save-AzureVhd `
 -Source "https://<storage account>.blob.core.windows.net/vhds/<name>.vhd" `
 -LocalFilePath "c:\temp\<name>.vhd"
```

This process is very inefficient, because the data has to be downloaded from Azure and then uploaded back again. The download will incur a cost since it is egress (outbound) traffic. A better option is to ask the Azure fabric to perform the copy for you. This is possible using the Start-CopyAzureStorageBlob cmdlet, which performs an asynchronous, server-side copy of BLOBs between storage accounts. This is what's required to move VHDs, since a VHD is stored as a page BLOB in Azure. Because the Start-CopyAzureStorageBlob cmdlet is asynchronous, several copy jobs can be run concurrently.

The example PowerShell script that follows copies a BLOB between two accounts. The data never leaves Azure; there is no traffic to your local machine. The first two commands in the script variables are storage contexts—think handles—to each of the two storage accounts: the source and the target. You will need the storage key for each of the storage accounts, and both the names and keys should be stored in variables as referenced in the script. The status of the copy is checked using the Get-AzureStorageBlobCopyState cmdlet.

```
#Source Storage Account
$StorageContextSource = New-AzureStorageContext `
    -StorageAccountName ` $storageAccountsource `
    -StorageAccountKey $storageKeySource
#Target Storage Account
$StorageContextTarget = New-AzureStorageContext `
    -StorageAccountName ` $storageAccounttarget `
    -StorageAccountKey $storageKeyTarget
$blob1 = Start-AzureStorageBlobCopy -SrcContainer $srcContainerName `
    -SrcBlob $srcBlobName -SrcContext $StorageContextSource `
    -DestContainer $destContainerName -DestBlob $destBlobName `
    -DestContext $StorageContextTarget `
    $blob1 | Get-AzureStorageBlobCopyState
```

I found a nice script from some MVPs that leverages this cmdlet to copy VMs between Azure subscriptions. This script is available here:

http://blogs.msdn.com/b/microsoft_press/archive/2014/01/29/from-the-mvps-copying-a-virtual-machine-from-one-windows-azure-subscription-to-another-with-powershell.aspx

More information on the asynchronous copy API is available here:

http://blogs.msdn.com/b/windowsazurestorage/archive/2012/06/12/introducing-asynchronous-cross-account-copy-blob.aspx

Microsoft also has developed a very powerful tool, AzCopy, that enables the uploading, downloading, and copying of data related to Azure. It is available at http://aka.ms/AzCopy. There you will find a lot of examples and documentation that can help you get started. The tool also supports the server-side copy between storage accounts. It is simple to use because only the URLs of the source and target and the associated storage keys need to be passed. Here's an example:

```
AzCopy
/Source:https://sourceaccount.blob.core.windows.net/mycontainer/mycontainer1
/Dest:https://destaccount.blob.core.windows.net/mycontainer2 /SourceKey:key1
/DestKey:key2 /Pattern:vm.vhd
```

Notice that in all of these examples, the storage keys are required. PowerShell lets you quickly get the key without having to go into the Azure portals and then save the key to a variable that you can pass to the various commands. The PowerShell script that follows first lists all the storage accounts that exist for your subscription and provides the name, location, and resiliency type. The second command stores the primary storage key for the specified storage account into a variable, which is then displayed:

```
PS C:\> Get-AzureStorageAccount | ft label, location, accounttype -AutoSize
Label                  Location    AccountType
-----                  --------    -----------
savtechstoreeastazia   East Asia   Standard_LRS
savtechstoreeastus     East US     Standard_GRS
```

```
savtechstorenortheurope North Europe Standard_LRS

PS C:\> $StorageKey = (Get-AzureStorageKey `
-StorageAccountName 'savtechstoreeastus').Primary

PS C:\> $StorageKey
ROEwNVyfTaOB....01LgDsFeGv1tUw==
```

A number of graphical tools are available from various third parties. The one I use is CloudXplorer from ClumsyLeaf Software (`http://clumsyleaf.com/products/cloudxplorer`). I consider CloudXplorer an essential tool. Once you install it and add your storage accounts and keys, you can graphically manage, upload, download, and copy your Azure Storage accounts. A free version is available, but the paid version provides additional functionality. Figure 3.14 shows the basic interface—an Explorer-like experience that will be familiar to any Windows user. To add storage accounts, use the File ➤ Accounts menu option.

FIGURE 3.14
CloudXplorer
interface viewing
one of my storage
accounts

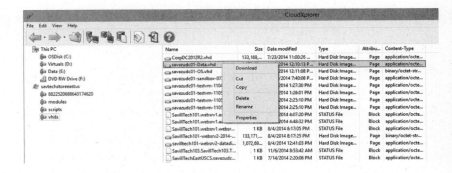

Azure Storage Explorer is another free tool:

`http://azurestorageexplorer.codeplex.com/`

It provides a similar Explorer experience. You can find other tools here:

`http://blogs.msdn.com/b/windowsazurestorage/archive/2014/03/11/windows-azure-storage-explorers-2014.aspx`

These tools use the same REST APIs as the PowerShell cmdlets. You can use them in your own applications as well. You'll find a great walk-through for writing your own storage management tool here:

`http://blogs.msdn.com/b/jnak/archive/2010/01/11/walkthrough-windows-azure-blob-storage-nov-2009-and-later.aspx`

If you are feeling adventurous, the full REST API for storage services is available here:

`http://msdn.microsoft.com/en-us/library/azure/dd179355.aspx`

Mount VHD will mount an Azure VHD within an Azure VM and is a free tool:

`http://mountvhdazurevm.codeplex.com/`

Many people and companies have created ingenious tools related to Azure Storage. Check them out.

Performing a Bulk Import/Export

Using the various tools to upload and download data results in data being sent over the Internet. Though encrypted, your data is still being sent over the Internet, which means bandwidth usage and potential high latencies. If you are transferring large amounts of data, it may take a significant amount of time. If you need to import or export very large amounts of data, transferring it over the Internet may not be practical.

For these scenarios, Microsoft has an Import/Export service, which enables organizations to copy large amounts of data to BitLocker encrypted drives, send the drives to an Azure datacenter, and then import that data into the specified Azure Storage account. The inverse is also possible. Data from your Azure Storage account can be copied to drives and sent to your location.

A special drive preparation tool is used to prepare the drives and encrypt them with BitLocker. The process is outlined here:

```
http://azure.microsoft.com/en-us/documentation/articles/storage-import-export-
service/#create-an-import-job-in-the-management-portal
```

As of this writing, the following conditions exist:

◆ Each drive can be up to 4 TB in size and must be a 3.5 SATA II/III drive.

◆ Each Import/Export job can consist of up to 10 hard drives.

◆ Each customer may have up to 20 active jobs per storage account.

◆ Only block and page BLOBs are supported. (IaaS VM VHDs are stored in page BLOBs.)

The decision to use the Import/Export service depends on the amount of data that needs to be transferred and the amount of time that the data can be aged. It may take a few days to ship the drives, which may impact the availability of services that need the data. You should keep in mind that it may take several days to copy large amounts of data over the Internet anyway. If your organization needs to move large amounts of data or VMs that can be offline for a few days, the Import/Export service is a great choice. If the amount of offline time is too great, another option is to use Import/Export with a delta sync, which only synchronizes changes, i.e., the deltas. You will need some mechanism to replicate the delta that occurs between the time the data was copied to the drive and when it becomes available in Azure. Other replication and migration options are available for VMs, as you'll see in Chapter 8.

Understanding StorSimple

I will only cover StorSimple at a very high level, because it is not an Azure Storage service but rather a Microsoft solution that uses Azure Storage. It is a very interesting solution. Most organizations retain very large amounts of data, and that data grows exponentially over time. Traditionally, that data growth means that organizations have to continually purchase additional (and expensive) storage. However, there is a smaller set of that data, the working set, that is consistently used by the organization, and the amount of that data remains fairly constant, as shown in Figure 3.15. It is only the working set data that organizations need to have readily available.

FIGURE 3.15
Typical data growth
and usage over time at
organizations

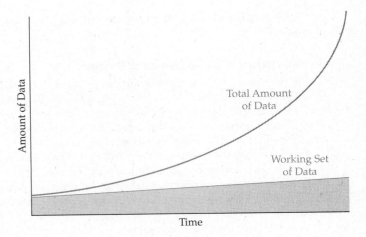

StorSimple is a storage appliance that has a certain amount of local storage (both HDD and SSD) and can also leverage Microsoft Azure Storage. The StorSimple appliance acts as an iSCSI target. At a block level it leverages tiers of storage, including deduplication and compression to store the data. As data is accessed more frequently, it is stored on a higher tier. For example, the most used data will be stored in the SSD tier, less used data would be stored in the HDD tier, and rarely used data will be stored in Azure Storage. This reorganizing of data happens automatically using algorithms built into StorSimple. What this means is data that exists but is rarely used would be uploaded to Azure Storage and then deleted from the local storage. The most used data remains local (as well as being stored in Azure for protection), which gives the highest performance while providing essentially an infinite total capacity size.

To the end user, all of the data looks like it's available locally on StorSimple. Data that has been moved to Azure Storage maintains a local thumbprint on the StorSimple storage. That thumbprint represents the Azure stored data. If data that has been off-loaded to Azure is accessed, the StorSimple device automatically downloads it and makes it available. Obviously, this impacts storage performance, because the data has to be downloaded over the Internet. It is also possible to pin certain data to always be kept locally. You can also configure data to be off-loaded to Azure as soon as possible.

StorSimple has many different tiers: SSD Linear (not deduplicated), SSD Deduplicated, and HDD (which is deduplicated and compressed). In the final Azure Storage tier, the data is not only deduplicated and compressed, but it's also encrypted using a key known only to the StorSimple appliance. Initially, data is written to the SSD Linear tier, and then over time, it is deduplicated in SSD. Finally, depending on its usage, it may be moved to the HDD tier or even Azure Storage.

This automatic tiering may sound very familiar—Storage Spaces in Windows Server 2012 R2 does something similar with its HDD and SSD tiers. Currently, StorSimple is based on Linux, but I expect this to change. I also don't think it would be much of a leap for the StorSimple algorithms for off-loading to Azure to find their way into the next version of Windows Server and become part of Storage Spaces. This would allow you to add the Azure Storage tier to

Storage Spaces, and then the StorSimple appliances could be based on Windows Server vNext. This is all pure conjecture on my part, but it would make complete sense. Microsoft pushes Storage Spaces, and they now own StorSimple.

The StorSimple appliances come in different sizes. Microsoft is giving them away if you purchase certain amounts of Azure credit. This offer is intended to help you use Azure Storage more easily. There are key scenarios where StorSimple is a great solution. It's great as storage for file servers and archive servers. It can be used for low- to mid-range Hyper-V VM storage and SQL workloads, including SharePoint. It should not be used for high-disk IOPS, such as Hyper-V and SQL scenarios, because it will not deliver the required storage performance. StorSimple should not be used as a backup target; once it hits 80 percent full on local storage, all future writes basically go directly to Azure. At that point, the storage performance would be terrible during the backup.

The StorSimple 8000 series features a new set of capabilities, which includes the ability to be managed through the Azure portals, and now has a virtual appliance. This means in the event of an on-premises disaster, you can start the virtual StorSimple appliance—which runs as a VM in Azure—and armed with the encryption key, you can read and access the data stored in Azure. Services in Azure can then connect to the virtual StorSimple appliance via iSCSI and access the data.

For more information on StorSimple, visit this site:

www.microsoft.com/en-us/server-cloud/products/storsimple/

The Bottom Line

Understand the types of storage exposed to a virtual machine.   By default, an IaaS VM will have a C: drive containing the operating system, which is 127 GB in size, and a D: drive, whose size will vary based on the VM size. By default for Windows VMs, the D: drive contains the paging file. The C: drive is stored on the durable, persistent Azure Storage service. The D: drive is stored on disks local to the host and should be considered nonpersistent. Any operation that results in the VM being moved to another host—which could include maintenance, resizing of VMs, or failures—will result in loss of the D: drive content. Additionally, data drives can be added to a VM; they are also stored on Azure Storage, which means their content is durable and persistent even in the event of failures.

Master It   Why should data that you care about not be stored on the D: drive?

Know when to use Azure Files.   Azure Files enables Azure Storage to be accessed via the SMB protocol. Any scenario that needs a shared or central storage location is a good candidate for leveraging Azure Files, which includes centralized storage of data, configuration, logs, and performance information.

Master It   What version of SMB is supported by Azure Files?

Understand how StorSimple uses Azure Storage.   StorSimple is an on-premises storage appliance that supports different tiers of storage based on its internal SSD and HDD storage. StorSimple can use Azure Storage as an infinite cloud tier. The least used data is moved to Azure Storage, but thumbprints are maintained on-premises. To the users connecting via iSCSI, the data appears to still be stored locally. In the event data that has been moved to Azure is accessed, it is pulled down from Azure at a block level. Additionally, all data on the StorSimple appliance is saved to Azure to provide protection in the event of a StorSimple appliance failure or loss. The StorSimple 8000 series tightly integrates with Azure for management and access to the data. In the event of a disaster, a virtual StorSimple appliance, which essentially is an Azure VM, runs the StorSimple software and can access the data stored in Azure through the shared encryption key.

Master It   What are good use cases for StorSimple?

Chapter 4

Enabling External Connectivity

When services run on-premises, they are already part of your network infrastructure and are readily available for access and integration with other services. When a public cloud service is used, specifically Azure, the services are accessed via the Internet, or at least *initially* via the Internet. This chapter focuses on Azure networking basics and how to enable connectivity to VMs running in Azure.

In this chapter, you will learn to

- ◆ Understand how communication to services running in a VM from the Internet works

- ◆ Use load balancing capabilities

- ◆ Differentiate between a stopped and a deprovisioned VM

Cloud Services

Before I start talking about the various networking technologies related to accessing your VMs running in Azure, I want to relate to you a small part of a movie I enjoyed when I was younger, *The Princess Bride*. If you've not seen it, you should. I think it is about halfway through the movie that the grandpa (played by Peter Falk, who I'll always remember as Columbo) stops reading the story to his sick grandson.

"She doesn't get eaten by the eels at this time. The eel doesn't get her. Now, I'm explaining to you because you look nervous."

I mention this because, as I begin to talk about networking, you will get nervous, but it's important to understand the basic networking features. There will seem to be serious limitations and even unworkable scenarios. Do not be nervous. The Dread Pirate Roberts (aka the Man in Black) really is Westley, the farmboy hero—a hero who rescues the princess time and time again. So, dread not; more will be revealed in Chapter 5, "Using Virtual Networks." Virtual networks will be your very own man in black. You will be able to resolve all the limitations I introduce here. Many of the concepts I cover in this chapter will just get better.

Cloud Service Basics

All VMs live in a cloud service. In Chapter 2, "When to Use IaaS: Cost and Options," when you created a VM and a default cloud service, you used the name that was specified, which was globally unique across the Azure `cloudapp.net` namespace. This became the DNS name of your cloud service, and your VM resides there. It is possible to create a cloud service without any resources, but that empty cloud service is really just a reserved DNS name in the `cloudapp.net` namespace—it is not actually deployed to the Azure fabric. At the time when a resource is created in the cloud service, it is deployed to the fabric. Until a resource is deployed into a cloud service, the cloud service does not really exist; it's just a name holder. Once this is understood, the fact that networking features cannot be used on an empty cloud service will make sense. Once a VM is deployed, the cloud service instantiates onto the Azure fabric. Finally, a cloud service can only be considered "running" and its associated assets available if it has at least one resource (for example, a VM) running inside that cloud service.

You can use PowerShell to test whether a cloud service name is available and then create that new empty cloud service. Take a look at the following PowerShell script:

```
$servicename = 'SavillTech102'
$serviceexists = Test-AzureName -Service $servicename
if (!$serviceexists)
{
    New-AzureService -Location "East US" -ServiceName $servicename
}
```

In the example script, I store my desired name for the cloud service in a variable and then test to see if the name is available. If the name is available, then the cloud service is created in the East US region. Note the exclamation mark (!) in the `if` statement; the exclamation mark means *not*. If the test for the `$serviceexists` variable returns `false` (which is the return value if the desired cloud service name is available), then the code that creates the cloud service runs.

As an alternative, you can create a cloud service inside an affinity group. This construct is used to ensure services are kept very close together. To ensure consistency of hardware and to keep your services physically close together for the lowest latencies, affinity group services are created within the same compute stamp. However, due to changes to the networking architecture, affinity groups are rarely used today, but I will touch on them briefly in the next chapter.

You don't have to create cloud services in advance; they can be created as part of your VM creation process. It is good, however, to know how to create services in advance because some automated processes involve precreated services, and to create them, you need to check for valid names.

To delete an empty cloud service, you can use the following:

```
Remove-AzureService $servicename -Force
```

So, let's review:

◆ Every cloud service contains one or more resources; for IaaS, this means one or more VMs.

◆ Each cloud service is bound to a specific Azure region and cannot span Azure regions.

◆ The full name of the cloud service is your custom name with a suffix of `cloudapp.net`—for example, `savilltech102.cloudapp.net`—which can be resolved to the virtual IP (VIP) address for the cloud service.

◆ A VM must be deployed to the cloud service to instantiate the cloud service on the Azure fabric before any details can be viewed in the Azure portal.

As shown in Figure 4.1, the name, along with other details such as the Internet-accessible address, is shown in the portal on the dashboard for the cloud service.

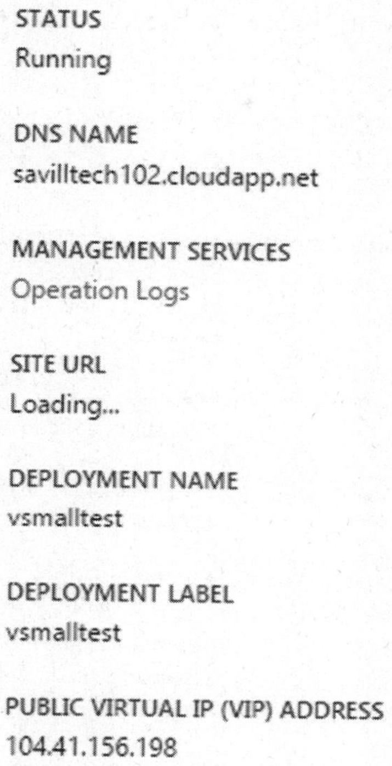

FIGURE 4.1
Basic information
about a running cloud
service

STATUS
Running

DNS NAME
savilltech102.cloudapp.net

MANAGEMENT SERVICES
Operation Logs

SITE URL
Loading...

DEPLOYMENT NAME
vsmalltest

DEPLOYMENT LABEL
vsmalltest

PUBLIC VIRTUAL IP (VIP) ADDRESS
104.41.156.198

By default, a cloud service is automatically placed into a resource group of the same name. This enables the cloud services to be used in the new Azure portal. (The new Azure portal requires all resources to be in a resource group.) Cloud services are not specific to IaaS VMs. Platform as a Service (PaaS) also uses cloud services to host various types of web and worker roles. However, you cannot mix PaaS and IaaS workloads in a single cloud service. As of this writing, a cloud service can support up to 50 VMs. Typically, you will have far fewer, but you will need multiple cloud services if you have more than 50 VMs. For the most up-to-date limits, visit this site:

```
http://azure.microsoft.com/en-us/documentation/articles/azure-subscription-
service-limits/
```

The cloud service provides a number of features and benefits to services, including:

◆ Health monitoring for services and logging

◆ Load balancing

◆ Automatic scaling

◆ Automatic assigning of a VIP address for Internet accessibility

You can view details about a cloud service using the `Get-AzureService` PowerShell cmdlet, as shown here:

```
PS C:\> Get-AzureService $servicename

ServiceName             : SavillTech102
Url                     :
https://management.core.windows.net/<GUID>/services/hostedservices/SavillTech102
Label                   : SavillTech102
Description             :
Location                : East US
AffinityGroup           :
Status                  : Created
ExtendedProperties      : {[ResourceGroup, SavillTech102],
[ResourceLocation, East US]}
DateModified            : 11/13/2014 12:01:37 PM
DateCreated             : 11/13/2014 11:52:58 AM
ReverseDnsFqdn          :
WebWorkerRoleSizes      : {}
VirtualMachineRoleSizes : {}
OperationDescription    : Get-AzureService
OperationId             : 110160c0-bd7b-2e77-b839-6d049023cd55
OperationStatus         : Succeeded
```

Did you notice that the VIP address of the cloud service is not returned? There is no simple cmdlet that allows you to view the VIP of a cloud service. Initially, I used the following script:

```
$servURL = Get-AzureDeployment -ServiceName $servicename -Slot "production" | `
    Select-Object -expandproperty Url | Select-Object -expandproperty DnsSafeHost
[System.Net.Dns]::GetHostAddresses($servURL) | `
    foreach {echo $_.IPAddressToString }
```

This code finds the expanded DNS name of the cloud service, performs a DNS lookup, and outputs the IP address. It's not very pretty, but it works. Another option is to dump or debug information for the cloud service. In the Role element, this shows the VIP address, but it is hard to use in any kind of script because address information is part of a large XML output. Here's the code I used:

```
Get-AzureRole -ServiceName $servicename -Slot Production -InstanceDetails -Debug
```

My final solution was the next PowerShell script, which works great and provides easy-to-understand output:

```
$d = Get-AzureDeployment -ServiceName $servicename -Slot Production
$d.VirtualIPs[0].Address
```

An easier way to look at the properties of a cloud service is through the Azure portal. A number of tabs provide information areas and actions, as shown in Figure 4.2. The main

Dashboard tab shows key attributes of the cloud service, such as status, VIP, DNS name, location, deployment name (the name of the first VM deployed to the cloud service to instantiate the service on the fabric), and the endpoints. (I will cover endpoints later in this chapter. They are ways to access VMs running in the cloud service from the Internet.) A CPU utilization chart is also displayed for the VMs running in the cloud service. For each VM, the CPU chart can be customized for frequency and update, and to display either relative or absolute information.

FIGURE 4.2
Cloud service information via the Azure portal

Each cloud service supports a specific number of cores. These are shown on the dashboard in the usage overview section. The processor cores used in the cloud service that has the focus are displayed, as are the cores used by the entire Azure subscription. This can help you stay ahead of the limit. As you approach limits, you can contact support and ask for a core limit increase or perhaps start a new subscription.

Linked resources are resources that may be used by the cloud service but are not stored within the cloud service. Typically, these are storage accounts and SQL databases. Linking resources enables those services to be viewed through the cloud service dashboard. The Monitor tab provides basic metrics about the instances running in the cloud service. By default, only the CPU usage values are shown. If you click the Add Metrics button, details on the disk and network can be added for selected instances, as shown in Figure 4.3. Note that memory is not shown because the memory use does not change. Hyper-V technologies, like Dynamic Memory and hot-add of memory, are not used in Azure. This means that a small VM deployed with 1.75 GB of memory always has 1.75 GB of memory; a chart showing that number would not be very interesting.

FIGURE 4.3
Cloud service instance information through the Monitor tab

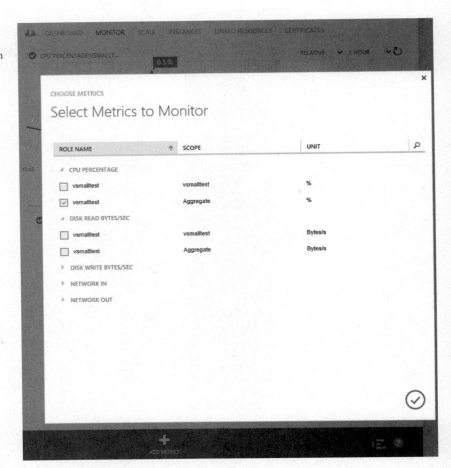

I will cover the Scale tab in Chapter 9, "Customizing Azure Templates and PowerShell Management." The Instances tab shows the instances running in the cloud service. For IaaS, this means virtual machines. The status, size, update domain, and fault domain are shown; VMs can be started, stopped, and connected to from the tab. I will cover the concepts of update domain and fault domain when we discuss availability sets and auto-scale in Chapter 9. The Linked Resources tab enables the management of resources linked to the cloud service, which as previously mentioned, includes the storage accounts and SQL databases. The Certificates tab is specific to applications published to a cloud service—for example, if you were provisioning a PaaS.

Although the cloud service has a default name in the `cloudapp.net` DNS namespace, there are scenarios where you need more. You might want to use a custom DNS name or be able to perform a reverse DNS lookup. (For that, you'll need a pointer record.) A custom name is useful if, for example, you want to make services hosted in Azure available through the Internet, perhaps on a website. Internet accessibility is provided through the cloud services VIP address. However, you typically don't give people IP addresses—you give them hostnames, such as `www.savilltech.net`. By default, your cloud service has a DNS name, `<cloud service>.cloudapp.net`, but it is unlikely you want to give your customers that name either.

The solution is to create your own DNS records in your own DNS zone. (In this context, the DNS record in your DNS zone is also called a vanity name.) Using this method, you have two options. Both are performed on the DNS servers for the domain (for example, `savilltech.net`) that you want to make the service available through.

Create a host record. You can create a host (A) record in your DNS zone with a vanity name that resolves to the IP address of your cloud service. There is some risk here if your cloud service VIP address changes, which could happen if you deprovisioned all VMs in the cloud service. The risk can be avoided through a reserved IP address. This will be covered in detail later in this chapter.

Create an alias record. You can create an alias (CNAME) record in your zone with a vanity name that resolves to the DNS name of the cloud service.

Both of these solutions are completely invisible to Azure. You are simply creating a DNS record (the name you share with your customers) in your own DNS zone. When the customer uses that DNS name, it either resolves to the IP address of your cloud service VIP address or redirects to the DNS name of the cloud service. Either way, the customer will find their way to the cloud service without ever seeing the redirect.

In July 2014, Microsoft added support for pointer records that enables reverse DNS for the cloud service VIP address. This is documented in a Microsoft blog here:

```
http://azure.microsoft.com/blog/2014/07/21/announcing-reverse-dns-for-azure-
cloud-services/
```

To use the reverse DNS lookup, you have to opt in to the service and specify the DNS suffix to be used for the reverse lookup. The PowerShell script would look like this:

```
Set-AzureService -ServiceName "savilltech101" `
    -Description "savilltech101 with Reverse DNS" `
    -ReverseDnsFqdn "savilltech101.cloudapp.net."
```

You can also add the reverse lookup when you create a cloud service by adding `-ReverseDnsFqdn` as part of the `New-AzureService` cmdlet.

A reverse FQDN can also point to a vanity domain (your domain), such as `websrv.savilltech.net`, provided `websrv.savilltech.net` is an alias (CNAME) on your DNS server that resolves to the cloud service DNS name. In my example code, I used `savilltech101.cloudapp.net`. Azure performs a check to ensure that you own the DNS name you are trying to configure for reverse DNS. Now, if someone performs a reverse IP lookup for the IP address of your cloud service VIP, it will resolve to the configured FQDN.

Using a Virtual IP

I've mentioned VIP a number of times, and so far the information I have given is for the Internet-addressable IP address for the cloud service. That VIP use provides a container for instances such as VMs. In this section, I will explore how it is used.

Figure 4.4 shows a high-level picture of a cloud service with two VMs and a VIP that provides direct communication capability with the Internet. The VIP is assigned when the cloud service is instantiated onto the Azure fabric—that is, when an instance in the VM is running. The VIP will remain constant provided the cloud service does not become deallocated, which occurs when all instances in the cloud service are deallocated. To avoid this risk, ensure that the cloud service always has at least one instance (VM) allocated.

FIGURE 4.4
Cloud service VIP
high-level view

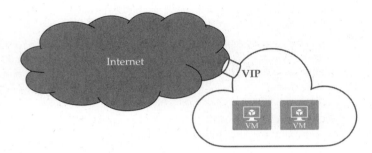

RUNNING, STOPPED, AND DEALLOCATED STATES FOR VMS

There are three primary states for a virtual machine, as shown in the following graphic: Running, Stopped, and Stopped (Deallocated). Running is self-explanatory—the VM is running, consuming processor and memory, and you are paying for the VM.

Stopped and Stopped (Deallocated) mean very different things, and the route to these states is different. Prior to June 2013, you paid for a VM in Azure once it was created. It didn't matter what its state was. If it was created, you paid for it. This drove many organizations to create elaborate processes to delete and recreate VMs as needed to save on the Azure spend. Remember, a key value proposition for Azure is that resources are only paid for as needed. In June 2013, this changed. Stopped VMs no longer result in user charges. However, there are two different types of shutdown for a Windows Azure IaaS VM: Stopped and Stopped (Deallocated), which I will refer to as Deallocated going forward.

If you stop a VM from within the guest OS of the VM or you use the `Stop-AzureVM` cmdlet with the `-StayProvisioned` parameter, then the VM stays allocated in the Azure fabric. This means the VM remains provisioned on the Azure fabric, which means it still has a slot on a server, still has reserved resources on the Azure fabric, and it keeps the IP address it was dynamically assigned via DHCP (Dynamic IP or DIP), which I will cover soon. This is not the same as the cloud service VIP.

A VM shutdown this way is considered Stopped, but not Deallocated; it will continue to be billed. It shows as Stopped in the Azure portal.

If you stop a VM from the Azure portal by using the Shut Down button, then the VM is actually deallocated from Azure resources. It no longer has resources reserved and loses its network configuration. When you restart the VM, it's reprovisioned in Azure, has resources assigned, and a network adapter added, and it is provided with a new IP lease.

This deallocation deprovisioning also happens when the `Stop-AzureVM` cmdlet is used without the `-StayProvisioned` parameter. The VM shows as Stopped (Deallocated); VMs in this status do not incur any billing. You should be aware that, if every VM in a cloud service is in a Stopped (Deallocated) state, then the cloud service might lose its VIP. When VMs are restarted, they could be assigned new VIPs. If consistency of the VIP is important, then ensure at least one VM in each cloud service stays provisioned or use a reserved IP.

To summarize:

For shutdowns from within the VM or accomplished using `Stop-AzureVM -StayProvisioned`, billing continues, and the VM resources remain reserved, including the leased IP address.

For shutdowns from within the Azure portal or that are accomplished using `Stop-AzureVM` without the `-StayProvisioned` parameter, billing stops, all resources reserved for the VM are deprovisioned (including network adapters), and the IP address lease is lost.

Make sure you use the correct stop action for your VMs to ensure you are billed only for VMs when you expect to be. Technologies such as Azure Automation can be used to automate the deprovisioning and restarting of VMs based on a schedule or trigger to help minimize cost.

The actual VIP address assigned to a cloud service comes from one of the many IP blocks Microsoft owns. Microsoft constantly acquires new blocks of IP addresses to meet the Azure demand, so the IP addresses change over time. Microsoft maintains an XML file that is updated weekly here:

```
www.microsoft.com/en-us/download/confirmation.aspx?id=41653
```

This file lists the IP blocks used by Azure for each of its regions. This can help you plan for specific firewall exceptions that may be required based on your use of Azure services in specific regions.

Sometimes, you might see slightly strange behavior when accessing the Internet from an Azure VM. For example, when I access certain websites from an Azure VM in the United States, I occasionally get redirected to the wrong country's version. I once went to Yahoo.com and was redirected to the French version, which was very puzzling. The reason for this is that the different IP ranges are assigned to various organizations by the specific countries, who then sell them to Microsoft. It takes time for the fact that an IP range has changed between countries to properly propagate through Azure. Although the IP routing works correctly, some organizations will believe certain IP blocks are in France, for example, and will redirect you accordingly. It's a transitory issue, but one to be aware of because it could potentially impact your services.

RESERVED IPs

In the previous section, I walked you through finding the VIP address for your cloud service. As I explained, once the VIP for your cloud service is allocated, it will never change as long as the cloud service stays provisioned on the Azure fabric. Your cloud service must contain a provisioned instance—in other words, at least one VM whose status is Running or Stopped, but not Stopped (Deprovisioned). As an alternative, you can reserve a VIP address for your Azure subscription for a specific region. Each Azure subscription provides five free reserved VIPs. Additional VIP addresses can be purchased if needed for about $3 per month. The detailed pricing can be found here:

http://azure.microsoft.com/en-us/pricing/details/ip-addresses/

These are reserve IPs for the cloud service. Later in the chapter, you'll learn how to use those IPs with the VMs running in the cloud service.

The new Azure portal supports the assignment and creation of a reserved IP during VM creation through the Optional Config ➤ Network ➤ IP Addresses ➤ Reserved IP Address blade shown in Figure 4.5. It is, however, more likely that you will manage these through PowerShell. The first step is to create a new reserved IP. The next PowerShell script creates a new reserved IP address and then lists all the reserved IPs for the subscription.

```
New-AzureReservedIP –ReservedIPName "SavSiteVIP" –Label "SavSiteVIP" `
    –Location "East US"
Get-AzureReservedIP
```

FIGURE 4.5
Configuring a reserved IP using the new Azure portal

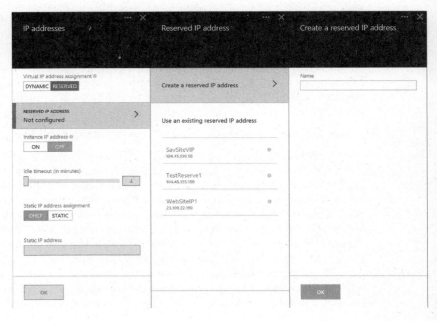

Notice that you do not specify a specific IP address—you have no control over this. What the command does is reserve an IP address from the Azure allocation that is permanently assigned for the life of your Azure subscription. You can use that reserved IP address with any service within your subscription. The reserved IP is bound to a specific Azure region and cannot be transferred between Azure subscriptions.

You cannot assign a reserved IP directly to a new cloud service because a reserved IP is implemented in the Azure fabric. Until a VM is created within a cloud service, the cloud service is not instantiated on the fabric. Therefore, you have to apply the reserved IP to the cloud service when you create the first VM in the cloud service. The example code that follows uses a reserved IP that I previously created. Notice that I am creating the VM in a new cloud service that is located in the same region as the reserved IP:

```
$ReservedIP = Get-AzureReservedIP -ReservedIPName 'SavSiteVIP'
New-AzureVMConfig -Name "JohnVM" -InstanceSize Small `
    -ImageName $images[62].ImageName | Add-AzureProvisioningConfig `
    -Windows -AdminUsername localadmin -Password Pa55word123 | New-AzureVM `
    -ServiceName "JohnApp" -ReservedIPName $ReservedIP -Location "East US"
```

The reserved IP is now assigned and used by the cloud service that I created using PowerShell. Note that the cloud service could have been precreated, in which case the `Location` parameter would not have been required.

I'm often asked whether you can bring your own public IP address for use as a VIP address in Azure as the VIP. The answer is no. You cannot take an IP address assigned to your organization by your carrier and use it in Azure. IP routing on the Internet is more complicated and it simply would not work. Likewise, you cannot take the Azure VIP and use it on-premises. If the desire is for failover of services from on-premises to Azure or vice versa, there is a solution, but it involves DNS. I will cover this in Chapter 11, "Completing Your Azure Environment," where I will talk about Azure Traffic Manager.

PRODUCTION AND STAGING

In some of the previous PowerShell scripts, I used the parameter -Slot Production, which is not something you use with IaaS. For IaaS, your slot will always be production. Slots are an interesting capability for PaaS solutions in Azure. In PaaS, you create your application and deploy to the Azure fabric. Now imagine that you want to test and then deploy a new version. One option would be to just replace your existing code with the updated code, but that makes it hard to roll back code and properly prepare the environment. Instead, for PaaS there are two slots: production and staging. Both of these slots have a VIP. The new code can be deployed, configured, and tested in the staging slot. Once you are ready for the code to go live, you perform a VIP swap. The staging environment takes over the VIP of the production environment, and what was the production environment now takes the staging VIP. Essentially you are switching the live environment, as shown in Figure 4.6. Your end users access via the VIP, and that VIP now points to the environment (slot) with the new code. The Move-AzureDeployment cmdlet can be used to switch the slots.

You can find more information on the production and staging slot mechanics for PaaS here:

```
http://azure.microsoft.com/en-us/documentation/articles/cloud-services-how-to-
manage/
```

FIGURE 4.6
Using the PaaS VIP
Swap capability

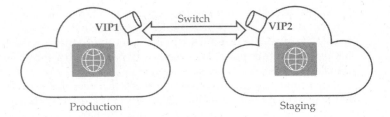

Production   Staging

Dynamic IP Addresses

VIPs are assets of cloud services—not the virtual machines running inside the cloud service. The VMs running with a cloud service are able to use the VIPs, as you will see shortly. Each VM needs its own IP address to enable initial communication between the VMs running within the cloud service. The IP address assigned to a VM in a cloud service is known as the dynamic IP (DIP).

As the name suggests, the DIP is always assigned by the Azure fabric using DHCP. You can never statically assign an IP address within the VM. The VM will always be set to use DHCP. If you view the IP address assigned by Azure, for example using IPCONFIG, and attempt to statically configure the VM with that IP address, it may work initially, but eventually it will break and you will lose communication with the VM. Always use DHCP within the VM; the IP address must be assigned by the Azure fabric to ensure the correct IP, gateway, DNS, and other configurations. Although the IP address is assigned by DHCP, it is an infinite lease, and the VM will retain that IP address unless it is deprovisioned from the Azure fabric. If you stop paying for a VM, or if some service healing that requires aspects of the VM environment to be recreated is performed, the address may change.

For VMs in a cloud service but not in a virtual network, the IP address will be allocated from the 10/8 or 100.64/12 network. The 100/8 network is reserved for service providers (per RFC 6598). It works like a subnet reserved for internal use only (per RFC 1918), such as 10/8, 172.16/12, and 192.168/16. VMs placed in the same cloud service are not necessarily on the same subnet, but Azure enables automatic routing between VMs within a cloud service. You will not be able to ping the Azure gateway for the subnet of a particular VM; this ability is disabled. The ability of VMs within a cloud service to automatically communicate via IP is shown in Figure 4.7.

FIGURE 4.7
IPv4 communication
between VMs in the
same cloud service

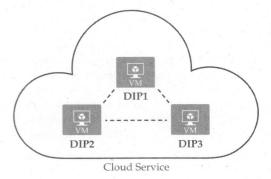

Cloud Service

To view the DIP assigned to a VM from within the VM, use standard networking methods such as running `IPCONFIG` or using Network and Sharing Center. The IP address can also be seen through the Azure portal on a VM dashboard/blade. Using PowerShell, you can see the DIP for a VM by using the `Get-AzureVM` cmdlet. In the following example, I output all VMs in my subscription and their IP addresses along with the status. Note that if a VM is not provisioned, there is no IP address. If it is just stopped, it still has an IP address because the VM is still present on the Azure fabric (and you are still paying for it).

```
PS C:\> Get-AzureVM | ft Name, IpAddress, Status -AutoSize

Name           IpAddress       Status
____           _____       _____
test           10.241.152.157  ReadyRole
websrv1                        StoppedDeallocated
websrv2                        StoppedDeallocated
vsmalltest     100.66.198.37   ReadyRole
websrv1                        StoppedDeallocated
sandbox                        StoppedDeallocated
savazudc01     10.7.115.13     ReadyRole
testvm         10.7.115.100    StoppedVM
websrv1                        StoppedDeallocated
```

As of this writing, only IPv4 is supported in Azure, and the following types of traffic are supported:

◆ TCP

◆ UDP

◆ ICMP

Multicast and broadcast type traffic is not supported and will not work in Azure. A VM that is not in a virtual network can have a single NIC with a single IP address that is automatically assigned. The Azure-provided gateway enables the VMs in the cloud service not only talk to each other, but also to communicate with the Internet.

The actual speed of the NIC depends on the VM size. Microsoft has no official NIC speed table and no guarantee of speed. There are big differences in the network speed possible based on the VM size. One of my customers was using a small-sized VM. They believed they were having CPU problems, because they could not get throughput until they increased the size of the VM to large. The large-sized VM gave them extra processors and memory, but it also gave them a greater network egress allowance. As it turned out, egress had been the bottleneck with the small-sized VM. Table 4.1 shows the speeds I found based on my testing. These are not guaranteed to be 100 percent accurate, and they could change at any time. They are not guaranteed speeds, but they are the most I've seen. Think of these numbers as nothing more than a guide. Note that there is no limit in ingress traffic.

Note also that the A8 and A9 VMs are designed for compute-intensive workloads. In addition to the regular network adapter used for network and storage traffic, a 32 Gbps RDMA network adapter is used for communication between the instances. Learn more about the RDMA adapter here:

`http://msdn.microsoft.com/en-us/library/azure/dn689095.aspx#BKMK_RDMA`

TABLE 4.1:   VM network speed based on VM size

VM Size	Maximum Egress Speed (Mbps)
A0	5
A1	250
A2	500
A3	1,000
A4	2,000
A5	500
A6	1,000
A7	2,000
A8	2,000
A9	4,000
B1	100
B2	200
B3	400
B4	800
D1	500
D2	1,000
D3	2,000
D4	4,000
D11	1,000
D12	2,000
D13	4,000
D14	8,000

What about if you have VMs in more than one cloud service? Can they communicate if they are part of the same Azure subscription and are located in the same region? The answer is no. The only communication between VMs in different cloud services is through the same mechanisms used by parties on the Internet, as shown in Figure 4.8. They are accessed via the cloud service VIP, which I will cover in the next section (remember, Buttercup does not get eaten by eels). Although I've discussed a number of major limitations, they are limitations only because there is no virtual network; a virtual network will resolve the limitations.

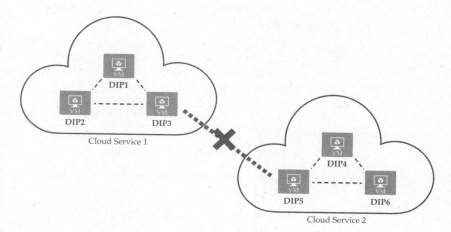

FIGURE 4.8
No communication exists between VMs in different cloud services except via the VIP.

Azure has its own DNS service that can be updated dynamically. This internal DNS service is automatically configured for VMs within a cloud service and enables all VMs within a cloud service to resolve the names of the other VMs in the same cloud service. The DNS server and the DNS zone are all configured as part of the DHCP configuration. Name resolution spans across cloud services only through a virtual network. The name resolution uses a default DNS zone that cannot be modified. This can be viewed using the `IPCONFIG` command. The example output shown here provides information for the DNS zone used for my cloud service, `b5.internal.cloudapp.net`:

```
C:\Users\localadmin>ipconfig

Windows IP Configuration

Ethernet adapter Ethernet:

   Connection-specific DNS Suffix  . : SavillTech102.b5.internal.cloudapp.net
   Link-local IPv6 Address . . . . . : fe80::8004:aed9:b742:f647%12
   IPv4 Address. . . . . . . . . . . : 100.66.198.37
   Subnet Mask . . . . . . . . . . . : 255.255.254.0
   Default Gateway . . . . . . . . . : 100.66.198.1
```

Using Endpoints and Load Balancing

Thus far the cloud service we've discussed has an Internet routable IP address and the VMs within that cloud service each have a DIP that can be used for communications within the service and out to the Internet. No link between the VM DIPs and the cloud service VIP enables services running in the VMs to be made accessible via the cloud service VIP to the Internet. The link that is required is known as an endpoint, and it enables traffic to the cloud service VIP to be forwarded to a specific VM or VMs.

Endpoint Basics

Endpoints are very simple. IP services are offered over one or more ports. For example, HTTP is offered over port 80, whereas HTTPS is offered over port 443. Remote Desktop Protocol (RDP), which enables a remote desktop connection to a Windows machine, uses port 3389. Endpoints on the VIP enable specific ports to be forwarded to specific ports on the VMs within the cloud service.

By default, when a Windows VM is created in Azure, two endpoints are automatically configured:

◆ RDP (port 3389), which enables Remote Desktop connections

◆ WS-Management (port 5986), which enables remote management, primarily through PowerShell

A Linux VM has a single endpoint that is automatically created: SSH (port 22).

These default endpoints enable basic communication and manageability from the Internet for an Azure VM. As you progress through your Azure usage, you will likely not want communication directly from the Internet and will disable it. You will only add specific endpoints when you want to make a service such as HTTP available to the Internet.

A cloud service hosts multiple VMs, which means the endpoints cannot use the same port on the cloud service VIP for multiple VMs. The mapping needs to be 1:1 unless you are using load balancing. The actual port that the cloud service VIP listens on likely will be completely different. Figure 4.9 shows two VMs running in a cloud service and how the cloud service VIP accepts and directs packets from the RDP. In this case, packets received on port 52577 on the cloud service VIP will be forwarded to the VM1 port 3389. Packets received on port 52845 on the cloud service VIP will be forwarded to the VM2 port 3389. Azure automatically generates the unique ports on the cloud service VIP. Those port assignments can be changed if required.

FIGURE 4.9
Example RDP
endpoints for two
VMs in a cloud service

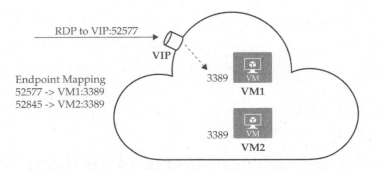

You can view the endpoints for a VM in the legacy Azure portal by using the Endpoints tab of the VM. In the new Azure portal, you will find the endpoints in the Configure lens of the VMs blade, as shown in Figure 4.10. You will find other useful information, including some hints of features to come such as a static private IP address, on the blade as well.

FIGURE 4.10
Viewing configuration
information for a VM

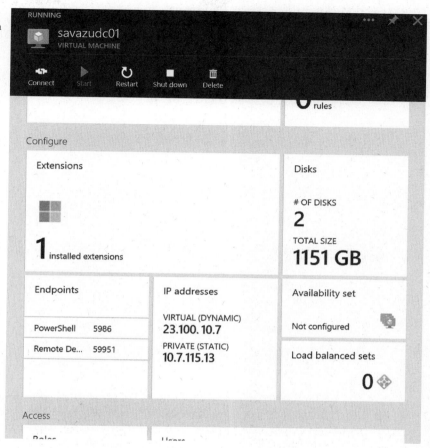

To view the endpoints for a VM from PowerShell, use the `Get-AzureEndpoint` cmdlet as shown next. Note that for PowerShell, the actual local port used for the cloud service VIP endpoint port is used for the first VM created in the cloud service. As the first VM in the cloud service, the port was available. If this type of direct mapping is not desired, you should change the endpoint. For example, you might want to obfuscate the actual ports for services from easily attempted connections. Endpoints can be changed through the portals by selecting an endpoint and then typing a new value for the public port.

```
PS C:\> Get-AzureVM -Name savazudc01 -ServiceName savilltecheastuscs | `
Get-AzureEndpoint

LBSetName         :
LocalPort         : 5986
Name              : PowerShell
Port              : 5986
Protocol          : tcp
```

```
Vip                          : 23.100.10.7
ProbePath                    :
ProbePort                    : 0
ProbeProtocol                :
ProbeIntervalInSeconds       :
ProbeTimeoutInSeconds        :
EnableDirectServerReturn     : False
Acl                          : {}
InternalLoadBalancerName     :
IdleTimeoutInMinutes         :

LBSetName                    :
LocalPort                    : 3389
Name                         : Remote Desktop
Port                         : 59951
Protocol                     : tcp
Vip                          : 23.100.10.7
ProbePath                    :
ProbePort                    : 0
ProbeProtocol                :
ProbeIntervalInSeconds       :
ProbeTimeoutInSeconds        :
EnableDirectServerReturn     : False
Acl                          : {}
InternalLoadBalancerName     :
IdleTimeoutInMinutes         :
```

Remember that the endpoint provides for forwarding communications only from a port on the VIP endpoint to a port on the specified VM. You need to ensure that the VM itself can accept traffic on its assigned port. For example, ensure that the required firewall exceptions are enabled inside the guest OS so that the port can accept traffic.

To view all endpoints that are configured on the VIP for a cloud service, view the cloud service in the Azure portal or use this PowerShell script:

```
$servicename = 'SavillTechEastUSCS'
$VMs = Get-AzureVM -ServiceName $servicename
foreach ($VM in $VMs)
{
    Write-Output $VM.Name
    Get-AzureEndpoint -VM $VM |ft Name, Port, LocalPort, Protocol `
        -autosize -HideTableHeaders
}
```

Creating Endpoints

During the creation of a VM, the option to change the default endpoints and add additional endpoints is available. However, it is more likely that you will customize these after VM creation. To add a new endpoint using the new Azure portal, perform the following steps:

1. Select the VM you wish to add an endpoint to by clicking Browse and choosing Virtual Machines, and then selecting your VM.

2. From the Configure lens, select the Endpoints part.

3. In the Endpoints blade, review the current endpoints. Click the Add button at the top of the blade.

4. When the Add An Endpoint blade (shown in Figure 4.11) opens, specify a name, such as HTTP, for the new endpoint.

FIGURE 4.11
Adding a new endpoint

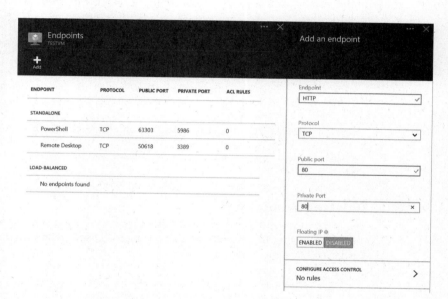

5. Specify the protocol to be used: TCP or UDP.

6. Next, select the Public Port number; this is the port that will be listened to on the cloud service VIP. Typically, you will choose a standard port since the port will be accessed through the Internet and your customers will not know your special ports. So, if you are offering HTTP, you would use port 80; if offering HTTPS, you would use port 443; and so on.

7. Specify the Private Port number. This is the port that the VM listens on to offer the service. This may be the same port number as the public port.

8. A Floating IP is specifically for use in SQL Server Always On configurations; it is also known as Direct Server Return (DSR). Unless you are configuring an always-on SQL server, leave the option set to Disabled.

   Ignore the Configure Access Control settings for now.

9. When you are finished, click OK to create the endpoint.

You can also add an endpoint by using PowerShell. The following code adds the same HTTP endpoint that you just created using the portal. The code, like most PowerShell code, uses a pipe (|) to pass objects between commands. First, the VM object to be updated is found; then, that VM object is used to add an endpoint; and finally, the update is applied to the VM.

```
Get-AzureVM -ServiceName $serviceName -Name "testvm" |
    Add-AzureEndpoint -Name "Http" -Protocol "tcp" -PublicPort 80 -LocalPort 80 |
    Update-AzureVM
```

In Chapter 9, I will talk about creating entire VM provisioning configurations that are used when creating a new VM via the `New-AzureVMConfig` cmdlet. The `Add-AzureEndpoint` cmdlet can be used as part of a VM configuration. For example, a rich VM configuration could look like this:

```
$NewVM = New-AzureVMConfig -Name $VMName -InstanceSize 'Basic_A2' `
            -ImageName $2012R2imgs[0].ImageName  |
        Add-AzureProvisioningConfig -Windows -AdminUsername $admin `
            -Password $myPwd -NoRDPEndpoint -NoWinRMEndpoint |
        Add-AzureDataDisk -CreateNew -DiskSizeInGB 100 -DiskLabel 'datadisk' `
            -LUN 0 |
        Add-AzureEndpoint -Name "Http" -Protocol "tcp" -PublicPort 80 `
            -LocalPort 80
New-AzureVM -ServiceName $serviceName -VMs $NewVM
```

Deleting Endpoints

You can remove endpoints through the Azure portal in the same location where you view them by selecting the endpoint and choosing the Delete action. To delete an endpoint using PowerShell, use the following:

```
Get-AzureVM -ServiceName $serviceName -Name "testvm" |
    Remove-AzureEndpoint -Name "Http" |
    Update-AzureVM
```

As previously mentioned, during the creation of a VM using the portal, the default endpoints can be deleted to suppress and prevent them from being created. However, if you are creating a VM using PowerShell, a different method is required. There are two primary ways to create a VM through PowerShell. If you are using the "quick create" VM option, only the basic settings can be configured. You can use the `New-AzureQuickVM` cmdlet with the `-NoWinRMEndpoint` parameter to suppress a WS-Management endpoint and prevent it from being created. (It is not possible to suppress the creation of the Remote Desktop endpoint for good reason; you need to be able to connect to the VM once it's created.) When you use the richer VM provisioning configuration option, it is possible to suppress both WS-Management and RDP endpoint creation using the `-NoRDPEndpoint` and `-NoWinRMEndpoint` parameters. For a Linux VM, automatic SSH endpoint creation can be suppressed by provisioning the VM using the `-NoSSHEndpoint` parameter. The RDP and SSH endpoints can be suppressed when you create a VM using a full provisioning configuration because other means for communicating with the VM that don't require the use of the cloud service VIP can be enabled.

Before you think about deleting or suppressing the creation of the RDP or SSH endpoints, make sure that you have another means to get to the VM. For example, if you are using a virtual network, you can use direct communication from your network to the Azure network. (That solution will be covered in the next two chapters.) In a worst-case scenario, you could always add an RDP or SSH endpoint to the VM if needed. Also, don't disable RDP or SSH from within the VM, as you will lock yourself out of the VM. (Don't panic if you do lock yourself out; in Chapter 9, you'll learn how to enable access through the use of the VM agent.)

Endpoint Access Control Lists

By default, an endpoint is accessible to the entire Internet, and it's important you practice defense in-depth by having layers of protection for services that are exposed to the Internet. You can define access control lists (ACLs) that, based on the source IP, can allow or deny access to specific subnets. This approach can be useful to blacklist certain IP addresses, or even whole countries, and allow only certain IP addresses or subnets to connect. Note that in the future this ability will be deprecated in favor of the network security group capability.

Each endpoint can have up to 50 rules defined. Each rule has the following properties:

◆ Order (a number that controls the order in which rules are applied)

◆ Description (a name for the rule)

◆ Remote Subnet (the IP subnet that rule should apply to)

◆ Permit/Deny

If you specify a remote subnet, use the Classless Inter-Domain Routing (CIDR) format: `<network>/<number of bits that make up the subnet mask>`. For example, 10.20.0.0/16 is the equivalent of 10.20.0.0 with a subnet mask of 255.255.0.0.

By default, every endpoint already has a rule that denies all traffic. When an endpoint is added, a rule is created to allow all inbound traffic for that port. The rules that define the access are added manually.

Because multiple rules can be defined for an endpoint, the Order property controls precedence: the lower the Order value, the higher its precedence. Order 1 has the highest precedence. Table 4.2 defines two rules. The first rule denies access to the 175.10.1.0/24 subnet, whereas the second enables access to subnet 175.0.0.0/8.

TABLE 4.2:   ACL rule example

RULE #	REMOTE SUBNET	ENDPOINT	PERMIT/DENY
10	175.10.1.0/24	HTTP	Deny
20	175.0.0.0/8	HTTP	Permit

To define endpoints using PowerShell, you must follow three steps. First, create an ACL object; the rules will be applied to this object. Here's the syntax:

```
$acl1 = New-AzureAclConfig
```

The next step is to add rules to the ACL configuration object:

```
Set-AzureAclConfig –AddRule –ACL $acl1 –Order 10 –Action Deny `
        –RemoteSubnet "175.10.1.0/24" –Description "Deny 175.10.1.0/24"
Set-AzureAclConfig –AddRule –ACL $acl1 –Order 20 –Action Permit `
        –RemoteSubnet "175.0.0.0/8" –Description "Allow 175.0.0.0/8"
```

You can remove rules from an ACL configuration using the `-RemoveRule -ID <rule ID>` parameters.

Finally, apply the ACL configuration object to an endpoint:

```
Get-AzureVM -ServiceName $serviceName -Name "testvm" |
        Set-AzureEndpoint -Name "Http" -ACL $acl1 | Update-AzureVM
```

To remove an ACL from an endpoint, use the following PowerShell code:

```
Get-AzureVM -ServiceName $serviceName -Name "testvm" |
        Remove-AzureAclConfig -Name "Http" | Update-AzureVM
```

Instance-Level IP Addresses

Endpoints provide a method for specific ports to be forwarded from the cloud service VIP to a VM. However, if you have a service that uses a dynamic range of ports, such as an FTP server, then creating endpoints for every possible port is not possible. Additionally, you may want traffic that is outbound from the VM to be marked with a specific source IP address that is owned by the VM. Instance-level public IP (PIP) addresses enable an Internet-addressable IP address to be assigned to a specific VM. All traffic to the PIP is sent directly to the VM. This does not replace the cloud service VIP, and a VM can still be sent traffic via endpoints on the cloud service. The assigned PIP provides an additional method for traffic to reach the VM. PIPs should be used with care, because any traffic sent to a PIP goes directly to the VM. Good firewall protection and security on the VM to mitigate attacks is a requirement for VMs that are accessed through a PIP. Figure 4.12 shows a VM receiving traffic via an endpoint and via a PIP. Note that the VM does not see the PIP—it sees only its DIP.

A PIP is assigned to a VM using the `Set-AzurePublicIP` cmdlet. The only action associated with the cmdlet sets a name for the new PIP; no precreation is required. The next PowerShell script assigns a PIP to a VM, views the PIP details by viewing the instances in the cloud service, and then removes the PIP from the VM. An instance-level PIP can also be assigned using the new Azure portal via the IP addresses part in the Configure lens.

```
Get-AzureVM -ServiceName $serviceName -Name TestVM |
        Set-AzurePublicIP -PublicIPName testpip | Update-AzureVM
```

```
Get-AzureRole -ServiceName $serviceName -Slot Production -InstanceDetails

Get-AzureVM -ServiceName $serviceName -Name TestVM |
      Remove-AzurePublicIP | Update-AzureVM
```

As of this writing, it is not possible to use a reserved IP address with PIP.

FIGURE 4.12
Example of PIP access
for a VM

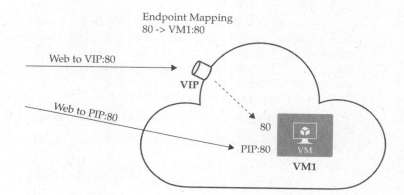

Load-Balanced Sets

Typically, an endpoint on the cloud service points to a specific VM. However, when high availability and load balancing are required, a single endpoint needs to point to multiple VMs; it also must have the intelligence to direct incoming traffic only to VMs that are currently available. Load-balanced sets enable this capability and include a probe capability that checks the health of the possible VM targets. Request clients are only sent to healthy members of the load-balanced set. The basic idea is shown in Figure 4.13; this particular set includes three members.

FIGURE 4.13
Example showing
load-balanced set
in action for a web
service

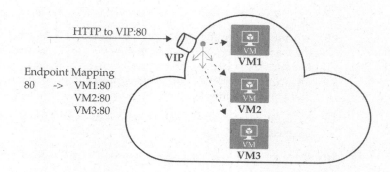

An Azure load-balanced set is a Layer 4 load balancer that works with TCP and UDP workloads. By default, it uses a 5 tuple load-balancing algorithm, which specifically uses the following:

◆ The source IP address

◆ The destination IP address

◆ The protocol type (TCP or UDP)

◆ The source port

◆ The destination port

Using a 5 tuple algorithm ensures a good distribution of traffic. It also ensures that all traffic from a specific session will be sent to the same specific member of the load-balanced set. If, however, a different session is created or a workload (such as Remote Desktop Gateway traffic) uses different ports or protocols, then the traffic will be distributed among the various members of the set. I will cover this in greater detail shortly.

You can create a load-balanced set through the new Azure portal using these steps:

1. Open the blade for the VM that will initially join and create the load-balanced set.

2. In the Configure lens, select the Load Balanced Sets part.

3. When the Load Balanced Sets blade opens, any existing load-balanced sets will be displayed. Click the Join command at the top of the blade.

4. When the Join A Load Balanced Set blade opens, make sure the type is set to Public. Next, set the endpoint name and port (for example, HTTP and port 80) for this VM when it joins the set.

5. Click the Load Balanced Set menu part to open the Choose A Load Balanced Set blade and select the Create A Load Balanced Set item. When the Create A Load Balanced Set blade (shown in Figure 4.14) opens, enter a name for the new load-balanced set, unless you are adding a second machine to the set. If this is a second machine joining the set, you can just select a set that already exists.

Notice how many blades have been opened thus far in this process. This is why journeys are so important; they enable you to jump between the various activities you currently have going on.

6. Select the protocol the VM uses and the public port for listening on the VIP.

7. If the VM is an Always On SQL server, enable the Floating IP option.

8. You must next configure the protocol and port to be used for the probe. They are used by the load balancer to check which members of the set are available. Specify the interval in which the probe is performed along with how many retries are allowed before the member is considered unresponsive and will no longer be sent incoming requests. Note that you can define ACLs in the same way as a regular endpoint.

9. Click OK on the open blades to submit the Azure job that creates the new Azure load-balanced set.

10. Once the set is created, repeat the process for the other VMs that will join the set.

FIGURE 4.14

Creating a new load-balanced set

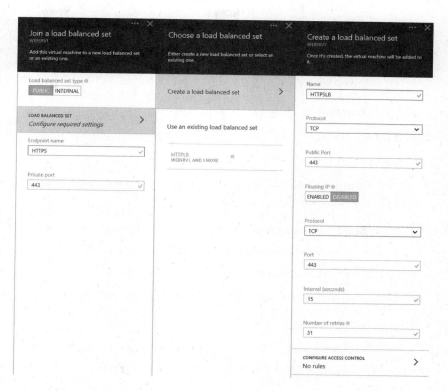

PowerShell can also be used to create a load-balanced set, but you don't create the load-balanced set first—you just add an endpoint but specify that it's part of a load-balanced set and configure the options.

```
Get-AzureVM -ServiceName "savilltech101" -Name "websrv1" |
      Add-AzureEndpoint -Name "HTTP" -Protocol tcp -LocalPort 80 `
      -PublicPort 80 -LBSetName "LBHTTP" -ProbePort 80 `
      -ProbeProtocol http -ProbePath "/" | Update-AzureVM
Get-AzureVM -ServiceName "savilltech101" -Name "websrv2" |
      Add-AzureEndpoint -Name "HTTP" -Protocol tcp -LocalPort 80 `
      -LBSetName "LBHTTP" | Update-AzureVM
```

When you use PowerShell, another option is available for setting the distribution mode for a load-balanced set. Typically, a 5 tuple distribution algorithm is used to distribute traffic, but there are times when this causes problems. If a client closes a connection and then reconnects, they will likely use a new local port. That new local port would not match the 5 tuple, and therefore the traffic would be directed to a different set member. Likewise, if a communication uses multiple ports or protocols, the 5 tuple mode would distribute the connections to different members, which likely would break the communication. Two additional distribution modes can be configured using PowerShell, which help enable additional stickiness: 2 tuple and 3 tuple.

For a 2 tuple distribution mode, only the source and destination IP is used to map traffic to target members. This means any traffic from a specific IP will always go to the same member of the load-balanced set no matter which port or protocol is used. The 3 tuple distribution mode uses protocol in addition to the source and destination IP address. All traffic using the same Layer 4 protocol type (TCP or UDP) from an IP address will always be routed to the same member of the distribution set. Microsoft has a great blog post that goes into detail about these distribution modes:

```
http://azure.microsoft.com/blog/2014/10/30/azure-load-balancer-new-distribution-
mode/
```

I recommend reading the post. It features two graphics showing how the 5 tuple differs from 2 tuple distribution mode when distributing traffic from multiple connections from the same source IP address.

To set the distribution mode to a mode other than the default 5 tuple, PowerShell must be used. Add the -LoadBalancerDistribution parameter with one of these values:

◆ -LoadBalancerDistribution "SourceIP" (use 2 tuple distribution mode)

◆ -LoadBalancerDistribution "SourceIPProtocol" (use 3 tuple distribution mode)

If the -LoadBalancerDistribution parameter is not specified, the default 5 tuple distribution mode is configured. Here's an example of a script for creating a load-balanced set using 2 tuple:

```
Get-AzureVM -ServiceName "savilltech101" -Name "websrv1" |
    Add-AzureEndpoint -Name "HTTP" -Protocol tcp -LocalPort 80 -PublicPort 80 `
    -LBSetName "LBHTTP" -ProbePort 80 -ProbeProtocol http -ProbePath "/" `
    -LoadBalancerDistribution "SourceIP" |
    . Update-AzureVM
```

You can change the distribution mode at any time. The current distribution mode can be viewed using the Get-AzureEndpoint cmdlet against a VM object. To change the distribution mode, use the following:

```
Set-AzureLoadBalancedEndpoint -ServiceName "savilltech101" -LBSetName "LBHTTP" `
    -Protocol tcp -LocalPort 80 -ProbeProtocol http -ProbePort 80 `
    -LoadBalancerDistribution "sourceIP"
```

Another option configurable through PowerShell is idle connection time-out by configuring the -IdleTimeoutInMinutes parameter. This enables the time-out to be modified from the default 4 minutes to a shorter, or more likely a longer, time to maintain the same connection between a client and your service. This can be up to 30 minutes.

Internal Load-Balanced Sets

Load-balanced sets are a powerful mechanism for distributing traffic coming in via the cloud service VIP to multiple VMs. The sets not only provide high availability of service, but also distribute the load. Consider a more advanced deployment consisting of multiple tiers of service. Perhaps a front-end web tier uses a load-balanced set on the cloud service VIP that then communicates to a backend service, such as a database, that also requires load balancing and fault tolerance. For this to work, a separate internal load-balanced set is needed to handle traffic between the web VMs and the database VMs. Creating a load-balanced set on the cloud service VIP for the database VMs does not make sense because the traffic between the web VMs and the database VMs exists entirely within the cloud service. Sending traffic from the web VMs to the database VMs out via the Internet does not make sense. An internal load-balanced set is exactly what the name suggests: a load-balanced set created within the cloud service (or, looking forward, a virtual network). It includes an additional IP address that represents the internal load-balanced set that services can communicate with. From that additional IP address, traffic is distributed accordingly, as shown in Figure 4.15.

FIGURE 4.15
Load-balanced set and internal load-balanced set in action

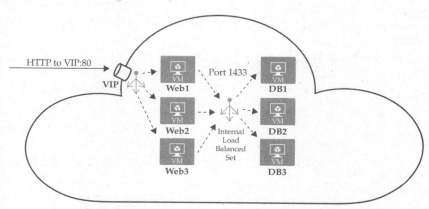

In Microsoft documentation, the IP for the internal load-balanced set is called a VIP. This can be a little confusing, since we usually think of the VIP as externally addressable. For internal load-balanced sets, it's a virtual IP on the Internet network. In terms you might be more used to, it is really just an additional DIP. When creating an internal load-balanced set in a virtual network, you can assign an IP address from the virtual network address space. In a nonvirtual network environment, the IP is always assigned by the cloud service.

Creating an internal load-balanced set using the portal is basically the same as creating a regular load-balanced set—the difference is you configure the load-balanced set type as Internal and not Public. I will therefore focus instead on configuring using PowerShell. In this example, I'll use a subnet name because I'm creating the set on a virtual network, which you will as well if you use this (every Azure subscription should use a virtual network when focusing on IaaS).

```
#Create a new internal load balancer in a specific cloud service on a subnet
Add-AzureInternalLoadBalancer -InternalLoadBalancerName ILBSQL `
    -SubnetName DBSubnet -ServiceName savilltech101

#Add an endpoint to first VM on the internal load balancer
Get-AzureVM -ServiceName "savilltech101" -Name "dbsrv1" |
    Add-AzureEndpoint -Name "intwebep" -LBSetName "intdbeplb" -Protocol tcp `
        -LocalPort 1433 -PublicPort 1433 -ProbePort 1433 -ProbeProtocol tcp `
        -ProbeIntervalInSeconds 10 -InternalLoadBalancerName ILBSQL |
    Update-AzureVM
```

```
#Add an endpoint to the second VM on the internal load balancer
Get-AzureVM -ServiceName "savilltech101" -Name "dbsrv2" |
      Add-AzureEndpoint -Name "intwebep" -LBSetName "intdbeplb" -Protocol tcp `
        -LocalPort 1433 -PublicPort 1433 -ProbePort 1433 -ProbeProtocol tcp `
        -ProbeIntervalInSeconds 10 -InternalLoadBalancerName ILBSQL |
      Update-AzureVM

#View the state of the internal load balancer
Get-AzureService -ServiceName savilltech101 | Get-AzureInternalLoadBalancer
```

Once again, ACLs can be defined on the load balancer, and as you deploy multitiered services to Azure, the ability to create the internal load balancers is a critical one.

The Bottom Line

Understand how communication to services running in a VM from the Internet works. VMs are housed in a cloud service, and that cloud service has an Internet-addressable IP, the virtual IP (VIP). Endpoints map ports on the VIP to ports on specific VMs. This enables inbound communication from the Internet to be sent to specific VMs, thereby offering services out to the Internet.

Master It Can a VM have its own Internet-addressable IP to accept all traffic sent to it?

Use load-balancing capabilities. You can create a load-balanced set, which consists of one or more members that will have traffic sent to them based on the distribution mode configured. A probe is configured to enable the load-balancer component to detect whether a member is not responding and therefore is not eligible to receive traffic. An internal load balancer works in a similar fashion but does not use the cloud service VIP. Rather, it has its own internal IP address and enables load balancing within a cloud service or virtual network.

Master It What are the available distribution modes for a load-balanced set?

Differentiate between a stopped and a deprovisioned VM. A stopped VM is one that, while not running, is still provisioned on the Azure compute fabric. It is deployed to a cluster and has resources reserved for it. A stopped VM still incurs cost, the same as if it were running. It also maintains items such as the VM's DIPs. A deprovisioned VM is not deployed to the Azure fabric. No costs are incurred, other than the storage cost for its virtual hard disks. When a deprovisioned VM is restarted, it is provisioned to the Azure fabric and gets new resources, including a new virtual NIC and a new DIP.

Master It Is there any way to help automatically deprovision and then restart at different times of the day?

## Chapter 5

Using Virtual Networks

Virtual networks are the foundation for all the true enterprise networking configurations you need to use in Azure, especially, but not limited to, IaaS. This chapter explains what virtual networks are, how they should be architected, how to deploy them, and what capabilities are exposed when they are used. This chapter resolves many of the limitations that were exposed for networking in a cloud service without a virtual network and prepares you for connecting Azure to your on-premises locations.

In this chapter, you will learn to

◆   Articulate virtual network and virtual subnet basic concepts

◆   Use multi-NIC VMs

Virtual Network Basics

Take a look at Figure 5.1. You will recall from Chapter 4, "Enabling External Connectivity," that VMs that are in different virtual networks are isolated from one another. The key limitations include:

◆   No communication between cloud services other than via endpoints on the cloud service VIP

◆   No name resolution between cloud services

◆   No control of IP namespace

◆   No control of Domain Name System (DNS) configuration

◆   No ability to reserve IP addresses for VMs, even if deprovisioned

◆   Limited scalability due to the maximum number of VMs within a cloud service (50) that are able to communicate

A Very Brief History of the Affinity Group

Virtual networks solve all of these limitations and more. Up until a year ago, before I talked about virtual networks I would introduce the concept of an affinity group. Affinity groups were containers for virtual networks and a very important architectural component. This is no longer the case. I will briefly cover what an affinity group is and explain why it is not used anymore.

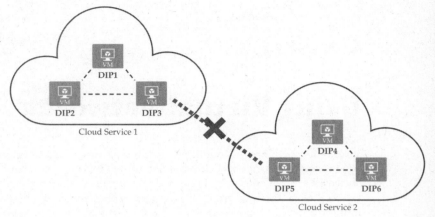

FIGURE 5.1
Communication of VMs in different cloud services

In Chapter 2, "When to Use IaaS: Cost and Options," I talked about the architecture of Azure datacenters and how compute stamps (racks of servers) are deployed. The servers in a stamp use the same hardware generation—for example, the same processor—and traditionally had better network connectivity intrastamp (within) than was available interstamp (between). An affinity group was bound to a specific stamp, which provided two key benefits:

◆ Very low latency for communications between the VMs in the affinity group

◆ Consistent performance due to the guarantee of the same hardware specifications within the stamp

Additionally, a single cluster network manager handled network configuration within each cluster.

Problems arose as Microsoft introduced new generations of hardware. The new VM sizes, such as the A8 and A9, were deployed in separate stamps and could not become part of an existing affinity group–based virtual network. Fortunately, at the same time, Microsoft had redesigned its networking and offered very fast connectivity and low latency throughout an entire Azure region. With the introduction of a regional network manager, it became possible to create a regional virtual network that is no longer bound to a specific stamp. Instead, it can be deployed over an entire Azure region. This enables VMs on different stamps (and therefore hardware of different sizes and generations) to be deployed as part of the same virtual network. As you read this, all virtual networks have been migrated to regional virtual networks, even if they were created as affinity group–based networks.

Is there still a benefit to affinity groups? An affinity group guarantees all VMs deployed are in the same Azure stamp. This means an affinity group can still be useful if you want to ensure you're deployed to exactly the same type of hardware. However, remember that because Microsoft levels the performance of dissimilar hardware, you should always see performance parity—even across dissimilar hardware. If you must be 100 percent sure that your network is on the same hardware type, then deploy to an affinity group, but because affinity groups can actually limit functionality, I recommend avoiding them unless you must use them.

Virtual Networks 101

You will remember that in Chapter 4 I told you to dread not—the Man in Black would come to your rescue. He has. In this case, however, your personal Man in Black is not Westley, the farm-boy hero, but a virtual network. Virtual networks bring high levels of control and configuration to administrators. Fundamentally, a virtual network enables the IP space in the virtual network to be defined and includes breaking that space into virtual subnets. Virtual machines are placed in a virtual network when they are created, which results in the entire cloud service being part of the virtual network. Thus, the first VM created in a cloud service must be joined to the virtual network. Virtual networks can connect disparate cloud services to each other, as well as to on-premises networks. Figure 5.2 shows a high-level view of a virtual network. Virtual networks are, however, bound to a specific Azure region and, as of this writing, are limited to a maximum 2,048 VMs.

FIGURE 5.2

VM communication in a virtual network

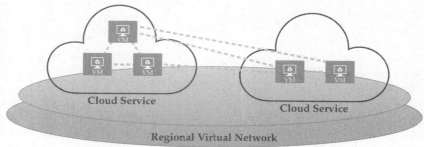

The IP space chosen for the virtual network should not overlap any IP space used on-premises or in any other service used by your organization. For example, if your organization uses the 10.0.0.0/8 IP range on-premises, you would likely choose the 172.16.0.0/12 range in Azure to avoid any risk of overlap. Always consider that, even if you don't want to connect Azure to your on-premises network today, you may want to connect in the future.

Once you decide the IP address range you wish to use for the Azure network, you can then divide that address range into subnets for use by different types of service. I like to create different subnets for my Azure infrastructure servers, such as domain controllers, and another for my Azure application services, such as SQL servers. The Azure gateway requires its own IP subnet for VPN as well.

Subnets can be as large as /8 and as small as /29 (using CIDR subnet definitions). Remember, Classless Interdomain Routing (CIDR) subnet definitions show the number of bits in the IP address that defines the network. An /8 provides a subnet mask of 255.0.0.0. (I doubt you would ever have a subnet anywhere close to this size.) Gateway functionality between subnets in a virtual network is provided automatically by the virtual network. However, you cannot ping the gateway for each subnet, nor will tracer type utilities work. Also, the subnets you define cannot have overlapping address spaces.

Typically, the IP space used in Azure would be chosen from RFC 1918:

◆ 10.0.0.0–10.255.255.255 (10/8 prefix)

◆ 172.16.0.0–172.31.255.255 (172.16/12 prefix)

◆ 192.168.0.0–192.168.255.255 (192.168/16 prefix)

However, as of November 2014, this is no longer a requirement. A number of customers have very large IP address spaces that are Internet routable. Those customers want to use those addresses in Azure in the same way the addresses are used on-premises. The update to Azure virtual networks announced at TechEd Europe 2014 allows virtual networks to use non-RFC 1918 IP address ranges. If you plan to use non-RFC 1918 IP addresses in Azure, it is obviously important that you use only non-RFC 1918 addresses for IP spaces you own in your organization. For most organizations, the use of RFC 1918 ranges is still the best option; non-RFC 1918 use would be on an exception basis.

UNDERSTANDING CIDR NOTATION

When defining virtual networks, CIDR notation is used. CIDR notation combines the IP network address and the associated mask that defines which part of the IP address represents the network. It is presented in the format of *xxx.xxx.xxx.xxx/n*, where *xxx.xxx.xxx.xxx* is the IP network and *n* represents the number of bits used for the subnet mask.

An *n* value of 24 indicates a subnet mask of 255.255.255.0. Since each part of the address is 8 bits, 24 bits means the first three parts are all 1s and therefore 255.

192.168.1.0/24 equates to an IP range of 192.168.1.0–192.168.1.255.

Within a virtual network subnet, the protocol reserves the first and last IP addresses of a subnet: a host ID of all 0s is used for the network address, and a host ID of all 1s is used for broadcast. In addition, Azure reserves the first three IP addresses in each subnet (binary 01, 10, and 11 in the host ID portion of the IP address) for internal purposes. Figure 5.3 shows an example of a virtual network with three subnets. Note that in this example, the virtual network is a small address space (10.7.115.0/24), and within it I've divided some of that space into the subnets. Under usual circumstances, the gateway subnet (10.7.115.0/29) would allow six usable IP addresses (10.7.115.1 to 10.7.115.6). But, as shown in Figure 5.3, notice that the address space shows only three IP addresses are usable (.4 to .6). This is because Windows Azure has reserved the first three usable addresses (.1 to .3) for its own purposes.

FIGURE 5.3
Viewing the address space for virtual subnets

virtual network address spaces

ADDRESS SPACE	STARTING IP	CIDR (ADDRESS COUNT)	USABLE ADDRESS RANGE
10.7.115.0/24	10.7.115.0	/24 (251)	10.7.115.4 - 10.7.115.254
SUBNETS			
Static-Net	10.7.115.8	/29 (3)	10.7.115.12 - 10.7.115.14
App-Net	10.7.115.16	/28 (11)	10.7.115.20 - 10.7.115.30
Lab 173_0	10.7.115.64	/27 (27)	10.7.115.68 - 10.7.115.94
Subnet-1	10.7.115.96	/27 (27)	10.7.115.100 - 10.7.115.126
Gateway	10.7.115.0	/29 (3)	10.7.115.4 - 10.7.115.6

add subnet   add gateway subnet

Once you define subnets and add virtual machines to those subnets, you must allocate an IP address for each VM. The address will be allocated from the subnet IP address range as an infinite lease. This means that even though Dynamic Host Configuration Protocol (DHCP) is used to assign the IP address to the virtual machine, the actual IP address will never change as long as the virtual machine is provisioned, which means you are paying for it.

Within a virtual network, most IP-based protocols, such as TCP, UDP, and ICMP, will work, although you should be aware that multicast, broadcast, IP-in-IP encapsulated packets, and Generic Routing Encapsulation (GRE) packets are blocked. The GRE blocking is very logical when you consider that, behind the scenes, Azure leverages Hyper-V Network Virtualization, which itself uses GRE. This could change in the future. Multiple virtual networks can be connected via on-premises connectivity or through the Azure fabric.

This is really all a virtual network is: an IP address space you define and then divide into subnets, and virtual machines are then assigned to a subnet when the virtual machine is created. You cannot move existing virtual machines into a subnet or move a virtual machine out of a subnet. The configuration must be done at the time of virtual machine creation. Although I am talking exclusively about IaaS virtual machines, PaaS web and worker roles can also leverage VPNs.

WARNING Once VMs are created, it's difficult to move them into a virtual network. It is critical that, before any real workloads are created in Azure, you work with your on-premises network team, identify the IP space for use in Azure, create your Azure virtual network, and be ready for VMs to join the VPN.

Creating a Virtual Network

The easiest way to introduce the core concepts for a virtual network is to create one. As of this writing, VPNs must be created through the legacy Azure portal. Follow these steps:

1. In the Azure portal, select the Networks navigation item.

2. Select the New action, and select the Custom Create option as the Virtual Network setting.

3. Enter a name for the new virtual network and select the region. Use a descriptive name so you can identify the network going forward. Click the Next arrow.

4. Specify the DNS servers for the virtual network. If you don't have this information, leave it blank. You can identify the DNS servers later. If you previously defined DNS servers in Azure, they will appear in the drop-down list. For now, do not configure the VPN as either site-to-site or point-to-site. Click the Next arrow. Figure 5.4 shows the DNS Servers and VPN Connectivity page.

5. On the final screen, you configure the subnets available in the virtual network. By default, a subnet has been added at the start of the IP address space. You can change the address space used from the default 10.0.0.0/8 to anything you want by clicking in the Starting IP field and changing the IP to meet your needs, as shown in Figure 5.5.

6. Change the name of the default subnet to a useful name, such as **InfraVMs**. Likely, you will also want to change the size of the subnet from the default /11 to something smaller based on the number of VMs you expect to have in the subnet.

FIGURE 5.4
Virtual Network
connectivity options

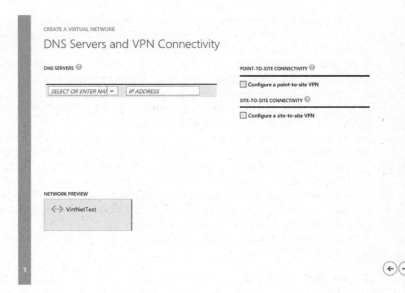

FIGURE 5.5
Defining IP subnets

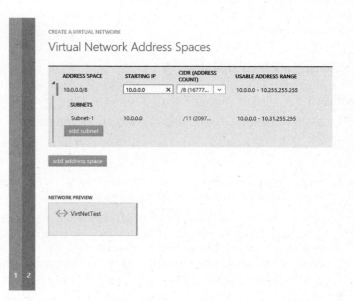

NOTE Before administrators could reserve IP addresses for VMs in a virtual network, I used a dedicated subnet just for groups of servers, such as domain controllers. Because only my domain controllers were in this subnet, no one else would take their address, even if the virtual machines were deallocated at some point in the future and lost their IP addresses. With reserved IP addresses, that is no longer necessary, but as a best practice, I recommend creating a dedicated virtual subnet for VMs where IP addresses are reserved.

7. Now, click Add Subnet to create additional subnets for your domain servers, application servers, DMZ VMs, and so on, as shown in Figure 5.6. Click the check mark icon to complete the virtual network creation.

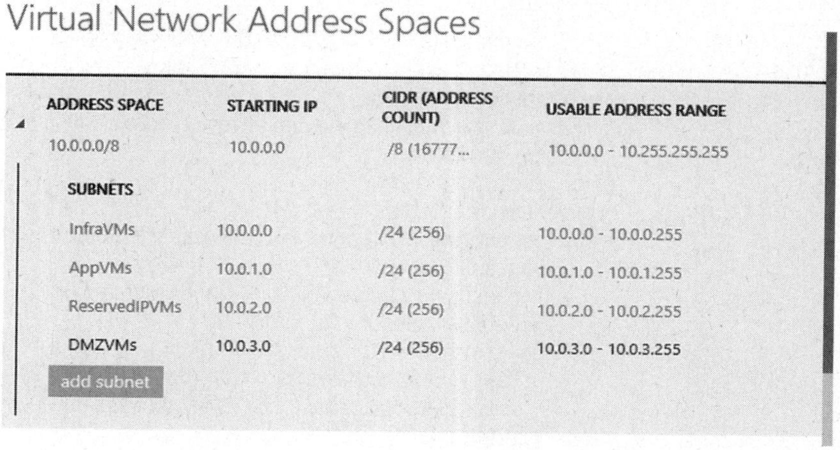

FIGURE 5.6
Example of a virtual network with virtual subnets defined

Virtual Network Address Spaces

ADDRESS SPACE	STARTING IP	CIDR (ADDRESS COUNT)	USABLE ADDRESS RANGE
10.0.0.0/8	10.0.0.0	/8 (16777...	10.0.0.0 - 10.255.255.255
SUBNETS			
InfraVMs	10.0.0.0	/24 (256)	10.0.0.0 - 10.0.0.255
AppVMs	10.0.1.0	/24 (256)	10.0.1.0 - 10.0.1.255
ReservedIPVMs	10.0.2.0	/24 (256)	10.0.2.0 - 10.0.2.255
DMZVMs	10.0.3.0	/24 (256)	10.0.3.0 - 10.0.3.255

add subnet

Postcreation, you can add additional subnets, but you cannot change existing subnets through the portal. The one exception to that rule is the last subnet you defined. You can modify the subnet size and the starting IP, and it can even be deleted.

There are no PowerShell cmdlets to create and modify virtual networks. Instead, the process is to export the virtual network configuration to XML, modify the XML, and then reimport the XML to update the virtual network. Do not try to change subnets where VMs are already deployed because the import will fail. When the XML file is imported, it redefines the virtual networking for the subscription. So, you could create a virtual network just by editing the XML configuration, adding the completely new virtual network, and then importing the XML to apply the configuration.

To dump the entire configuration of the virtual networks, use the following:

```
Get-AzureVNetConfig | select -ExpandProperty xmlconfiguration
```

The result will be a huge amount of information. Here's an example output:

```
PS C:\> AzureVNetConfig | select -ExpandProperty xmlconfiguration
<?xml version="1.0" encoding="utf-8"?>
<NetworkConfiguration xmlns:xsd="http://www.w3.org/2001/XMLSchema"
xmlns:xsi="http://www.w3.org/2001/XMLSchema-instance"
xmlns="http://schemas.microsoft.com/ServiceHosting/2011/07/NetworkConfiguration"
>
  <VirtualNetworkConfiguration>
    <Dns>
      <DnsServers>
        <DnsServer name="savazudns01" IPAddress="10.0.0.10" />
```

```
          </DNSSERVERS>
        </DNS>
        <LOCALNETWORKSITES>
          <LOCALNETWORKSITE NAME="DC1">
            <ADDRESSSPACE>
              <ADDRESSPREFIX>10.5.0.0/16</ADDRESSPREFIX>
              <ADDRESSPREFIX>10.10.0.0/16</ADDRESSPREFIX>
            </ADDRESSSPACE>
            <VPNGATEWAYADDRESS>99.99.99.99</VPNGATEWAYADDRESS>
          </LOCALNETWORKSITE>
        </LOCALNETWORKSITES>
        <VIRTUALNETWORKSITES>
          <VIRTUALNETWORKSITE NAME="VIRTNETTEST" LOCATION="EAST US">
            <ADDRESSSPACE>
              <ADDRESSPREFIX>10.0.0.0/8</ADDRESSPREFIX>
            </ADDRESSSPACE>
            <SUBNETS>
              <SUBNET NAME="INFRAVMS">
                <ADDRESSPREFIX>10.0.0.0/24</ADDRESSPREFIX>
              </SUBNET>
              <SUBNET NAME="APPVMS">
                <ADDRESSPREFIX>10.0.1.0/24</ADDRESSPREFIX>
              </SUBNET>
              <SUBNET NAME="RESERVEDIPVMS">
                <ADDRESSPREFIX>10.0.2.0/24</ADDRESSPREFIX>
              </SUBNET>
              <SUBNET NAME="DMZVMS">
                <ADDRESSPREFIX>10.0.3.0/24</ADDRESSPREFIX>
              </SUBNET>
            </SUBNETS>
              <DNSSERVERSREF>
              <DNSSERVERREF NAME="SAVAZUDNS01" />
            </DNSSERVERSREF>
          </VIRTUALNETWORKSITE>
        </VIRTUALNETWORKSITES>
      </VIRTUALNETWORKCONFIGURATION>
    </NETWORKCONFIGURATION>
```

To export the XML to a file that can then be modified, use the following:

```
Get-AzureVNetConfig -ExportToFile d:\temp\MyAzureNetworks.netcfg
```

Replace the file destination location (d:\temp\) with one that that is appropriate for your environment.

The format of the XML file is very intuitive. The first section, <DnsServers>, defines the DNS servers that are available to be linked within specific virtual networks. The DNS servers are defined at the Azure subscription level and can be used by any virtual network within the subscription. A DNS entry consists of a name and IP address.

The next section, `<LocalNetworkSites>`, specifies the IP space used by your on-premises locations and the IP address of the VPN gateway. This is used for two primary purposes:

◆   To define connections between Azure virtual networks and on-premises locations

◆   To identify to Azure networking which IP destinations should be routed via VPN connections—that is, your on-premises—and which should be sent to the Internet (although forced tunneling is possible)

The final section, `<VirtualNetworkSites>`, is our primary interest. This defines the actual virtual networks and the regions they reside in—for example:

```
<VirtualNetworkSite name="VirtNetTest" Location="East US">
```

This identifies a virtual network named VirtNetTest in the East US Azure region. If you had an affinity group–bound virtual network, you would see something like this:

```
<VirtualNetworkSite name="SavTechNet115" AffinityGroup="SavTech115">
```

As you read this, all affinity group–bound virtual networks should have been converted to regional virtual networks, which means you should not see any virtual network bound to an affinity group. If you do see `AffinityGroup=`, it means you have an old virtual network that has not been converted, and many networking features will not work because they rely on the regional network manager. The only solution is to create a new regional virtual network and move resources. However, if you contact Azure support, they likely can expedite the conversion of your virtual network to a regional one.

The IP address space of the virtual network is defined in the `<AddressSpace>` section, and then each individual virtual subnet is defined in the `<Subnets>` section. Finally, one of the previously defined DNS servers is referenced, which means that DNS server will be configured via DHCP as the DNS server for the machines on the virtual network. If you modify the XML—for example, if you add a new virtual network to apply the new configuration—run the following PowerShell command:

```
Set-AzureVNetConfig -ConfigurationPath d:\temp\MyAzureNetworks.netcfg
```

TIP   Until you are familiar with virtual networks, I recommend that you use the web interface for management.

Adding a VM to a Virtual Network

Once the virtual network is created, the next step is to add virtual machines. Here are some key rules:

It's all or none.   All VMs in a cloud service must be part of the same virtual network. If a cloud service has an existing VM that is not part of a virtual network, then no VMs in that cloud service can join a virtual network. Likewise, if a cloud service has a VM that is part of a virtual network, then all VMs created in that cloud service must join that same virtual network.

First wins.   The first VM created in a cloud service sets the virtual network affiliation for the entire cloud service.

Regions matter... VMs can only be part of virtual networks in the same region as the cloud service. If a cloud service is in the East US region, the virtual network must be in the East US region.

...but resource groups don't. Resource groups do not affect virtual network affiliation. A VM can be in a different resource group from the virtual network.

Plan well. You cannot (easily) move VMs between virtual networks postcreation. Carefully plan virtual networks and VM architecture before deployment.

Subnets VMs are added to virtual subnets, which are part of a virtual network.

A VM can be added using the Azure portal or using PowerShell. To add to a virtual network using the Azure portal, follow these steps:

1. Create a new VM in a new cloud service using the normal process in the new Azure portal. (Chapter 2 showed you how to use the Azure portal to create a new VM in a new cloud service.)

2. Ensure that the location for the new VM matches the region for the virtual network you wish to join.

3. Select Optional Configuration and then select Network.

4. Select Virtual Network and select the virtual network to join, as shown in Figure 5.7. The virtual subnets will now be available for you to select. Choose the required subnet.
   The cloud service is represented as a domain name, which you can change using the Network blade.

FIGURE 5.7
Selecting a virtual network for a new VM

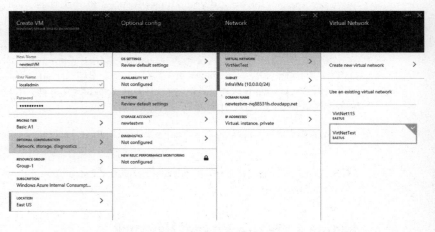

5. Click OK on the blade to save changes and proceed with other configurations.

6. Once you've completed the configurations, click Create.

To join a VM to a virtual network using PowerShell, the VM provisioning configuration option must be used. You cannot use the quick create method. There are two parts of the configuration:

- Specifying the virtual subnet as part of the VM configuration (`Set-AzureSubnet 'App-Net'`)

- Specifying the virtual network as part of the VM creation into a cloud service (`-VNetName 'VirtNet115'`)

Here's a basic example:

```
New-AzureVMConfig -Name "TestVM55" -InstanceSize 'Basic_A2' `
    -ImageName $2012R2imgs[0].ImageName |
    Add-AzureProvisioningConfig -Windows -AdminUsername localadmin `
      -Password Pa55word!123 |
    Set-AzureSubnet 'App-Net' |
    New-AzureVM -ServiceName "SavillTech103" -Location 'East US' `
      -VNetName 'VirtNet115'
```

Note that you can continue to use other features in conjunction with joining a virtual network. For example, you can specify a reserved VIP for the cloud service. To specify a reserved IP for the VIP, add the `-ReservedIPName '<VIP Name>'` to the `New-AzureVM` part of the example.

VMs can be moved between virtual subnets that are part of the same virtual network using PowerShell. Here's an example:

```
Get-AzureVM -ServiceName $Service –Name $VMName |
    Set-AzureSubnet –SubnetNames Subnet-2 | Update-AzureVM
```

MOVING A VM BETWEEN VIRTUAL NETWORKS OR INTO A VIRTUAL NETWORK

Once a VM is created, there is no way to move it between cloud services or into, out of, or between virtual networks. The only solution is to delete the virtual machine and recreate it. This is not as bad as it seems. What is a virtual machine? A virtual machine is primarily virtual hard disks (VHDs) that contain the OS, data, and most of its state. The rest of the VM in Azure—the VM size, location, cloud service membership, and so forth—is likely the part you want to change. Therefore, a good way to "move" a VM is to delete the VM but retain its VHDs. Then, create a new VM in the target cloud service/virtual network and attach it to the VHD files of the old VM. This essentially moves the VM. It's similar in concept to taking the hard drive out of one computer and putting it in a new computer.

To find the VHDs attached to VMs, use the following PowerShell code, and make note of the disk names:

```
Get-AzureDisk | Where-Object {$_.AttachedTo -ne $null } |
    Format-Table -auto "DiskName","DiskSizeInGB","AttachedTo"
```

To delete the VM, use the following PowerShell code. This code will not delete the associated VHDs.

```
Remove-AzureVM -ServiceName $Service -Name $VMName
```

The next code shows how to use existing VHDs in the new VM. (Remember, you will need to add the virtual network and other configurations.)

```
New-AzureVMConfig -Name $VMName -InstanceSize 'Basic_A2' `
    -DiskName 'OSDiskName' |
    Add-AzureDataDisk -Import 'DataDisk0' -LUN 0|
    New-AzureVM -ServiceName "SavillTech103" -Location 'East US'
```

Reserved IP for VM

VMs inside a virtual network receive their IP address from the Azure fabric, the same way VMs get their IP addresses outside of a virtual network. The difference is that inside a virtual network, and specifically on a virtual subnet, the IP addresses are assigned from the IP ranges configured as part of the virtual subnets. Remember that each IP address lease is an infinite lease. Apart from service healing operations, an IP address will never change as long as the VM is provisioned in Azure.

Whether on-premises or in Azure, you should avoid reliance on the IP address of a VM wherever possible. Ideally, you will leverage DNS to communicate with OS instances. Then, if the IP address does change, the DNS record would automatically update via dynamic DNS, and clients can continue communication even after an IP change. However, there are circumstances where you need to ensure that the IP address of a VM never changes, even if it is deprovisioned or healed. In some instances, you need to use the IP address for a specific VM. For example, for DNS services in Azure, the IP addresses for domain controllers are specified directly in the virtual network configuration.

You can reserve specific IP addresses through the Azure portal during the VM creation, as shown in Figure 5.8. After a VM is created, you can use the IP addresses part of the Configure lens, as shown in Figure 5.9, to configure a static IP address. You can only configure an IP address that is available in the virtual subnet and that is within the range of the virtual subnet. If you try to configure other addresses, you will receive an error, like the example shown in Figure 5.10.

FIGURE 5.8
Setting a reserved IP during VM creation

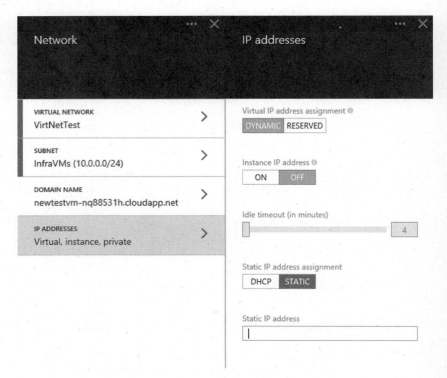

FIGURE 5.9
Setting a reserved IP
for an existing VM

FIGURE 5.10
Error trying to set
an IP outside of the
virtual subnet range

To configure a static IP address using PowerShell, you must first check whether the desired IP address is available. If it's not available, the ones that are appear. An example output is shown here:

```
PS C:\> Test-AzureStaticVNetIP -VNetName VirtNet115 -IPAddress 10.7.115.13

IsAvailable          : False
AvailableAddresses   : {10.7.115.12, 10.7.115.14}
OperationDescription : Test-AzureStaticVNetIP
OperationId          : d889a14c-850d-396d-9fcb-236b8480b8c4
OperationStatus      : Succeeded


PS C:\> Test-AzureStaticVNetIP -VNetName VirtNet115 -IPAddress 10.7.115.14

IsAvailable          : True
AvailableAddresses   : {}
OperationDescription : Test-AzureStaticVNetIP
OperationId          : 6f454243-b47c-319c-ae58-4463e60b8b82
OperationStatus      : Succeeded
```

To apply an IP address, you use an object representing the target VM and then the IP address applied to that object:

```
$staticVM = Get-AzureVM -ServiceName savilltecheastuscs -Name savazudc01

Set-AzureStaticVNetIP -VM $staticVM -IPAddress 10.7.115.13 | Update-AzureVM
```

To check the static IP address configuration, use the following code:

```
Get-AzureStaticVNetIP -VM $staticVM
```

Note that at no time was the networking configuration inside the VM modified. The VM is always configured to use DHCP and never a static IP address within the OS. The IP reservation is through the Azure network fabric, which ensures that the VM always gets the same IP address.

To remove a static IP address from a VM, use the following code:

```
Remove-AzureStaticVNetIP -VM $staticVM
```

Configuring DNS

VMs in Azure always get their IP configuration via DHCP. For VMs outside of a virtual network, the DNS configuration always points to Azure DNS, which provides name resolution for VMs within the cloud service but not between cloud services. For VMs in a virtual network, you can still use Azure DNS, which will provide name resolution via the fully qualified domain name (FQDN) across cloud services, provided they are part of the same virtual network.

In most environments, leveraging virtual networks using a custom DNS server configuration is desirable. For example, you can use domain controllers in your organization to offer consistent name resolution across different services and different locations. You can set the DNS servers through the virtual network configuration in the browser and by exporting the XML configuration file of a virtual network and modifying the DNS configuration.

DNS servers are global to the Azure subscription. To add a new DNS configuration to an Azure subscription, use the New-AzureDns cmdlet. For example, to add a new DNS server, savazudns01, with an IP address 10.0.0.10, you'd use:

```
New-AzureDNS -Name "savazudns01" –IPAddress "10.0.0.10"
```

Ensure that whatever DNS server you use supports dynamic DNS. This enables OS instances to register their own hostname to IP address records. Microsoft has a nice article that talks about DNS options in Azure here:

```
http://msdn.microsoft.com/en-us/library/azure/jj156088.aspx
```

I recommend checking this out if you wish to further investigate the DNS options and capabilities.

Using Multiple Network Adapters

Normally, an Azure VM has a single virtual network adapter, which has a single IP assigned by the Azure fabric. At TechEd Europe 2014, Microsoft announced supports for VMs (Windows or Linux) with more than one virtual NIC, provided the VM is part of a virtual network. Each virtual NIC should be placed in a separate virtual subnet (although it can be placed in the same virtual subnet) and must be part of the same virtual network. The goal of this functionality is to enable certain types of network virtual appliances, such as Citrix NetScaler and Riverbed Steelhead WAN optimizers, to run in Azure.

Figure 5.11 shows an example configuration for a VM with multiple network adapters. Each NIC connects to a different virtual subnet, and the default NIC also receives traffic via endpoints defined on the cloud service VIP.

FIGURE 5.11

Example of a VM using multiple NICs

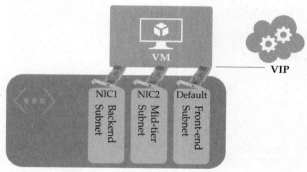

Azure Virtual Network

The additional NICs must be configured at the time of the VM creation and must be done via PowerShell. Additional network interfaces are added via the `Add-AzureNetworkInterfaceConfig` cmdlet—for example:

```
Add-AzureNetworkInterfaceConfig -Name "Ethernet1" -SubnetName "Midtier" `
    -StaticVNetIPAddress "10.1.1.111" -VM $vm
```

Don't forget that you also need to set the network configuration for the default NIC added as part of a standard VM. Building on my earlier example of creating a VM, in this example I add two more virtual NICs, each connected to a different virtual subnet:

```
New-AzureVMConfig -Name "3NICVMTST" -InstanceSize 'ExtraLarge' `
    -ImageName $2012R2imgs[0].ImageName |
    Add-AzureProvisioningConfig -Windows -AdminUsername localadmin `
        -Password Pa55word!123 | Set-AzureSubnet 'Frontend' |
        Set-AzureStaticVNetIP -IPAddress "10.0.0.10" |
        Add-AzureNetworkInterfaceConfig -Name "Ethernet1" -SubnetName "Midtier" `
        -StaticVNetIPAddress "10.1.1.10" |
        Add-AzureNetworkInterfaceConfig -Name "Ethernet2" -SubnetName "Backend" `
        -StaticVNetIPAddress "10.1.2.10" |
    New-AzureVM -ServiceName "SavillTech103" -Location 'East US' `
        -VNetName 'MultiNet'
```

Notice that the default network adapter is added to the front-end virtual subnet with a static IP address; then additional network adapters are added, each with its own static IP address in the mid-tier and backend subnets. Also notice I used an extra-large VM size. The reason is that multiple NICs are only supported on certain size virtual machines. As of this writing, the VMs that support more than one NIC are shown in Table 5.1, but you'll find the current numbers here:

```
http://msdn.microsoft.com/en-us/library/azure/dn848315.aspx
```

TABLE 5.1:   Azure VM NIC limits

VM SIZE	NUMBER OF NICS
Large (A3) and A6	2
Extra Large (A4) and A7	4
A9	2
D3	2
D4	4
D13	4
All other sizes	1

http://msdn.microsoft.com/en-us/library/azure/dn848315.aspx

Note that the VM cannot forward traffic between the NICs; it cannot act as a Layer 3 (IP) gateway. Instead, the intention is that the appliance using the multiple NICs receives traffic on a NIC, terminates the connection, and then makes a new connection to the next system via a different NIC. This is common in many types of network appliances.

Network Security Groups

A virtual network can be thought of as a trust boundary. Each virtual network is completely isolated from other virtual networks unless you choose to connect them. (I will discuss connecting virtual networks in Chapter 6, "Enabling On-Premises Connectivity.") Within the virtual network, each virtual subnet is automatically connected to every other virtual subnet through an Azure-provided gateway functionality. In Chapter 3, "Customizing VM Storage," I talked about endpoint ACLs. Network security groups (NSGs) replace endpoint ACLs, and the two technologies are mutually exclusive.

In some scenarios, virtual subnets should be isolated from one another. Consider your datacenter. You likely have a separate network that connects to the Internet, your DMZ. There will be another network for your datacenter, another network for high-impact servers, and so on. Between these different networks are firewalls, which primarily are tasked with ensuring that only specific traffic for specific hosts is allowed to traverse the network boundaries. This same functionality can be enabled between virtual subnets in an Azure virtual network using NSGs. NSGs provide segmentations within a virtual network by defining rules between virtual subnets and even for specific VMs. They can also be used to control Internet-bound traffic based on the virtual subnet. These groups can control connectivity to on-premises networks, such as through site-to-site VPNs.

Figure 5.12 shows an example use case with three virtual subnets: a front-end that receives traffic from the Internet, a mid-tier subnet that receives communication from the front-end and the backend networks, and then the backend network. Note that the mid-tier and backend networks cannot communicate directly to the Internet, nor can the front-end and backend networks directly communicate.

FIGURE 5.12
Traffic control can be achieved using network security groups (NSGs).

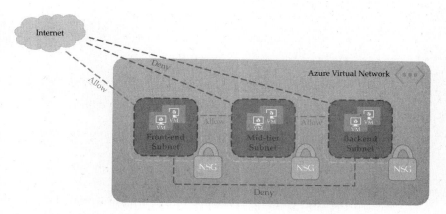

NETWORK SECURITY GROUP RULES

There are two primary steps to using NSGs. First create one or more rules, and then apply the rules to a virtual subnet or VM. Note that rules can be applied to both a VM and the virtual subnet that the VM resides in. The rules assigned to the virtual subnet are applied first; then the rules are applied to the VM. This configuration effectively gives the VM two layers of protection.

NSG rules use 5 tuple:

- ◆ Source IP
- ◆ Source port
- ◆ Destination IP
- ◆ Destination port
- ◆ Protocol

The source and destination IPs can be presented as ranges in CIDR format. Protocols are specified as TCP or UDP, or by using the wildcard character (*). Additionally, the following attributes are used:

- ◆ Name (identifier for the rule)
- ◆ Type (inbound/outbound)
- ◆ Access action (Allow/Deny)
- ◆ Priority between 100 and 4096

The priority attribute allows multiple rules to be applied, and in the event of a conflict, the rule with the highest priority (lowest number) wins.

A number of default rules are defined and accomplish the following:

◆ Allow full inbound/outbound communication between NSGs within the virtual network address space

◆ Allow inbound communication from the Azure Load Balancer

◆ Allow outbound traffic to the Internet

◆ All other inbound and outbound traffic is denied

The explicit rules are documented here:

```
http://msdn.microsoft.com/en-us/library/azure/dn848316.aspx
```

These rules have very low priorities (65000 and lower), which means you can override the defaults with your own rules.

When you create rules, you can use three special system-provided identifiers for certain special types of traffic:

VIRTUAL_NETWORK   Identifies traffic within the virtual network address space and for connected networks, such as another virtual network or on-premises network

AZURE_LOADBALANCER   Identifies traffic from the Azure infrastructure load balancer

INTERNET   Identifies traffic from an IP address space external to the virtual network that is reachable from the Internet

CREATING NETWORK SECURITY GROUP RULES

You create NSG rules by using PowerShell—specifically the `Set-AzureNetworkSecurityRule` cmdlet, which creates rules applied to an NSG that you created using the `New-AzureNetworkSecurityGroup` cmdlet.

The first step is to create a new NSG. NSGs are region specific and can be used only within the region specified at creation. The following code creates a new NSG in the East US region:

```
New-AzureNetworkSecurityGroup -Name "NSGFrontEnd" -Location "East US" `
    -Label "NSG for FrontEnd in East US"
```

The next step is to apply a rule to the newly created NSG. The following script creates a rule that allows all traffic from the Internet:

```
Get-AzureNetworkSecurityGroup -Name "NSGFrontEnd" |
    Set-AzureNetworkSecurityRule -Name WEB -Type Inbound -Priority 100 `
    -Action Allow -SourceAddressPrefix 'INTERNET'  -SourcePortRange '*' `
    -DestinationAddressPrefix '*' -DestinationPortRange '*' -Protocol TCP
```

Next is a rule that enables inbound SQL communication:

```
Get-AzureNetworkSecurityGroup -Name "NSGFrontEnd" |
    Set-AzureNetworkSecurityRule -Name SQL -Type Inbound -Priority 110 `
```

```
-Action Allow -SourceAddressPrefix '10.0.1.0/24'  -SourcePortRange '*' `
-DestinationAddressPrefix '10.0.2.0/24' `
-DestinationPortRange '1433' -Protocol TCP
```

Notice I added the rule to my front-end NSG, which is likely not where I would want to apply it. Most likely, the rule would be applied to a backend network.

To remove a rule from an NSG, use a script similar to this:

```
Get-AzureNetworkSecurityGroup -Name "NSGFrontEnd" |
    Remove-AzureNetworkSecurityRule -Name SQL
```

To view the rules applied to an NSG, you'd use PowerShell. Notice in the example in Figure 5.13 that the default rules that are present for all NSGs are shown and cannot be removed.

FIGURE 5.13
Viewing rules defined
in an NSG

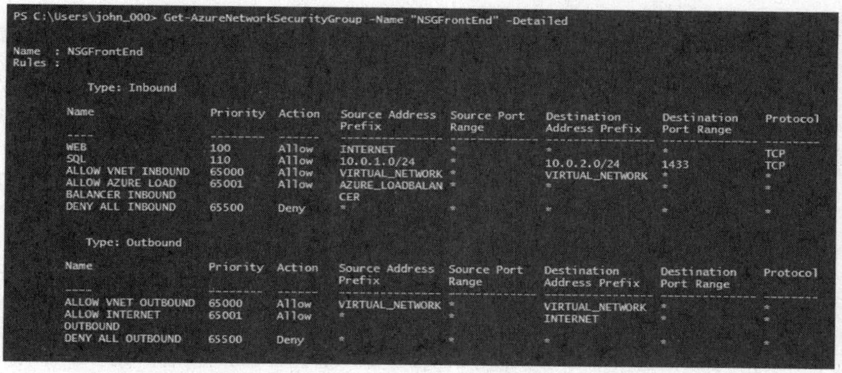

APPLYING NETWORK SECURITY GROUPS

To apply an NSG to a VM, use the following:

```
Get-AzureVM -ServiceName $service -Name $VM |
    Set-AzureNetworkSecurityGroupConfig -NetworkSecurityGroupName "NSGFrontEnd"
```

To remove an NSG assignment from a VM, use this:

```
Get-AzureVM -ServiceName $service -Name $VM |
    Remove-AzureNetworkSecurityGroupConfig `
    -NetworkSecurityGroupName "NSGFrontEnd"
```

To apply an NSG to a virtual subnet, use the following:

```
Get-AzureNetworkSecurityGroup -Name "NSGFrontEnd" |
    Set-AzureNetworkSecurityGroupToSubnet -VirtualNetworkName 'VNetTest' `
    -SubnetName 'FrontEndSubnet'
```

To remove a Network Security Group from a virtual subnet use:

```
Get-AzureNetworkSecurityGroup -Name "NSGFrontEnd" |
    Remove-AzureNetworkSecurityGroupFromSubnet -VirtualNetworkName 'VNetTest' `
    -SubnetName 'FrontEndSubnet'
```

Note that if you are already using ACLs on endpoints, they will need to be removed before using NSGs. NSGs and endpoint ACLs are mutually exclusive. Remember also that once you apply an NSG, no traffic will be allowed unless a rule allows it. For example, if you wish to use Remote Desktop Protocol (RDP) on a VM from the Internet and that VM has an NSG applied to it either explicitly or via the virtual subnet, you will need an Allow rule for RDP traffic from the Internet. The script that follows creates and applies such a rule specifically for destination port 3389:

```
Get-AzureNetworkSecurityGroup -Name "NSGFrontEnd" |
    Set-AzureNetworkSecurityRule -Name RDPIN -Type Inbound -Priority 101 `
    -Action Allow -SourceAddressPrefix 'INTERNET'  -SourcePortRange '*' `
    -DestinationAddressPrefix '*' -DestinationPortRange '3389' -Protocol '*'
```

If you apply an NSG to VMs or subnets, make sure you remove it from the VM or subnet before you delete that VM or subnet. If you fail to do so, the NSG can end up in a "limbo" state, and that can be hard to fix. (By the time you read this, I expect a fix to be in place. Fingers crossed!)

The Bottom Line

Articulate virtual network and virtual subnet basic concepts. A virtual network is an administrator-defined IP space that is divided into virtual subnets. Virtual machines are joined to virtual networks at time of creation, and their IP addresses will be allocated from the virtual subnet specified in the provisioning configuration. All VMs in a cloud service must be part of the same virtual network.

Master It Why must the IP space used in the virtual network not conflict with the space used on-premises?

Use multi-NIC VMs. Azure enables certain VMs to be configured with multiple virtual network adapters. Each network adapter must be connected to a different virtual subnet within the same virtual network. Additional network adapters can be configured only during the creation of a virtual machine.

Master It What VMs can use multiple NICs?

Chapter 6

Enabling On-Premises Connectivity

Right now, your on-premises locations have resources, and after working through Chapter 5, "Using Virtual Networks," you have defined virtual networks in Azure that also have resources deployed. In Chapter 4, "Enabling External Connectivity," I discussed endpoints as a way to connect to services running in virtual machines via the cloud service VIP. If you require a lot of connectivity between on-premises resources and the virtual machines in Azure, using the endpoints is not practical. To compound the problem, data is sent over the Internet, and depending on the type of traffic, that data may not be encrypted.

A site-to-site (S2S) VPN connection between on-premises and Azure provides a better solution. Using S2S avoids the endpoints completely and allows direct communication between the systems.

In this chapter, you will learn to

◆ Explain the connectivity enabled with a site-to-site VPN

◆ Understand the key benefits of Azure ExpressRoute over standard site-to-site VPNs

Using S2S Virtual Private Networks

Figure 6.1 represents the current state of the technologies I have covered so far:

◆ The VMs are running in cloud services.

◆ The VMs are part of virtual networks that you define.

◆ The VMs can be accessed over the Internet through endpoints configured on the cloud service VIP.

◆ The VMs also can be accessed through a dedicated public instance IP.

Although accessing cloud services via endpoints works when only limited access is required—such as accessing web services via port 80—trying to use endpoints for all communication that is common between end services is not practical or even possible. There is a limit to the number of endpoints that can be configured per VM (25) and per cloud service (150).

S2S VPN Basics

Although the number of endpoints is limited on the Azure side and restricts the possible on-premises–to–Azure communications, Azure-based services have no ability to communicate with on-premises resources unless those resources are accessible to the Internet, which is highly unlikely. Depending on the type of communication, Internet traffic may be encrypted, but for

FIGURE 6.1
Communication from
on-premises to Azure-
based services via
endpoints

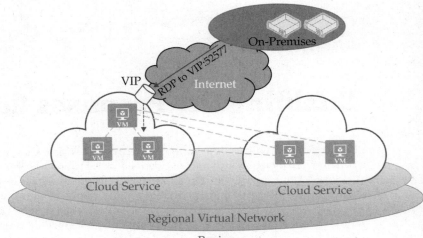

many types of traffic, it is not encrypted. If services in Azure are being used exclusively by
on-premises resources, the idea of publishing those services in Azure to the Internet so they can
be accessed is highly illogical, and they would be blocked by most security teams.

The most basic and most accessible solution for securely linking Azure virtual networks
to on-premises resources is the S2S VPN. Note that the emphasis here is on linking Azure
virtual networks to on-premises rather than linking VMs to on-premises. All mechanisms for
connecting Azure to on-premises rely on the VMs being part of a virtual network. There are
no options for connecting on-premises resources to VMs that are not part of a virtual network
other than through the cloud service VIP or an instance-level public IP. One easy way to think
about this is that the virtual network in Azure acts as a branch office to the main network
on-premises.

The S2S VPN uses IPsec to provide an encrypted connection between Azure and your
on-premises network. Two types of gateway are supported by Azure: static and dynamic.

Static Routing Gateways   A static routing VPN, also known as a policy-based VPN, routes
traffic based on a customer-defined policy. Typically, traffic is allowed based on an access
list of entries that are manually added to a routing table. (That quickly becomes impractical
in a large network.) A static routing VPN must connect to a static routing gateway. Internet
Key Exchange version 1 (IKEv1) is used for the initial security association configuration.
Static routing is the most simple to configure, but there are numerous limitations. Static
gateways do not support coexistence with point-to-site VPN, cannot be used to link to virtual
networks, and permit only a single VPN connection to on-premises.

Dynamic Routing Gateways   A dynamic routing VPN, also known as a route-based VPN,
uses a tunnel interface for forwarding packets. Protocols are used to locate networks and
automatically update routing tables, which makes it more suitable for larger networks.
Although Border Gateway Protocol (BGP) is not supported, it is on the Azure road map and
may be available by the time you read this. (BGP enables tighter integration with on-premises

networking infrastructure.) A dynamic routing VPN requires a dynamic routing gateway device, such as a Windows Server 2012 Routing and Remote Access Server, and employs IKEv2. Dynamic routing enables additional capabilities, such as linking separate virtual networks and connecting to multiple on-premises locations, and it can coexist with point-to-site VPN.

You can read a great MSDN article on VPN device types and the key differences between them here:

`http://msdn.microsoft.com/en-us/library/azure/jj156075.aspx`

The article includes details on the various types of on-premises gateways that are supported for connecting via the Azure S2S gateway. Basically, all of the major VPN devices are supported, and in many cases, Azure helps you configure your local device. (I will cover this in more detail later in this chapter.)

A number of different encryption algorithms are available for use with traffic sent via IPsec, specifically AES256, AES128, and 3DES. The particular algorithms supported depend on whether the gateway is static or dynamic. This is detailed here:

`http://msdn.microsoft.com/en-us/library/azure/jj156075.aspx#bkmk_IPsecParameters`

The key point is that all are supported on both static and dynamic gateways with the exception of AES128, which is not supported for dynamic VPN. The encryption algorithm used not only impacts the security of the data sent over the Internet, but also affects the speed possible from on-premises to Azure: the higher the encryption, the more computation required, which reduces the available bandwidth. This will make more sense when I walk you through some of the Azure gateway internals later in this chapter. The algorithm used is negotiated upon gateway connection: AES256 first, then AES128 (if supported), and finally 3DES.

Once an S2S gateway has been established, your environment will look like the one shown in Figure 6.2. Full Layer 3 communication is enabled between on-premises and the connected Azure virtual network for supported traffic: IPv4, TCP, UDP, and ICMP.

FIGURE 6.2
Communication from on-premises to Azure-based services with S2S gateway

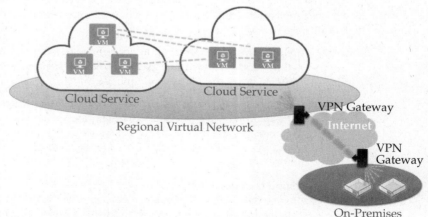

Creating an S2S Gateway

Once your virtual networks are created in Azure, it's easy to enable the S2S VPN and bring cross-premises connectivity. If you followed the steps in the previous chapter to create a virtual network, you did not enable S2S virtual private networking. So the first step in creating your gateway is to enable an S2S VPN and the configuration required to use it. Two actions are involved:

◆ Define the IP ranges used on-premises and your local VPN gateway Internet-accessible IP address.

◆ Enable the option to use S2S connectivity.

Because the virtual network will be configured, use the legacy Azure portal at https://manage.windowsazure.com. The steps that follow walk you through defining a local network (which represents your on-premises address space) and then enabling the S2S connectivity for the virtual network. Remember, it is important to properly define your local network to ensure that Azure routes traffic to your locations rather than out to the Internet.

1. Log on to the Azure portal.

2. Navigate to the Networks node.

3. Select the Local Networks tab.

NOTE   If you had configured S2S connectivity during the initial virtual network creation, you would have been prompted for your local network IP definition as part of the wizard. Because the S2S is being added postcreation, it is necessary to manually create a local network that represents the IP space of your on-premises environment in addition to specifying the IP address of your on-premises VPN gateway.

4. Click the New icon and select Virtual Network ➤ Add Local Network.

5. Enter a name for the new local network, such as **CorpOnPrm**, and the VPN IP address of your gateway device; then click the Next arrow. If you don't know the IP address of your gateway device, you can leave it blank and add it later.

6. The next screen allows the address space for your on-premises to be defined. This should encompass all of the IP space that will be communicated from Azure to your on-premises resources.

◆ If you have six datacenters and your gateway will route traffic to the other datacenters, the address space must cover all six datacenters so Azure knows to route traffic to those IP addresses via the S2S VPN.

◆ If you are going to add additional VPN connections, such as one VPN connection for each datacenter, you should define separate local networks for each datacenter, with each network having the IP address space defined only for that datacenter. This will allow Azure to know which VPN connection should be used for each part of the IP address space.

The distinction is shown in Figure 6.3 and Figure 6.4. In Figure 6.3, I show one S2S VPN connection to one datacenter. That datacenter then routes traffic to the other datacenters. A single local site definition encompasses the address space of all sites.

FIGURE 6.3
Local network definition when a single S2S VPN connection is used

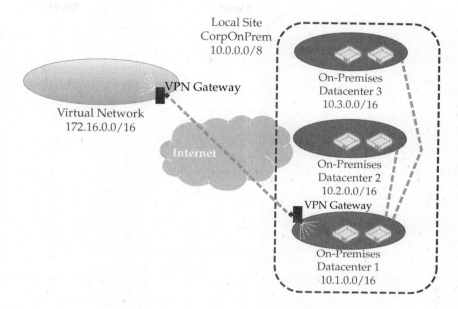

FIGURE 6.4
Local network definitions when multiple S2S VPN connections are used

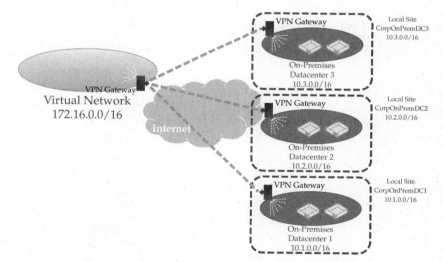

In Figure 6.4, I show an S2S VPN connection for each datacenter. The local site definition for each site encompasses the IP space of just that datacenter and any other IP spaces that would be routed from that connection. Multiple S2S VPNs are covered later in this chapter. For now, just know that you can connect a virtual network to multiple on-premises locations, something that was not possible until 2014.

Set your IP address space as shown in Figure 6.5, and click the check mark icon to complete creation.

FIGURE 6.5
Configuring the IP
address space for a
local site

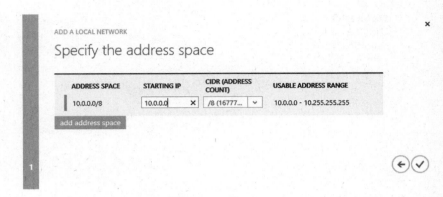

The new local network will be shown in the list of local networks. It can be selected and then modified using the Edit action, which would be required if you did not populate the gateway IP address during initial creation of the local network but now wish to configure ahead of the actual S2S VPN creation.

The next phase in enabling S2S connectivity for the virtual network is simple:

1. Navigate to the Networks node and, on the Virtual Networks tab, select the virtual network you previously created.

2. Select the Configure tab.

3. In the S2S connectivity section, check the connect to the local network box, as shown in Figure 6.6.

FIGURE 6.6
Enabling S2S
connectivity and
selecting the local
network that will be
connected to via the
VPN connection

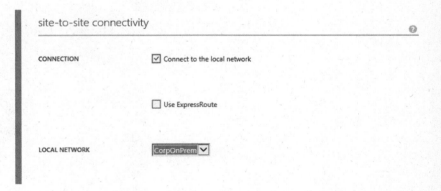

When the additional select fields become available, ignore the Use ExpressRoute option (for now), and from the Local Network drop-down list, select the local network definition you created earlier. This is the local network that will be connected via the VPN connection.

If the local network you select conflicts with the IP address space of the virtual network, your selection will be flagged by a red exclamation warning sign, as shown in Figure 6.7.

FIGURE 6.7
Address spaces
overlap

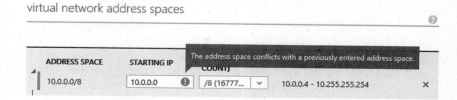

This warning occurs when an overlap between the Azure virtual network address space and the local network address space that would cause routing issues is detected. You will need to resolve the issue before proceeding by changing one of the network definitions.

4. Click Save to complete the change.

So far, you have prepared the environment for the gateway, but it does not actually exist yet, as shown in the virtual network dashboard shown in Figure 6.8.

FIGURE 6.8
The connectivity
is defined, but the
gateway resource is
not created.

The final step is the actual creation of the gateway, which is achieved by clicking the Create Gateway button on the dashboard and selecting either Dynamic Routing or Static Routing, as shown in Figure 6.9. Whether you choose Dynamic Routing or Static Routing depends on the gateway on your premises and the levels of functionality required. Remember that, whenever possible, dynamic routing is preferred. If you are using Windows Server 2012 RRAS as the local gateway device, you select the Dynamic Routing option. No other configuration is required; you have already preconfigured everything. Specific encryption configurations are made on the local gateway side and are negotiated with Azure upon connection.

FIGURE 6.9
Creating the gateway

The gateway can also be created using PowerShell:

```
New-AzureVNetGateway -VNetName <virtual network name> `
    -GatewayType <type static/dynamic>
```

Azure gateway creation takes around 5 minutes, as the Azure-side resources must be provisioned. The status of the gateway creation and its configuration can be checked by using this PowerShell command:

```
Get-AzureVNetGateway -VNetName <virtual network name>
```

Once the configuration is complete, click the Download VPN Device Script link. The link provides a list of supported VPN devices (such as those from Cisco and Juniper as well as Microsoft's own RRAS). For these listed devices, Azure will generate a complete configuration script that can be used to complete the configuration of your local network infrastructure gateway. The configuration file will automatically be populated with the Azure-site gateway IP address and the master key that secures the initial connection. Both of those pieces of information are also available via the virtual network dashboard page. The IP address is shown under the virtual network connectivity picture as the gateway IP address. When you click the Manage Key icon, the key can be copied for use.

Once your side of the VPN gateway is configured, click the Connect action on the virtual network dashboard. This will trigger a connection and open cross-premises connectivity. To trigger the connection from PowerShell, use the following:

```
Set-AzureVNetGateway -Connect -LocalNetworkSiteName <your site name> `
    -VNetName <azure virtual network name>
```

You can also trigger the connection from your on-premises side. If you are using RRAS, you can use this command:

```
Connect-VpnS2SInterface -Name <Azure Gateway IP address>
```

Figure 6.10 shows a completed connection.

FIGURE 6.10
A completed gateway connection

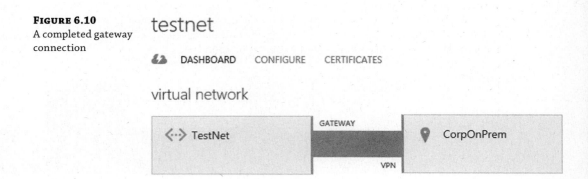

If you are using Windows Server 2012 RRAS, the downloaded configuration file is actually a PowerShell script, which you can view to see the configuration being performed. It boils down to adding a new S2S interface using IKEv2. Once connected, the state of the VPN connection can be checked locally via PowerShell by using the `Get-VpnS2sInterface` cmdlet.

TIP The Azure web interface can be a couple of minutes behind the actual connected state. Even if the virtual dashboard doesn't show the connection, it doesn't mean the connection hasn't completed. Often, it's easier to check the connection status by looking at your local gateway.

I walk through the entire process in a video you'll find here:

`http://youtu.be/O8wUnt4mDUc`

I recommend watching the video if you are setting up for the first time. I cover the virtual network creation, the gateway configuration, and the on-premises side configuration for using Windows Server 2012 RRAS.

At this point, Azure is an extension of your datacenter. IP traffic can be routed between Azure and your on-premises over an encrypted IPsec connection. You are now hybrid!

TROUBLESHOOTING THE AZURE GATEWAY

If you experience problems with the Azure gateway, there are limits to what you can do since you have no direct access to the Azure-side gateway resources. Use PowerShell to start diagnostics. The results are sent to a storage account, which can then be viewed to aid troubleshooting.

Begin by connecting to an Azure storage context. (I covered this in Chapter 3, "Customizing VM Storage.") Then start the diagnostics for a defined period of time in seconds (I used 5 minutes in the example that follows) and specify a container within the storage account. While the diagnostics are running, the state of monitoring can be checked. The code lines that follow show how to trigger the diagnostics and check the status.

```
PS C:\> $context = new-azurestoragecontext -storageaccountname 'mystorage' `
    -storageaccountkey 'mystoragekey'

PS C:\> Start-AzureVNetGatewayDiagnostics -CaptureDurationInSeconds 300 `
    -StorageContext $context -VNetName VirtNet115 -ContainerName logs

Error         :
HttpStatusCode : OK
Id            : 7d22ecc5-2b2d-4dac-b6a9-5bbcacb46365
Status        : Successful
StatusCode    : OK
RequestId     : 36c5a2b91c1f32fba78119d986096078

PS C:\> Get-AzureVNetGatewayDiagnostics -VNetName VirtNet115

DiagnosticsUrl    :
State             : InProgress
```

```
OperationDescription : Get-AzureVNetGatewayDiagnostics
OperationId          : 4e94513b-653b-33d9-a9b6-e3ce00acbe7f
OperationStatus      : Succeeded
```

Once the diagnostic time expires, run the Get-AzureVNetGatewayDiagnostics cmdlet again. The return will show that the diagnostics are ready and provide the URL for accessing the diagnostic data text file. As an alternative, you can download the txt file directly from your storage account by navigating to the container you specified when you started the diagnostics.

```
PS C:\> Get-AzureVNetGatewayDiagnostics -VNetName VirtNet115

DiagnosticsUrl       :
     https://storageaccount.blob.core.windows.net/logs/VNetGatewayDiagCapture_
UTC_12_7_2014_8
_21_49_PM_300.txt?sv=2014-02-4&sr=c&si=GatewayReadOnly&sig=sgbVDEZ1nPGO%2Fiavw
kwhqgxXKTudwfdTL6h2hgVCNCU%3D
State                : Ready
OperationDescription : Get-AzureVNetGatewayDiagnostics
OperationId          : b87171f1-fd76-3884-81b6-57f0d10c8f6d
OperationStatus      : Succeeded
```

A huge amount of data is generated, and the file is useful to Microsoft support. They can help you ascertain the cause of problems. Still, it is useful to know how to run the diagnostics.

Very basic logs about the gateway can be viewed via the Management Services tab in the Azure portal. Select the Operation Logs tab, set the type of the logs to Networks, and then select the specific virtual network in the Service Name drop-down list. As of this writing, logs related to the following activities are available:

Gateway creation and deletion

ExpressRoute circuit creation and deletion

ExpressRoute circuit link authorization, creation, and deletion

ExpressRoute BGP session creation, deletion, and update

The list is expected to expand over time.

Azure Gateway Internals and Maximum Speed

It is useful to understand what is happening behind the scenes when the Azure gateway is created and why you will experience varied speeds for communications between on-premises and Azure via the S2S VPN gateway.

As of this writing, the Azure side of the gateway is provided by two, single-vCPU virtual machines that are paired in an active/passive configuration. One of the VMs acts as the gateway endpoint; the other takes over in the event the active experiences a problem or requires an update. This keeps the Azure side of the gateway highly available and enables the 99.9 percent Azure S2S VPN SLA. This is also why it takes 5 to 6 minutes to create the gateway: the two VMs have to be provisioned on the Azure fabric.

Each VM has its own IP, which is allocated from a virtual subnet that was automatically created when S2S connectivity was enabled. A small subnet is created (three usable IP addresses) from the next available IP range in the virtual network. In Figure 6.11 you can see that a 10.0.2.0 subnet was automatically created for exclusive use by the S2S gateway. Notice that it uses a /29 mask, which leaves only three usable IP addresses, but this is all the gateway needs.

FIGURE 6.11
Example gateway subnet automatically created by Azure

virtual network address spaces

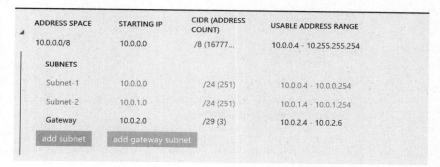

ADDRESS SPACE	STARTING IP	CIDR (ADDRESS COUNT)	USABLE ADDRESS RANGE
10.0.0.0/8	10.0.0.0	/8 (16777...	10.0.0.4 - 10.255.255.254
SUBNETS			
Subnet-1	10.0.0.0	/24 (251)	10.0.0.4 - 10.0.0.254
Subnet-2	10.0.1.0	/24 (251)	10.0.1.4 - 10.0.1.254
Gateway	10.0.2.0	/29 (3)	10.0.2.4 - 10.0.2.6

add subnet   add gateway subnet

You can view the Microsoft S2S VPN gateway FAQ here:

http://msdn.microsoft.com/en-us/library/azure/dn133803.aspx#BKMK_VNETFAQConnectivity

You'll learn why the subnet needs two IP addresses (for the two VMs). The FAQ also stresses that you should never use this subnet for your own VMs, a very important point. Below is an important part of the Azure FAQ:

"What is the 'gateway subnet' and why is it needed?

"We have a gateway service that we run to enable cross-premises connectivity. We need 2 IP addresses from your routing domain for us to enable routing between your premises and the cloud. We require you to specify at least a /29 subnet from which we can pick IP addresses for setting up routes.

"Please note that you must not deploy virtual machines or role instances in the gateway subnet."

MANAGING THE SUBNET USED BY THE GATEWAY

The gateway subnet created by Azure uses the first IP address space in the virtual network in which a /29 subnet will fit. I prefer to have my gateway as the first subnet rather than at the end or in the middle. However, during the creation of a virtual network, you are forced to create at least one virtual subnet at the start. The trick is to change the address space for the first virtual subnet so that it does not start at the first available address. Instead, start at least eight addresses later.

Begin at 10.0.0.8 (which leaves 0 through 7 preceding) or for simplicity a class C address space. Eight addresses are all that's needed. For example, if my virtual network address space began at 10.0.0.0/8, I would change the first virtual subnet address space to start from 10.0.1.0 rather than 10.0.0.0. Then, when I add the gateway later, the subnet would use 10.0.0.0. In the following graphic, I've changed the default virtual subnet postcreation, but you can change it during creation as well.

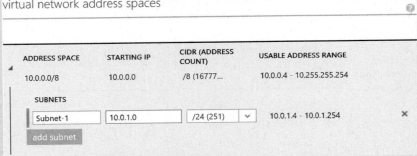

Now when I enable S2S connectivity, I see the gateway subnet created at the start of the virtual network IP range, as shown here:

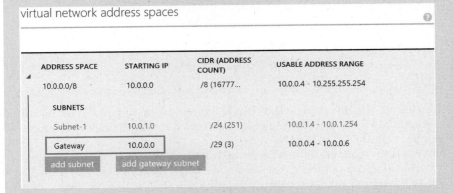

Although this approach does not change functionality, I find that it provides consistency and makes for easier viewing of a virtual network configuration. (It also satisfies my obsessive-compulsive tendencies.)

The fact that the Azure side of the VPN gateway is a single-core VM leads to the next aspect of the connection—the transfer speed. Typically, the speed will be between 80 Mbps and 100 Mbps. At those speeds, the processor is running at 100 percent and cannot process additional data. Computationally, that makes IPsec very expensive—exactly how expensive depends on the particular cryptographic algorithm you configure. The physical distance between your on-premises location and the Azure datacenter also has an impact on the transfer speed: the greater the distance, the higher the latency.

Finally, the latency itself, as speed, is one aspect of a connection, but latency can often be more important than the speed. A connection with a high latency means that many workloads will not function correctly. Imagine trying to run an application that connects to a SQL database over a connection with a 60 ms latency; that would not be pretty. But if the actual amount of data required is very low, a high-speed connection is not required. Not coincidentally, the average latency I see between resources on-premises and those in Azure over an S2S VPN is around 60 ms. Again, the exact value depends on your distance from the Azure datacenter, as well as the route the packets take between your location and Azure. The data is traveling over the Internet, so the exact path can vary and can be affected by other Internet traffic. If you are using the S2S VPN, it is important to consider this latency in your designs. You do not want to separate the tiers of a highly integrated application that are not tolerant of latency by the VPN connection. I would try to keep all tiers either on-premises or in Azure. If that is not possible, use some other clever cache to keep data near to the location where it is required.

Enabling a High-Performance VPN Gateway

In November 2014, Microsoft introduced a new high-performance gateway option. It provides a more performant S2S VPN gateway by increasing the Azure-side gateway VMs. The maximum speed rises from 80 Mbps to 200 Mbps. If the configuration changes, this could change in the future. I've seen transfer speeds higher than 200 Mbps with high performance—I've never seen more than 80 Mbps on the standard gateway. Note that this option will not improve latency, which is still primarily governed by the fact that the connection runs over the Internet.

You must use PowerShell to create a high-performance gateway. Configure your new gateway using the `-GatewaySKU` parameter with the `New-AzureVNetGateway` cmdlet. The default value is `'Default'`, but if you change the setting to `'HighPerformance'`, it will create a high-performance gateway.

An existing gateway can be switched between `Default` and `HighPerformance` by using the `Resize-AzureVNetGateway` cmdlet and specifying the new gateway SKU. For example, here's the code I used to resize my gateway from `Default` to `HighPerformance`:

```
Resize-AzureVNetGateway –VNetName VirtNet115 –GatewaySKU HighPerformance
```

The high-performance gateway carries a price premium, which as of this writing is 49 cents per gateway hour in addition to the egress data charges that apply to a standard gateway. A standard gateway is priced at 3.6 cents per gateway hour as detailed here:

http://azure.microsoft.com/en-us/pricing/details/virtual-network/

That's a significant price difference. In reality, the price for the high-performance gateway is more consistent with the pricing for two medium-sized VMs, while the default gateway is heavily subsidized. Also remember these prices do not include any discount your organization receives.

A high-performance gateway not only gives increased bandwidth, but it also increases the maximum number of S2S tunnels from 10 to 30, which means that you will have more connections to on-premises locations and/or other virtual networks.

Note that high-performance gateways are only available for dynamic gateways and ExpressRoute. Static gateways are not supported.

Using Forced Tunneling

For services (think VMs) running in the Azure virtual network, the Azure network routing will decide whether the data should be sent out via the standard connection to the Internet or if it should be sent to the on-premises location via the S2S VPN whenever the VMs send traffic out of the Azure virtual network IP range. The local on-premises IP range is known through the local network configuration that was defined and used as part of the S2S VPN creation.

There may be times when all traffic from Azure should be sent via the on-premises S2S VPN connection, even if the target for the communication does not reside on-premises. For example, if you have a web-filtering solution that checks targets before allowing the communication to the Internet and audits the traffic sent, you will want all of your traffic sent via the S2S VPN. This type of solution is known as *forced tunneling*. This capability is supported by Azure when you employ a dynamic gateway. (Forced tunneling is not supported for static gateways.)

The configuration for forced tunneling is applied to a virtual subnet, enabling some virtual subnets to have forced tunneling applied while others can communicate directly with the Internet. The application of forced tunneling is facilitated through the addition of a route to the virtual subnet routing table, which is hidden. By default, the virtual subnet routing table defines three routes:

Intra-VNet (Virtual Network) Routes Directly to the destination VMs in the same virtual network

On-premises Routes To the Azure VPN gateway

Default Route Directly to the Internet. Note that packets destined to the private IP addresses (RFC 1918, such as 10.0.0.0/8) not covered by the first two rules will be dropped.

A new default route is added specifying that the default route is via the Azure VPN gateway instead of the Internet, forcing all traffic through the tunnel and via on-premises. If you're using ExpressRoute, this approach is not used, and instead a default route is advertised via the ExpressRoute BGP peering session.

The following PowerShell script creates a new routing table and adds a default rule that specifies all IP traffic must use the VPN gateway. The routing table is then applied to two virtual subnets: a middle tier and backend tier. Finally, a default local site is configured for the VPN gateway; this is needed in a scenario where the VPN gateway in Azure is connected to multiple on-premises local networks.

```
#Create a new routing table
New-AzureRouteTable -Name "FTRouteTable" `
    -Label "Routing Table for Forced Tunneling" `
    -Location "East US"

#Add default route for all IP addresses to use the VPN gateway.
#This is the only rule allowed
Set-AzureRoute -RouteTableName "FTRouteTable" -RouteName "DefaultRoute" `
    -AddressPrefix "0.0.0.0/0" -NextHopType VPNGateway

#Apply the routing table to subnets
Set-AzureSubnetRouteTable -VNetName "MultiTier-VNet" -SubnetName "Midtier" `
    -RouteTableName "FTRouteTable"
```

```
Set-AzureSubnetRouteTable -VNetName "MultiTier-VNet" -SubnetName "Backend" `
    -RouteTableName "FTRouteTable"

#Set the default site to a local network definition
# connected to the Azure VPN Gateway

#Single element variable must be used for site name
$DefaultSite = @("CorpMainDC")
Set-AzureVNetGatewayDefaultSite `
    -VNetName "MultiTier-VNet" -DefaultSite $DefaultSite
```

The results of this configuration script are shown in Figure 6.12. The front-end tier, which communicates with the Internet, continues to talk to the Internet directly since it has no alternate policy applied, whereas the middle and backend tiers have their Internet communication forced through the VPN connection.

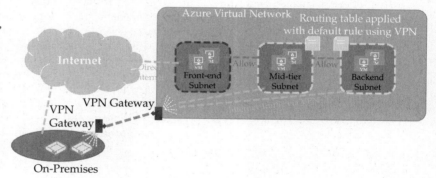

FIGURE 6.12

Three-tier application, with two tiers forced through the VPN connection for Internet communication

To view the content of a route table, use the `Get-AzureRouteTable` cmdlet. The `Get-AzureRouteTable` cmdlet optionally allows a specific routing table (via the `-Name` parameter) and a level of detail (using the `-DetailLevel` parameter) to be specified. To view the routing table that is associated with a virtual subnet, use the following:

```
Get-AzureSubnetRouteTable -VNetName "MultiTier-VNet" -SubnetName "Midtier"
```

To remove a route table from a virtual subnet, use this:

```
Remove-AzureSubnetRouteTable -VNetName "MultiTier-VNet" -SubnetName "Midtier"
```

If you want to remove routes and entire route tables, take a look at the Help entry for the `Remove-AzureRouteTable` cmdlet. To remove the default local site from a VPN gateway, use the `Remove-AzureVNetGatewayDefaultSite` cmdlet. For this operation, specify the virtual network using the `-VNetName` parameter.

Connecting a Virtual Network to Multiple On-Premises Gateways

When embracing a hybrid environment between Azure and on-premises, ensuring that connectivity is available is critical, as is having connections between the primary locations. For example, each on-premises datacenter should have a connection directly to Azure. This provides the most optimal connection path and ensures that connectivity to Azure continues even in the event of a datacenter failure.

The initial S2S VPN gateway supported only a single connection; Azure could only be connected to a single on-premises location. Organizations had to pick one location for connection to Azure and then route all communications to and from Azure through that location. In the event of a disaster, organizations had to use scripting to move the S2S VPN connection to a new gateway location at a different on-premises location. This limitation was removed, and the standard Azure VPN gateway can now concurrently connect to 10 gateways. A high-performance Azure VPN gateway can concurrently connect to 30 gateways.

NOTE   A dynamic VPN gateway is required for more than one connection.

It is important to understand that behind the scenes the Azure-side gateway infrastructure does not change. There are still the same two virtual machines in the active/passive arrangement. The configuration changes to enable the multiple connections, however, because the multiple connections are through the same VMs. The amount of bandwidth does not change, and all the connections share the bandwidth limit (about 80 Mbps for a standard gateway and 200 Mbps for a high-performance gateway). Therefore, if you connect to 10 locations using the standard gateway, each connection may experience transfer speeds of about 8 Mbps.

As noted earlier, if you intend to connect an Azure virtual network to multiple on-premises locations, it is important to create a distinct local network entity for each location within the appropriate IP space. This allows Azure to route the traffic to the correct VPN tunnel. When connecting to multiple local sites, your connectivity will look something like Figure 6.13.

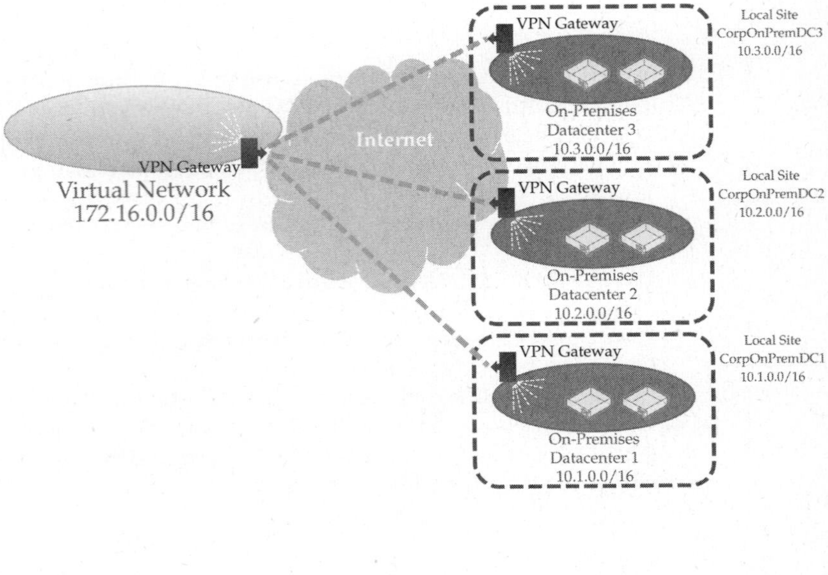

FIGURE 6.13
Virtual network connected to three on-premises locations

To enable multiple VPN connections, it is necessary to use PowerShell to export the network configuration for your virtual network; then, make changes to add an additional local network site reference for the gateway configuration to the downloaded XML file; and finally, apply that updated network configuration back to Azure. It's a fairly simple process as described here:

```
http://msdn.microsoft.com/en-us/library/azure/dn690124.aspx
```

I advise you to follow those instructions; there is little benefit in repeating them here. The key points are:

◆ Define local network definitions for each VPN connection location and ensure that each definition includes the IP address for the Internet-accessible VPN gateway for that location.

◆ Create a regular S2S VPN connection to one of the local network locations using the portal or through PowerShell.

◆ Export the network configuration and then add the other local site definitions to the gateway section—for example, a definition that reads as follows:

```
<Gateway>
  <ConnectionsToLocalNetwork>
    <LocalNetworkSiteRef name="CorpOnPremDC1"><Connection type="IPsec"
/></LocalNetworkSiteRef>
  </ConnectionsToLocalNetwork>
</Gateway>
```

would be changed to read:

```
<Gateway>
  <ConnectionsToLocalNetwork>
    <LocalNetworkSiteRef name="CorpOnPremDC1"><Connection type="IPsec"
/></LocalNetworkSiteRef>
    <LocalNetworkSiteRef name="CorpOnPremDC2"><Connection type="IPsec"
/></LocalNetworkSiteRef>
    <LocalNetworkSiteRef name="CorpOnPremDC3"><Connection type="IPsec"
/></LocalNetworkSiteRef>
  </ConnectionsToLocalNetwork>
</Gateway>
```

Then the revised configuration would be imported back into Azure.

Note that it is not possible to add redundant VPN connections from a virtual network to a local network. There would be minimal benefit on the Azure side; the redundant paths would be connected via the same Azure instance VM. You cannot add two VPN connections to two different local site definitions with different gateway IP addresses; both local sites would have the same IP spaces defined. This would cause an error, and Azure would reject the configuration. Microsoft provides useful information that covers many common questions in the FAQ available here:

```
http://msdn.microsoft.com/en-us/library/azure/dn133803.aspx#BM_MultiSiteandVNet
```

Virtual Network–to–Virtual Network Connectivity

Virtual networks are region based: East US, West US, and so on. It's likely you will add services in multiple regions or may even have different Azure subscriptions within the same region, each with a separate virtual network, and want to connect them.

One way to connect different virtual networks is to connect them via your on-premises infrastructure. In this scenario, each virtual network has a VPN gateway that connects to your main datacenter. Your datacenter network infrastructure then provides the routing between them. This is not ideal for a number of reasons:

◆ Egress charges are incurred for traffic to Azure; you pay for all communication between the virtual networks routes via a network external to the Azure region. (As you will see, this happens anyway for routing between virtual networks in different regions, but not for virtual networks within a region.)

◆ The traffic experiences double latency: the traffic going to the datacenter and then the traffic going from the datacenter back to Azure.

◆ Load is added to your internal network infrastructure.

◆ Bandwidth on your VPN connection is used that would be better spent on traffic required between Azure and your on-premises infrastructure.

> ### CONNECTING AN ON-PREMISES VPN GATEWAY TO MULTIPLE AZURE VPN GATEWAYS USING A CISCO ASA
>
> In my testing, I experienced a problem when I used a Cisco ASA device to connect to multiple Azure networks. By default, the device creates a new crypto map for each connection, and Cisco allows only one crypto map per interface on the ASA. The solution is to change the ID number for each additional connection but use the same crypto map.

At the same time that Microsoft added support for multiple connections from the Azure VPN gateway, they added support for connecting different virtual networks using the Azure backbone network. Note that this connectivity between virtual networks uses the VPN gateway on your virtual network and the same gateway VMs. The bandwidth between the virtual networks is limited to the capabilities of the VMs (80 Mbps), but the latency will be very low since the traffic stays within the Azure network. Essentially, a VPN connection between virtual networks is created using the same IPsec encryption. It just does not travel via the public Internet.

If you connect virtual networks within the same region, there is no cost. However, if you connect virtual networks in different regions, you need to pay the network egress costs, and since traffic between regions would always be egress for one of them, you pay for all network traffic. Remember, though, this communication is over Azure's own network and not over the public Internet. It is still encrypted using IPsec.

An example of the virtual network–to–virtual network connectivity is show in Figure 6.14. Remember that it's critical that each virtual network have its own unique IP space. They cannot overlap or, once again, the routing will fail and the configuration will be rejected when it is

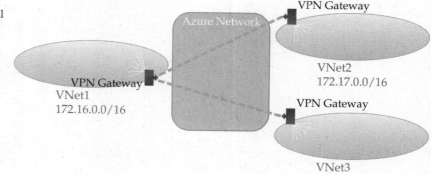

applied to Azure. The virtual networks you connect to can be in different regions, different subscriptions, and completely different Azure accounts because this connection is really just a VPN tunnel between two VPN gateways and is completely independent of Azure subscription details.

You can mix connections to on-premises locations and other virtual networks, but the total number of tunnels must be equal or less than the tunnel limit: 10 for standard and 30 for the high-performance network. For example, with a standard Azure VPN gateway, you could use six tunnels for connectivity to on-premises locations and four tunnels for connectivity to other virtual networks. As expected, there can be no IP address overlap in any of the virtual networks or local networks that are connected together via VPN. Additionally, no redundant connections can be created.

Microsoft has provided detailed instructions for creating a virtual network–to–virtual network connection here:

`http://msdn.microsoft.com/en-us/library/azure/dn690122.aspx`

At a high level, the steps performed are as follows:

1. Separate virtual networks are created, each with a unique IP address space.

2. Local networks are created for each of the virtual networks that a specific virtual network will be connecting to. For example, if you are connecting three virtual networks (A, B, and C) that are each in different Azure subscriptions, in the subscription containing virtual network A, you would create a separate local network for the IP space for virtual networks B and C. Yes, a *local* network since, to this virtual network, those remote virtual networks are essentially remote networks. In the subscription for virtual network B, you would add local networks for virtual networks A and C, and so on.

3. Gateways will be created in each virtual network, and the IP address of each virtual network's gateway is configured as the IP address of the VPN gateway for its corresponding local network in each of the other virtual networks. The IP address of the gateway for virtual network A is configured as the VPN IP address for the local network representing virtual network A in the subscription for virtual network B. I show this in Figure 6.15.

FIGURE 6.15
IP address and local
networks

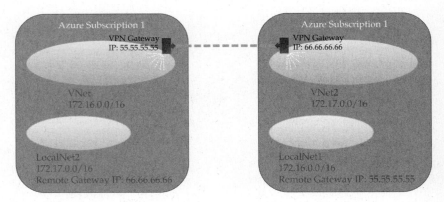

Using Point-to-Site Virtual Private Networking

Point-to-site VPN capability is available and gives specific machines connectivity to Azure that leverages a special client downloaded from the Azure management portal. The clients receive an IP address from a pool defined as part of the Azure point-to-site VPN configuration. If you need this kind of VPN, it is available as an option. Microsoft has plenty of documentation, including a blog post here:

```
http://blogs.msdn.com/b/piyushranjan/archive/2013/06/01/point-to-site-vpn-in-
azure-virtual-networks.aspx
```

For most virtualization-type communications in the datacenter, you will want to use the S2S VPN options, so I'm not going to cover point-to-site in detail.

The point-to-site option is useful in scenarios where you have individual machines that need to connect to a particular virtual network in Azure instead of an entire location. Consider the case of a consultant working from home or an offshore developer who needs communication with VMs running in Azure.

The same gateway used for your S2S VPN connections can be used for point-to-site connections. To enable the point-to-site option:

1. Navigate to the Networks node.

2. On the Virtual Networks tab, select a virtual network that you previously created.

3. Select the Configure tab.

4. In the Point-To-Site Connectivity section, select the Configure Point-To-Site Connectivity check box.

5. When prompted, as shown in Figure 6.16, enter an address space.

   The address space you enter must not conflict with other address spaces, such as those used in the virtual network or in local networks. This IP range is used to allocate IP addresses to the point-to-site VPN clients that connect. Each VPN connection is assigned an IP address from this range. Only a single class C is required, since the maximum number of point-to-site connections is 250. Azure will handle the routing between the point-to-site VPN connections and your virtual network.

6. Click Save to apply the configuration change.

7. If you do not already have a gateway created for the virtual network, you should create the gateway. Be sure that you select a dynamic gateway.

FIGURE 6.16
Configuring the IP space to be used for point-to-site clients

point-to-site connectivity

CONNECTION   ☑ Configure point-to-site connectivity

ADDRESS SPACE	STARTING IP	CIDR (ADDRESS COUNT)	USABLE ADDRESS RANGE	
192.168.1.0/24	192.168.1.0 ⌄	/24 (254) ⌄	192.168.1.1 - 192.168.1.254	✕

add address space

The next step is to create and upload a certificate that will authenticate the VPN clients. Find details on creating and using certificates for point-to-site here:

http://msdn.microsoft.com/library/azure/dn133792.aspx

Once you completed the configuration, the option to download the VPN client (both 32-bit and 64-bit) becomes available in the dashboard, and the number of connected point-to-site connected clients appears, as in Figure 6.17.

FIGURE 6.17
Downloading the VPN client for Azure and viewing connected users

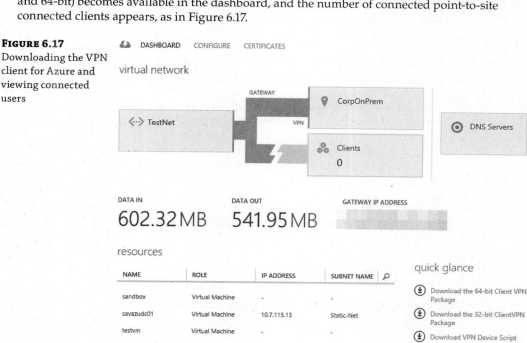

DASHBOARD   CONFIGURE   CERTIFICATES

virtual network

NAME	ROLE	IP ADDRESS	SUBNET NAME
sandbox	Virtual Machine	-	-
savazudc01	Virtual Machine	10.7.115.13	Static-Net
testvm	Virtual Machine	-	-

DATA IN **602.32 MB**   DATA OUT **541.95 MB**   GATEWAY IP ADDRESS

quick glance

⬇ Download the 64-bit Client VPN Package
⬇ Download the 32-bit ClientVPN Package
⬇ Download VPN Device Script

Using ExpressRoute

At this point, the benefit of establishing an S2S VPN between your on-premises locations and Azure virtual networks should be clear. Azure is an extension of your datacenter with full Layer 3 routing between them. IPv4 TCP and UDP communication is enabled. Additionally, multiple locations can be connected to a virtual network, as can other virtual networks. There are, however, limitations to using the S2S VPN, which for some scenarios and organizations may make it nonoptimal or even unfeasible:

Data Security   The connection is over the public Internet, and even though the connection is encrypted, this can be a showstopper for some organizations.

Latencies   Because the connection is over the Internet, the path taken by packets can vary, which also makes the speed and latency variable. Typically latencies around 60 ms are experienced, which blocks certain hybrid scenarios that need lower latencies.

Transmission Speed   The maximum speed is limited to 200 Mbps when using the high-performance gateway and around 80 Mbps with the standard gateway.

Connection Limits   There is a limit to the number of locations and the number of virtual networks that can be connected via the S2S gateway.

Cost   Egress traffic results in charges, and for scenarios where there is significant egress traffic, these costs could become a factor.

ExpressRoute Fundamentals

To address the previously listed limitations, Microsoft introduced ExpressRoute. ExpressRoute provides direct Layer 3 connectivity between your on-premises network and your services running in Azure. Notice that I said *services running in Azure* rather than your virtual networks. VMs must still reside in virtual networks to be connected via on-premises, but the ExpressRoute connection can be used for other types of communication between on-premises and Azure, such as replication traffic and even Azure storage access.

ExpressRoute does not leverage the public Internet. Instead, it uses dedicated connectivity through a service provider that provides high security and isolation. Additionally, because a dedicated connection is used, a predictable, fast path gives fast connection speeds and very low latencies. Because a dedicated path is used, there is no need for cryptography on the wire. (Encryption typically uses large amounts of CPU, introduces latency, and can reduce overall speed.) Latencies experienced with ExpressRoute are in the order of low single-digit milliseconds.

The fast speeds, and especially the low latencies, make it possible for the new hybrid scenarios and services in Azure to be leveraged by on-premises resources. Scenarios such as using storage in Azure from on-premises, backup and recovery, Big Data, media services, and hybrid applications with tiers mixed between Azure and running on-premises are now plausible.

There are two types of ExpressRoute service provider: Network Service Providers and Exchange Providers. The version you use will depend on your requirements, physical location, and existing network connectivity.

Using an ExpressRoute Exchange Provider

An Exchange Provider is also known as an Ethernet Exchange Point (EXP), which is similar to an Internet Exchange Point (IXP) except an EXP is not connecting Internet connections. An EXP is a location where different service providers are connected and exchange traffic between their networks. For example, an EXP would have connectivity to Verizon, AT&T, Comcast, and so on. Sometimes these facilities are also known as "fiber hotels" since they essentially have fiber coming into the facility from all the different carriers and provide the interconnections.

In many ways, ExpressRoute via an Exchange Provider is the easiest to understand. Figure 6.18 shows an example configuration. As can be seen, the Azure resources exist in a typical virtual network; however, that virtual network is connected to an ExpressRoute Exchange Provider. Multiple large fiber links between the Azure cages and the EXP exchange infrastructure create virtual circuits that allow communication at the desired speed between Azure ports and the customer ports. Each customer's virtual network is logically isolated from other customers hosted in Azure who may also be using ExpressRoute. The customer then either hosts their servers at the EXP directly or has a dedicated fiber connection from their datacenter to the EXP. The EXP then handles the Layer 2 routing between the Azure virtual network(s) and the customer on-premises resources, basically enabling the IP routing between them. Customers using an Exchange Provider require a pair of physical cross-connections with an active-active BGP session configuration for each physical cross-connection to make the link highly available and resilient to failures.

FIGURE 6.18
Example of connectivity via an ExpressRoute Exchange Provider

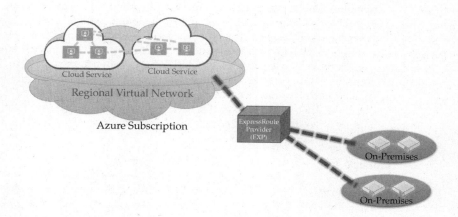

To use an Exchange Provider, you must meet specific requirements related to the configuration of the virtual network and the on-premises connectivity to the EXP. For example, the virtual network gateway must be configured to use a /28 subnet and the IP range set forth in IETF document RFC 1918. The complete list of prerequisites for using an Exchange Provider and a full deployment workflow are documented here:

http://msdn.microsoft.com/en-us/library/azure/dn606306.aspx

This should be considered the definitive guide for deploying ExpressRoute with an Exchange Provider. The article also includes the step-by-step PowerShell commands to use, but in most cases when deploying ExpressRoute, you will work with the Exchange Provider and likely Microsoft.

As of this writing, ExpressRoute using an Exchange Provider is available in a number of bandwidth options, specifically 200 Mbps, 500 Mbps, 1 Gbps, and 10 Gbps. A number of

Exchange Providers can be used. Microsoft maintains a list of the partners available and the Azure regions in which they operate in the "Service Providers and Locations" section of the page:

```
http://msdn.microsoft.com/en-us/library/azure/dn606309.aspx
```

Pricing information for Exchange Provider–based ExpressRoute can be found here:

```
http://azure.microsoft.com/en-us/pricing/details/expressroute/
```

The price tiers are based on the port speed of the connection. Pricing includes unlimited inbound traffic and limited amounts of outbound traffic. Outbound traffic that exceeds the tier limit is priced per GB of additional outbound traffic. Additional charges from the EXP for the configuration and ongoing support of the connection are also incurred.

Using an ExpressRoute Network Service Provider

A Network Service Provider ExpressRoute connection is based on an MPLS (Multiprotocol Label Switching) cloud connection. Many organizations today leverage MPLS to connect their datacenters and locations together. At a very high level, MPLS works by adding a label to the IP packets and then using those labels to switch traffic on the service provider's backbone. MPLS operates between Layers 2 and 3 in the OSI model. Note that ExpressRoute is technology agnostic and will work with any VPN technology; I mention MPLS here because it is the most popular. After the label has been added to packets, it can be used to filter actions. For example, you can group packets with the same label and isolate others based on their label. MPLS creates a virtual routing table for each customer and distributes traffic to the various edge routers that a customer connects to. This enables the connectivity over the MPLS cloud. A route distinguisher is used to make each customer's network unique. All of the connections could be using 192.168.0.0/16, but the distinguisher ensures that each connection is unique. Azure effectively is added into the routing of your network. You are connected to your services in Azure via your existing MPLS. Figure 6.19 shows this arrangement.

FIGURE 6.19
Example of connectivity via an ExpressRoute Network Service Provider

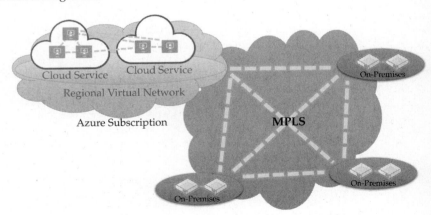

A benefit of using a Network Service Provider rather than an Exchange Provider for ExpressRoute is that if MPLS is already being used, no additional hardware is required. Enabling connectivity to Azure via the MPLS is a configuration change that can be made quickly and simplifies onboarding. As with an Exchange Provider, the virtual network gateway must use a /28 address space, and the virtual network must use an IP space from RFC 1918. You'll find the full list of requirements and the step-by-step deployment guidance here:

http://msdn.microsoft.com/en-us/library/azure/dn643736.aspx

As of this writing, ExpressRoute using a Network Service Provider is available in a number of bandwidth options, including 10 Mbps, 50 Mbps, 100 Mbps, 500 Mbps, and 1 Gbps. Note that the fastest speed for a Network Service Provider is significantly lower than that offered by an Exchange Provider, but I expect over time the numbers will increase for all types of ExpressRoute. You can use several different Network Service Providers; a listing of the Network Service Provider partners can be found in the "Service Providers and Locations" section here:

http://msdn.microsoft.com/en-us/library/azure/dn606309.aspx

Pricing information for Network Service Provider–based ExpressRoute can be found on the Network Service Provider tab here:

http://azure.microsoft.com/en-us/pricing/details/expressroute/

The price tiers are based on the port speed of the connection and include unlimited inbound traffic and (unlike Exchange Provider) also include unlimited outbound traffic. Note that you also would be paying charges for your standard MPLS service.

ExpressRoute Key Points

ExpressRoute provides the premium connectivity option between on-premises and Azure services. Here are key points that you need to understand to get the most out of your ExpressRoute connectivity:

Expanded Services   ExpressRoute can be used to connect to more than just virtual networks hosting VMs. It can be used to connect to storage, backup, media services, and more. The complete list of services that can be communicated to via ExpressRoute is available here:

http://msdn.microsoft.com/en-us/library/azure/dn606292.aspx#BKMK_
ExpressRouteAzureServices

Expanded Regional Connectivity   Once you are connected by ExpressRoute to an Azure region, all regions within that continent can be connected via the ExpressRoute circuit. For example, connections to virtual networks in East US and West US regions could be made using the same ExpressRoute circuit. You would not be able to connect to services outside of the continental United States via a US ExpressRoute circuit.

Expanded High-Availability and Disaster-Recovery Capabilities   A single virtual network can be connected to multiple ExpressRoute circuits, and each of those circuits can be through different service providers. This provides additional high-availability and disaster-recovery capabilities, and the total throughput would be aggregated through the multiple providers based on the virtual network gateway size.

Expanded Subscription Connectivity   Multiple virtual networks across multiple subscriptions can be connected to the same ExpressRoute circuit. When this is done, all the virtual networks become part of the same routing domain and can therefore communicate with each other. If there is a requirement to isolate virtual networks that are connected to the same ExpressRoute circuit, you can leverage Network Security Groups to control the traffic access between virtual subnets. Another option would be to use separate ExpressRoute circuits for the different virtual networks. It's very important that no IP overlap exist between virtual networks connected via an ExpressRoute circuit. The owner of the circuit has to authorize the connections to other Azure subscription services, and the owner gets billed for the usage.

Expanded Provider Connectivity Each subscription supports up to 10 circuits and enables connectivity to multiple providers.

On-Premises VLAN Stretching Existing VLANs on-premises cannot be stretched to Azure. VLANs are a Layer 2 concept, which are not supported in Azure.

Internet Traffic VMs in a virtual network can still access the Internet through the regular Azure Internet connection unless a default route (0.0.0.0/0) is defined to use the ExpressRoute connection. Adding the default route will force Internet-based traffic to route via the ExpressRoute connection.

Bandwidth Bursts It is possible to burst bandwidth up to double the selected bandwidth. There are two connections in an active-active configuration to provide high availability. Both can be used in burst scenarios at no extra cost. For example, if you have a 1 Gbps circuit, you could burst to 2 Gbps.

Migration to ExpressRoute You can migrate a virtual network from using S2S VPN to using ExpressRoute, but there will be a small amount of downtime associated with the move.

Site-to-Site and ExpressRoute Dual Use As of this writing, you cannot use ExpressRoute and S2S VPN for the same virtual network. This would typically be designed for resiliency purposes in cases where the ExpressRoute connection was unavailable. Dual use is on the road map. In a static routing environment, the ExpressRoute would be primary and the S2S VPN would be secondary. In a dynamic routing (using BGP) environment, the customer would be able to control the routing and preference.

Uptime SLA ExpressRoute has a 99.9 percent uptime SLA.

Azure Auditing ExpressRoute integrates with Azure Auditing, which means information on the ExpressRoute connection can be found through Management Services by selecting ExpressRoute on the Operations Logs tab in the portal. Information about circuit and gateway creation, circuit link updates, authorizations, and BGP session status is currently shown, and this list will continue to grow over time.

Microsoft has a free eBook specifically on ExpressRoute, and I recommend that anyone considering using ExpressRoute read it. You can download it here:

```
http://go.microsoft.com/fwlink/?LinkId=506748
```

The Bottom Line

Explain the connectivity enabled with a site-to-site VPN. An S2S VPN connects a virtual network to another network, which could be an on-premises location or another virtual network. Once connected, Layer 3 routing is provided between the networks. When a virtual network is connected to on-premises resources via the S2S VPN, Azure essentially becomes an extension of your datacenter.

Master It What is the difference between a standard S2S gateway and a high-performance gateway?

Understand the key benefits of Azure ExpressRoute over standard site-to-site VPNs. Although an Azure S2S VPN provides IP connectivity between an on-premises location and Azure, it operates over the public Internet and uses CPU-heavy cryptography to ensure security. These factors result in high latencies, limited maximum speeds, and no dedicated path. ExpressRoute operates over dedicated connections that result in low single-digit latencies and higher speeds. ExpressRoute also provides connectivity to other Azure services, not just VMs in a virtual network. When deciding between S2S VPN and ExpressRoute, you should take time to fully understand the requirements, how workloads between Azure and on-premises will interact, and the tolerance of each workload to latency.

Master It What is the difference between using a Network Service Provider and an Exchange Provider?

Chapter 7

Extending AD to Azure and Azure AD

At this point, I hope it is clear I am taking you on a journey to a rich environment consisting of resources in Azure and on-premises. The book started with cloud basics and looked at compute, storage, and networking. Chapter 6, "Enabling On-Premises Connectivity," culminated in full network connectivity between on-premises and Azure resources in a fully hybrid environment. With this connectivity in place, the next logical integration between Azure and on-premises is authentication and directory services, which for most companies means Active Directory (AD) integration. This chapter explores integrating with AD for Azure resources. Azure AD is a very different technology from on-premises Active Directory, and this chapter explains how to use its capabilities.

In this chapter, you will learn to

- ◆ Build an Active Directory architecture that integrates with Azure resources

- ◆ Understand the difference between Active Directory Domain Services and Azure AD

Using Active Directory Domain Services in Azure

Active Directory Domain Services (also known as ADDS, but more commonly referred to as just Active Directory) is the building block of nearly every organizational service. Active Directory provides a variety of services; the ones that come to mind first include:

- ◆ Authentication and authorization

- ◆ Directory services used by applications

- ◆ Group Policy

In a hybrid environment, Azure resources become an extension of your organization's infrastructure. It is logical to want some—or potentially all—of those Azure-based resources to also become part of your on-premises Active Directory and thus enable seamless authentication, management, and integration.

Making Active Directory Available in Azure

Two things are required for Active Directory to be leveraged by computers, users, and services:

- ◆ The ability to locate a domain controller or specific service, which for Active Directory means DNS name resolution for DNS servers hosting the domain DNS partitions

◆ The ability to communicate with the located domain controller using a variety of protocols, such as Lightweight Directory Access Protocol (LDAP), Kerberos, RPC, or Netlogon

A complete list of protocols is available here:

```
http://technet.microsoft.com/en-us/library/dd772723(v=ws.10).aspx
```

The key point is that communication is required over a wide range of TCP and UDP ports. Another good article that discusses port requirements for many Microsoft services can be found here:

```
http://support.microsoft.com/kb/832017
```

Fortunately, both DNS name resolution and the ability to communicate are easy to accomplish once you have connectivity between Azure and on-premises established using either the site-to-site VPN connectivity or ExpressRoute. Connectivity to domain controllers (initially on-premises) will already be in place via Layer 3 routing. If there are specific firewalls between on-premises and Azure that restrict traffic flow or if you are using network security groups (NSGs) in Azure, it's important to make sure the required traffic can flow. Specifically, you must be sure that the port requirements mentioned in the Microsoft articles I recommended are met.

WHAT ABOUT NAT?

One other question related to traffic flow is the use of network address translation (NAT) and even double NAT. Imagine that all your on-premises internal traffic uses the IP space at 99.0.0.0/8. Until recently, Azure only supported RFC 1918 address spaces for virtual networks. (This is no longer the case, but hey, we're imagining.) So, you might have wished to use NAT to make the Azure-based resources appear to be part of the 99.0.0.0/8 address space. Though this is possible, it's not recommended for Active Directory, and that recommendation has nothing to do with Azure. It is just not recommended in general for use with Active Directory. If NAT is something you want to use, I advise reading the following articles. Make sure that you are aware of the guidelines and Microsoft's official support position on using NAT with Active Directory.

```
http://blogs.technet.com/b/ad/archive/2009/04/22/dcs-and-network-address-
translation.aspx
```

```
http://support2.microsoft.com/default.aspx?scid=kb;EN-US;978772
```

Once IP connectivity is established, the next step is to configure the Azure resources to use your on-premises DNS servers to enable name resolution for domain services. (Most likely DNS services are provided by your domain controllers, but that is not necessarily the case.) Ascertain the IP addresses and names for your on-premises DNS servers by talking to your AD and networking teams. Although you could examine your machines' network configuration to ascertain the DNS servers—for example, `ipconfig /all` shows the DNS servers configured— this would show the DNS servers your machine in your location is configured to use. Based on the point of connection to Azure, other DNS servers in your organization may be preferred—or even required—if network traffic is controlled between Azure and on-premises. Working with the AD and networking teams will ensure the correct configuration.

After you've identified the DNS servers that Azure resources should use, your next step is to configure them for the Azure virtual network. You will remember that in Azure all VMs obtain their IP configuration through the Dynamic Host Configuration Protocol (DHCP). As part of the virtual network configuration, different virtual subnets are created and carve up the available address space. VMs obtain their configuration from a virtual subnet that defines the IP address, the subnet mask, gateway, and the DNS server configuration. You can modify the DNS servers configured for a virtual network, which will then be configured on the VMs via DHCP. To change the DNS server configuration, follow these steps:

1. Open the Azure management portal (https://manage.windowsazure.com).

2. Select Networks in the navigation area.

3. Select the network whose DNS configuration you wish to change.

4. Select the Configure tab.

5. In the DNS Servers section, enter the name and IP address for each DNS server you want the VMs in Azure to be configured to use, as shown in Figure 7.1. The name configured for the DNS server is a logical name for your identification purposes. The VMs in the Azure network are only sent the IP address.

6. Click Save.

FIGURE 7.1
Configuring DNS servers for a virtual network

testnet

DASHBOARD   CONFIGURE   CERTIFICATES

dns servers

dnsserver1	192.168.1.10
dnsserver2	
SELECT OR ENTER NAME	IP ADDRESS

The changes will not take effect until clients renew their DHCP lease. For this reason, and others, it's good to configure the site-to-site connectivity and integration with AD before adding regular services to Azure. The DNS servers added are part of a subscription list of DNS servers. If you navigate to the top-level Networks area, there is a DNS Servers tab, which when selected shows all the DNS servers that are configured in the subscription. These servers may currently be used by one or more virtual networks, as shown in Figure 7.2. By default, a subscription can register nine DNS servers. You can increase that limit to a maximum of 100 by contacting Azure Support.

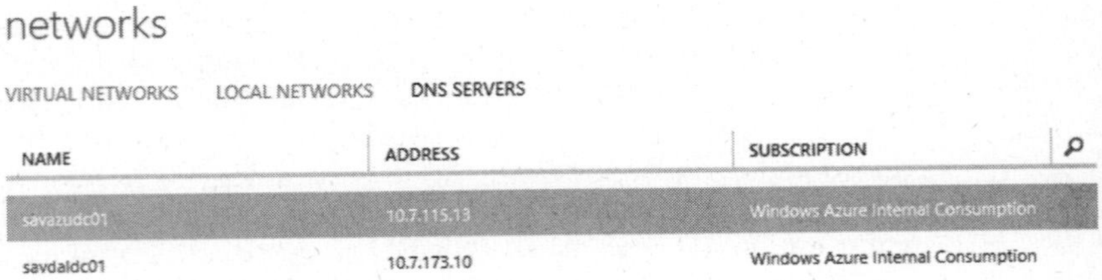

FIGURE 7.2
Viewing DNS servers
registered for
subscription

networks

VIRTUAL NETWORKS   LOCAL NETWORKS   **DNS SERVERS**

NAME	ADDRESS	SUBSCRIPTION	
savazudc01	10.7.115.13	Windows Azure Internal Consumption	
savdaldc01	10.7.173.10	Windows Azure Internal Consumption	

DNS servers that are no longer used by virtual networks should be deleted to avoid taking up a registration slot in your subscription. Although DNS servers can be registered automatically when you're configuring them for a network, you can also register them separately via the New ➤ Network Services ➤ Virtual Network ➤ Register DNS Server menu item, which enables a name and IP address for a new DNS server to be configured.

You can also register DNS servers with PowerShell by using New-AzureDNS—for example:

```
$newdns1 = New-AzureDns –Name "dnsserver1" –IPAddress "10.7.173.10"
```

Normally a VM will use the DNS configuration of the virtual network it is part of, but it is also possible to specify a separate DNS configuration on a per-VM basis by adding the -DnsSettings parameter to the New-AzureVM cmdlet and passing a DNS server object as created in the previous PowerShell line.

The VMs in Azure should now be able to resolve domain service records, which will then allow them to join the domain and use domain services. To test whether name resolution is working correctly:

1. Run IPCONFIG /ALL and ensure the DNS servers configured are the ones specified in the virtual network configuration. If they aren't, try running ipconfig /renew to force the machine to update its IP configuration.

2. Try to resolve a domain record. In this example, the domain is savilltech.net, and I am looking for a nonsite-specific Kerberos server.

   ```
   Nslookup
   Set q=srv
   _kerberos._tcp.savilltech.net
   ```

The response should be a list of domain controllers in your domain.

Active Directory Site Configuration

In the NT 4 domain days, things were simple. A domain was created with a single writable domain controller known as the Primary Domain Controller (PDC) and one or more optional Backup Domain Controllers (BDCs) that received changes from the PDC. Clients could authenticate to the PDC or BDCs. Replication would flow simply from the PDC to the BDCs, and clients would authenticate against any domain controller, regardless of physical proximity to a DC. NT 4 domains had no concept of geography.

Active Directory completely changed this. The PDC/BDC model was removed (mostly), and all domain controllers can make changes. Through multimaster replication, the directory is kept synchronized between all the domain controllers. The replication topology is automatically generated by the Intersite Topology Generator (ISTG), which creates different models of replication depending on whether domain controllers are in the same physical site (a ring of replication) or in different sites (a least-cost-spanning tree). This enables efficient replication. You provide the site information to Active Directory by defining AD sites (which are IP address spaces) and then defining IP site links. Those links tell the ISTG which sites have direct communication and the connection speed to enable the replication topology to be generated. Figure 7.3 shows a basic example of replication topology. In the figure, each site has three domain controllers, which use a ring topology to replicate changes. One domain controller from each site replicates any changes intersite, which then propagate to the remaining domain controllers in the site through the ring of replication.

FIGURE 7.3
Example of AD replication within sites and between them

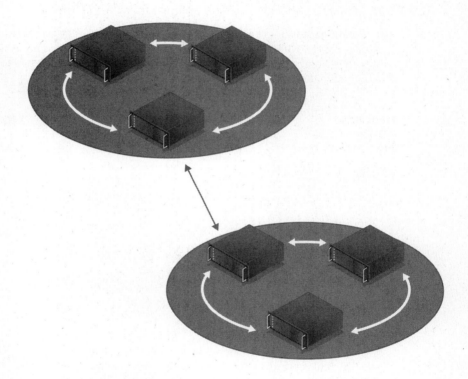

In addition to being used for the replication of Active Directory data, the sites are used by AD clients and other services that want to use services in their local site or as close to their local site as possible. For example, a user logs on to a machine. That machine has an IP address that will be part of a subnet. The subnet is associated with an AD site. The site enables clients to locate domain controllers and other services. If no domain controller or service is found in the local site, services in the closest site can be used. Closeness is determined based on the site links and their speed (or cost) between sites.

As you can see, an accurate site and site link topology are critical for the health of AD replication, the efficient utilization of AD, and any service that is site aware. When extending your infrastructure to Azure, it's critical that Azure also become part of your site and site link definition, even if you don't place DCs in Azure—but especially if you *do* place DCs in Azure.

The Azure virtual networks are an IP space you have allocated, which corresponds perfectly to an Active Directory site. Your Azure virtual network will become a new site in Active Directory. You likely have an existing naming scheme for your Active Directory. Follow your existing scheme for your Azure site(s), but try to incorporate the fact that the site is in Azure and some information about the corresponding virtual network when you name the Azure site. An AD site name can be up to 63 characters in length, and since site names are used as part of DNS names, they cannot contain characters not allowed in DNS. The details on site names can be found in the Site names section here:

```
http://support.microsoft.com/kb/909264
```

Azure-based sites can be named `Azure-<Region>-<virtual network name>`—for example, `Azure-EastUS-VNet113`. In my basic lab environment, I named my Azure-based site `Azure`, as shown in Figure 7.4. The figure also shows that the IP space assigned to the site matches IP space assigned to the virtual network.

FIGURE 7.4

An AD site for my Azure virtual network

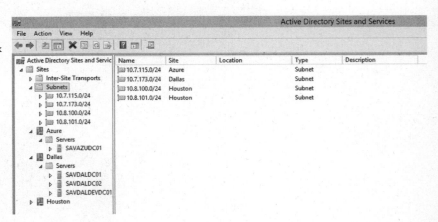

Once the Azure virtual network is defined as a site, the next critical step is to define the site link that represents the connection between on-premises and the Azure virtual network. Remember that the site links are used by the ISTG to decide how data should be replicated and which domain controllers should replicate with each other. Most likely, one of your on-premises locations has a link to Azure using either site-to-site virtual private networking or through ExpressRoute. The on-premises site should have an IP site link to the Azure site. Do not just add all sites to the `default-first-site-link`. Instead, create specific site links between locations that are connected. Remember to configure the interval desired for replication and follow your organization's existing cost scheme to accurately represent the speed of connection between your on-premises location(s) and Azure. If you have multiple on-premises sites connected to your virtual network, add multiple site links representing that connectivity. My basic setup in my lab environment appears in Figure 7.5, and Figure 7.6 shows the appropriate site links in AD that represent the physical connectivity.

FIGURE 7.5
Demonstration lab environment with two on-premises locations and an Azure virtual network

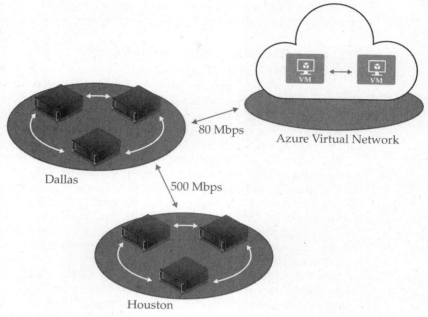

FIGURE 7.6
AD site links that represent the lab environment

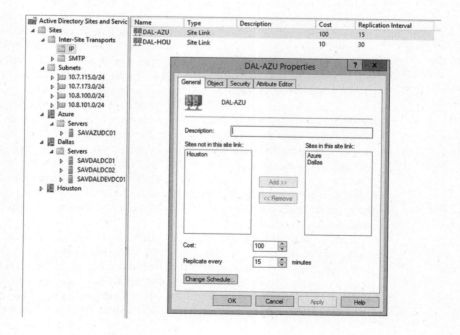

Defining the sites and site links before creating services in Azure ensures optimal AD integration and avoids erroneous traffic and suboptimal AD functionality.

Placing a Domain Controller in Azure

Just reading the title of this section will leave many AD administrators in a panicked state. AD contains information about every object in your organization. It controls who can access what. Domain controllers have the sacred duty of storing and servicing the directory content. The idea of placing one of these sacred objects outside of your own datacenter, where you can no longer nurture and protect it, seems sacrilegious. However, it's important to dismiss your initial emotional responses and take a look at the reality of the situation.

In Chapter 12, "What to Do Next," I will look at many of the concerns about leveraging public cloud services, and Azure specifically. A big part of this is a concern about the security of services running in Azure. Spoiler alert: these concerns are not based on the realities of Azure. The datacenters that host Azure services are some of the most secure and resilient datacenters you will ever see. The physical security can stop a tank. Azure has been audited and certified for almost every major standard there is, which speaks to how secure and well processed the services are. Azure datacenters are used by governments, financial institutions, and the largest organizations in the world. They are secure.

However, *you* are responsible for ensuring that your services are secure. If you place a domain controller in Azure with the default RDP port open for login, that is a bad (but easily avoided) thing. I will talk later in this chapter about some best practices for hosting domain controllers in Azure to maximize security. Do you host domain controllers in branch offices today? How secure are they? Remember that Azure will likely be a substitute for branch offices, for disaster recovery, or even other datacenters. You need to afford Azure domain controllers the same services that would accompany those on-premises facilities to be able to properly meet requirements.

This is not to say you should always place a domain controller in Azure, but you should consider it depending on how integrated with Active Directory your Azure resources are. If services running in Azure are highly dependent on Active Directory to function, consider what will happen if the link to on-premises is unavailable. How would the services continue to function? Even while the link to on-premises is available, how much traffic will be sent from resources in Azure to domain controllers on-premises? Remember that you pay for egress traffic. Consider also how sensitive your traffic is to latency if you are using the site-to-site VPN gateway. (Site-to-site VPN gateways commonly introduce around 60 ms of latency.) On the flip side, if you place one or more domain controllers in Azure, you must take into account the replication traffic between the domain controllers on-premises and those in Azure. If the majority of change is sourced on-premises, then most replication traffic will be ingress to Azure and therefore free of charge. For most organizations, the replication traffic will not be a significant consideration. The more important factor will be having domain controllers close to the resources using Active Directory in Azure and ensuring availability even if the link to on-premises is unavailable.

Some organizations will consider creating a separate domain, or even separate forest in Azure, which then has trusts to on-premises. The key to success here is in determining what domain services need to be part of the trusted domain and then leveraging those services and trusted domains. If creating a separate domain or forest makes it difficult to manage services, then I would argue it will be detrimental to your organization's chances of being successful in a hybrid environment. Remember, Azure is an extension of your datacenter.

DOMAIN CONTROLLER IN AZURE CONSIDERATIONS

Assuming you make the decision to create a domain controller in Azure, there are some special factors and operational practices for running a domain controller in Azure to consider. Prior to Windows Server 2012, virtualizing a domain controller was supported, but there were problems in organizations that used checkpoint functionality. Checkpoint functionality creates a point-in-time saved state of a VM and then reverts a VM back to a previous point in time when a checkpoint is applied. This is a huge problem for any kind of directory service, including Active Directory, that generally expects time to move forward. These services would be unaware that they had been reverted to a previous point in time. Problems arise when a reverted domain controller tries to replicate with a DC that has already received newer updates. This is cumbersome to fix.

Windows Server 2012 solved this by adding Active Directory virtualization safeguards through the use of a new attribute named VM-GenerationID. VM-GenerationID provides a unique ID that stays consistent, providing nothing changes with the VM's view of time. For example, application of a checkpoint would result in a VM-GenerationID change. The Active Directory service would detect the change to VM-GenerationID and go into a "panic" mode to protect Active Directory from any risk of corruption or bubbles of replication. The service would reset its invocation ID, dump its Relative ID (RID) pool, and set SYSVOL as nonauthoritative. Although this protects Active Directory, it causes a lot of additional replication and work on other domain controllers to correct that state.

VM-GenerationID support was added as part of the Windows Server 2012 Hyper-V server release, and since Azure runs on Hyper-V, Azure also supports VM-GenerationID. This is both good and potentially bad. It should be noted, though, that Windows Server 2008 R2 Active Directory does not support this functionality, which means you should think carefully before running Windows Server 2008 R2 domain controllers in Azure.

On the good side, if an unplanned failure occurs and the VM that contains Active Directory running in Azure has to be service healed and is shunted back in time slightly, there will not be any corruption. On the bad side, if the VM running Active Directory was deprovisioned (removed from the Azure fabric) and then reprovisioned, the VM would get a new VM-GenerationID and cause Active Directory to go into the panic mode. You don't want this to happen frequently. Although you can shut down VMs running Active Directory in Azure, you should not deprovision them. Shut them down from within the OS so that they stay provisioned on the Azure fabric. Do not shut them down from the portal. This does mean that you will need to continue paying for the shutdown VMs.

There are two other considerations for domain controllers running in Azure that relate to storage and networking. First, remember that Active Directory has a database, and this database should not be stored on storage that uses caching. You cannot place it on the Azure VM OS drive. Domain controllers assert Forced Unit Access (FUA) and expect the I/O subsystem to honor the request, thus ensuring that sensitive writes are persisted to durable media. Instead, ensure that a data disk is added to the Azure VM and configured for no caching. When running the DC promotion process, ensure the Active Directory database, logs, and SYSVOL are placed on the data disk rather than the C: drive.

Second, all VMs in Azure have their IP configuration assigned by DHCP. As a result, when running the promotion process for the domain controller, a warning will be generated, as you will probably make the domain controller a DNS server and DNS servers should not have their IP configuration assigned via DHCP. What the promotion process does not know is that, using

PowerShell, your domain controller Azure VMs will be reserved an IP address, as discussed in Chapter 5, "Using Virtual Networks." Your domain controllers will always have the same IP address, even in the event the VM is moved between hosts or reprovisioned—actions that normally would make a VM be allocated a new IP address by the Azure fabric.

These points are very important. To summarize factors you must consider for domain controllers running in Azure:

◆ Use Windows Server 2012 and later DCs—ideally the latest OS.

◆ Do not shut down and deallocate DCs in the Azure management portal (instead, shut down or restart the VM within the guest OS).

◆ Store the Active Directory database, logs, and SYSVOL on a data disk with no caching.

◆ Assign a reserved IP address.

Microsoft has an official page with guidelines for domain controllers in Azure. Take time to read it. The page features any updated guidance:

http://msdn.microsoft.com/library/azure/jj156090.aspx

CREATING A DOMAIN CONTROLLER IN AZURE

The process for creating a DC in Azure is the same you'd use when creating a DC on-premises. Keeping in mind the key considerations for the configuration outlined in the previous section, you can ignore the warning that you are using a dynamically assigned IP address. Microsoft has some basic documentation on creating a DC in Azure here:

http://azure.microsoft.com/en-us/documentation/articles/virtual-networks-install-replica-active-directory-domain-controller/

When you create a domain controller, the most time-consuming part is replicating the existing directory content from an existing domain controller to the new DC. When you create the first DC in Azure, this traffic will need to travel over the site-to-site VPN or ExpressRoute connection, but since this is ingress traffic, there is no associated cost. The only real consideration is how long it will take to copy over the data. If you have a very large AD database and a large amount of SYSVOL content, be prepared to wait. For additional domain controllers created in Azure, the replication would be from the existing domain controller and, therefore, copied over the local Azure network.

An alternative to copying the AD database over the on-premises–to–Azure connection during the promotion process is to leverage the Install From Media (IFM) capability. IFM works by seeding the initial AD content for the new domain controller from a system state backup of an existing domain controller or, preferably, by using ntdsutil.exe to specifically create the media to be used for an IFM domain controller promotion. Learn more about creating the IFM required media using ntdsutil.exe here:

http://technet.microsoft.com/en-us/library/cc770654(v=WS.10).aspx

Once the media that contains the AD data required to create a new domain controller has been created, it must be made available to the VM running in Azure. This is still ingress data to Azure, but it can be done in advance of the domain controller promotion, and the actual domain controller promotion will not be dependent on data being retrieved from on-premises. Another option would be to create a new domain controller on-premises on Hyper-V and then move that VM into Azure. That approach would, however, involve even more data, since both AD and the OS would need to be moved, but it is an option. You can even upload a VHD of a replica DC from on-premises Hyper-V. For a walk-through of this method, see this article:

```
http://support.microsoft.com/kb/2904015
```

When you create DCs in Azure, make sure they are Global Catalog (GC) servers. GC servers are used for many types of domain operations, including certain group enumerations. Beginning with Windows Server 2012, all DCs are also Global Catalog servers by default.

If you do place multiple domain controllers in Azure for resiliency and load balancing, and those DCs are configured as GCs and they are DNS servers, and none of them hold Flexible Single Master Operation (FSMO) roles, then make sure that they are placed in an availability set. This will ensure that the domain controllers are placed across Azure fault domains. If you do so, a server failure—or even an entire rack failure—will not take down all of your domain controllers in Azure. In addition, you won't have to worry that, during maintenance operations in Azure, all of your domain controllers could be offline at the same time.

Another change you will have to make relates to the DNS records published by domain controllers. By default, DCs publish service DNS records in a generic portion of the DNS namespace and a site-specific portion of the namespace for the site the DCs are located in. If a client can't find a DC in its local site DNS space (maybe the local DC is offline), the client will query the generic portion of the DNS namespace. In a default configuration, the client will just as likely be returned a DC in a random branch office or Azure instead of one in a hub or central location. That isn't a desirable situation. It's unlikely you want services and users in on-premises locations authenticating and using domain controllers in Azure.

To ensure that clients without a local DC available are returned only records from the central locations and not your DCs running in Azure, you need to configure DCs in Azure (the same way you configure DCs in branch offices) to register only site-specific DNS service records. To perform this change, you need to edit the Group Policy for the default domain controllers and enable the DC Locator DNS Records Not Registered By The DCs option. (You will find this option by selecting Computer Configuration ➤ Administrative Templates ➤ System ➤ Net Logon ➤ DC Locator DNS Records.) Set it to the following:

```
LdapIpAddress Ldap Gc GcIPAddress Kdc Dc DcByGuid
Rfc1510Kdc Rfc1510Kpwd Rfc1510UdpKdc
Rfc1510UdpKpwd GenericGc
```

These settings are explained fully in the *Windows Server 2003 Active Directory Branch Office Guide*, but essentially, they stop DCs from registering any nonsite-specific entries. The problem is that configuring these settings makes the change for all DCs, so contrary to what the Microsoft document says, I prefer to change the settings on DCs using the following Registry multistring value:

```
HKEY_LOCAL_MACHINE\SYSTEM\CurrentControlSet\Services\
    DNS\Parameters\DnsAvoidRegisterRecords
```

You can set the same options used by the DC Locator DNS Records Not Registered By The DCs Group Policy setting, but each value should be placed on an Enter-delimited line, as shown in Figure 7.7. After this change is applied and the DC rebooted, the generic portions of the DNS namespace (_ldap._tcp.) should contain service records for only DCs that didn't receive the Registry change: the domain controllers not in Azure or branch offices. Check out the official Microsoft article on this change here:

```
http://support.microsoft.com/kb/306602
```

FIGURE 7.7
Suppressing the creation of generic DNS records for a domain controller

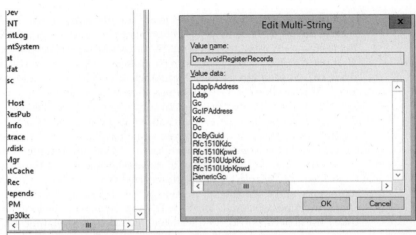

Computer\HKEY_LOCAL_MACHINE\SYSTEM\CurrentControlSet\Services\DNS\Parameters

READ-ONLY DOMAIN CONTROLLER AZURE CONSIDERATIONS

The baby step that many IT teams consider when they realize they need a domain controller in Azure is to deploy a read-only domain controller (RODC) instead of a writable domain controller. RODCs were introduced in Windows Server 2008 primarily as a solution for branch offices where hardware could not be physically secured but the site required a local domain controller. RODCs had a number of key features that made them attractive for locations that could not physically secure hardware:

Read-Only Database The read-only copy of the database prevents any changes from replicating to the rest of the domain if the server is compromised.

Filtered Attributes A filtered attribute set prevents certain attributes in AD from being replicated to the RODC. For example, attributes containing very sensitive data could not be replicated.

Limited Password Caching The only passwords that are cached on an RODC are for accounts specified, such as those used at the location. If the server is compromised, any password attack would only expose limited accounts. Deleting the RODC object from AD management tools gives the option of resetting any passwords that were cached on the RODC.

Limited Administrator Rights An individual can be made an administrator of an RODC without being made a domain administrator.

For organizations that are unsure about the security of Azure, placing an RODC in Azure instead of a typical read-write DC (RWDC) provides a level of comfort. However, Azure is not a branch office. In a branch office, users log on, and some basic directory interaction is performed. In Azure, there are likely services running that interact with Active Directory, and many applications do not support RODCs—they expect to be able to write to the DC and do not understand the referral to an RWDC that the RODC returns if a write is attempted. Therefore, the decision to use RODCs in Azure will depend on whether the services running in Azure will work with an RODC. Even if they do, you should consider how much write activity they perform and what the impact on their functionality will be if every write has to travel back to on-premises, especially on the high-latency site-to-site VPN connection. Ultimately, is Azure a physically insecure branch office? No. But it will take some time to gain that trust.

If you decide to go that route, see these articles for more guidance on RODC deployments:

```
http://technet.microsoft.com/library/dd728028(WS.10).aspx
```

```
http://technet.microsoft.com/en-us/library/dd734758(WS.10).aspx
```

JOINING ACTIVE DIRECTORY IN AZURE

As part of the regular SYSPREP specialize phase when deploying an operating system from a template, it is possible to join a domain through configuration in the unattend.xml answer file. When deploying a VM to Azure, you cannot specify an answer file; Azure uses this mechanism for its own deployment process. As part of the VM provisioning configuration, it is possible to specify domain joining configuration.

To configure an Azure-provisioned VM to join a domain, use the following PowerShell with the provisioning configuration:

```
Add-AzureProvisioningConfig -WindowsDomain `
    -Password 'password' `
    -Domain 'savilltech' `
    -DomainPassword 'password' `
  -DomainUserName 'Administrator' `
    -JoinDomain 'savilltech.net'
```

Optionally, you can specify an OU for the machine using the parameter:

```
-MachineObjectOU 'OU=AzureVMs,DC=savilltech,DC=net'
```

Active Directory Federated Services in Azure

As mentioned at the start of this chapter, Active Directory consists of more than just Domain Services. Other capabilities, such as Rights Management Services, Certificate Services, and Federation Services, can be hosted in Azure VMs like other workloads. Active Directory Federation Services (AD FS) requires some additional consideration and has an important role, as you'll see in the next section.

Best practices for AD FS that apply on-premises apply equally to Azure, but there are certain changes in technology. For example, the Azure load-balancing capability needs to be used instead of configuring load balancing within the VMs themselves. Microsoft has some great guidance for AD FS in Azure available here:

```
http://msdn.microsoft.com/library/azure/jj156090.aspx#BKMK_WhyADFS
```

Notice as you read that Azure did not leverage network security groups (NSGs); they did not exist at the time the article was written. Instead of using basic ACLs to control traffic as the article suggests, now you can use the richer NSG functionality.

Azure Active Directory

Thus far, this chapter has been devoted to leveraging Active Directory Domain Services in your Azure environment. There is also an Azure service called Azure Active Directory, or Azure AD for short. Is this the same thing? No, not at all. When you think about traditional Active Directory, it brings to mind a true directory service that has a hierarchical structure (based on X.500) that uses DNS as its locator mechanism, and that you can interact with via LDAP. For authentication, it primarily uses Kerberos. In addition to actually joining machines to the domain, Active Directory enables organizational units (OUs) and Group Policy Objects (GPOs) for managing policy.

Azure AD, though having some aspects of a directory service, is really an identity solution. It allows users and groups to be created, but in a flat structure without OUs or GPOs. You cannot join a machine to Azure AD. There is no Kerberos authentication. You cannot query it via LDAP. This is fine, as those things do not make sense on-premises, where all types of communication are possible. Azure AD is focused on identity throughout the Internet, where the types of communication are typically limited to HTTP (port 80) and HTTPS (port 443). Azure AD can be used by all types of devices, not just corporate assets. Authentication is done through a number of protocols, such as Security Assertion Markup Language (SAML), WS-Federation, and OAuth. It is possible to query Azure AD, but instead of using LDAP, you use a REST API called AD Graph API. These all work over HTTP and HTTPS. This is a key point: Azure AD works using Internet protocols.

Why Do You Need Azure AD?

Look around you right now. Consider a 5' radius. How many different devices are around you? Your phone, that's one; laptop or desktop computer, that's two; maybe a table, that's three; and so on. When I speak at conferences, I ask people to raise their arms and keep them up while I go from one upward regarding the number of devices people have on them. The average is between 2 and 3 and has gone as high as 6 (that guy was sitting by himself). The point is that in this day and age we are accustomed to using many different devices. We expect to be able to use all these devices from anywhere to perform both personal and work-related tasks. Often, users are leveraging not just services within their organization, but also services hosted externally. Users access Office 365, Salesforce, Twitter, Amazon—the list goes on. Traditionally, the way this access is managed is by each user having a separate identity (account or credential) on each service or some corporate credential, such as Twitter, being shared between people (which is never a good idea). This is problematic in a couple of ways:

Passwords   Humans are not good at remembering lots of different passwords. This means they choose ridiculously easy passwords, they write them down on a sticky note and attach it to their monitor, or use the same password for all of them. In that last case, if one service is compromised. the attacker now has access to any system they use. And when they forget a password or ID, it causes a lot of helpdesk work.

Provisioning and Deprovisioning   When a new employee is hired (provisioned), there is a long process to create all these accounts. If someone leaves the company, all those accounts have to be deprovisioned very quickly or that person retains access to corporate services even though he or she is no longer an employee. This is even more difficult if the individual had access to a shared account such as the corporate Twitter account.

The solution is to avoid the separate identity on each partner service, and this is achieved through federation. Federation is a special type of trust relationship. Essentially, an out-of-band relationship is created between organizations based on a shared secret that enables a user's home identity to be used on systems within federated organizations. The Microsoft federation solution, as mentioned earlier, is AD FS. I'll walk you through the basics of an AD FS interaction based on the example shown in Figure 7.8:

FIGURE 7.8
Overview of federated interaction between organizations

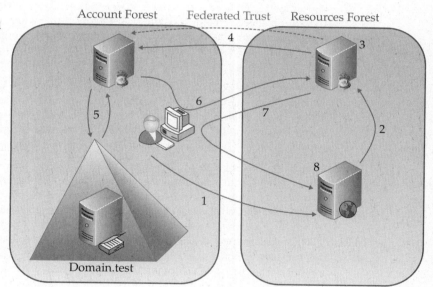

1. The user in the account forest tries to access a web server in another organization's forest that is connected to the account forest via a federated trust. The AD FS web agent on the web server checks for a security token for the user, which at this point will not exist.

2. Because the user has no security token, no access will be given, and the user will be redirected to the federation server in the resource forest.

3. The resource forest federation server will perform a "home realm discovery," during which the server will ascertain the home forest of the user. Home forests can be determined by prompting the user (via a web page, which by default displays all the forests that are trusted by the federation server in a drop-down list). As an alternative, the server can inspect a persistent cookie (if one exists) that is placed on the client by the

resource federated server after the first communication. This saves future requests and prompts for a home realm.

4. Once the home forest of the requesting user has been identified, the resource federation server redirects the user to the user's local federation server to continue processing.

5. Authentication then takes place through the user's local federation service. The local federation service, in turn, authenticates via Active Directory. Information pertinent to the token it will create is pulled from the AD. Different information may be designated for the different resource forests that trust the account federation.

6. The local federation server then issues the client a token specifically for the resource forest and redirects the user back to the federation server in the resource forest.

7. The resource federation server checks the token and confirms that it is digitally signed with the correct certificate. After the certificate is confirmed, the resource federation server creates its own local token for use when communicating with the web application. The user is then redirected to the web application server. This may remind you of referral tickets in a multiple domain forest; it works in a similar fashion.

8. The web application then checks the token. The token is a SAML token (version 2.0 format, which is an industry standard format and allows maximum support from different web applications). The web application reads the SAML token and authorizes use of the application and its content based on the access limitations specified in the token.

So, essentially the user asks for access to a partner site. The user has no permissions, so the website passes the user to a federation server in its forest. The federation server has no clue what to do with the user, so it forwards the user back to a federation server in the user's home forest. That server then checks out the user and gives the user a token to pass to the resource federated server. Now that the resource federated server has a token it can trust, it gives the user a local token to talk to the web server. Based on the content of the token from the user's home federation services, application access is granted.

This is not a trust that allows domain controllers from each domain to communicate with each other and browse the security directory. With a federation trust, the two organizations never actually communicate directly. All authentication and validation is done using web protocols and redirections. (I'll walk through those in a moment.) Visibility into your accounts is extended in a very controlled manner. Your partner organizations cannot see any information you don't explicitly allow as part of the token content. The partner organization cannot "ask" for information directly. The actual communication between the client and the web application and the AD FS servers is via HTTPS, so only port 443 needs to be opened between the client who will use AD FS to gain access to a website and the AD FS front-end services.

The federation relationships that need to be created and maintained are not easy to get up and running. Additionally, many companies you would want to federate with don't support true federation yet or will not federate with you directly. This leaves organizations unable to deliver a true Single Sign-On (SSO) experience. What does this have to do with Azure AD? Azure AD will do all of this for you.

What Is Azure AD?

As mentioned at the start of this section, Azure AD is primarily an identity solution that already has federations to all of the major services. Where federation is not available, another method is used to enable Single Sign-On. When you think about using Azure AD, consider that you will use it for authentication for Internet-based services, such as Office 365 and Azure, as well as many more, including Twitter and the thousands of other services that are already federated with Azure AD. Those services trust Azure AD without you having to do anything other than enable an application or service for use by your users. Figure 7.9 shows the gallery of applications available for use by your Azure AD users. Notice the number of applications. More than 2,400 different applications are federated through Azure AD, and the list grows daily. Go ahead and look for yourself. In the legacy Azure portal, navigate to Active Directory ➢ *<your Azure AD>* ➢ Applications ➢ Add ➢ Add An Application From The Gallery.

FIGURE 7.9
The application gallery screen for Azure AD

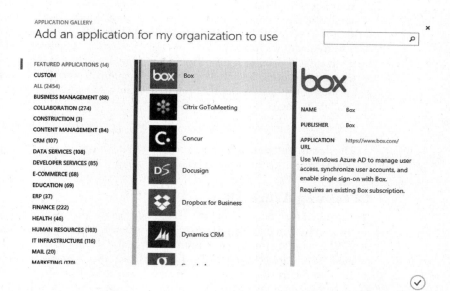

In my mind, this is the number-one value proposition for Azure AD. Azure AD already has federated with pretty much every Internet service that organizations use, which makes it easy for your organization's users to quickly use those applications using their single, on-premises identity. You can deliver SSO for users and solve those provisioning and deprovisioning pains. Consider that corporate Twitter account. With Azure AD, I add Twitter to Azure AD and specify the credential. The actual users will never see that credential or password—it's invisible to them. They will be able to use the application for their day-to-day operations. Figure 7.10 shows a high-level usage overview. Azure AD connects to your on-premises Active Directory and even other directories, such as HR systems, as you choose. Then, through Azure AD, users can access any application you have enabled through the Azure AD federations. Your organization has a single federation, and that is to Azure AD.

FIGURE 7.10
Azure AD federations
in action

Your users are likely already using cloud services out on the Internet. You may be aware of some; others you may not. Microsoft has a free Cloud App Discovery tool, which as of this writing is in preview. It provides great insight into the applications being used by collecting data from machines in your environment. That data is then analyzed and provided to you through a dashboard in Azure. The tool is available at http://appdiscovery.azure.com/.

If you have your own custom applications that you would like to enable for SSO, you can do so by adding the custom application to the Azure AD application list. Learn details on enabling this capability here:

http://msdn.microsoft.com/en-us/library/azure/dn151790.aspx

The documentation is very thorough and walks you through the configuration required in Azure AD and in your application.

Obtaining Azure AD

It's highly likely you already have Azure AD. Many Microsoft services use Azure AD for identity management, including services such as Microsoft Azure, Dynamics CRM, and Office 365. When you log on to Azure with a Microsoft ID, behind the scenes an Azure AD instance is created. Your name is used as the Azure AD instance name. You can see the instance if you look at the Active Directory area of the legacy Azure portal, as shown in Figure 7.11. Notice that the figure shows both my default Microsoft ID Azure AD instance and an organizational Azure AD instance used by my Office 365 subscription. You can create additional Azure AD instances for whatever needs you may have.

FIGURE 7.11
Azure AD instances

Three types of Azure AD SKUs are available: Azure AD, Azure AD Basic, and Azure AD Premium. Azure AD is free, though there is a cost associated with Azure AD Basic and Azure AD Premium (additional functionality comes with that cost). An article that details the key differences, including a comparison chart to make it easy to visualize those differences, is available here:

```
http://msdn.microsoft.com/en-us/library/azure/dn532272.aspx
```

The free Azure AD includes the following features:

◆ Self-service password change

◆ Basic security reports that show the geographical location and time your account was logged on

◆ Directory synchronization

◆ User-based provisioning of services

◆ Up to 500,000 objects

◆ SSO for up to 10 applications that are federated with Azure Active Directory

Azure AD Basic includes the following additional features:

◆ Enterprise SLA of 99.9 percent

◆ No limit to the number of objects

◆ Group-based provisioning of services

◆ Self-service password reset

◆ Customized branding on the logon and access pages

◆ Application Proxy

Azure AD Premium includes the following additional features:

◆ No limit to the number of SSO applications

◆ Self-service group management

◆ Advanced security reports and alerts to suspicious logon behavior based on learning how users log on

◆ Multifactor authentication security alert integration; when suspicious users log on, they must use another factor of authentication

◆ Self-service password reset; and that password, when synchronized, then replicates to on-premises Active Directory and provides a cloud-based password reset capability

◆ Usage reporting

◆ Multifactor authentication, such as requiring response to a call or text message

◆ A mobile logon application for cloud and on-premises users

◆ Licenses for Microsoft Identity Manager (MIM) to be used on-premises to enable synchronization of other directories

NOTE As of this writing, Azure AD Premium is only available as part of the Enterprise Mobility Suite. The Enterprise Mobility Suite also includes Microsoft Intune and Azure Rights Management Services (RMS).

The features available in the Premium SKU are great, but what is impressive to me is even the completely free SKU offers a great deal of functionality and scalability. It is a realistic identity option for many types of users. Remember that you can mix SKUs and enable some users to use the Basic features while others may use the Premium features. Both Basic and Premium are licensed on a per-user, per-month basis.

There will be times when you'll want to be able to manage your Azure AD instances through the regular Windows Azure portal. You may also wish to use your Azure subscription to manage your Azure AD users. This functionality might already be in place. However, if your Azure subscription is tied to a Microsoft ID, then you'll need to link your organizational Azure AD instance with your Azure subscription as follows:

1. Log on to Azure with your Microsoft ID (`https://manage.windowsazure.com`).

2. Navigate to the Active Directory workspace.

3. Select New ➤ App Services ➤ Active Directory ➤ Directory ➤ Custom Create.

4. Select Use Existing Directory from the drop-down list, select the "I am ready to be signed out now" check box, and click the check mark icon to complete the action.

5. You'll be logged out. When you log on again, you should log on as a global administrator for the Azure AD instance that you want to add to the organization's Azure subscription.

6. You'll be prompted to use the directory with Azure. Click Continue.

7. Click Sign Out Now.

8. Log back on to your Azure subscription as a regular Azure user (using Live ID).

9. Select the Active Directory workspace, and you'll see your organization's Azure Active Directory instance.

10. Look at the users, and you'll see a new user that's actually your Live ID—which is now part of your organizational Azure AD. This is what allows the access. If you ever want to disassociate your organizational Active Directory instance from your Azure subscription, just delete this user.

11. You can go one step further and make the organizational Azure Active Directory instance the main directory for your Azure subscription. This allows you to make users from the organizational Azure Active Directory coadministrators of the Azure subscription. From the Subscriptions menu, select Manage Subscriptions/Directory.

12. Select the subscription and then click Edit Directory, as shown in Figure 7.12.

FIGURE 7.12
Changing the directory for an Azure subscription

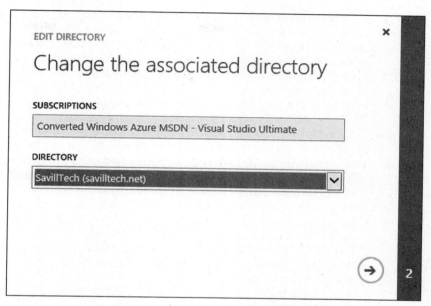

13. The selected directory is your organizational Azure Active Directory. (In this example, it is the only other directory available). Click Next ➤ Complete. If you wish to change your Live ID back to the one that was automatically created by Azure AD, just repeat this step and specify your built-in Azure Active Directory

14. Refresh the portal.

15. To add users from your organizational Azure Active Directory, navigate to the Settings workspace and select Administrators.

At this point, you can manage your organizational Azure Active Directory through the Azure portal, as well as give users access to your Azure subscription.

Connecting to Azure AD

Although it is possible to manually create users in Azure AD, for the best and most seamless experience, think about combining your on-premises Active Directory with Azure AD. You can do so by setting up directory synchronization (including password sync) and federation. This allows users working on their corporate assets to log on with their AD account. When they access Internet services, such as Office 365, authentication with Azure AD just happens via the federation. Users are seamlessly allowed access to all the services that Azure AD is federated with. Azure AD acts like your federation hub.

Setup is a two-phase process, although the second phase is optional. First, you populate Azure AD with users and groups based on the content of the on-premises Active Directory. The second phase is the establishment of a federation between the on-premises Active Directory and Azure AD. This enables Azure AD authentications to be performed by the on-premises domain controllers.

For the population of Azure AD from the on-premises Active Directory and later for the ongoing synchronization (both for changes made in the on-premises Active Directory and those made in Azure AD), there have historically been a number of solutions. It depends on when you first started leveraging Microsoft cloud services and the complexity (single domain, multiple domain, or multiple forests) of your on-premises directory. The solutions included the Directory Sync tool (DirSync), Azure Active Directory Synchronization Services (AAD Sync), and even the full MIM. The configuration of the services can be very complex.

To resolve the challenges of multiple synchronization technologies, different setup methodologies, and the relative complexity, Microsoft introduced Azure AD Connect as a single technology that enables the integration between on-premises Active Directory and Azure AD. Azure AD Connect is the recommended path for single forest deployment. It has an Express Settings mode, which in four clicks enables the configuration of synchronization from on-premises Active Directory to Azure AD. It even synchronizes user passwords (in a secure form) and synchronizes a hash of the hashed AD password to Azure AD. The Express Settings installation is the smallest footprint deployment of Azure AD Connect. It can be deployed to a single OS instance and can colocate with a domain controller.

Azure AD Connect works by initially connecting to the on-premises Active Directory, gathering some basic information, and then advising on the best path based on the AD configuration discovered. Behind the scenes, existing tools such as DirSync are used. This is hidden from the configuring administrator, and the entire configuration is simplified. Most customers are single forest and can use the Express Settings installation option. A Customize option is available for organizations with multiple forests or those who want to modify the sign-in options (including the configuration of ADFS enabling federation between Azure AD and on-premises), modify the filtering used for attribute synchronization, or change how IDs are mapped between on-premises and Azure AD (using `ImmutableID` normally). You'll find a great walk-through of both installation types here:

```
http://blogs.technet.com/b/ad/archive/2014/08/04/connecting-ad-and-azure-ad-only-4-
clicks-with-azure-ad-connect.aspx
```

I also recommend the following TechEd video that explains advanced synchronization concepts:

```
http://channel9.msdn.com/Events/TechEd/Europe/2014/EM-B316
```

Once synchronization is configured, the synchronization begins and changes are replicated. If you look in Azure AD, objects will be created for the on-premises users and groups. By default, synchronization runs every three hours. To trigger a synchronization on-demand in the most supported way, run the following PowerShell script:

```
PS C:\> .\Program Files\Windows Azure Active Directory Sync\
    DirSync\ImportModules.ps1
PS C:\> Start-OnlineCoexistenceSync
```

Behind the scenes, MIM is still being used. Azure AD Connect uses AAD Sync, which uses MIM. It's also possible to launch the `miisclient.exe` (MIIS was an earlier name for MIM), which can be found in the `C:\Program Files\Windows Azure Active Directory Sync\ SYNCBUS\Synchronization Service\UIShell` folder. Using MIIS, you can perform further customization and even troubleshoot. Fair warning: you should not attempt this unless you are familiar with MIM. I wrote an article on customizing the objects replicated based on the OU container they are in:

http://windowsitpro.com/windows-server/control-dirsync-object-synchronization

You'll also find my troubleshooting article useful if you are alerted that AD synchronization is not working:

http://windowsitpro.com/azure/azure-active-directory-sync-problems

Both leverage miisclient.exe. And yes, you read that right. Once synchronization has been configured, if no synchronization occurs for 24 hours, Microsoft will send you an email warning that synchronization is unhealthy. This enables you to initiate troubleshooting. Although using miisclient.exe was necessary when using DirSync, the new Azure AD Connect has its own Sync Rule Editor that can be used for most changes. For information on the more advanced Azure AD Connect configuration, see http://aka.ms/aadsync.

Earlier I mentioned federation between your on-premises Active Directory and Azure AD. It was also discussed as an optional second step in the process for setting up Azure AD. Azure AD Connect can deploy this federation for you, or you can deploy it manually. The decision to add federation depends on how you want authentication in Azure AD to work. There are two options, as shown in Figure 7.13.

FIGURE 7.13
Authentication options using Azure AD

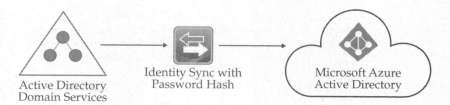

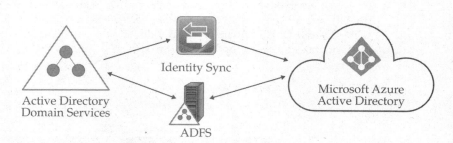

In the first option (shown at the top of Figure 7.13), as part of the synchronization to Azure AD, the user's password (the hash of the hash, thus removing any risk of exposing your user's credentials in the event of an attack) is also synchronized to Azure AD. The user's on-premises AD account and their identity in Azure AD shares the same username and password. Essentially SSO has been enabled, since the end user uses the same credential. Authentication in Azure AD occurs against the Azure AD authentication service.

The second option is shown at the bottom of Figure 7.13. Although the identity synchronization still occurs, the password hash does not need to be synchronized (although it can be as a backup authentication option). Federation is configured between the on-premises Active Directory and Azure AD. When authentication is required for an Azure AD identity, the authentication occurs via federation against the on-premises Active Directory domain controllers.

The first option is the simplest and used by many small to medium-sized companies. The second option is used by organizations that want tighter control and centralized authentication. With the first option, if a user is disabled on-premises, it will take some time for the disabled status to synchronize to Azure AD. An on-premises disabled user would continue to be able to use services until the disabled status had synchronized. Using the second option, when users are disabled on-premises, they are immediately disabled, since authentications for Azure AD take place against the on-premises Active Directory. Organizations that use the first option tend to do so because they are intimidated by stories of how hard federation is to configure and use. With the new Azure AD Connect, this isn't the case. I urge you to use federation (the second option) where possible. Remember, you can still enable the password hash synchronization option and use it in a fallback authentication scenario if the federation is unavailable for some reason.

Using Azure AD

Azure AD really "just works," and that's the point of anything "as a Service." I do want to explain basic operational tasks that will allow you to maximize Azure AD benefits, especially around using federated applications and the available reports. Azure AD is managed through the Azure portal in the Active Directory area. Select the Directory tab, and then select a specific Azure AD instance.

Once an Azure AD instance is selected, the default dashboard shows common actions that can be performed, such as adding a custom domain name to your Azure AD and upgrading to the Premium Azure AD SKU. The Users tab shows all the users in the Azure AD and the source of the account. In Figure 7.14, you can see accounts that were sourced from an on-premises Active Directory and synchronized to Azure AD, accounts that were created in Azure AD directly, and a Microsoft account that has been added to the Azure AD to give the account rights to the Azure AD. The Directory Integration tab shows the current status of synchronization and has guidance on how to configure and next steps.

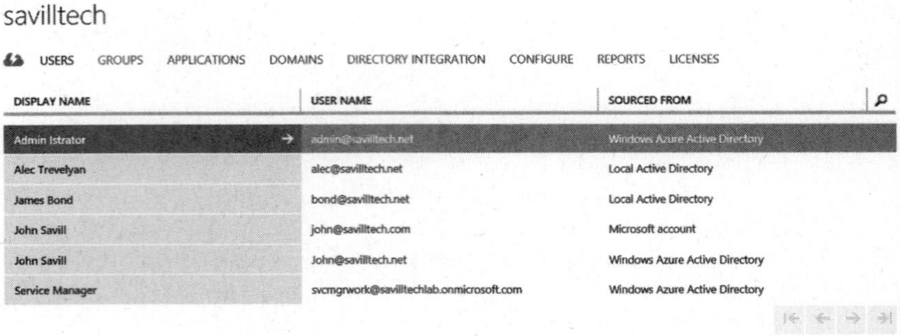

FIGURE 7.14
Active Directory
Users tab

savilltech

| | USERS | GROUPS | APPLICATIONS | DOMAINS | DIRECTORY INTEGRATION | CONFIGURE | REPORTS | LICENSES |

DISPLAY NAME	USER NAME	SOURCED FROM	
Admin Istrator	admin@savilltech.net	Windows Azure Active Directory	→
Alec Trevelyan	alec@savilltech.net	Local Active Directory	
James Bond	bond@savilltech.net	Local Active Directory	
John Savill	john@savilltech.com	Microsoft account	
John Savill	John@savilltech.net	Windows Azure Active Directory	
Service Manager	svcmgrwork@savilltechlab.onmicrosoft.com	Windows Azure Active Directory	

GRANTING ACCESS TO APPLICATIONS

The Applications tab enables the management of application assignment to Azure AD users. To assign a new application to users and groups, follow these steps:

1. In the Applications tab, select the Add action.

2. Select the option Add An Application From The Gallery.

3. When the application gallery opens, notice the Featured Applications list. Other applications are broken into various categories. You can also search for specific applications. As mentioned earlier, different applications support different levels of federation and SSO. Featured Applications support true federation and have APIs available that enable the Azure AD provisioning process not only to federate, but also to create any identities required on the application side. Other applications may support federation but do not expose APIs to enable objects to be created on the application side. Still others do not support federation, XAML, or oAuth. Instead, Azure AD caches the username and password to enable SSO. For the end user, the experience is the same; the process is seamless.

4. From the gallery, select the application you want to enable and click the check mark icon. Once the application is added, the next step is to provision that application for specific users or groups.

5. When you select an application, you will be able to see the type of SSO that is available for that application:

   ◆ Windows Azure AD Single Sign-On, which means a true federation is being used

   ◆ Password-Based Single Sign-On, where the username and password for the target is cached and then sent to the remote application during logon

   ◆ Existing Single Sign-On, which simply adds a link to the application on the user application portal and assumes SSO is enabled through another mechanism

   Azure AD will make the best selection based on the methods supported by the application.

6. Select Assign Users to begin the process of assigning an application to users or groups, as shown in Figure 7.15. Select the Assign Users action to open the Users tab.

7. Select a user or users and select the Assign action.

8. The options presented will depend on the application being added. For example, with Twitter it is possible to let users enter their own credentials, which will be cached the first time they try to use the application. Or, as Figure 7.16 shows, a credential can be entered for the user. That credential will then be used for the user's connection to the application. The benefit of doing this is that it enables users to access an application as a corporate resource without knowing the details of the connection. If they leave the organization, they cannot take an important password with them. Click the check mark icon to complete the provisioning of the user(s) for the application.

FIGURE 7.15
The Quick Start
screen for an
application

FIGURE 7.16
Configuring a
credential to be used
by the user when
connecting to the
application

Assign Users

This action will allow the selected user to authenticate to the Twitter application from within the Access Panel. Users can enter and update their Twitter credentials using the Access Panel at any time.

☑ **I want to enter Twitter credentials on behalf of the user**

User Name

corptwitter@savilltech.com　　×

Password

••••••••••••

Remember that with the Basic or Premium Azure AD it is also possible to provision based on group membership. With group-based provisioning, as users are added to groups, they are automatically provisioned for the applications associated with the group. This happens within a few minutes of a user being added to a group.

Once users are provisioned for applications, they can access those applications through the Azure AD Access Panel, which is available at https://myapps.microsoft.com (Figure 7.17). The first time a user selects an application, they will be prompted to install the Access Panel

Extension. Once installed, the applications can be launched and connected to using the configured credential. The Profile tab on the Azure AD Access Panel allows users to see their information and change their password.

FIGURE 7.17
The Azure AD Access Panel showing applications assigned to a user

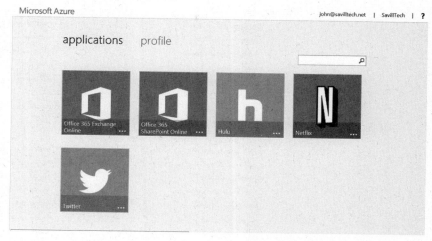

Applications are available for Android and iOS. You will find iOS My Apps here:

`https://itunes.apple.com/us/app/my-apps-windows-azure-active/id824048653?mt=8`

and Android My Apps here:

`https://play.google.com/store/apps/details?id=com.microsoft.myapps`

It's important to note that, although the Azure AD Access Panel provides a simple way to access applications provisioned for users, Azure AD also supports industry standard protocols such as SAML 2.0, WS-Federation, and OpenID Connect. This makes sign-in to Azure AD from a variety of platforms such as .NET, Java, Node.js, and PHP very simple.

USING AZURE AD REPORTS

Azure AD has many capabilities, and reports are the final feature I want to talk about. Figure 7.18 shows a screenshot of the available reports. Many are self-explanatory, but others require some additional elucidation. Take a look down the list of the reports shown in the figure, or better yet, look at the list via your own Azure AD.

Behind the scenes, Azure AD uses technologies such as machine learning to analyze usage patterns of users. It understands the geographic region logons are coming from, it can aggregate access across different Azure AD instances to identify irregular types of activity, and it even uses information gathered from other sources. Any access initiated via the Azure AD Access Panel will be included in the reports, even if the authentication takes place on-premises via federation. Here are a few reports I find useful:

Sign Ins from IP Addresses with Suspicious Activity This report looks at access attempts to accounts across multiple Azure AD instances from a single IP address, which would likely indicate some kind of attack.

FIGURE 7.18
Azure AD Reports tab

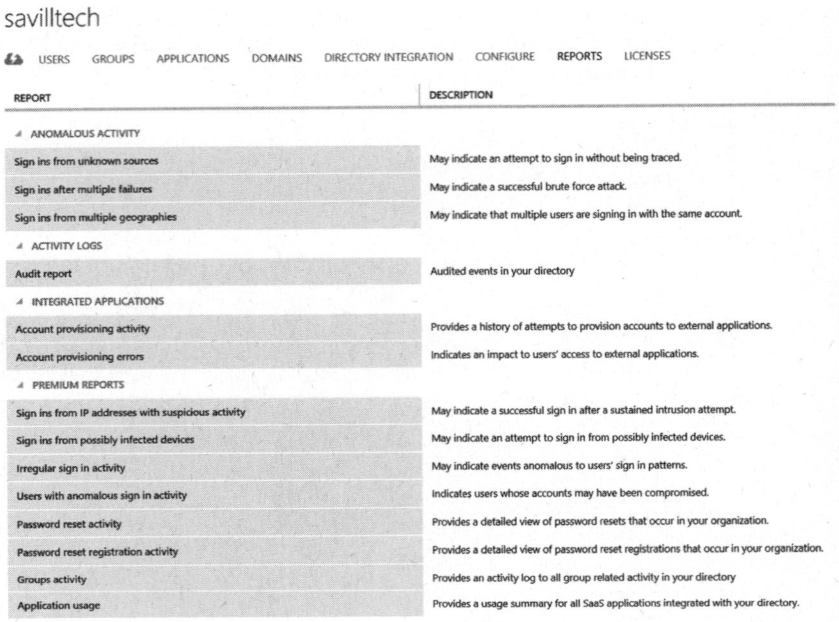

savilltech

| USERS | GROUPS | APPLICATIONS | DOMAINS | DIRECTORY INTEGRATION | CONFIGURE | REPORTS | LICENSES |

REPORT	DESCRIPTION
▲ ANOMALOUS ACTIVITY	
Sign ins from unknown sources	May indicate an attempt to sign in without being traced.
Sign ins after multiple failures	May indicate a successful brute force attack.
Sign ins from multiple geographies	May indicate that multiple users are signing in with the same account.
▲ ACTIVITY LOGS	
Audit report	Audited events in your directory
▲ INTEGRATED APPLICATIONS	
Account provisioning activity	Provides a history of attempts to provision accounts to external applications.
Account provisioning errors	Indicates an impact to users' access to external applications.
▲ PREMIUM REPORTS	
Sign ins from IP addresses with suspicious activity	May indicate a successful sign in after a sustained intrusion attempt.
Sign ins from possibly infected devices	May indicate an attempt to sign in from possibly infected devices.
Irregular sign in activity	May indicate events anomalous to users' sign in patterns.
Users with anomalous sign in activity	Indicates users whose accounts may have been compromised.
Password reset activity	Provides a detailed view of password resets that occur in your organization.
Password reset registration activity	Provides a detailed view of password reset registrations that occur in your organization.
Groups activity	Provides an activity log to all group related activity in your directory
Application usage	Provides a usage summary for all SaaS applications integrated with your directory.

Sign Ins from Possibly Infected Devices   This is another good report to consider. How can Azure AD possibly know if a device may be infected? There is no Azure AD agent running on the machine to return a health status. You probably have read reports of Microsoft taking down large botnets. When Microsoft takes these down, it can gather information related to machines that communicate with the botnet servers and knows those devices are likely infected with malware. This is how it can flag machines as possibly infected: they were communicating as part of a botnet.

Irregular Sign In Activity   This report is based on the machine learning capabilities. Azure learns the typical working practices of people, and when sign-in activity deviates from that norm, it is flagged.

Sign Ins from Multiple Geographies   Azure understands where a sign-in is physically based. If it sees a sign-in from London, then three minutes later from New York, it knows there is no way to travel that distance. Azure then flags the sign-in as suspicious. It is possible to configure exceptions to the alerts—for example, you might not want to be alerted for rapid authentications from London and New York.

Note that some reports are open to any level of Azure AD, whereas others are Premium SKU only. The Premium SKU reports tend to rely more heavily on the machine learning–based algorithms, which involve a greater level of ongoing monitoring.

To enable a faster response, you can configure email alerts for certain types of activity. An email message is sent to administrators when more than 10 records occur in one of the reports.

The Bottom Line

Build an Active Directory architecture that integrates with Azure resources. For Azure resources to integrate with Active Directory, it is necessary for the resources using AD to be able to resolve AD DNS records and communicate via a number of ports to domain controllers. Virtual networks can be configured to use specific DNS servers. For VMs in the virtual network, that is configured via DHCP. Also, you can place domain controllers in Azure to enable local connectivity to domain controllers.

Master It Why is it important to define a separate AD site for Azure and a site link?

Understand the difference between Active Directory Domain Services and Azure AD. Active Directory provides a rich directory service set of capabilities with an X.500-based hierarchical structure. AD can be communicated with using protocols such as LDAP and primarily uses Kerberos for authentication. It allows machines to be joined to the directory and can enable rich policy deployment. Azure AD is primarily an identity system aimed at enabling identity across cloud-based systems. Therefore, it uses protocols designed for the Internet over HTTP and HTTPS. Azure AD's number-one feature is its ability to enable SSO for thousands of applications for an organization's users. Other key features include multifactor authentication and reporting.

Master It How does on-premises Active Directory link to Azure AD?

Chapter 8

Setting Up Replication, Backup, and Disaster Recovery

With Azure now tightly integrated with your on-premises environment, the next step is to ensure it is resilient to failure and highly available to the levels you need. Azure itself may be providing that resiliency and disaster recovery (DR) capability for services running on-premises. This chapter presents the various options available for services exclusively hosted in Azure and those in a hybrid environment.

In this chapter, you will learn to

- ◆ Plan your disaster recovery strategy

- ◆ Understand the sources that can be protected with Azure Site Recovery

The Need for Disaster Recovery and DR Basics

Modern organizations have a range of applications that are used internally, by partners, and by customers. These applications range from those that are nice to have but not essential to doing business, to those that quite literally shut down the company if they are not available. Even the briefest outage to these business-critical applications can cause organizations harm in multiple ways, including the following:

- ◆ Financial loss through not being able to perform normal business functions

- ◆ Damage to reputation through publicly visible outages that erode confidence in the organization for external parties

- ◆ Potential compliance gaps to regulatory requirements

In 2011, there were 14 natural disasters that caused $1 billion in damage; 2012 was not much better. A number of research studies have found that 96 percent of organizations are susceptible to damage from natural disasters but only 20 percent were actually concerned, and an even smaller number have taken or are taking steps to protect themselves in the event of a disaster. Often because the problem seems so great and there is no clear place to start, they take no action at all. The key to effective disaster protection is to break the challenges into realistic "bites" that can be tackled and enable protection one step at a time.

Planning for Disaster Recovery

Given the threat of damage, both from natural disasters and other sources, it is important to ensure that business-critical applications are always available, both within the primary datacenter through high-availability technologies, such as Failover Clustering in Windows, and to alternate locations through DR technologies. Often a single technology can be leveraged for high availability and DR. To provide DR, the data related to an application must be available in the alternate location, which means data replication. Also, there must be a means of running the application and connecting to it, which means compute and network resources.

It is important to understand which applications are critical to your organization. This can only be ascertained with the involvement of the business groups. Next, it is critical to understand the applications and services on which those business-critical applications depend. Protecting the business-critical application without its dependent applications would result in a nonfunctional solution in the event of a system outage or disaster scenario.

For example, consider a typical line-of-business (LOB) application that runs on several application servers. That application may also leverage a SQL database that runs on a separate infrastructure. It may publish services through a corporate reverse-proxy that is Internet facing. It may require Active Directory for authentication. For the LOB application to be functional, all those dependent services must be available. When planning for high availability and disaster recovery, you must protect applications and services that the target application depends on at the same or a higher protection level.

Consider also how the systems will be used in the event of a disaster. If the services are run by users who have no way to access the service, then that particular service has limited use. Plan for remote access for users in the event the primary facility is unavailable and users cannot make their way to the office. This could be a VPN-based solution, or you could use DirectAccess, which is part of Windows Enterprise Edition. Perhaps it's a virtual desktop running on-premises or in Azure through Virtual Desktop Infrastructure (VDI) or session virtualization technologies. The key point is to ensure users can do their jobs. Make sure that your systems can handle all employees (as opposed to the typical 5 percent) working remotely. Remember, the disaster may not affect your datacenter at all. Perhaps an ice storm has rendered travel to the workplace impossible. Be prepared for remote work for everyone (or a snow day and relaxing in front of a fire with a warm mug of cocoa).

There are many ways to provide resiliency and availability to services within a location and between locations; there is no single "best" technology. Rather, it is important to use the best availability technology for specific applications and services. Many availability solutions leverage the Failover Clustering feature that was covered in Chapter 7, "Extending AD to Azure and Azure AD." A cluster-enabled application is protected from the failure of a node and will either seamlessly transition to another node or restart on another node without any administrator intervention.

Traditionally, a physical location was the boundary for a cluster for a number of reasons:

Access to Shared Storage   Cluster applications historically required access to shared storage. SAN storage was connected using technologies such as iSCSI and Fibre Channel. Making shared storage available to a remote SAN was typically not possible due to the latencies introduced with remotely accessing storage, and having a remote site dependent on storage in a remote site defeated the point of having a multisite cluster, which was to protect from a site failure. The solution was to have SAN-level replication, which historically was not available or prohibitively expensive.

Intolerance of Latency   The nodes in a cluster required high-quality interconnection and were not tolerant of latency. This network was used for heartbeats between nodes to ensure that all nodes were healthy and available. Cluster resources required an IP address that could not be changed between locations. Most multisite environments used different IP networks at the different locations, which meant that using clustering in a multisite environment required complex VLAN configurations and geo-networks.

Access to the Quorum Disk   Clusters used a special quorum disk, which provided the foundation for partitioning protection. The quorum disk was a resource that always had to be available. Typically, that meant the cluster and the quorum disk had to reside in one physical location.

Windows Server 2008 and a new shift in many datacenter applications removed these barriers to multisite clusters. Key datacenter applications, such as SQL Server and Exchange, introduced options that did not require shared storage. Instead, they leveraged their own data replication technologies. Failover Clustering introduced changes that enabled multiple IP addresses to be allocated to a resource—whichever IP addresses were required for the site currently hosting the resource was used, which allowed access. Failover Clustering also enabled more flexible heartbeat configurations, which tolerated higher latency networks. Reliance on a quorum disk was removed, and additional quorum models based on number of nodes were offered. Even a file share, which could be located at a third site, was allowed. The ability to run clusters over multiple locations without shared storage enabled certain DR options that will be discussed later in this chapter.

USING CLUSTERING IN AZURE

Failover Clustering can be used in Azure. However, as of this writing, because each vmNIC has only a single IP address, you must take some additional steps for the cluster to function correctly. It is also possible to have a cluster stretch on-premises to Azure; some nodes are on-premises, whereas others run in Azure. In general, the normal clustering processes can be used. Here are some caveats:

- Use a file share witness, not a disk witness.

- Create a fake IP address for the Azure side of the network. This is because in Azure virtual networks, all IP addresses are assigned via DHCP. The cluster IP address given is actually the same IP address as one of the hosts in the cluster on the Azure side. You can send traffic into an Azure VM only via two IP addresses: (1) the IP address assigned by the Azure infrastructure to the VM, and (2) at most one VIP that is a load-balanced IP.

  Because the cluster will be used for a workload—for example, SQL Server AlwaysOn—it's important that the SQL Server IP address be contacted rather than the cluster IP, which is why the cluster on the Azure side is given the fake, unusable address.

- The cluster IP address for the on-premises side should be a valid IP address and can be static or dynamically assigned.

Realize that the IP address for the Azure side is useless; it is there only to satisfy the need for an IP address. That Azure-side address enables the cluster name to come online. To manage the cluster from the Azure side in the event of a failover, you will need to be connected to the actual cluster node and launch Failover Cluster Manager.

After you've created a cluster as you normally would, follow these steps:

1. Open Failover Cluster Manager.

2. Select the cluster, and in the details, look at Cluster Core Resources.

3. Right-click the IP address for the Azure network, and select Properties.

4. Rename it to Azure Dummy 169.254.1.1 in the General tab.

5. Select the Advanced Policies tab and ensure only the Azure nodes are selected as possible owners; then click OK.

6. You will now force this IP address to 169.254.1.1. If it's in the actual network, do not perform any checks.

This can be done using PowerShell. Use the following code; be sure to enter it on one line without any breaks:

```
Get-ClusterResource "Azure Dummy 169.254.1.1" | Set-ClusterParameter
-Multiple @{"Address"="169.254.1.1";"SubnetMask"="255.255.0.0";
"Network"="Cluster Network 1";"OverrideAddressMatch"=1;"EnableDHCP"=0}
```

7. For the other IP address (the on-premises valid IP address), right-click and select Properties.

8. Select the Advanced Policies tab and ensure only the on-premises cluster nodes are selected as possible owners, and click OK.

The cluster should now be good to go!

There are some specific configurations for certain services. One example is SQL Server; Microsoft has a detailed paper on clustering SQL in Azure available here:

http://msdn.microsoft.com/en-us/library/dn425027.aspx

When you are designing a DR solution, typically you can choose any of the many options available. Each offers different levels of recoverability. You will need to determine a recovery point objective (RPO), which is the point you wish to recover to in the event of a disaster. For example, you can specify that only 30 minutes of data should be lost. You also will need to determine a recovery time objective (RTO), which is how quickly you need to be running in the event of a disaster. Should your systems be available within 4 hours in the event of a disaster? You can specify that. It's important to understand the RPO and RTO requirements for each of your systems when designing your DR solution. Different systems will likely have different requirements.

It is important to be realistic about the capabilities of your organization. Alternatives to implementing new DR solutions for services may be to host the service in a public cloud infrastructure; this solution provides site resiliency as part of the service. Using the public cloud as the DR location can also be an option.

Create detailed processes for use in the event of a disaster to facilitate the failover, and update those processes any time a system changes or a new system is added. DR tests should be performed at least every six months. Do not assume any amount of IT knowledge in your instructions; IT personnel may not be available in the event of a disaster.

There are fundamentally three types of disaster recovery:

Planned "Look, a storm is coming. Let's move our production workloads to the DR location now and notify our users to follow the DR processes for service access."

In your DR process there should be no unplanned data loss or unplanned outage. Note I am saying *no unplanned*. There may be data loss and there may be an outage, but this would be known in advance and accepted as part of the failover per the RPO and RTO the recovery was designed to meet.

Unplanned "Where did that storm come from? And where has our datacenter gone? Didn't it used to be where that big lake is? Damn."

In an unplanned DR, steps could not be taken ahead of the disaster. There could be additional data loss and a longer outage period depending on the replication in place and the processes followed. However, even in an unplanned disaster if your protection was designed correctly, your outage window and data loss should still be within the RPO and RTO for unplanned disasters.

Test "Let's test a failover process in case there is a storm one day. Just make sure you don't affect production."

The key point in a test is that the production systems should not be impacted in any way, nor should the replication of data to the DR location from production be paused or affected. Typically, this means clones of the DR systems are created and attached to separate networks to enable the failover process to be tested without affecting production.

Of those three types, which is the most important? Test!

Regardless of how good your planning is, you have to test the failover process—and test it regularly—perhaps a full test every 6 months. I know some companies that alternate the "primary" location and run that way for 6 months. It's the perfect way to identify any problems or systems that have been omitted from the DR plan. Remember, your DR plan will be a living document that will constantly change as the systems in your organization change and the capabilities of those systems change. It is critical that, as part of your change control process, you include a step that identifies whether the DR plan should be updated to reflect the change. You don't want to find problems in your DR in the event of an actual disaster: it will be too late.

Asynchronous vs. Synchronous Replication

As discussed earlier in this chapter, the core of disaster recovery requires having the application data available in the DR location. This may require the data to be stored somewhere that is available to both locations such as in the public cloud, but more commonly, it requires the data to be stored in both locations. It further requires that the replication technologies used to keep the replica copy of the data be synchronized with the primary (live) copy of the data.

The mode of the replication can be either asynchronous or synchronous. Asynchronous mode allows transactions to be committed on the primary before the transaction has been sent to the replicas or has been acknowledged. The exact mechanism for asynchronous replication differs, but the key point is that the primary source can carry on working independently of the replica receiving and acknowledging the data. This gives the best performance on the primary replica, although there is always a slight risk of data loss in a failure situation as data is committed on the primary before it's committed—or potentially even sent—to the replica.

Synchronous mode ensures no transactions are committed on the primary until they are acknowledged on the replica, thus ensuring no risk of data loss. This does incur some performance impact due to the additional delay caused by waiting for the acknowledgments from the replica. The higher the latency between the primary and the replica, the greater the performance impact.

Nearly every type of cross-site replication leverages asynchronous as the replication type because of the performance impact synchronous replication imposes across high-latency links. Synchronous replication is typically reserved for replication within a datacenter for highly critical data that cannot risk any kind of data loss.

SQL Server is a good example of a workload that leverages both asynchronous and synchronous replication. Its AlwaysOn technology provides replication of SQL databases between a primary replica and one or more secondary replicas. Within a datacenter, synchronous AlwaysOn replication may be used, but between locations, the asynchronous AlwaysOn replication is typically used. SQL AlwaysOn allows switching between replication types, which opens up some interesting failover solutions. You can run in asynchronous under normal operating conditions but switch to synchronous prior to failover to ensure no data loss.

Many storage solutions, such as SANs, offer replication at a storage level from one SAN to another. Very high-end SANs may offer a synchronous replication capability; however, this is typically expensive and is specific to the type of SAN used. The benefit of using SAN-level replication (where available) is that a cluster can use the SAN storage in multiple locations as a single logical storage device. This enables clusters to span multiple locations with "shared" storage. Some very large organizations leverage this type of SAN replication for their tier 1 workloads.

Planning for Service Protection

Later in this chapter, I will talk about replicating OS instances from on-premises to Azure. This works for Hyper-V VMs, VMware VMs, physical systems, and more. All can be replicated to an Azure VM. However, just because the capability exists does not mean that it should be your first choice. Typically, there are several ways to make a service highly available and replicate its data. Here is a list of various options:

◆ Native application replication or multimaster solution

◆ Native application DR capability to a hot or warm standby

◆ OS/guest-level replication using an agent in the OS that captures changes to disk and replicates those changes to a target system

◆ Replication that operates at the hypervisor level (Hyper-V Replica), captures changes to virtual storage, and applies those changes to a replica platform

◆ Storage-level replication, such as found in SANs, or a solution that replicates to Azure, such as StorSimple

◆ Restoring a backup

◆ No plan at all, thus leaving the industry in disgrace if a failure ever occurs

Not surprisingly, the list is in order of preference, and you will not pick one solution. Do not settle on the lowest common denominator that could be used for every workload you have. If you do, most likely you will settle at OS- or hypervisor-level replication. Instead, pick the highest option available for the workload. Your first instinct might tell you that this is not a good idea and that it will complicate your failover processes. A failover that involves multiple technologies all being used together (as you'll learn later in this chapter) employs orchestration technologies that enable a big red button that you can press and perform the failover using many different technologies. It's more important to provide the best possible protection for workloads. This is probably best understood by looking at some examples:

Microsoft Exchange Microsoft Exchange is a distributed architecture service consisting of various roles that deliver the complete service, including the mailbox servers that store the email messages. Exchange uses database availability groups (DAGs); mailbox servers are grouped together. Mailbox databases (which store emails) are replicated between certain mailbox servers within the DAG. This is an example of a native application replication capability. The benefit over OS, hypervisor, or storage replication is that when a mailbox server fails, the other mailbox servers know about the server failure. Although they have a replica of the mailbox database, they will take additional actions, such as contacting the hub transport servers (which mail routes through) to check if any messages have been lost. If lost messages are discovered, they are fetched from the hub transports that cache emails for a period of time specifically so they can be restored in the event a mailbox server fails. Restoring these messages would not be possible for a nonapplication-aware recovery solution.

SQL Server SQL Server is another example. SQL Server has AlwaysOn, which enables both asynchronous and synchronous replication. It is an application-aware replication that enables various recovery and additional usability features beyond a non-OS-aware method. If you do decide to use a hypervisor replication feature, you should not use SQL replication technologies. The use of both is not supported, as documented by Microsoft here:

http://support.microsoft.com/kb/956893

If you decide to use a Hyper-V Replica to replicate a VM running SQL Server—whether to another Hyper-V server or to Azure—it's important that all the disks of the VM be replicated at the same point in time. You don't want the log disk to replicate at a different time than the database disk, as this would cause inconsistencies in a recovery. You therefore need to run on write order preservation across disks. You can set this via PowerShell with the -EnableWriteOrderPreservationAcrossDisks 1 parameter:

```
Set-VMReplication -VMName <vm-name> -EnableWriteOrderPreservationAcrossDisks
```

Active Directory Active Directory has its own multimaster replication. File services have Distributed File System Replication.

I hope the point is clear. If the application or service has its own native replication solution, always use that first; it's going to give the most resiliency. It is best illustrated using SQL Server, but it would equally apply to any application-aware replication or high-availability capability.

Figure 8.1 shows an example of replication from on-premises to Azure, a very common DR approach. Notice that SQL Server is running in a VM on-premises and in Azure. The application has to be running on the source and on the target to facilitate the application-aware replication.

Depending on the application, this may mean paying for two licenses: one for the on-premises instance of the application and one for the Azure instance. This is the case for SQL Server, which allows passive failover instances provided the SQL licenses are covered by Software Assurance per the SQL Server Licensing Guide at `http://go.microsoft.com/fwlink/?LinkId=230678` for on-premises DR but not for replication to Azure. Also note the Azure VM is running and is incurring cost based on the size of the VM.

FIGURE 8.1
Replication using application functionality

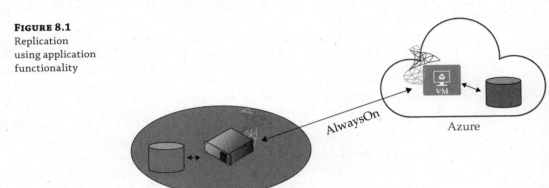

Figure 8.2 shows an example of the same scenario, but this time a hypervisor replication technology is being used. The illustration would also apply to the Azure Site Recovery Scout technology, which is covered later in the chapter. Notice that this time there is no VM running in Azure—only storage is used. In the event of a failover, a VM is created and attached to the storage. This is because the replication is external to the application. In this case, the replication is even external to the OS; no application or OS is needed on the target. You only pay for the VM in Azure in the event of an actual failure (which will hopefully never happen) and during the routine testing (which you are doing, right?). There is the cost of the Azure storage, but this is typically very low.

FIGURE 8.2
Replication using hypervisor/external functionality

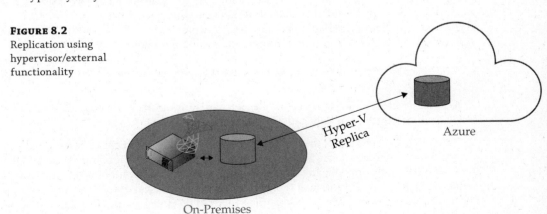

This difference could add up to a lot of money, especially if Azure is being used as DR for a large number of VMs. Having the VMs running to use application replication and high availability means more cost. Using an external replication means the VM does not need to be running. It's a trade-off: the highest level of protection and functionality against cost. For some workloads, those that are most critical and require the highest level of protection and integrity, application methods might be used, and the additional cost might be acceptable. For less critical workloads, you might use the cheaper methods that don't require a VM to be running. Basically, try to use the best possible/least costly method for each workload.

Remember that this approach is not just for on-premises to Azure, but also for one Azure region to another Azure region. Although you want to provide protection against an Azure region failure, that's not likely to happen. Still, you need to consider how you will ensure the availability of your services. But doesn't Microsoft already do this for your IaaS services in Azure? Yes and no—but mostly no—and what they do provide may not meet your requirements.

Let's start smaller. What happens if a server, rack, or cluster fails in an Azure datacenter? Essentially, the Azure service healing will take care of reprovisioning the VM on another host. Although there is no firm time frame for reprovisioning, it typically happens in a few minutes. No action is required on your part.

Now consider what happens when an entire Azure region goes down. Obviously, this would be a huge outage, and thus far, it has never happened. But you should consider it as a possibility. In Chapter 3, "Customizing VM Storage," I covered the types of storage replication that are available. The only type that provides protection from an Azure region failure is geo-redundant. If you have data or VMs that you want Azure to replicate to its partner region, ensure the data or VM is stored in an account that is configured as geo-redundant. Data is synchronized asynchronously, and there can be up to a 15-minute delay. This means that the RPO for Azure Geo-redundant Storage is 15 minutes. If the possibility of losing 15 minutes of data is not acceptable, you need to use another method of data replication.

If the storage replicated contains the virtual hard drives for your virtual machines, what would happen in the event of an Azure region failure? The Geo-redundant Storage account would become active in the paired region, thus allowing the content to be accessed. The VHDs for the virtual machines would be available to be used by VMs. All the other tasks to make a VM available would need to be done. These include the following:

- Creating virtual networks

- Enabling Azure to on-premises connectivity

- Creating cloud services in the target region

- Creating the VMs in the virtual networks and cloud services along with any required endpoints.

- Connecting the new VMs to the VHDs in the geo-replicated storage account.

- Ensuring that the new VM is connected to the existing storage and is in the same OS instance

- Configuring any other load balancing or configurations required

This stresses the importance of not creating VMs that you care about via the portal, as there is no consistent way to recreate the VM in the event of a disaster without going back into the portal and manually creating the VM. Imagine doing this for a hundred VMs! If you create services in Azure using a provisioning process that stores the configurations used in the creation, then in the event of a disaster, that same provisioning process can be re-executed in a DR mode that recreates all the services and VMs but attaches to existing storage instead of creating new disks. If you intend to use the replicated storage in your DR plan, you need to ensure you have the process in place to recreate your critical services in the event of an Azure region disaster.

Using the Azure storage replication to provide protection might not be ideal for some organizations or specific workloads. The fact that up to 15 minutes of data may be lost in any failover might be unacceptable. Then, once you notice that the failure has occurred, additional downtime is incurred while processes are run on the paired datacenter to recreate services. Recovery time, availability of services, and data integrity may be insufficient, which means you are back to the same logic as providing protection for on-premises workloads. Is there an application-level replication, for example SQL AlwaysOn, between Azure regions? You could create domain controllers in two Azure regions and use multimaster replication to keep them synchronized and so on. Remember that just because Azure has Geo-redundant Storage does not mean you have to use it for your protection. Instead, you can use locally redundant storage in each region, create VMs in each region, and then use application or other methods to synchronize and fail over, all within your own control.

My personal recommendation? Carefully consider taking this approach if you have critical services in Azure and manage your own replication and failover rather than relying on the Azure failover. Once again, it will cost more, since the primary and the failover VMs are running in both regions, but you have the benefit of control over when you fail over. For Microsoft to deem a region down, there would have to be a huge problem, and given the impact taking down a region would have on customers, this would not be Microsoft's first course of action. Instead, they will try to resolve the problem. During this time, your service may be affected. If you are managing your own replication and failover, you can choose to fail over at any time.

Orchestrating Failover with Azure Site Recovery

I have advocated using the best possible technology for the replication of your workloads. This means you may be using combinations of technologies: SQL AlwaysOn, multiple domain controllers, hypervisor replication such as Hyper-V Replica, and OS replication such as InMage Scout. If this is an on-premises to on-premises failover, it may also involve SAN failovers. Employing a failover using different technologies also means ensuring failover occurs in a specific order. For example, the SQL database needs to fail over before failing over the application workloads, and so on. There might also be a need to run scripts at certain points.

One option would be to fail over manually, but this goes against a key principle that the DR process should be as simple as possible. Remember, a disaster has happened; the IT team might not be available. Think big red button. An option to automate would use a script, such as something created with PowerShell, which would be a good option. PowerShell can work with almost any product. This, however, raises another question: where does the PowerShell run during the disaster? Consider, too, the amount of work involved in the creation and maintenance of the script, especially given the various technologies and the need to fail services over in a specific order—and you must enable options, such as testing failover.

Another option would be to use a technology such as System Center Orchestrator to orchestrate failover, but once again, there would be a big emphasis on creating complicated runbooks. Microsoft released some Hyper-V Replica runbooks that leverage System Center Orchestrator to enable an orchestrated failover process. They are available here:

```
http://blogs.technet.com/b/privatecloud/archive/2013/02/11/automation-
orchestrating-hyper-v-replica-with-system-center-for-planned-failover.aspx
```

Though a nice solution, the runbooks are focused on Windows Server 2012 and have not been updated for Windows Server 2012 R2. But if you wish to go this route, they're a great starting point.

ASR Version 1, Hyper-V Recovery Manager

This section covers the Azure Site Recovery solution, which enables not only the orchestration of failovers, but also the actual replication of data and applications. However, before I cover that functionality, I want to first cover how it started and then describe how it has evolved to where it is today.

Hyper-V introduced a replication technology called Hyper-V Replica in Windows Server 2012. This enables an asynchronous replication of Hyper-V VM virtual hard disks between two Hyper-V servers. In Windows Server 2012, the frequency was fixed at 5 minutes, but in Windows Server 2012 R2, the frequency could be configured as 30 seconds, 5 minutes, or 15 minutes. Additionally Hyper-V Replica can be extended so the replica VM has its own replica to another Hyper-V server, essentially a replica of the replica, which can replicate every 5 or 15 minutes. This is shown in Figure 8.3. In addition to the replication, Hyper-V Replica also enables alternate IP information to be injected into the replica VM in the event of a failover. This ability is useful when you consider that most DR locations will be using a different IP subnet, which means changing the VM's IP address during a failover enables the VM to function correctly without manual changes being required.

FIGURE 8.3
Hyper-V Replica in extended replica

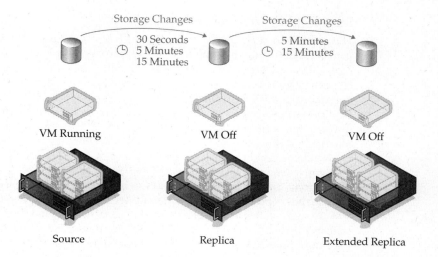

Hyper-V Replica provides the technology to replicate Hyper-V VMs, but you still must perform the initial configuration, maintain the failover process, and then perform the failover in the event of a disaster. Microsoft released an Azure-based solution, Hyper-V Recovery Manager (HRM), which runs as a service in Azure and communicates to on-premises Hyper-V servers via System Center Virtual Machine Manager (SCVMM), which would run in both the primary and DR locations. No VM data replicates to Azure. HRM is an orchestration manager and enables the desired "red button" effect. It is accessed through an Azure website and enables recovery plans to be created. Specific sets of VMs can be failed over in desired order, and even scripts that are hosted in libraries on the on-premises SCVMM servers can be run. Figure 8.4 shows this option. Notice that although SCVMM communicates to the Azure service, the actual replication of VMs is still directly between the on-premises locations and not via Azure. HRM is still very much alive and is one of the technologies that are part of Azure Site Recovery.

FIGURE 8.4
Hyper-V Recovery
Manager architecture

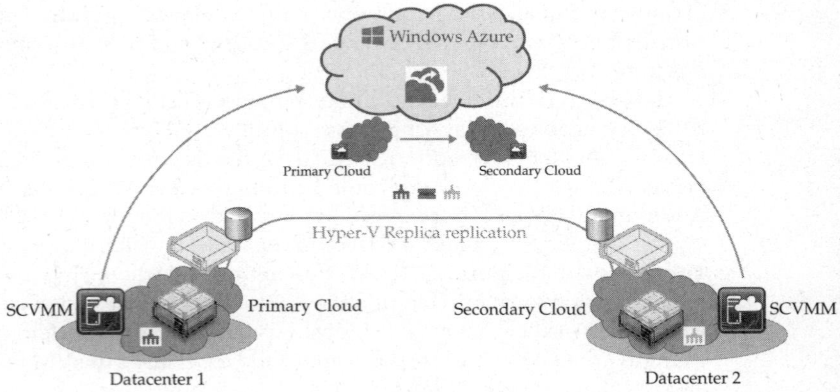

Replicating to Azure with ASR

The ability to orchestrate the failover of VMs between Hyper-V instances on-premises is valuable, but the number-one request I hear from customers is for the ability to replicate to Azure. This is logical, since Azure uses Hyper-V. So, how hard can it possibly be to replicate Hyper-V VMs to Azure? There are many factors to consider, but this capability is now available. You can replicate VMs from an on-premises Hyper-V server to Azure using the Hyper-V Replica technology, and of course, you have the ability to fail those VMs back. At the time of the introduction of the ability to replicate Hyper-V VMs to Azure, the Azure recovery service was renamed to Azure Site Recovery (ASR). HRM technology became one of the channels available to provide protection and orchestration through ASR. The ability to replicate from Hyper-V to Azure leverages the same Hyper-V Replica technology used for on-premises to Azure. The replication is transparent to the guest OS, but things work differently on the Azure side.

Like the on-premises Hyper-V Replica technology, changes to the virtual hard disks of the VM are replicated to Azure at a defined interval. The option for periodic application-consistent snapshots is available. As part of the configuration of the Azure-targeted HRM, networks in the Azure Virtual Network are selected to map to on-premises virtual networks. This enables

VMs in Azure to get the required IP connectivity. No VM is created in Azure until a failover is performed. When a VM is created during a failover, the VM automatically gets an IP address for its new virtual NIC from whatever virtual subnet it has been mapped to. This protection is shown in Figure 8.5.

FIGURE 8.5
Hyper-V Replica to
Azure architecture

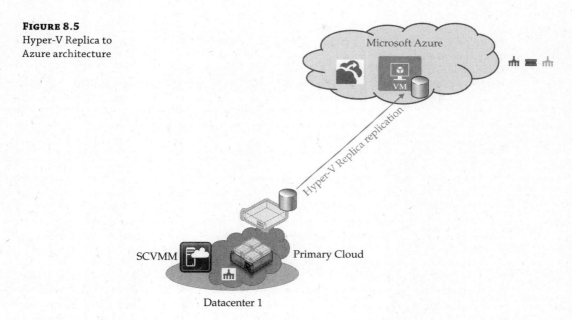

Note that as shown in Figure 8.5, SCVMM is used for the management of the replication; however, Microsoft also has a solution targeted at smaller locations to enable direct replication from Hyper-V servers to Azure without requiring SCVMM. More information on this option is available here:

```
https://weblogs.asp.net/scottgu/azure-premium-storage-remoteapp-sql-database-
update-live-media-streaming-search-and-more
```

What is different with Hyper-V Replica to Azure is that there is no VM in Azure during the normal protection of a VM. Instead, the VHD files for the VM are stored in an Azure storage account (which must be configured as geo-redundant), and the Hyper-V Replica Log (HRL) files are sent from on-premises to the storage account at the configured interval. There is a task in Azure that asynchronously takes the HRL files and applies the changes into the VHD. A separate task periodically applies and cleans up the HRL files and runs approximately once an hour. Therefore, the HRL files have been applied but not cleaned up *or* have not been applied yet. This is different from on-premises Hyper-V Replica, where the HRL files are immediately applied to the target VHD. If you examine the Azure storage account that is the target for a replica, you can see the VHD and a number of HRL files. Figure 8.6 shows an example storage account that contains a replicated Hyper-V VM. Note that in the event of a failover to Azure, the HRL files are immediately applied as part of the failover. Look at the first characters of each filename. Notice most start with `hrl/`. These are the log files. At the bottom is the VHD file. Ignore the `prunelock` and `syncsessionlock` files at the top of the figure. These are used by the Azure protection service for synchronization and are visible only because there is no hidden file concept in Azure.

FIGURE 8.6

Example content of container in Azure storage account

8822520688643174620-202009-905241119147727871

NAME	URL	LAST MODIFIED	SIZE
905241119147727871-prunelock	https://savtechstoreeastus.blob.co	12/25/2014 6:16:36 AM	512 B
905241119147727871-syncsessionlock	https://savtechstoreeastus.blob.co	7/24/2014 6:14:48 PM	512 B
hrl/b0a72979-1200-4769-87bc-544c649df493_83f8638b-8dca-4152-9eda-2ca8b33...	https://savtechstoreeastus.blob.co	12/25/2014 6:06:54 AM	1.2 MB
hrl/b0a72979-1200-4769-87bc-544c649df493_83f8638b-8dca-4152-9eda-2ca8b33...	https://savtechstoreeastus.blob.co	12/25/2014 4:22:09 AM	2.17 MB
hrl/b0a72979-1200-4769-87bc-544c649df493_83f8638b-8dca-4152-9eda-2ca8b33...	https://savtechstoreeastus.blob.co	12/25/2014 5:23:15 AM	70.04 MB
hrl/b0a72979-1200-4769-87bc-544c649df493_83f8638b-8dca-4152-9eda-2ca8b33...	https://savtechstoreeastus.blob.co	12/25/2014 2:06:55 AM	1.27 MB
hrl/b0a72979-1200-4769-87bc-544c649df493_83f8638b-8dca-4152-9eda-2ca8b33...	https://savtechstoreeastus.blob.co	12/25/2014 5:36:52 AM	1.55 MB
hrl/b0a72979-1200-4769-87bc-544c649df493_83f8638b-8dca-4152-9eda-2ca8b33...	https://savtechstoreeastus.blob.co	12/25/2014 5:51:55 AM	1.43 MB
hrl/b0a72979-1200-4769-87bc-544c649df493_83f8638b-8dca-4152-9eda-2ca8b33...	https://savtechstoreeastus.blob.co	12/25/2014 3:06:58 AM	1.45 MB
hrl/b0a72979-1200-4769-87bc-544c649df493_83f8638b-8dca-4152-9eda-2ca8b33...	https://savtechstoreeastus.blob.co	12/25/2014 4:06:57 AM	1.35 MB
hrl/b0a72979-1200-4769-87bc-544c649df493_83f8638b-8dca-4152-9eda-2ca8b33...	https://savtechstoreeastus.blob.co	12/25/2014 1:06:55 AM	1.24 MB
vhd/b0a72979-1200-4769-87bc-544c649df493_83f8638b-8dca-4152-9eda-2ca8b3...	https://savtechstoreeastus.blob.co	12/25/2014 6:07:44 AM	127 GB

In the event of a failover to Azure, a VM is created and attached to the storage. It is at this point you start paying for the provisioned VM. Once a VM has failed over, the Azure replication is not reversed. There is no ongoing replication back to on-premises. It is for this reason that the VM storage must be stored in Geo-redundant Storage; without geo-redundancy, there is no way to ensure a level of protection from failure. When the VM is ready to fail back to on-premises from Azure, a delta resynchronization occurs when the Optimized For Low Downtime option is selected. Alternatively, an Optimized For Resources option is available that would incur greater downtime. A task is run to bring the on-premises version of the VM up to date, and then the VM is stopped in Azure. Another resynchronization is performed to capture any final changes, and then the on-premises VM is started and the VM in Azure is deleted. At this point, the replication once again runs from on-premises to the Azure storage account.

It is important to note that, in the event of a failover, the VM is running in Azure. The source VM must fit within the capability profile of an Azure VM. The capability profile is documented here:

```
http://msdn.microsoft.com/en-us/library/dn469078.aspx
```

The following are some key characteristics as of this writing, but check the Microsoft page often as I suspect these will change over time. Azure VMs can be expected to support more features such as VHDX and Generation 2 VMs.

◆ The guest OS must be 64 bit and supported on Azure.

◆ The OS disk must be between 20 MB and 127 GB. (It can be a dynamic disk; it will be converted on the Azure side to a fixed size.)

- ◆ The number of data disks must fit based on the compute size of the VM, and each disk must be between 20 MB and 1,023 GB.

- ◆ The connection must be made through a single NIC and a single IP.

- ◆ The VM must be a Generation 1 VM.

It's important to consider these requirements when deploying to on-premises if you intend to protect them with ASR. The biggest customer problems I have seen are using VHDX and Generation 2 VMs; today, neither will work in Azure, but by the time you read this, a conversion may be in place.

Just like the orchestration between on-premises locations with the first version of HRM, when protecting Hyper-V VMs to Azure with ASR, you create a recovery plan. Include the various groups of VMs and the order of the failover, in addition to the ability to run PowerShell through integration with Azure Automation. (I will touch on this in more detail later in this chapter.)

OS-Level Replication with InMage Scout

InMage Scout is a recent Microsoft acquisition. It has been integrated into Azure Site Recovery as another available channel to enable replication, and ultimately disaster recovery, for additional workloads. InMage Scout uses an agent, the Mobility Service, running within the source OS that needs to be replicated. The agent captures all write-to-disk actions while still in the source OS's memory. It then fractures the write request to send the request to the local InMage Scout Process Server, after which the write continues to disk. Capturing the write in memory and sending it to another system minimizes any additional overhead on the source OS.

The InMage Scout Process Server does all the heavy lifting related to compressing, deduplicating, and encrypting the data, which it then sends over the network to its reciprocal server at the target location, the InMage Scout Master Target Server. The data is sent near-synchronously, which means it isn't done at the same time the write occurs on the local disk—which would affect the performance of the primary workload—but it also isn't sent at some scheduled interval, such as every 5 minutes. Instead, the data is sent as quickly as possible, which means perhaps a second of latency depending on network conditions.

When the InMage Scout Master Target Server receives the data, it then performs the writes to the target replica storage. The way this works is the Master Target is a virtual machine (VM); the disks for all the target replica VMs are attached to this Master Target VM, which enables it to perform all the required disk writes. In the event of an actual failover, those virtual disks are disconnected from the Master Target Server and attached to the actual replica VMs, which are then created and started. The actual target VMs aren't running during replication because the disks aren't even attached to the target VMs. There's also an InMage Scout Configuration Server that provides a centralized management point for the entire solution and the point of entry for management and failover operations.

The InMage Scout Process Server runs on Windows Server 2012 and can run as a physical or virtual instance. A physical instance is typically used for larger-scale environments. The InMage Scout Master Target Server is always a VM because it needs to have the virtual hard drives attached for all the VMs that are being replicated to. When replicating to Azure, the InMage Scout Master Target Server is an Azure IaaS VM that is still attached to the disks for the replica VMs.

Figure 8.7 shows the various components working together; the key for the figure follows.

1. These are the workloads being migrated—for example, VMs running on VMware. Inside the OS instances being migrated is the Mobility Service, which captures the changes to the filesystem that are sent to the Process Server.

2. The Process Server receives the changes to the filesystem, caches them, and then forwards them to the Master Target over a secure channel.

3. Configuration Sever is the centralized management component that runs in the customer's Azure subscription. This communicates with all other roles to control configuration via HTTPS. (The other roles poll the Configuration Server.)

4. The Master Target runs in your Azure subscription as a virtual machine. It receives the changes to OS instances being migrated and writes those changes to virtual hard disks that are attached to the Master Target. At migration time, the disks are attached to the VMs that will run the workload in Azure.

5. The Azure Multi-tenant portal is used for the configuration that runs outside of your Azure subscription but communicates to your Configuration Server instance.

FIGURE 8.7
InMage Scout
components

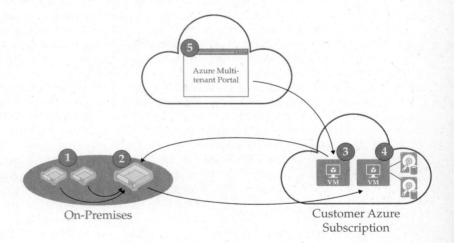

On-Premises   Customer Azure
                           Subscription

Both Windows and Linux are supported. Because the agent runs within the OS being replicated, that source OS can be a physical or virtual instance. The replication process is completely independent of any hardware or hypervisor. The InMage Scout channel enables many options, which include the following:

◆ On-premises VMware to on-premises VMware replication

◆ On-premises VMware to Azure

◆ On-premises physical systems to Azure

I expect this list to grow over time to basically anything to anything.

Other Supported Technologies

Remember the key point of replication and DR: where possible, leverage native application capabilities before OS or hypervisor replication. So far, all the ASR channels I've covered have operated at the hypervisor or OS level. ASR also supports management of SQL Server AlwaysOn replication. This enables your recovery plan to also manage the failover of an application-level SQL Server AlwaysOn protected database.

ASR also includes integration with many of the major SAN vendors. See the Microsoft announcement here:

```
http://azure.microsoft.com/blog/2014/10/27/san-replication-based-enterprise-
grade-disaster-recovery-with-asr-and-system-center/
```

This integration consists of the orchestration of the SAN-based replication and failover using the SAN's own native replication technologies for a SAN-to-SAN environment. This doesn't replicate data to Azure but instead provides another integration with Azure Site Recovery to orchestrate the SAN portion of a DR failover. It also helps with the initial and ongoing replication configuration. This is achieved through SMI-S integration, which is managed through System Center Virtual Machine Manager.

Finally, ASR integrates with Azure Automation. Azure Automation is the ability to run PowerShell workflows in Azure through the creation of runbooks. (I will cover runbooks in Chapter 11, "Completing Your Azure Environment.") Through PowerShell, it is possible to perform almost any action. The integration with Azure Automation can be embedded in your recovery plans, along with the other channels. Through ASR, it is possible to control almost anything, although you must create the Azure Automation runbooks.

As part of an Azure Site Recovery recovery plan, items such as virtual machine failover (from any hypervisor with a mixture of Hyper-V Replica and InMage Scout channels), SQL Server database failover, SAN failover, and Azure Automation (read anything else) can all be orchestrated. This single recovery plan becomes your big red button. The recovery plans can be run in planned, unplanned, and test modes. Visit the Microsoft official ASR page:

```
http://azure.microsoft.com/en-us/services/site-recovery/
```

Figure 8.8 shows a high-level view of the capabilities of ASR.

FIGURE 8.8
The different channels of ASR

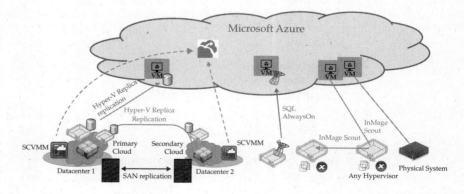

Enabling Hyper-V VM Protection to Azure with ASR

Many channels are available with ASR. You can provide protection for the various workloads supported. In this section, I will walk you through enabling protection of an on-premises Hyper-V VM to Azure using ASR. Due to space constraints, I will not go into detail on each step; my goal is to explain the process. Each of the different channels uses a similar method for configuration. The Azure portal does a great job of walking you step-by-step through the actions required. Additionally, Microsoft has great documentation available at these sites:

http://azure.microsoft.com/en-us/documentation/articles/hyper-v-recovery-manager-azure/

http://blogs.technet.com/b/systemcenter/archive/2014/07/01/microsoft-azure-site-recovery-your-dr-site-in-microsoft-azure.aspx

1. In the Azure portal, create a new Site Recovery Vault (New ➤ Recovery Services ➤ Site Recovery Vault). Follow the onscreen prompts to configure a name. Select the new vault, and then review the list of types of recovery available in the Setup Recover drop-down list box. Select the option "Between an on-premises Hyper-V site and Microsoft Azure," as shown in Figure 8.9.

2. A Registration key file is generated through the portal, which is valid for 5 days. Copy the registration file to the SCVMM server.

3. Once you select a recovery option, the steps required to implement your solution are displayed. Follow the steps by clicking the links under each step. They will guide you through importing the CERT file into Azure (which enables secure communication between Azure and SCVMM), downloading, and installing the Azure Site Recovery Provider on the SCVMM server (VMMASRProvider_x64.exe). Note that you must stop the VMM service before installation. (System Center Virtual Machine Manager is the service name.) All settings are stored in Registry locations: HKEY_LOCAL_MACHINE\ SOFTWARE\Microsoft\Hyper-V Recovery Manager and HKEY_LOCAL_MACHINE\ SOFTWARE\Microsoft\Microsoft System Center Virtual Machine Manager Server\DRAdapter. (You will have to delete both to wipe the configuration.) During the installation of the ASR provider, you will select the registration key file that you copied to the SCVMM server earlier. The SCVMM server will then register with the Azure portal. (The SCVMM server will be available on the Resources tab on the Recovery Vault screen.) Once this is complete, there will be a connection between SCVMM and Azure.

4. The next step is performed from the dashboard. Download and install the Microsoft Azure Recovery Services Agent, and install it on the Hyper-V hosts that will replicate to Azure (MARSAgentInstaller.exe).

5. Your environment is ready to replicate VMs to Azure, so the specific SCVMM clouds to be protected must be selected. Back on the site recovery vault dashboard (the page with all the steps), select Set Up Protection For VMM Clouds From Step 4. Select the cloud you want to protect, and then select Configure Protection Settings. Notice that Azure knows all the clouds in SCVMM, and specific clouds can be selected.

6. Select Microsoft Azure as the target and configure accordingly. (Only geo-replicated storage accounts are available as targets.) When you're finished, click Save. Note that this does not start the replication. It does enable the configuration so you can replicate. After the save, a job is created, and the configuration is performed on SCVMM and in Azure.

7. Optionally, you can map networks between on-premises and Azure. I recommend you do because it allows ASR to place VMs in the correct network and Azure cloud services during failover. The subnet names between your SCVMM logical network and Azure virtual networks must match or you will get a warning and the first subnet on the network will be used. Select the network, as shown in Figure 8.10. In this example, the on-premise subnet is named Lab 173_0, so I created a subnet in my virtual network to match.

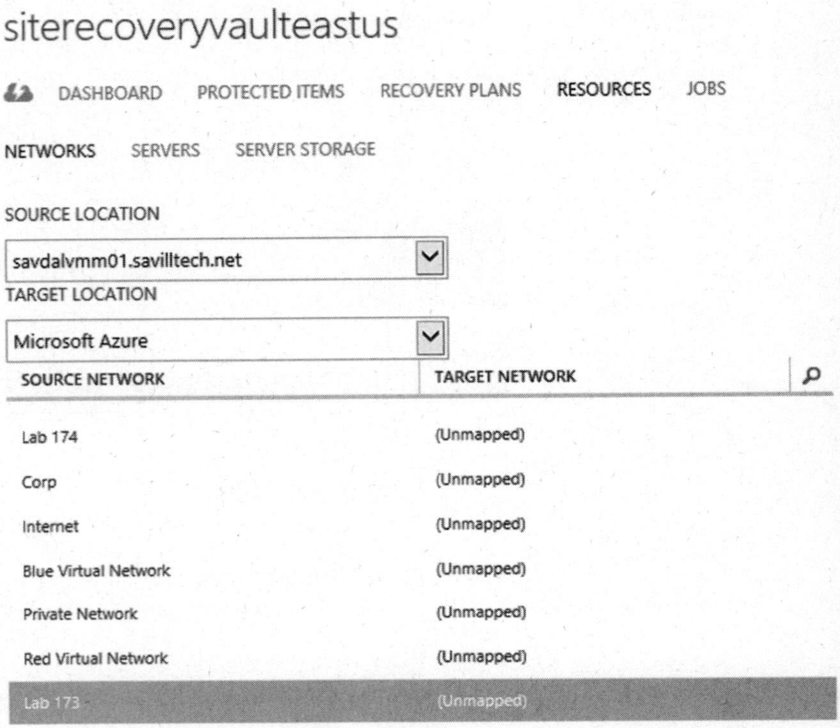

FIGURE 8.10
Mapping networks
in ASR

siterecoveryvaulteastus

DASHBOARD   PROTECTED ITEMS   RECOVERY PLANS   **RESOURCES**   JOBS

NETWORKS   SERVERS   SERVER STORAGE

SOURCE LOCATION

savdalvmm01.savilltech.net	⌄

TARGET LOCATION

Microsoft Azure	⌄

SOURCE NETWORK	TARGET NETWORK	🔍
Lab 174	(Unmapped)	
Corp	(Unmapped)	
Internet	(Unmapped)	
Blue Virtual Network	(Unmapped)	
Private Network	(Unmapped)	
Red Virtual Network	(Unmapped)	
Lab 173	(Unmapped)	

8. In SCVMM, ensure that the VM has the OS set correctly. You will find it in the cloud being
    protected. The hard drive in the hardware configuration for OS is labeled as containing
    the OS. You will need to shut down the VM to change the OS disk configuration, as shown
    in Figure 8.11. This process is described in detail in the Microsoft documentation. One
    recent update also allows the OS drive to be selected in the Azure portal.

FIGURE 8.11
Configuring the disk
containing the OS in
SCVMM

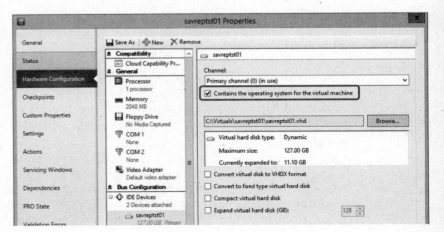

9. Under the actual cloud in the Azure portal, select the Virtual Machines tab. Now, select Enable Protection and select the VM, and jobs will run to first enable the protection. Once initial replication is complete, the Finalize Protection job will run. You are now ready to fail over the VM. You will see that a globally unique identifier (GUID) named *container* has been created in the storage account. That GUID contains the replicated VHD that you saw in Figure 8.6. The replication status can be seen from the Hyper-V server. The VM is now replicating to Azure.

10. Use the Recovery Plans tab to create a recovery plan that can be used to perform a failover. Select Create, provide the necessary information, and make sure you test.

Quite a lot of steps are involved in enabling the connection between your on-premises and Azure, but you only have to do this process once. From this point on, it's easy to modify the configuration, test, and even perform failovers, all from a simple Internet-accessible web portal. I walked you through only one of the channel types, but it is probably the most complicated. All of the others have a similar pattern of actions, and the Microsoft portal has detailed step-by-step guidance for each of the other options.

HANDLING STATIC IP ADDRESSES WITH AZURE SITE RECOVERY

Azure Site Recovery has a number of replication channels available. Each channel has different ways to handle static IP addresses.

For site-to-site solutions, if a VM has a static IP address, then ASR automatically reserves an IP address for the virtual machine when protection is enabled. This IP is injected into the VM during a failover.

For site-to-Azure solutions, you would perform the IP injection as part of your recovery plan by calling an Azure Automation runbook. What follows is an example Azure Automation runbook that sets a VM with a static IP:

```
workflow SavillTestStaticIP
{
    param(
        [Object]$RecoveryPlanContext
    )

    $AzureConnectionName = "SavillTech Internal Consumption"
    $VMMVMGUID = "nnnnnnnn-nnnn-nnnn-nnnn-nnnnnnnnnnnn";
    $IP = "10.7.115.14"

    Connect-Azure -AzureConnectionName $AzureConnectionName
    Select-AzureSubscription -SubscriptionName $AzureConnectionName

    $VMContext = $RecoveryPlanContext.VmMap.$VMMVMGUID
```

```
        Write-Output $VMContext
        if ($VMContext -ne $null)
        {
            InlineScript
            {
                Get-AzureVM -ServiceName $Using:VMContext.CloudServiceName `
                -Name $Using:VMContext.RoleName | `
                Set-AzureStaticVNetIP -IPAddress $Using:IP | Update-AzureVM
            }
        }
    }
```

Note that the actual VM to be modified is automatically fetched from the recovery plan and stored in the $VMContext variable.

Licensing of Azure Site Recovery

Remember that cost difference between application-level replication that requires the VM to be running on the target and using storage replication where the target VM is not running? Those savings apply with ASR because nearly all of the ASR technologies work by not having the VM running in Azure until a failover, thus saving the cost of the VM compute. There is, however, a license associated with protecting an OS instance with Azure Site Recovery, which should be considered if cost is a major factor in your DR. The pricing may be closer between using an application-level replication and Azure Site Recovery.

The pricing details for ASR are documented here:

```
http://azure.microsoft.com/en-us/pricing/details/site-recovery/
```

There are essentially two prices:

◆ Where replication is between customer on-premises locations and ASR is providing only management/orchestration of failover, the price is $16 per VM per month as of this writing.

◆ Where replication is to Azure, the price is $54 per VM per month as of this writing. If you purchase replication to Azure as part of an Enterprise Agreement (EA), then 100 GB of Geo-redundant Storage is included along with 100 GB of egress data. This is used for the storage of the replicated VM to help you avoid additional storage and network costs.

Microsoft bills based on the average number of VMs that were protected during the month. For example, if 20 VMs were protected for half the month and no VMs were protected for the second half of the month, then the billing would be based on 10 VMs. Note also that the prices may change, so check the official Microsoft page for accurate pricing. Also, you may receive a discount depending on your EA with Microsoft and your Azure purchasing commitment.

Migrating VMs to Azure

Why migration in the DR chapter? Consider: what is a migration? It can be thought of as the protection or replication of an environment to Azure and a failover of the environment to

Azure. The workload stays in Azure, never to fail back. This means the same technologies used for replication and DR can be used as part of a migration, and this is exactly what Microsoft has done with the Microsoft Migration Accelerator available here:

http://azure.microsoft.com/en-us/features/migration-accelerator/

The Microsoft Migration Accelerator uses the InMage Scout technology that enables migration to Azure from basically any source, including VMware, Amazon Web Services, physical systems, and more. The same architecture that I outlined earlier in the "OS-Level Replication with InMage Scout" section is used by Microsoft Migration Accelerate and offers a migration with very little downtime. The Microsoft Migration Accelerator works by capturing changes within the running OS, which enables the smallest amount of downtime but also requires more resources on the target to accept the changes and apply those changes to a target disk.

Microsoft has an alternate migration technology available, the Microsoft Virtual Machine Converter (MVMC). MVMC can migrate from VMware or physical systems to Hyper-V or Azure (both Windows and Linux OS instances). This solution is available here:

www.microsoft.com/en-us/download/details.aspx?id=42497

The MVMC works differently from the Microsoft Migration Accelerator. It converts the actual disks to VHD format, uploads them to Azure, and then creates a VM in Azure that attaches to the uploaded VHDs. The conversion is done while the source environment is offline, which means longer downtime for the migration but fewer resources required on the target.

A Migration Automation Toolkit (MAT) also is available here:

https://gallery.technet.microsoft.com/Automation-Toolkit-for-d0822a53

The MAT provides an improved experience for using MVMC by performing a scan of VMware environments and providing an easy-to-use interface to perform bulk migrations. Longer term, I don't expect Microsoft to maintain two different migration technologies and expect the InMage Scout–based solution to become the standard. But, for today, you have a choice of the migration technology you want to use.

Just because technically it is easy to migrate workloads to Azure does not mean it should be undertaken without careful planning. It is important to understand the dependencies between services. You want to avoid moving a service to Azure that is heavily used by something still running on-premises and then find that the service performs poorly because of the latency between on-premises and Azure. Likewise, consider where the users of a service will use the service from. Is there any specific network requirement between clients and the service? It's important to understand the requirements of the workloads. Will they work in Azure? For example, does a service require IPv6? Is it a 32-bit OS? Does it need multiple IP addresses per NIC? Does it have an OS disk larger than 127 GB? The list goes on. It's important that a workload fit within the capabilities of Azure and that consideration be given to the interdependencies between workloads when they are migrated.

Backing Up to Azure

It is possible to create a VM in Azure, attach a number of data disks to it, and run the VM as a backup server, such as System Center Data Protection Manager. This is likely something you will need to do if you have important workloads in Azure and you want to back them up. There is no native backup of VMs in Azure by the Azure service itself. In the IaaS world, you are responsible for your own backups.

The Azure Backup service provides application-aware backup, item-level recovery, and multiple recovery points that enable restoration of various previous points in time. It is relatively cheap—the first 5 GB are free and anything greater than that is 20 cents per GB per month, but this is subject to change. The details can be found here:

http://azure.microsoft.com/en-us/pricing/details/backup/

The key benefit is that this backup storage is off-site and geo-redundant. It provides an organization with confidence that the backup data is safely stored until needed. Now, you might ask why Azure Backup is 20 cents per GB, whereas basic Azure page BLOB storage is only 3 cents per GB. It's comparing apples to oranges. An Azure BLOB is basically just that—a binary large object you can place data in. Azure Backup is a backup service that provides application-aware backup, item-level recovery, and multiple recovery points that enable restoration of various previous points in time. Azure Backup does not charge egress for restored data; you don't need to pay for data out of Azure.

To use Azure Backup, your backup software simply needs to support Azure Backup. For Windows Server (2008 SP2 and later), an add-on agent to the Windows Backup feature is available that provides support for Azure Backup. The agent also works with Windows Server 2012 Essential and System Center Data Protection Manager (DPM). The agent is downloaded from the Azure portal via the Quick Start screen in a backup vault you have created. Once installed and registered to the backup vault, the ability to back up data to the Azure Backup service will be available. An agent is also available for Windows client operating systems. This enables Windows clients to back up to Azure Backup. The Windows client agent is available here:

http://support.microsoft.com/kb/3015072

For System Center Data Protection Manager, Azure Backup acts as a secondary backup target. The primary backup target for DPM is locally mounted disks, but Azure Backup can be used for off-site storage and even longer retention options. You configure the use of Azure for off-site retention on a per-protection group basis within DPM by checking the I Want Online Protection option, as shown in Figure 8.12. The specifics of the cloud protection can be configured as shown in Figure 8.13.

FIGURE 8.12
Enabling cloud protection for a DPM protection group

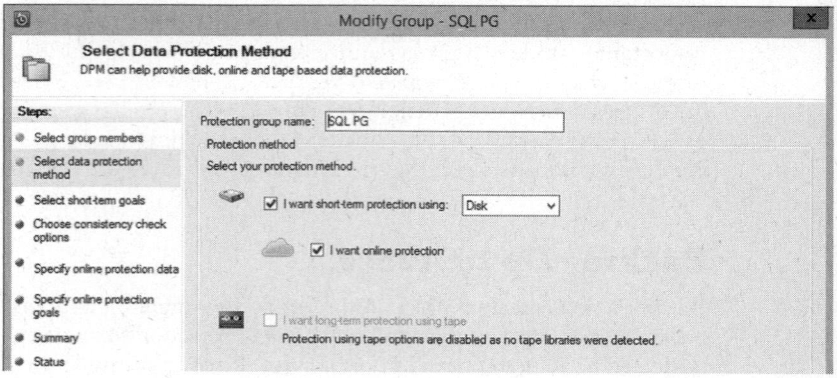

FIGURE 8.13
Configuring the
online protection
details in DPM

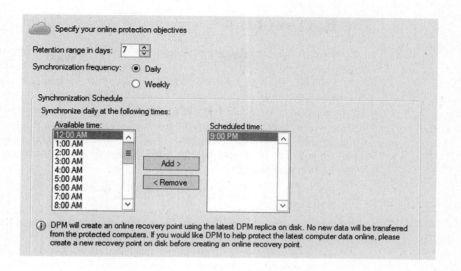

Azure Backup supports 120 recovery points as of this writing; each are point-in-time states of the data protected. Backed-up data is stored efficiently, with only the delta between points stored. For example, you may want a daily recovery point to keep 120 days of backups in Azure. Perhaps you are using Azure for longer-term retention, which means you could configure weekly recovery points, or even every 4 weeks for a monthly recovery point. In the most extreme example, you could set a recovery point every 4 weeks, which would enable 3,360 days of recovery (7 days × 4 weeks × 120 recovery points), or 9 years. This should be plenty, even for organizations that need to meet the strictest backup retention requirements. Microsoft has an interesting article on long-term retention here:

http://azure.microsoft.com/blog/2014/09/11/announcing-long-term-retention-for-azure-backup/

You can also access the Azure Backup FAQ here:

http://msdn.microsoft.com/en-us/library/azure/jj573031.aspx

Here you will find answers to many common questions. I recommend taking a look if you intend to use Azure Backup. One interesting point is that there is no maximum size for an Azure Backup vault; however, no single data source (a VM, SQL database, and so on) can exceed 1.65 TB.

Remember also that you can back up with Azure by leveraging StorSimple, which I discussed in Chapter 3. StorSimple uses Azure BLOBs to store data, both as a backup of its locally held content and as a means of moving the least used data to be exclusively stored in Azure. A thumbprint remains on the StorSimple appliance, which provides a seamless experience to users of the device who believe all data is still locally stored on the StorSimple device. In reality, some of the data exists only in Azure; it is pulled down from Azure automatically when needed.

The Bottom Line

Plan your disaster recovery strategy. Discovery of the environment, understanding how businesses use systems, ascertaining the dependencies between systems, planning how the DR plan will be activated, drawing up communications plans, and so on are all critical. However, the single most important part of DR planning is to have a good test routine. The number-one cause of DR failover problems is because organizations never tested the failover process. They only discover in the event of an actual failure that some replication was not working or that a dependent system had been missed. Create a good testing routine to ensure your DR plan works, but ensure the test does not impact or interfere with the ongoing production systems.

Master It Why is it important that DR be part of the change control plan of an organization?

Understand the sources that can be protected with Azure Site Recovery. Azure Site Recovery uses a number of channels to provide protection. This includes Hyper-V Replica for Hyper-V to Hyper-V on-premises and Hyper-V to Azure. Another channel uses InMage Scout, which provides protection from VMware to VMware on-premises, VMware to Azure, physical to Azure, and more. SQL Server AlwaysOn is also integrated and allows ASR to manage SQL Server failover, as is SAN management through SMI-S integration via SCVMM. Finally, ASR also integrates with Azure Automation and enables any action possible through PowerShell workflows to be part of a recovery plan.

Master It Why is it recommended that you map networks between on-premises and Azure?

Chapter 9

Customizing Azure Templates and PowerShell Management

It's Chapter 9, over two-thirds of the way through the book, and many times I've talked about using PowerShell with Azure and shown you PowerShell commands. However, I haven't walked you through the process of configuring your PowerShell environment to work with Azure. I've been guilty of taking you to the toy store, showing you all the great toys available, and then taking you back home to play with sticks in the garden. In this chapter, I'll walk you through using PowerShell with Azure in detail. In addition, I'll show you how to customize templates for use in Azure.

In this chapter, you will learn to

◆   Understand why you should use availability sets

◆   Enable PowerShell management of Azure

Using Availability Sets and Autoscale

Before I cover PowerShell—I'm not doing this on purpose, I promise—I want to cover a critical feature in Azure that will help ensure the availability of your multi-instance services: the availability set. Back in Chapter 2, "When to Use IaaS: Cost and Options," you saw how Azure services are provided. Inside Azure datacenters are stamps (also known as cluster and scale units), which consist of a number of racks. Each rack contains a number of blades, which provide services such as compute and storage. A cloud service lives within a specific stamp; the VMs in that cloud service are distributed among the blades and racks within the stamp. Each rack can be thought of as a possible unit of failure, a fault domain, since all the blades in a rack use a common top-of-rack switch. This introduces a point of failure along with other shared infrastructure.

Availability Set Basics

If you are deploying multiple instances of a service for load-balancing and availability purposes, it is important that they be separated over different blades (a possible unit of failure) and ideally different racks (another unit of possible failure) for two reasons:

◆   If there is a failure on a blade or rack, not all of the instances of a service are taken down, thus leaving the service available.

◆   During routine planned Azure maintenance where compute nodes (blades) and sometimes racks are taken down as part of patching and other maintenance, it is important not all instances be taken down at the same time.

The mechanism that tells Azure which VMs are offering the same service—and that therefore should be distributed among fault domains—is the availability set. When VMs are placed in an availability set, the VMs are distributed over two fault domains. As of this writing, these cannot be changed. Using the upgradeDomainCount attribute, you can specify up to 20 update domains (sometimes referred to as *upgrade domains*); the default is 5. For more information, see:

http://msdn.microsoft.com/library/azure/ee758711.aspx

Fault domains are racks in the stamp, which means that your VMs are distributed over two racks. If you have 10 VMs in an availability set, you might see 5 on one rack and 5 on the other. In an unplanned failure, you may lose half of your VMs because the fault domain (one rack) is lost. Note that when I say "lose the VMs," I mean that they become unavailable during maintenance or failure. Nothing in terms of the VM is actually lost—it's just unavailable during that time. Also, during planned maintenance operations, such as node updating and rack operations, the same fault domain units are used. During planned updates, you would also lose half your VMs during maintenance.

Update domains are the units used during updates to a service. The concept is focused on PaaS rather than IaaS. The idea is that as a PaaS deployment is updated with a new version of code, that rollout will be to one update domain at a time. This minimizes downtime for the service instances. Azure internal maintenance is not based on update domains.

The fault domain and update domain for the VMs in a cloud service can be viewed by looking at the Instance tab of the cloud service, as shown in Figure 9.1. All three of the VMs shown in Figure 9.1 are in the same availability set. Notice that they are split over two fault domains and three update domains.

FIGURE 9.1

Viewing the fault domain and update domain for VMs in a cloud service

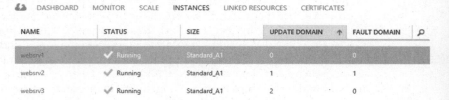

NAME	STATUS	SIZE	UPDATE DOMAIN ↑	FAULT DOMAIN	🔎
websrv1	✔ Running	Standard_A1	0	0	
websrv2	✔ Running	Standard_A1	1	1	
websrv3	✔ Running	Standard_A1	2	0	

The same information can be viewed using PowerShell—for example:

```
PS C:\> Get-AzureService -ServiceName savilltech101 | Get-AzureVM |
    Select Name, InstanceUpgradeDomain, InstanceFaultDomain | ft -AutoSize

Name     InstanceUpgradeDomain InstanceFaultDomain
----     --------------------- -------------------
websrv1 0                     0
websrv2 1                     1
websrv3 2                     0
```

In that code, I first fetch the object for my Azure cloud service. That object is then piped (passed) to the next command, which lists all VMs that are in the passed cloud service. Those

VMs are piped to the next command, which selects the name, update domain, and fault domain attributes. These attributes are piped to a `Format-Table` alias (`ft`) that auto-sizes the table based on the length of the content passed. A single (very long) line of PowerShell provides amazing information. All of this is made possible because PowerShell maintains the objects between commands rather than sending text strings. I digress, but all in the interest of building excitement for when I finally show you how to use PowerShell with Azure.

What if you need more than two fault domains to distribute your VMs over? I frequently hear this in scenarios where quorum is an issue. For example, there are three entities, and the majority is required to make quorum and offer a service—two out of three must be available. If your VMs are distributed over two fault domains, then like the VMs shown in Figure 9.1, two of the VMs would be on one fault domain and one on the other. If the fault domain with two VMs went down, then only one VM is left. That single VM would be unable to make quorum. Changes are coming in Azure related to the way Microsoft offers availability sets that will solve this problem. In the meantime, you can use the following trick to maximize the availability of VMs during maintenance: Use an availability set with two VMs in it and then a stand-alone VM, not in an availability set, as shown in Figure 9.2. (There is no guarantee that this strategy will work indefinitely.)

FIGURE 9.2
Increasing availability during routine maintenance

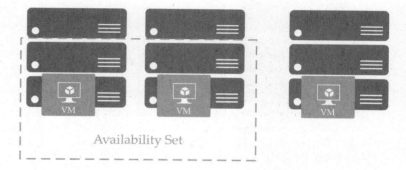

Availability Set

The reason this works is that the scheduled maintenance of VMs in availability sets is separate from that of VMs not in an availability set. That means your stand-alone VM should *not* be taken down at the same time as any VM in an availability set during standard maintenance. In the event of a rack failure or during top-of-rack switch maintenance, the stand-alone VM may be taken down at the same time as one of the VMs in the availability set. The "trick" only helps during normal node maintenance operations.

A QUICK WORD ON AZURE MAINTENANCE

You may be wondering why VMs are unavailable during Azure maintenance. If Azure runs Hyper-V, why can't VMs be live-migrated between nodes during Azure maintenance in the same way you do on-premises to avoid any impact on the VMs' availability? Although technically it is possible, doing so is not feasible in a mega-scale environment for a number of reasons.

First, it takes time to live-migrate VMs—a lot of time. If VMs had to be live-migrated during maintenance, it would greatly increase the amount of time required for maintenance.

Second, a lot of network bandwidth is required to move all that memory. It would be a huge cost (when you look on the scale of Azure services) to have all that additional networking infrastructure just for live-migrating VMs. If existing networking infrastructure was used, it would consume resources that normally would be used by VMs.

Third, there would also need to be a lot more spare hardware in Azure to accommodate moving the VMs while maintaining enough hardware to meet redundancy requirements.

I'm sure there are many other reasons, such as difficulty adhering to placement constraints, but essentially it's not practical to move VMs around when you look at the scale of Azure. So what is Microsoft doing to improve the downtime of services during their maintenance? As I write this book, a node may be down for 20 minutes during the planned maintenance. That is a pretty short amount of time, but those VMs are unavailable for those 20 minutes. Microsoft does not patch its servers. Instead, the nodes boot over the network, and to accomplish the update, the servers are booted to a new image that contains the updates. Microsoft has already removed one of the biggest update time consumers, the updating of the top-of-rack switch, and they are now working on clever technologies that enable the memory of VMs to be maintained in the physical memory of the host, even when the host is rebooted to a new image. VMs do not need to be shut down and restarted after patching; the VM is frozen during planned maintenance, thus reducing the time VMs are unavailable due to planned maintenance to less than a minute.

The key point is that there is downtime for VMs during Azure planned maintenance, but remember that planned maintenance is only part of the availability story. Should there be an actual unplanned event, such as a failure, live migration would not help. This is why the solution to keeping your service running during planned and unplanned events is to deploy multiple instances and place those instances in an availability set.

It is very important not to mix workloads in an availability set. Remember that the VMs in an availability set are distributed over two fault domains and not one fault domain for each VM. Imagine you have two IIS servers and two SQL servers. If you placed all four VMs in a single availability set, it is entirely possible they would be distributed as shown in Figure 9.3.

FIGURE 9.3
A single availability set with mixed workloads

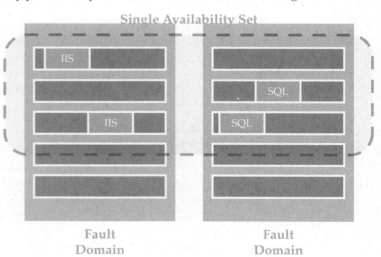

Azure has no way of knowing what is running in which VM, so it distributes the VMs among the two fault domains. In this case, if a rack failed, you would lose all your IIS or SQL instances, depending on which rack failed. The correct approach is shown in Figure 9.4. Each workload is placed in its own availability set. This ensures that the workloads are distributed over fault domains. Availability of the service is ensured even if a rack fails.

FIGURE 9.4
Separate availability sets
for each workload

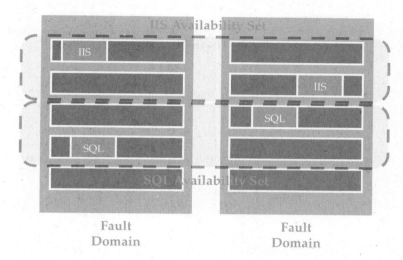

Fault
Domain

Fault
Domain

Never create an availability set with a single VM in it. Microsoft does not provide notification about planned maintenance downtime for any VM in an availability set. By virtue of the fact the VM is in an availability set, it is assumed that the service offered will not be impacted. There should be multiple instances deployed over separate fault domains. If you have only a single VM in an availability set, the service will be affected but you won't be notified. Microsoft provides notice of maintenance that will affect services not in an availability set and gives a window of 12 hours for that maintenance to occur. Sometime during that window, your single-instance VM will be unavailable for a period of time. Figure 9.5 shows a sample notification from Microsoft. Once again, you don't need to worry about maintenance when your VMs are in an availability set. Fault domains are updated at different times, therefore ensuring some of the VMs will be running at any given time.

Note that to receive the financially backed SLA of 99.95 percent for a VM, the VM must be in an availability set. If you have single-instance VMs, then the SLA does not apply. Essentially, there is no SLA. This does not mean that in the event of a problem you lose your VM. The storage containing the VM is highly available and protected. What is not guaranteed is how quickly the healing takes place and the VM is recreated on another node. It will come back at some point, and the only loss would be data on the temporary drive, which is always at risk on any VM and should never contain any data you need to keep. The SLA can be downloaded here:

www.microsoft.com/en-us/download/details.aspx?id=38427

Using Availability Sets

Placing a VM in an availability set can be done during the VM creation or any time afterward, although modifying availability set membership of a running VM will cause the VM to reboot.

It is likely that the VM will need to be provisioned on a different fault domain (rack). Up to 50 VMs can be placed in a single availability set. This is the same number of VMs that can be in a single cloud service. A VM cannot be a member of multiple availability sets.

FIGURE 9.5
Sample notification of upcoming maintenance

The following are the planned start times, provided in both Universal Time Coordinated (UTC) and United States Pacific Daylight Time (PDT). The maintenance will be split into two windows and will impact Virtual Machines or Cloud Services in either half of the maintenance. **We expect each half of the maintenance to finish within 12 hours of the start time.**

Region	PDT	UTC
US West (First half)	20:00 August 1	03:00 August 2
US West (Second half)	20:00 August 2	03:00 August 3

Region	PDT	UTC
US South Central (First half)	18:00 August 1	01:00 August 2
US South Central (Second half)	18:00 August 2	01:00 August 3

When placing VMs in an availability set, it's important to remember that all the VMs in the availability set are part of the same cloud service and, therefore, the same compute stamp. Different compute stamps have different generations of hardware and capabilities, which affects which series and size VMs can be part of it. As of this writing, the following VMs are supported by the various scale units:

- Type 1: A0–A4
- Type 2: A0–A7
- Type 3: A8–A9
- Type 4: A0–A7 and D1–D14
- Type 5: G1–G5 (Godzilla)

This means that your cloud service is bound to one of these types, depending on the first VM created. Therefore, if your cloud service is currently running on a type 1 scale unit, then you can add only A0–A4 VMs. If it is running on a type 4 scale unit, you have the broadest range of VMs supported.

To give yourself the most flexibility when creating a new cloud service, make the first VM deployed a D series VM. As a result, you will be deployed to a type 4 scale unit and have the widest range of VM sizes available. Remember that using a virtual network means VMs in different cloud services can communicate directly with each other, so having multiple cloud services is not a problem and does not in any way hamper communication between your workloads.

Note also that VMs can only be resized to a size supported on the scale unit where the VM is deployed. This means that you cannot resize an A4 VM to an A8, and possibly not a D series depending on the scale unit deployed to. If you need to perform a resize outside of the sizes available in the configuration option, you should delete the VM but select the option to keep the attached storage. Then, create a new VM in a new cloud service (or in an existing cloud service that supports the new size) and reattach the disks from the old VM.

This is important when considering membership of availability sets and the size and series of VMs you want in the availability set. Under normal circumstances, the VMs in an availability set should be of similar configuration; they are providing a similar service and therefore will likely be the same VM series and size. You want a similar experience for users of the service. However, there may be times when you want to mix various sizes and series of VM. If you need to have a range of VM series and sizes in your availability set, make sure your cloud service is bound to a compute stamp that supports the sizes and series you need in the availability set. Make sure that the first VM you create guides the stamp type required.

To add a VM to an availability set during creation on the legacy Azure portal, either select an existing availability set in the cloud service the VM is being provisioned to or select Create An Availability Set on the second page of the creation wizard. If you select Create An Availability Set, you will be prompted for a name for the new availability set. The new set will be created and the VM will be added to it.

To add a VM to an availability set using the preview Azure portal, select the Optional Configuration node of the Create VM blade. In the Optional Config blade, select Availability Set and select the availability set you wish the VM to be part of. As of this writing, there is no way to create a new availability set during VM creation using the preview Azure portal.

To set an availability set when creating a VM using PowerShell, use the `-AvailabilitySetName` parameter as part of the `New-AzureVMConfig` cmdlet:

```
$NewVMConfig = New-AzureVMConfig -Name "NewVM" -InstanceSize Small `
    -ImageName $img -AvailabilitySetName "NewAS"
```

To change a VM's availability set membership postcreation, such as adding to an availability set or removing from an availability set, use the Configure tab for the VM in the legacy Azure portal. Select a new availability set or remove an existing one, as shown in Figure 9.6. Notice that the other members of the availability set are also displayed on the tab.

To use the preview Azure portal, select the VM. From the Configuration lens in the VM's blade, select the availability set part. When the Availability Set blade opens, you can set the availability set membership. The New action allows you to create a new availability set, as shown in Figure 9.7.

To configure membership in a new availability set with PowerShell, you can use the `Set-AzureAvailabilitySet` cmdlet. Here's an example:

```
Get-AzureVM -ServiceName "savilltech101" -Name "testVM" |
    Set-AzureAvailabilitySet -AvailabilitySetName "NewAS" |
    Update-AzureVM
```

FIGURE 9.6
Modifying the availability set for an existing VM using the legacy Azure portal

FIGURE 9.7
Modifying the availability set for an existing VM in the preview portal

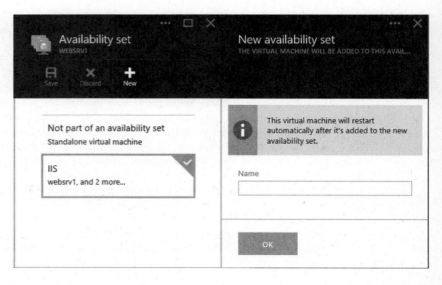

The example code fetches the object representing the VM and then pipes that object to the `Set-AzureAvailabilitySet` cmdlet. This sets the new availability set membership. The updated VM object is piped to the `Update-AzureVM` cmdlet and the change is applied. To remove a VM from an availability set, specify "" as the name of the new availability set.

Remember that, no matter which method is used, if you change the availability set configuration for a running VM, the VM will be rebooted and likely reprovisioned on another compute node. (You will lose the contents of the temporary drive—but you knew that.)

To view all VMs that are part of availability sets in your Azure subscription, use the following PowerShell code:

```
(Get-AzureService).servicename | foreach {Get-AzureVM -ServiceName $_ } |
    Where-Object {$_.AvailabilitySetName -ne $null } |
    Select name,AvailabilitySetName |
    Format-Table Name, AvailabilitySetName -AutoSize
```

Next is an example of the PowerShell code and what it returns:

```
PS C:\> (Get-AzureService).servicename | foreach {Get-AzureVM -ServiceName $_ } |
    Where-Object {$_.AvailabilitySetName -ne $null } |
    Select name,AvailabilitySetName |
    Format-Table Name, AvailabilitySetName -AutoSize

Name    AvailabilitySetName
----    -------------------
websrv1 IIS
websrv2 IIS
websrv3 IIS
```

That's all there is to availability sets. To summarize, remember the following points:

◆ For any service that needs to be highly available, deploy at least two instances and place them in an availability set.

◆ Do not mix workloads in an availability set; have one availability set for each type of workload. For example, create one availability set for the IIS tier of a service, one for the SQL tier, one for domain controllers, and so on.

◆ Availability sets are contained within a cloud service that exists within a specific compute stamp. The compute stamp governs the series and size of VMs.

Understanding and Configuring IaaS Autoscale

Placing VMs in an availability set tells Azure that the contained VMs need to be distributed among fault domains for protection against failures and ensures that during routine maintenance not all instances are taken down. There is another benefit. Azure now knows that all the VMs in an availability set collectively offer a service. Do you remember the pizza and Super Bowl example back in Chapter 1, "The Cloud and Microsoft Azure 101?" The key point was that the resources needed to offer a service vary over time. At times, you may need 20 VMs running to offer a service. At other times, you may only need 4. Although you could leave all

20 running 24/7, it will cost you; Azure bills based on provisioned services. A better approach would be to deprovision (shut down and remove unneeded VMs from your fabric to stop incurring charges) at a given point in time and restart them when they are needed. One option would be to create your own PowerShell script or other automation tool to deprovision and reprovision VMs as required. You can accomplish this with Azure Automation (a PowerShell workflow running in Azure, which I will cover in Chapter 11, "Completing Your Azure Environment"), but another option is available.

For VMs in an availability set, you can configure autoscaling. With the IaaS Autoscale feature, Azure provisions and deprovisions VMs as needed based on CPU utilization of the running VMs or a storage queue depth. Azure will not create new VMs; you must precreate all the VMs in advance and place them in an availability set. For example, you could precreate 20 web servers and place them in a single availability set. After you've created the machines and made them members of an availability group, you can configure autoscaling:

1. From the legacy Azure portal, select the Cloud Services workspace, and then select the cloud service that contains the availability group.

2. Select the Scale tab.

3. Select the availability set that you want to configure for Autoscale. Once selected, you can view the settings for the scale.

4. For IaaS, you can select the CPU metric to scale by. This allows you to configure:

   ◆ The range of virtual machines that can be scaled (minimum and maximum)

   ◆ The target CPU utilization for the virtual machines

   ◆ The number of virtual machines you need to scale up and down by

   ◆ A queue depth for scaling and similar options

   Notice that the maximum number of VMs is equal to the number of VMs you have in the availability set. The Queue option will be useful if you have some service running in your VMs that processes items from the queue. If the queue depth exceeds a certain threshold, that means the VMs are not handling the load, so adding additional VMs to process the queue content will help reduce the queue depth. The scale options are shown in Figure 9.8.

5. Select a schedule for when scaling should be applied.

6. Click Save.

Remember that it takes time to start VMs that are deprovisioned, which is why as part of the configuration there is a scale-up and scale-down wait time between actions to allow time for the scale action to take effect before reevaluating whether additional scale actions are necessary. The default 20 minutes is a good value. I don't recommend making this number less than 10 minutes.

The benefit of Autoscale is that it only starts the number of virtual machines that are required to provide the service capacity needed at any given time. Although there's some delay in the scaling actions, you only pay for the instances required and running, which saves you money. It's important that you have a means of load balancing the service that detects when instances are available—for example, a load-balancing endpoint for IIS VMs.

FIGURE 9.8
Enabling Autoscale for IaaS VMs in an availability set

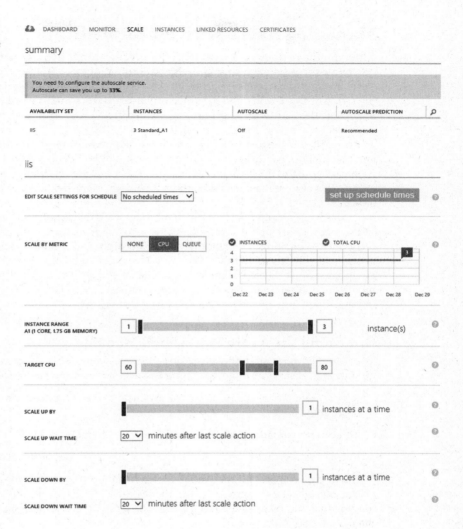

NOTE What about Scale-Up?

A common question I hear is about scaling a service up (making it bigger with more memory, CPU, or other resources) as opposed to scaling it out (adding more instances of the service). Perhaps you have a service that cannot run multiple instances, so scale-out is not an option.

Scale-up isn't available as a native Azure Autoscale capability. The size of an Azure VM can't be changed dynamically. To change the size of an Azure VM—which changes the CPU/memory—you have to deprovision the VM and then reprovision it—potentially on a new server. This introduces a period of unavailability for the service running inside the VM. In general, this isn't desirable and doesn't occur when you scale out.

If you want to implement scale-up, you can accomplish it fairly easily by creating an Azure Automation that checks the metrics of an Azure VM. If necessary, the VM unavailability will occur during scale-up.

Managing Azure with PowerShell

Although the various Azure portals offer great features, they are not designed for large-scale deployments or management. To achieve automation of actions and to access functionality not present in the portals, you can use PowerShell. A primer on PowerShell is outside the scope of this book, and I assume you have a certain amount of PowerShell competence to get the most out of this section. I will explain and give examples in as much detail as possible.

PowerShell is the direction for any kind of command-line interface management, scripting, and automation, not just across Microsoft technologies but across the entire IT landscape. If you are going to invest in one skill, I suggest becoming a PowerShell master. (I run an annual PowerShell Master Class online. If you are interested, I talk about the class on my site, www.savilltech.com.)

Azure has a number of PowerShell modules available for discrete areas of functionality. These modules are updated frequently by exposing features as they are added to Azure. I recommend checking weekly for new versions of the PowerShell modules for Azure. If there is a new feature in Azure that you cannot access through PowerShell, it is highly likely that an updated PowerShell module is available that you need to install. Features may take many months to become available in the Azure web-based portals (some never do), but they are used in PowerShell very quickly.

Obtaining the Azure PowerShell Modules

The Azure PowerShell modules are downloaded via the Web Platform Installer. You can get guidance on installing and configuring the Azure PowerShell environment here:

```
http://azure.microsoft.com/en-us/documentation/articles/install-configure-
powershell/
```

You can download the Microsoft Web Platform Installer here:

```
http://go.microsoft.com/fwlink/p/?linkid=320376&clcid=0x409
```

If you click the link for the Web Platform Installer, you will be prompted to run an executable. Select the Run action, and the installer will open and show the version of the Azure module that will be installed (see Figure 9.9). You will have to accept a license agreement before the installation will continue.

Once the Azure PowerShell module is installed, it will add a shortcut that opens a new PowerShell window with the Azure modules preloaded. You do not have to use this shortcut: it's just an easy option, because it handles the loading of the Azure modules for you. Behind the scenes, the Azure module location has been added to the system PSModulePath environment variable. This makes the Azure module globally accessible, but the change won't take effect until after a reboot. Before you use PowerShell for the first time after installing the Azure PowerShell environment, I recommend performing a quick reboot. As an alternative, you can force an update of the PSModulePath variable in a running PowerShell session by using the following PowerShell command (be sure to type it all on one line):

```
$env:PSModulePath =
    [System.Environment]::GetEnvironmentVariable("PSModulePath","Machine")
```

FIGURE 9.9
Installing the
Azure PowerShell
environment

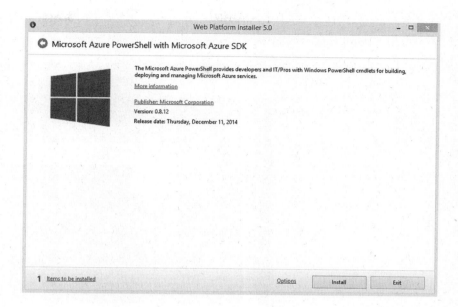

If you examine the properties of the Microsoft Azure PowerShell shortcut, you will see that it calls a start-up script:

```
."C:\Program Files (x86)\Microsoft
 SDKs\Azure\PowerShell\ServiceManagement\Azure\Services\ShortcutStartup.ps1"
```

You could manually run the script, but there really is no need. Assuming that the PowerShell module is installed correctly and the PSModulePath variable updated, you can load the Azure module in any PowerShell session using the following command:

```
Import-Module Azure
```

If you are new to PowerShell, I recommend using the Windows PowerShell ISE (Integrated Scripting Environment). This environment has a great command window that helps you find which cmdlet to use. It also features *IntelliSense*, as shown in Figure 9.10, which helps by auto-completing commands as you type. The ISE also features code snippets (press Ctrl+J). These precreated pieces of code or script for popular constructs, such as an if-else statement, can be inserted into your session.

To check the current version of the Azure module installed, use the command (Get-Module Azure).Version, as shown in Figure 9.10. You can compare your version to the version available via the Web Platform Installer to determine whether you need to download a newer version of PowerShell.

Configuring Azure PowerShell for Your Azure Subscription

Once the Azure PowerShell module is installed, the next step is to connect to your Azure subscription and enable it to be managed. There are two primary methods. The first method I describe is actually deprecated; it does not support the new Azure Resource Manager (ARM). ARM is the future of Azure. I am covering using management certificate methods for the sake of completeness.

FIGURE 9.10
Using the PowerShell
ISE for an enhanced
PowerShell experience

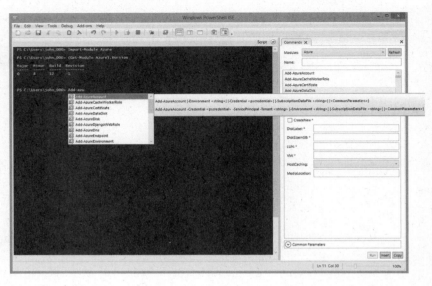

Azure can use management certificates to govern interaction with a subscription. A management certificate that is part of the Azure subscription can be used to connect to the subscription. The challenge with this approach is that it is not bound to a specific user, so auditing is difficult. As mentioned earlier, it does not support ARM, which means there is no support for granular access.

The certificate approach is accomplished through the generation of an Azure Publish Settings file that contains the certificate needed to connect to the subscription and the subscription ID. Here is an example of the file, which has a `.publishsettings` extension. The very long actual certificate has been removed.

```xml
<?xml version="1.0" encoding="utf-8"?>
<PublishData>
  <PublishProfile
    SchemaVersion="2.0"
    PublishMethod="AzureServiceManagementAPI">
    <Subscription
      ServiceManagementUrl="https://management.core.windows.net"
      Id="nnnnnnnn-nnnn-nnnn-nnnn-nnnnnnnnnnnn"
      Name="Windows Azure Internal Consumption"
      ManagementCertificate="MIIKLAIBA......==" />
  </PublishProfile>
</PublishData>
```

Creating the publish settings file is very simple. Run the PowerShell command `Get-AzurePublishSettingsFile`. This opens your web browser and requires you to authenticate. You should use the credentials for the Azure subscription for which you wish to generate a publish settings file. Once you authenticate, the browser will prompt you to save the automatically generated publish settings file. Save this file somewhere you can easily access. Once it's saved, you can open the file in Notepad and view your subscription ID and certificate. In the legacy Azure portal, if you choose Settings ➤ Management Certificates, you will see that a new certificate was generated. It is the partner certificate to the one you downloaded to the publish settings file. This is an important point. If you wish to stop the publish settings file from connecting to your Azure subscription, you should delete the partner certificate for that subscription from Azure.

The following lets you use a publish settings file to connect to an Azure subscription:

```
Import-AzurePublishSettingsFile '<publish settings file name>'
```

Your PowerShell session will then be connected to your Azure subscription.

The second, and preferred, method to connect to Azure from PowerShell is using the Add-AzureAccount cmdlet. This cmdlet opens a dialog that allows you to enter your credentials and be authenticated to Azure. This method authenticates with your account, which fully supports the Azure Resource Manager and allows access to resources secured with role-based access control (RBAC).

The challenge with this approach is that the connection is interactive; you have to enter credentials in a dialog. This is not ideal if you want connectivity to be "headless" (accomplished with no interaction). The solution is to use a PowerShell credential object. The next PowerShell script creates a credential object with a username and password, and then uses that credential object with the Add-AzureAccount cmdlet:

```
$securepassword = ConvertTo-SecureString -string "<your password>" -AsPlainText `
    -Force
$cred = new-object System.Management.Automation.PSCredential `
    ("<your logon>", $securepassword)
Add-AzureAccount -Credential $cred
```

Note that this script stores your password in plain text, which is likely not desirable. There are a number of options that use a method where the password is stored in an encrypted form rather than plain text. A third-party module that stores credentials in the Windows password vault is available here:

```
https://gallery.technet.microsoft.com/Manipulate-credentials-in-58e0f761/
```

Another option creates a secure, encrypted version of the password using the following:

```
$encryptedPassword = ConvertFrom-SecureString (ConvertTo-SecureString `
    -AsPlainText -Force "Password123")
```

Then take that output stored in the variable and use it in your script. Obviously if someone noted the entire value, they would get your password, but it's pretty long to quickly write down. To use in a script, enter the following:

```
$passwordAsSecureString = `
    ConvertTo-SecureString "<the value from previous command>"
```

If you don't want the password in the encrypted form visible in the script, you can save the entire credential in secure form to a file that would be accessible only as credentials for your user account when you attempt access from a specific machine, for example:

```
$credpath = c:\temp\MyCredential.xml
New-Object System.Management.Automation.PSCredential("<account>", `
    (ConvertTo-SecureString -AsPlainText -Force "Password123")) |
    Export-CliXml $credpath
```

To use the credential from the file in your script, you would use this:

```
$cred = import-clixml -path $credpath
```

Note that `Export-CliXml` and the PowerShell module specified both use the same crypto API (DPAPI) under the covers, so they have the same strengths and weaknesses. The difference is `Export-CliXml` saves to a file, whereas the PowerShell module saves to the Windows Registry in an encrypted form.

If you are using any of these approaches for presenting Azure credentials, the credentials variable only works with Azure AD accounts. You cannot use it with Microsoft IDs (Live IDs).

A word of caution: once you have used Add ➢ Azure Account to connect to Azure, a publish settings file will no longer work. If you import it, you will receive an error:

```
Get-AzureVM : Your Azure credentials have not been set up or have expired,
please run Add-AzureAccount to set up your Azure credentials.
```

Because you used an Azure Active Directory (AAD) account with Azure in PowerShell, it will take precedence. Going forward, you must specify an account. To resolve the issue, you could use `Remove-AzureAccount`. The cmdlet removes the Azure AD account from the PowerShell environment but will not delete anything from Azure.

```
Remove-AzureAccount -Name john@savilltech.com
```

The old certificate-based management with X.509 certificates should now work again.

NOTE   It is important to remember that Azure is moving to the Azure Resource Manager (ARM), which is not compatible with the old management certificates. Those old certificates don't understand RBAC and the like. My advice is to move away from using the certificates and publish settings files. Instead, use Azure AD accounts. Rather than importing a publish settings file at the start of your PowerShell session, you would use the `Add-AzureAccount` cmdlet.

Your PowerShell environment is now connected to Azure. If your credential has permissions for more than one subscription, the subscription you wish to work on can be selected. To view all of the subscriptions available to you, use the `Get-AzureSubscription` cmdlet. The output displays the subscription ID, name, and associated accounts. To select a specific subscription, select it via the ID or name. For example, to use the name, enter the following:

```
Select-AzureSubscription -SubscriptionName 'Windows Azure Internal Consumption'
```

Once you have selected a subscription, configure a default storage account to be used with the subscription. (Some PowerShell commands require a default storage account.) To view all of the storage accounts available, use the following to display the name, location, and type of the account:

```
Get-AzureStorageAccount | ft Label, Location, AccountType -AutoSize
```

Here's an example output:

```
PS C:\> Get-AzureStorageAccount | ft Label, Location, AccountType -autosize
Label                     Location      AccountType
-----                     --------      -----------
savilleastusGRS           East US       Standard_GRS
savilleastasiagrs         East Asia     Standard_LRS
savillmasterazurestore    East US       Standard_GRS
savtechstoreeastus        East US       Standard_GRS
savtechstorenortheurope   North Europe  Standard_LRS
```

To select a storage account, use the following:

```
Set-AzureSubscription -SubscriptionName 'Windows Azure Internal Consumption' `
    -CurrentStorageAccount 'savtechstoreeastus'
```

If you put all of these initial actions together, you can place them in a start-up file or at the top of a script. Here's an example:

```
Import-Module Azure
Add-AzureAccount
Select-AzureSubscription -SubscriptionName 'AzureSubscriptionName'
Set-AzureSubscription -SubscriptionName 'AzureSubscriptionName' `
    -CurrentStorageAccount 'AzureStorageAccountName'
```

Useful PowerShell in Azure

You can achieve almost anything in Azure using PowerShell. In this section, I will walk you through some of the most useful PowerShell commands I have used during my Azure interactions. Pay attention to the comments in the following PowerShell command listing so you can understand what each does.

```
#List all cloud services
Get-AzureService

#Set a variable
$cloudserv = 'savilltech101' #Cloud Service

#View all VMs in a cloud service
Get-AzureService -ServiceName $cloudserv | Get-AzureVM |
```

```
        Select Name, InstanceStatus, InstanceSize | ft -AutoSize

#View a specific VM
Get-AzureVM -ServiceName $cloudserv -Name 'websrv1'

#View all disks connected to a VM
Get-AzureDisk | Where-Object {$_.AttachedTo -ne $null } |
     Format-Table -auto DiskName,DiskSizeInGB,AttachedTo

#View all images available in Azure
Get-AzureVMImage | ft Label,ImageName,LogicalSizeInGB

#View all Azure locations
Get-AzureLocation

#Test if a cloud service name is in use. False return means it's available
Test-AzureName -Service 'CloudServiceNameToTestFor'
```

The Get-AzureLocation cmdlet returns all Azure locations and includes information about the various VM series and sizes supported. I created a PowerShell script for a customer that shows this information in a more readable format. Take a look:

```
$azurelocations = Get-AzureLocation
$out = @()
foreach ($location in $azurelocations)
{
    $VMSizes = $location.VirtualMachineRoleSizes
    $VMSizesStr = $VMSizes -join ', '
    $props = @{
    Name = $location.Name
    VMSizes = $VMSizesStr}
    $out += New-Object PsObject -Property $props
}

$out | Format-Table -AutoSize -Wrap Name, VMSizes
```

If you prefer, you can output the information to a graphical grid view using the following:

```
$out | Select Name, VMSizes | Out-GridView -Title 'Azure Regions'
```

This would produce an output similar to that shown in Figure 9.11. Note that you can produce either a grid view output or a text-based table for most PowerShell commands.

The next piece of code was designed to fetch the latest template available from Azure for a specific OS version. Azure maintains multiple versions of many OS templates based on patch levels. If you are creating a new VM in Azure based on an Azure template, you often want to use the most recent OS template. The code that follows stores the latest Windows Server 2012

R2 Datacenter image in a variable. You can change the code to accommodate any OS you need. I then use this variable in code to create VMs.

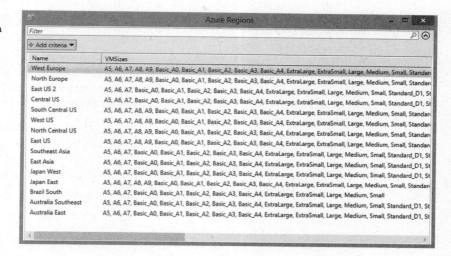

```
$images = Get-AzureVMImage
$2012R2imgs = @() #Create array of objects
foreach ($image in $images)
{
    if ($image.Label.Contains("Windows Server 2012 R2 Datacenter"))
    {
        $2012R2imgs += $image
    }
}

#put the newest first which is the highest patched version
$2012R2imgs = $2012R2imgs | Sort-Object PublishedDate -Descending

#Display detail of the image
$2012R2imgs[0] |  ft Label,ImageName,LogicalSizeInGB -AutoSize
```

Here's how I can use this to quickly create a new VM:

```
$admin = "localadmin"
$myPwd = "V3ryHardTh!ngT0Gue33"
$myVM = New-AzureQuickVM -Windows -name "TestVM" `
  -ImageName $2012R2imgs[0].ImageName `
  -ServiceName $cloudserv -Location 'East US' `
  -AdminUserName AdminJohn -Password $myPwd
```

You can use the next script to add additional data disks to your new VM:

```
Get-AzureVM -Name $myVM -ServiceName $cloudserv |
    Add-AzureDataDisk -CreateNew -DiskSizeInGB 1023 -DiskLabel 'datadisk1' -LUN 0 |
    Add-AzureDataDisk -CreateNew -DiskSizeInGB 1023 -DiskLabel 'datadisk2' -LUN 1 |
    Update-AzureVM
```

Alternatively, you can use Azure provisioning configuration to have more control over the VM creation. Of course, you can supplement my script with any (or all) the PowerShell scripts and commands previously discussed in the book. Notice that I disable the default RDP and management endpoints in this script since I am connecting the VM to a virtual network and will be connecting via my on-premises–to–Azure connection.

```
$NewVM = New-AzureVMConfig -Name 'TestVM' -InstanceSize 'Basic_A2' `
    -ImageName $2012R2imgs[0].ImageName   |
    Add-AzureProvisioningConfig -Windows -AdminUsername $admin -Password $myPwd `
        -NoRDPEndpoint -NoWinRMEndpoint|
        Set-AzureSubnet 'App-Net'
    #Could also add disks with Add-AzureDataDisk and even endpoints with
    #Add-AzureEndpoint
    #Could also set static IP with Set-AzureStaticVNetIP etc etc

New-AzureVM -ServiceName $cloudserv -VMs $NewVM
    #-VNetName 'VirtNet115' # if the first VM in cloud service to set the VNet

#Now I want to wait until its ready
$VMStatus = Get-AzureVM -ServiceName $mySvc -Name $VMName
While ($VMStatus.InstanceStatus -ne "ReadyRole")
{
  write-host "Not Ready. Status = " $VMStatus.Status
  Start-Sleep -Seconds 20

  $VMStatus = Get-AzureVM -ServiceName $mySvc -Name $VMName
}

#Create RDP file and save to enable connectivity
Get-AzureRemoteDesktopFile -ServiceName $mySvc -Name $VMName `
    -LocalPath c:\data\$VMName.rdp
```

Here are some other PowerShell cmdlets that you will find useful when working with VMs:

```
#Restart a VM
Restart-AzureVM -ServiceName $mySvc -Name $myVM

#Shutdown a VM
Stop-AzureVM -ServiceName $mySvc -Name $myVM

#Start a VM
Start-AzureVM -ServiceName $mySvc -Name $myVM
```

At the start of this section, I discussed the benefit of using the `Add-AzureAccount` cmdlet since it supports the Azure Resource Manager. The cmdlets I've shown you so far are just basic Azure commands. To interface with the Azure Resource Manager, you must use a different set of cmdlets. You can find them in the `AzureResourceManager` module. To switch modules and use the Azure Resource Manager cmdlets, run the following:

```
Switch-AzureMode -Name AzureResourceManager
```

To switch back to the regular Azure module:

```
Switch-AzureMode -Name AzureServiceManagement
```

I will cover some of the cmdlets used with the Azure Resource Manager later in this chapter, but for now, you can use the following command to see the cmdlets that are made available through the Azure Resource Manager:

```
Get-Command -Module AzureResourceManager | Get-Help | Format-Table Name, Synopsis
```

More information on the Azure Resource Manager cmdlets (with examples) can be found here:

```
http://azure.microsoft.com/en-us/documentation/articles/powershell-azure-
resource-manager/
```

Although the code I've shown you thus far barely scratches the surface, your environment will now be connected to Azure. You can use the PowerShell cmdlets and scripts discussed throughout this book to enable full management and automation of Azure through PowerShell.

Other Azure Interface Options

Azure exposes a REST API for full management capability. The API is what the Azure PowerShell cmdlets use to provide their management capabilities. It is possible to directly hook into the REST APIs in programs you may write. You will find the REST API documentation and example code here:

```
http://msdn.microsoft.com/en-us/library/azure/ee460799.aspx
```

The benefit of REST APIs is that they can be used by practically anything, even a basic web browser.

If you don't write your own programs using REST APIs or use PowerShell, Microsoft provides an Azure Cross-Platform Command-Line Interface (`xplat-cli`). The `xplat-cli` can be downloaded here:

```
https://github.com/WindowsAzure/azure-sdk-tools-xplat
```

You can find full documentation, which shows how `xplat-cli` can be installed, connected to Azure, and used, here:

```
http://azure.microsoft.com/en-us/documentation/articles/xplat-cli/
```

VM and Template Management

With a solid understanding of the core Azure infrastructure capabilities, how to architect services for resiliency, and how to manage your infrastructure via PowerShell, the next step is understanding the typical management actions you will need to take for the VMs running in Azure and how to use your own templates in Azure, as opposed to using the Azure provider ones made available through the gallery.

Maintaining VMs in Azure

One of the key points I have stressed throughout this book is that when using IaaS in Azure—that is, a VM in the cloud—Microsoft takes care of the network, storage, compute, and hypervisor aspects of the datacenter, but you are entirely responsible for everything that happens inside the VM. This includes but is not limited to the following:

- Patching
- Backing up
- Monitoring
- Upgrading applications
- Providing malware protection
- Configuring firewalls and your system

You likely already have solutions for each of these. You perform these functions on-premises. The goal would be to use those same solutions in Azure and avoid having to maintain different solutions to provide the same service. However, it is important to realize that Azure does have some special considerations; it is essentially a separate location connected on-premises through a site-to-site VPN or ExpressRoute. There is a finite amount of bandwidth and a certain latency. If you extend your on-premises solutions to cover the VMs in Azure, make sure you consider that fact and architect accordingly.

PATCHING

There are numerous solutions for patching. Common ones include Windows Server Update Services (WSUS) and System Center Configuration Manager (SCCM). Given that patches can be large in size, the best configuration is one where the VMs in Azure pull the patches from a location local to the Azure region. So, for WSUS, have a WSUS downstream server in Azure that hosts patches but pulls the configuration and policy from a central upstream server. For SCCM, place a distribution point in Azure.

BACKING UP

Follow the same best practices you use for on-premises backup with the exception that you cannot perform a bare-metal recovery of a VM in Azure; there is no way to Preboot eXecution Environment (PXE) boot an Azure VM. Instead, focus on protecting the data and application workloads. You can use a process to pull down the VHDs from the Azure storage account, or even create snapshots of VM storage within Azure, by creating a BLOB snapshot and then copying that content. If you want to try this approach, the PowerShell script that follows creates a snapshot of a BLOB, which can then be copied. Walk through the code and examine each step to better grasp what is being done. Microsoft has a script available here:

```
https://gallery.technet.microsoft.com/Create-an-Azure-IaaS-VM-04e09d68
```

I recommend using it if you wish to snapshot and handle both OS and data disks.

```
#This only snapshots the OS disk, you would also want to snapshot data disks
#by enumerating data disks with $DataDisk = $vm | Get-AzureDataDisk
$vm = Get-AzureVM -ServiceName 'savilltech101' -Name 'websrv1'
$osDisk= $vm | Get-AzureOSDisk
$sourceSAName=$osDisk.MediaLink.Host.split('.')[0]
$osDiskBlob= Split-Path $osDisk.MediaLink.PathAndQuery -Leaf
$Key=Get-AzureStorageKey $sourceSAName
$Cred = New-Object `
    Microsoft.WindowsAzure.Storage.Auth.StorageCredentials($sourceSAName, `
        $key.Primary)
$CloudStorageAccount = New-Object `
    Microsoft.WindowsAzure.Storage.CloudStorageAccount($cred, $true)
$CloudBlobClient = $CloudStorageAccount.CreateCloudBlobClient()
$BlobContainer = $CloudBlobClient.GetContainerReference("vhds")
$snapshot = $BlobContainer.GetPageBlobReference($osDiskBlob).CreateSnapshot()
$VMSnapshot=$snapshot.SnapshotQualifiedStorageUri.PrimaryUri.AbsoluteUri
#Copy it somewhere, e.g. Start-AzureStorageBlobCopy -AbsoluteUTI $VMSnapshot `
#    -DestBlob .....
#To list snapshots
$ListingOptions = New-Object `
    Microsoft.WindowsAzure.Storage.Blob.BlobListingDetails
$ListingOptions= "Snapshots"
($BlobContainer.ListBlobs($osDiskBlob,$true,$listingoptions,$null,$null) |
    where-object {$_.isSnapshot -eq "True"})
#To delete
$snapshot.Delete()
```

It is not possible to protect VMs at the hypervisor level. Instead, your focus will be on installing backup agents inside the VMs and protecting the content through that agent. The same consideration applies to the backup target. Try to keep the target of the backup within Azure; remember, you pay for egress. If your backup target is on-premises, you will pay for the egress data and be affected by the speed and latency from Azure to on-premises. Also, remember Azure has the Azure Backup service, which is a perfect target for backups. The backup can then be geo-redundant and provide protection from an Azure site failure. Most popular backup software supports VMs running in Azure, as well as using Azure Backup and the System Center Data Protection Manager.

MONITORING

The Azure monitoring is focused on whether the various compute, storage, network, and other Azure services are running; it is not focused on the health of the OS within your VM. You need to monitor the OS and services within your VM using a monitoring solution such as the System Center Operations Manager. Install the agent in each VM to get full insight into that VM's health. There is a basic integration into the Azure fabric to check on aspects of its health. An Azure management pack is available for Operations Manager and shows some level of information on the health of cloud services and storage accounts. It is very basic, so you should know that the best monitoring will come from your agents running inside each VM.

You cannot monitor the Azure network. For example, if you try to capture packets on the wire using promiscuous mode, you will not receive traffic. The only traffic monitoring you can do in Azure is for the traffic your VMs receive. This traffic would be captured by the agent inside the VM.

UPGRADING APPLICATIONS

It almost goes without saying, but you are responsible for any application and framework updates within your VMs. Ideally, you will be able to use the same infrastructure that you use for patching to deliver application and framework updates and avoid excessive infrastructure. If you want to move away from application updates, you need to look at Software as a Service (SaaS) solutions, such as Office 365.

PROVIDING MALWARE PROTECTION

It's critical that you run malware protection in your Azure VMs, the same way you run it on-premises. Be sure to keep those malware definitions current. In addition to using regular malware protection agents, there are some Azure-specific solutions that I will talk about in the "Using the Azure VM Agent" section later in this chapter. Although these solutions tightly integrate with Azure and cloud services, that level of integration is not required.

CONFIGURING FIREWALLS AND YOUR SYSTEM

Once again, make sure you have the firewall turned on. Only allow exceptions for specific services. I know of organizations that turn off the firewall; it's difficult to ascertain which exceptions are required to enable services to work. This is a very bad idea. Think defense in depth. You want a firewall at my Internet connection point, a firewall between your DMZ and your internal network, and then firewalls on all my servers and clients. Make sure you have disabled all the endpoints for each VM. You do not want RDP directly to your VMs from the Internet. Only add endpoints where you specifically want to offer services to the Internet.

Remember to apply policies to configure your VM. Most likely this will be achieved by joining the VM to a domain and then applying policy using Group Policy. It is also possible to apply configuration using PowerShell Desired State Configuration, which can be done during the VM provisioning.

Using the Azure VM Agent

I have repeatedly said that Azure does not care about the contents of your VM and provides no services to help in its management. This used to be true in the early Azure IaaS, but now you can install an optional Azure VM Agent into your VM. This agent is installed by default for new VMs, but you can disable it by deselecting the Agent option during provisioning in the portal. If you already have VMs deployed and wish to install the agent, follow these steps:

1. On the virtual machine, install the Azure VM Agent from

```
http://go.microsoft.com/fwlink/?LinkID=394789&clcid=0x409
```

2. After the installation is complete, tell Azure that the agent is installed inside the virtual machine, which will enable the various management actions. You do so by using PowerShell:

```
$vm = Get-AzureVM -ServiceName <cloud service name> -Name <vm name>
$vm.VM.ProvisionGuestAgent = $true
Update-AzureVM -Name <vm name> -VM $vm.VM -ServiceName <cloud service name>
```

After you run the PowerShell code, if you run the `Get-AzureVM` command and look at the virtual machine, you'll see that `GuestAgentStatus` is not blank.

The agent facilitates enabling a number of features. First, it allows you to install additional types of software, such as malware protection. Microsoft has partnered with a number of malware protection vendors, including Symantec and TrendMicro, and integrates their offerings via the Azure agent. Both the agent and malware definition files can be updated without connecting to the VM. The Microsoft malware protection is also available. Microsoft has a nice blog article that talks about antimalware integration here:

http://azure.microsoft.com/blog/2014/05/13/deploying-antimalware-solutions-on-azure-virtual-machines/

To enable the Microsoft antimalware via the Azure Agent, run the following PowerShell script for each VM:

```
#Get the VM
$vm = Get-AzureVM -ServiceName $servicename -Name $vmname
#Add Microsoft Antimalware Agent to the Virtual Machine
Set-AzureVMExtension -Publisher Microsoft.Azure.Security `
    -ExtensionName IaaSAntimalware -Version 1.* -VM $vm.VM
#Update the VM which will install the Antimalware Agent
Update-AzureVM -Name $servicename -ServiceName $name -VM $vm.VM
```

Additionally, a number of extra capabilities are exposed. To see a list of every extension available, run `Get-AzureVMAvailableExtension | Out-GridView` from PowerShell. Some useful ones include the following (these commands should all be written as one continuous line):

◆ `Set-AzureVMBGInfoExtension -VM $SandboxVM | Update-AzureVM`

This command installs the `BGInfo` extension and displays OS information as the wallpaper of the VM.

◆ `Set-AzureVMaccessExtension -VM $SandboxVM -UserName "localadmin" -Password "P@55word!" -ReferenceName Reset-Pass1 | | Update-AzureVM`

Use this command to reset a forgotten password inside the VM.

◆ `Set-AzureVMAccessExtension -VM $SandboxVM | Update-AzureVM`

To enable RDP access for a VM, try this command. It is useful if you accidentally disabled RDP to an Azure VM and can no longer communicate. It also enables the required firewall exception for RDP. Additional information is available here:

http://blogs.msdn.com/b/mast/archive/2014/03/06/enable-rdp-or-reset-password-with-the-vm-agent.aspx

You'll find a Microsoft blog post on the internals of the agent including the services it uses, the ports used for communication, and how to troubleshoot here:

```
http://blogs.msdn.com/b/mast/archive/2014/02/17/bginfo-guest-agent-extension-for-
azure-vms.aspx
```

The agent also enables integration with declarative, automation technologies such as Chef, Puppet, and PowerShell Desired State Configuration (DSC). This enables full configuration of VMs, either during provisioning or at a later time. With a declarative approach, you simply tell the system how you want it to look. For example, you might declare that you want IIS installed. The system then works out how to make that happen, handles errors, and so on. With an imperative approach, you would need to write code to check whether IIS was already installed, install IIS, check for errors, and so on. Here's some code that uses PowerShell to install IIS:

```
Import-Module ServerManager

#Check and install Web Server Role if not installed
If (-not (Get-WindowsFeature "Web-Server").Installed) {
    try {
        Add-WindowsFeature Web-Server -whatif
    }
    catch {
        Write-Error $_
    }
}
```

With PowerShell DSC, you would use this:

```
# Install the IIS role
WindowsFeature IIS
{
    Ensure       = "Present"
    Name         = "Web-Server"
}
```

Next, I want to show you a more complicated PowerShell DSC script that I use with my Azure VMs to install IIS and configure an additional website. You will notice the script connects to an Azure Files SMB share to pull down an additional PowerShell DSC provider (which provides functionality) along with some content for the new website. I also place all of the code I wish to run in a variable to stop PowerShell from generating a module not found error when it first runs validation. (I don't actually copy the required module until midway through the script.) That's why any single or double quotes within the $configString are escaped with the ` character; all the code is actually in a variable. Obviously, this is not for the faint of heart, but with a little PowerShell practice, it will make sense.

```
$hostname = (hostname).ToUpper()

Write-Verbose -Verbose:$true "[$hostname] Starting the node configuration"
```

```
#This is set automatically when called by Azure script extension
#Set-ExecutionPolicy unrestricted -Force

Write-Verbose -Verbose:$true "[$hostname] Enabling Remoting"

Enable-PSRemoting -Force

#uses
#http://gallery.technet.microsoft.com/scriptcenter
#              /xWebAdministration-Module-3c8bb6be

Write-Verbose -Verbose:$true "[$hostname] Copying Azure Files Content"

#Copy the modules to the folder
$username = "savillmasterazurestore"
$password = convertto-securestring -String "R6yw==" -AsPlainText -Force
$cred = new-object -typename System.Management.Automation.PSCredential `
        -argumentlist $username, $password

New-PSDrive –Name T –PSProvider FileSystem `
    -Root "\\savillmasterazurestore.file.core.windows.net\tools" `
    -Credential $cred
Copy-Item -Path "T:\DSC\xWebAdministration" `
    -Destination $env:ProgramFiles\WindowsPowerShell\Modules -Recurse
Remove-PSDrive -Name T

Write-Verbose -Verbose:$true "[$hostname] Applying DSC Configuration"

$configString=@"
Configuration SavillTechWebsite
{
    param
    (
        # Target nodes to apply the configuration
        [string[]]`$NodeName = `'localhost`'
    )
    # Import the module that defines custom resources
    Import-DscResource -Module xWebAdministration
    Node `$NodeName
    {
        # Install the IIS role
        WindowsFeature IIS
        {
            Ensure          = `"Present`"
            Name            = `"Web-Server`"
        }
        #Install ASP.NET 4.5
        WindowsFeature ASPNet45
```

```
                        {
                            Ensure = `'"Present`'"
                            Name = `'"Web-Asp-Net45`'"
                        }
                        # Stop the default website
                        xWebsite DefaultSite
                        {
                            Ensure       = `'"Present`'"
                            Name         = `'"Default Web Site`'"
                            State        = `'"Stopped`'"
                            PhysicalPath = `'"C:\inetpub\wwwroot`'"
                            DependsOn    = `'"[WindowsFeature]IIS`'"
                        }
                        # Copy the website content
                        File WebContent
                        {
                            Ensure       = `'"Present`'"
                            SourcePath   = `'"C:\Program
Files\WindowsPowerShell\Modules\xWebAdministration\SavillSite`'"
                            DestinationPath = `'"C:\inetpub\SavillSite`'"
                            Recurse      = `$true
                            Type         = `'"Directory`'"
                            DependsOn    = `'"[WindowsFeature]AspNet45`'"
                        }
                        # Create a new website
                        xWebsite SavTechWebSite
                        {
                            Ensure       = `'"Present`'"
                            Name         = `'"SavillSite`'"
                            State        = `'"Started`'"
                            PhysicalPath = `'"C:\inetpub\SavillSite`'"
                            DependsOn    = `'"[File]WebContent`'"
                        }
                }
        }
}
"@
Invoke-Expression $configString


SavillTechWebsite -MachineName localhost

Start-DscConfiguration -Path .\SavillTechWebsite -Wait -Verbose
```

Microsoft has a blog that links to some of their own solutions that I recommend reading:

http://azure.microsoft.com/blog/2014/08/08/automating-vm-configuration-using-powershell-dsc-extension/

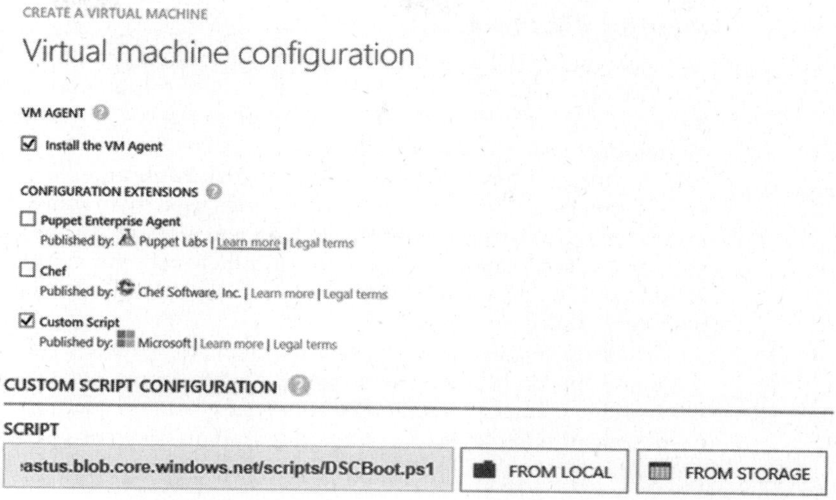

FIGURE 9.12
Specifying a script to
be used for initial VM
configuration

CREATE A VIRTUAL MACHINE

Virtual machine configuration

VM AGENT ⓘ

☑ **Install the VM Agent**

CONFIGURATION EXTENSIONS ⓘ

☐ **Puppet Enterprise Agent**
Published by: ⚠ Puppet Labs | Learn more | Legal terms

☐ **Chef**
Published by: 🍴 Chef Software, Inc. | Learn more | Legal terms

☑ **Custom Script**
Published by: ⊞ Microsoft | Learn more | Legal terms

CUSTOM SCRIPT CONFIGURATION ⓘ

SCRIPT

| astus.blob.core.windows.net/scripts/DSCBoot.ps1 | 📁 FROM LOCAL | ▦ FROM STORAGE |

During the initial provisioning of a VM, you can specify a script by entering a filename in the Custom Script Configuration area, as shown in Figure 9.12. You can also call the script at any time using PowerShell—for example:

```
Set-AzureVMCustomScriptExtensions –VM $vm -StorageAccountName $stor `
    -FileName "power.ps1" -run 'power.ps1' | Update-AzureVM
```

As I've experimented with PowerShell DSC, I've learned a few things. Here are some tips to help you as you begin to develop your own PowerShell DSC scripts for use in Azure:

◆ Make sure you enable remoting in your script.

◆ Do not require any interaction; the script runs in the background and you cannot interact with it.

◆ Use `Write-Verbose` in your script to aid troubleshooting; you want as much information as possible written to the log file.

◆ Give it time. The script runs asynchronously, so a VM may show as provisioned, but your script may still be running in the background even after you connect to the VM.

◆ View logs within the VM at `C:\WindowsAzure\Logs\Plugins\Microsoft.Compute.CustomScriptExtension\<version, e.g. 1.1>`. The main file is `CustomScriptHandler.log`. See your file execution for yourself.

If you are writing your script using PowerShell DSC, you will want to take a look at the example script in written using Azure DSC. It can help you in the deployment of VMs to Azure. You can download it here:

```
https://gallery.technet.microsoft.com/xAzure-PowerShell-Module-7dbf43b4
```

Moving VMs to Azure

As you know, an image is an OS disk that has been prepared for duplication. For Windows, this means SYSPREP generalize has been run. Although Azure has many images available for use in Azure, there will be instances where you need to move an existing VM from on-premises to Azure. At other times, you will need to create your own images in Azure as the basis for future VMs. In Chapter 8, "Setting Up Replication, Backup, and Disaster Recovery," I walked you through some of the technologies used to migrate OS instances from on-premises to Azure. In this section, I want to look in more detail at the process you need follow for a regular VM before moving it to Azure and then steps you will perform once it is in Azure. Note I am talking about VM disks and not images in this section—the VM disks that have not been generalized.

Assuming you are using Hyper-V on-premises, either as your hypervisor or as part of a migration approach, you need to ensure that the source VM is compatible with Azure. (As discussed in Chapter 8, you should have a Generation 1 VM and use VHD storage.) You also need to ensure that some other OS configurations are in place in the OS prior to moving to Azure:

◆ Ensure that Remote Desktop (RDP) is enabled.

◆ Ensure that the required firewall exception for RDP is enabled.

◆ Ensure that at minimum the Windows Server 2012 version of the Hyper-V Integration Services are installed in the VM.

◆ Ensure that the OS is supported in Azure.

It does not matter if the VHD type is Dynamic, since it will be converted to Fixed during the upload to Azure. Also, any network adapters will be removed. A new VM is created in Azure, so any network configuration will be lost and replaced with a new DHCP-based configuration.

To upload a VHD from a local area to an Azure storage account, I would use the following PowerShell script:

```
$sourceVHD = "D:\Software\VHDs\winiis05.vhd"
$destinationVHD = `
    "https://<storage account>.blob.core.windows.net/vhds/winiis053.vhd"
Add-AzureVhd -LocalFilePath $sourceVHD -Destination $destinationVHD `
    -NumberOfUploaderThreads 5
Add-AzureDisk -DiskName 'winiis05' -MediaLocation $destinationVHD `
    -Label 'winiis05' -OS "Windows"
```

The PowerShell script uploads the VHD, and once it is uploaded, the VHD is marked as an Azure disk that contains a Windows OS. With the disk uploaded, a new VM would be created in Azure and configured to use the newly uploaded VHD file. If you are using the New-AzureVMConfig cmdlet, you can pass to the existing disk by specifying -DiskName '<name>'. If you are adding data disks, then use Add-AzureDataDisk -Import '<data disk name>' -LUN 0 for each data disk.

Once you have created the VM in Azure using the uploaded VHD, there are some other changes to make:

◆ Move the pagefile to the temporary D: drive.

◆ Configure the VM to use Key Management Service (KMS) and to use the Azure KMS Servers. This ensures that the OS is activated. The KMS keys can be found here:

```
http://technet.microsoft.com/en-us/library/jj612867.aspx
```

Find the key for the OS version you have uploaded, configure that key (if not already using KMS), and then activate. Enter these commands in an elevated command prompt:

```
slmgr /ipk <KMS key>
slmgr /skms kms.core.windows.net
slmgr /ato
```

◆ Configure disks to automatically mount when added. Enter the next commands in an elevated command prompt:

```
Diskpart
SAN POLICY=OnlineAll
Exit
```

◆ Configure the RDP keep-alive. Enter the following commands in an elevated command prompt:

```
reg add "HKLM\SOFTWARE\Policies\Microsoft\Windows NT\Terminal Services"➤
/t REG_DWORD /vKeepAliveEnable /d 1
reg add "HKLM\SOFTWARE\Policies\Microsoft\Windows NT\Terminal Services"➤
/t REG_DWORD /vKeepAliveInterval /d 1
```

These configurations emulate many of the actions usually performed by Azure when creating a new VM. Azure populates a SYSPREP unattend answer file. If you look at a VM created in Azure, you can see the unattend.xml file it used. It is kept in the C:\Windows\Panther folder for troubleshooting purposes. If you look at the file, you will see most of the configuration is performed by one line:

```
<Description>Execute Unattend.wsf</Description><Path>cmd.exe /c "cscript
%SystemRoot%\OEM\Unattend.wsf //Job:setup //NoLogo //B
/ConfigurationPass:specialize"</Path>
```

The answer file remains in the C:\Windows\OEM folder, and if you poke around, you can learn a lot about what happens when Azure creates a VM. If you are interested in some of the internals that happen behind the scenes when you create a VM in Azure, I suggest watching Mark Russinovich's session from TechEd Europe 2013. At around 55 minutes, this video walks through the Azure VM provisioning process. You can find it here:

```
http://channel9.msdn.com/Events/TechEd/Europe/2013/WAD-B402#fbid=
```

Creating New VM Images

You can create your own custom images in Azure. These are OS environments ready for duplication. For Windows, SYSPREP generalize has been run for the image. This is the same process you would use to create an on-premises template.

1. Install the OS.

2. Configure it as required.

3. For Windows, run SYSPREP after selecting the generalize option and Enter System Out-of-box Experience (OOBE) for the action.

4. Ensure that your images do not have an unattend.xml file. Azure will create its own to enable the configuration of the OS inside the VM when deployed from your template.

Microsoft provides detailed instructions for creating both Windows and Linux images. They are available here:

http://msdn.microsoft.com/en-US/library/azure/dn790290.aspx

The Common Tasks For Managing Images section of the page includes links to articles that provide specific details. The key point is once your image is created, upload it to Azure in much the same way as you would an OS disk. Instead of using the Add-AzureVHD cmdlet, however, you will use the Add-AzureImage cmdlet to mark the VHD as an image instead of an OS disk. Here's an example:

```
Add-AzureVMImage -ImageName "Corp 2012 R2 DC" -MediaLocation $destinationVHD `
    -OS "Windows"
```

It is also possible to create new images in Azure based on VMs you have created in Azure. If you wish, you can choose to generalize them, but it is not required. Once you have an Azure VM configured as you would like, I recommend shutting it down (although shutdown is not required) and then saving it as an image. If the VM has additional data disks, they will also be saved as part of the image. For example:

```
Save-AzureVMImage -ServiceName $service -Name $name `
    -ImageName "CorpImage2" -OSState Generalized
```

If the VM has not been through the SYSPREP generalize process, use this:

```
Save-AzureVMImage -ServiceName $service -Name $name `
    -ImageName "CorpImage2" -OSState Specialized
```

The distinction is important. When a VM is created from the image, the -OSState setting tells Azure whether it is possible to perform configurations through an unattend.xml answer file. Using an answer file is only possible if the image has been generalized.

Once an image is created, it would be used the same way as any other image in Azure. What follows are some commented PowerShell commands that walk through the process of creating an image and then using it as part of a new VM creation:

```
#Capture an Azure VM to a template

#Recommend to stop first
```

```
Stop-AzureVM -ServiceName savtecheastus -Name sandbox

#Save the specified virtual machine to a new image (sandboximage in this example)
#Because this VM has NOT had SYSPREP run I use OSState Specialized but if it had
#been SYSPREP'd I would use -OSState Generalized
Save-AzureVMImage -ServiceName savtecheastus -Name sandbox `
    -ImageName "sandboximage" -OSState Specialized

#Save a reference to the new image
$sandboxImg = Get-AzureVMImage -ImageName sandboximage

#Set some variables I would use if setting a provisioning configuration
$admin = "localadmin"
$myPwd = "V3ryHardTh!ngT0Gue33"

#Create a new VM config using the new image. Below is assuming the image is
#not generalized.
$newVM = New-AzureVMConfig -Name "Sandbox2" -InstanceSize Basic_A1 `
    -ImageName $sandboxImg.ImageName

#If the image had been specialized I would add a provisioning config to command,
#for example:
#$newVM = New-AzureVMConfig -Name "Sandbox2" -InstanceSize Basic_A1 `
#    -ImageName #$sandboxImg.ImageName |
#    Add-AzureProvisioningConfig -Windows -AdminUsername $admin -Password -$myPwd

#Create a new virtual machine based on the above configuration
New-AzureVM -ServiceName savtecheastus -VMs $newVM -WaitForBoot -Verbose

#Remove an image
Get-AzureVMImage -ImageName sandboximage | Remove-AzureVMImage -DeleteVHD
```

You can also use the Azure portal to select a VM and create an image based on that VM via the Capture action. Once again, you do not have to shut down the VM first, but I recommend that you do. Once you select the Capture action, you will be prompted for a name and a description of the new image. Click the check box if you've executed SYSPREP and the VM is specialized. Figure 9.13 shows this option.

JSON and the Future of Templates

I want to finish with a quick word on the direction of Azure and the Microsoft on-premises solutions. I have covered in great detail deploying single VMs, and this is critical. However, most solutions are composed of multiple VMs and perhaps multiple tiers—for example, a web tier, a middleware tier, and a database backend tier. Remember that Azure started with PaaS as the primary model and then introduced roles. IaaS VMs blended into that existing model with no real way to model resources that were not cloud services. If yours is a large organization, you want to perform full modeling of services to enable activities such as change control. So far, all the actions performed (apart from PowerShell DSC for the OS configuration inside a VM) have been imperative. You have to write your own scripts with your own error handling

FIGURE 9.13
Creating a new image
from an existing
Azure VM

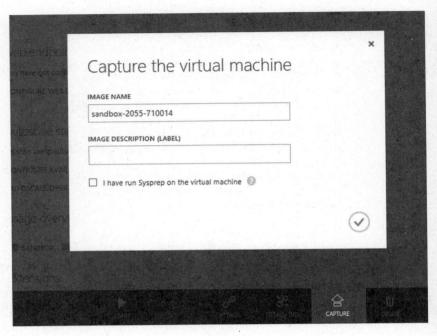

and your own checks to verify whether part of a script has already been performed. This is a big toll. Microsoft tried to help with this by creating scripts to deploy certain types of services. (Microsoft published a huge script for deploying SharePoint.) The problem is that people don't want to deploy resources à la carte, one by one. They want to deploy services in a resource-centric manner. This is why Microsoft has shifted focus to the resource groups and Azure Resource Manager mentioned in Chapter 2. The resource group becomes a life cycle container with all resources in the group sharing a common life cycle. This approach also enables features such as RBAC. Additionally, the resources in a resource group share a common identity, so they will be able to talk to each other using their identity, thus simplifying access between resources.

If you look at the preview Azure portal, there are options to deploy entire solutions such as SharePoint that consist of multiple virtual machines. This is made possible through the new resource group template. The template uses JavaScript Object Notation (JSON) to notate the desired configuration, which is then used in deployment. A resource group template is the preferred way to deploy resources to resource groups. Although the old imperative way (using PowerShell and APIs) is still available, you will want to adopt the resource group templates so that you no longer have to worry about handling errors and can just let Azure do it.

A number of these resource group templates are available in the Azure gallery, and you can create your own. Microsoft has an add-on for Visual Studio, which allows for a very intuitive JSON editing environment with IntelliSense to help guide you in the process. Additionally, through the integration it is also possible to perform deployments. You can find an overview of the Visual Studio JSON environment here:

```
http://azure.microsoft.com/blog/2014/11/26/azure-resource-manager-2-5-for-visual-
studio
```

To work with the templates, you need to use the Azure Resource Manager in PowerShell, which means switching mode using the `Switch-AzureMode AzureResourceManager` command and using `Add-AzureAccount` to authenticate.

To view the available gallery templates, use the following code. I've also included a sample of the returned data, but the gallery contains hundreds of templates and is the standard way services are now delivered.

```
PS C:\> Get-AzureResourceGroupGalleryTemplate
Microsoft                    Microsoft.WebSiteMySQLDatabase.0.2.2-preview
Microsoft                    Microsoft.WebSiteMySQLDatabase.0.2.3-preview
Microsoft                    Microsoft.WebSiteMySQLDatabase.0.2.4-preview
```

In my example, I returned three entries related to a SQL web farm. This might seem unusual since I'm an infrastructure-focused person, but take note of the name, Farm, and not just Server. These templates provide great insight into the capabilities. To download one to inspect it more closely, use the following PowerShell command. Notice that in the following example, first I look at basic information about the template and then I download it.

```
PS C:\> Get-AzureResourceGroupGalleryTemplate `
      -Identity  Microsoft.WebSiteMySQLDatabase.0.2.4-preview
Identity              : Microsoft.WebSiteMySQLDatabase.0.2.4-preview
Publisher             : Microsoft
Name                  : WebSiteMySQLDatabase
Version               : 0.2.4-preview
CategoryIds           : {azure, web, data}
PublisherDisplayName  : Microsoft
DisplayName           : Website + MySQL
DefinitionTemplates   : https://gallerystoreprodch.blob.core.windows.net/prod-
                        microsoft-windowsazure-gallery/Microsoft.WebSiteMySQLDatabase.
                        0.2.4-preview/DeploymentTemplates/Website_NewHostingPlan
                        _MySQL_NewDB-Default.json
Summary               : Enjoy secure and flexible development, deployment, and
                        scaling options for your web app plus a MySQL database.
Description           : <h3>Create and deploy web sites in seconds, as powerful
                        as you need them</h3>
                        <p>Leverage your existing tools to create and deploy
                        applications without the hassle of managing
                        infrastructure. Microsoft Azure Web Sites offers secure
                        and flexible development, deployment, and scaling
                        options for any sized web application. Use frameworks
                        and templates to create web sites in seconds. Choose
                        from source control options like TFS, GitHub, and
                        BitBucket. Use any tool or OS to develop your site with
                        .NET, PHP, Node.js or Python.<p>
                        <p>Use this Azure template to create a Website and
                        ClearDB MySQL Database together to start developing even
                        faster.<p>
```

```
<ul>
<li>Fastest way to build for the cloud</li>
<li>Provision and deploy fast</li>
<li>Secure platform that scales automatically</li>
<li>Great experience for Visual Studio developers</li>
<li>Open and flexible for everyone</li>
<li>Monitor, alert, and auto scale</li>
</ul>
<p>MySQL Database requires a credit card to be
associated with the subscription. To add credit card to
your subscription, <a
href="http://account.windowsazure.com/subscriptions"
target="_blank">click here</a>. Additionally, MySQL
Database is not available in certain regions and cannot
be created by users who have an Enterprise Agreement or
by co-admins. For more information, <a
href="http://go.microsoft.com/fwlink/?LinkId=268693"
target="_blank">click here</a>.<p>
```

```
PS C:\> Save-AzureResourceGroupGalleryTemplate `
    -Identity Microsoft.WebSiteMySQLDatabase.0.2.4-preview `
    -Path d:\azure\templates\


Path
----
D:\azure\templates\Microsoft.WebSiteMySQLDatabase.0.2.4-preview.json
```

Download the template in your environment and take some time to walk through it, either in Notepad or a tool like Visual Studio. Microsoft's article "Using Windows PowerShell with Resource Manager" goes through the parts of the template and discusses deploying the template using PowerShell. You will find the article here:

http://azure.microsoft.com/en-us/documentation/articles/powershell-azure-resource-manager/

The first part of the file walks through the parameters required to deploy the template. For example, it describes how to select a site to deploy to and an SKU for the database. These values are then used in the resources section to create the resources. One very nice feature is that templates understand dependences between the resources and will create resources in the correct order. You can reference resources as part of the creation of other resources. For example, you can reference a SQL resource as part of the configuration of an IIS resource. The required values are automatically populated at deployment time, which helps the Azure Resource Manager know that the SQL resources need to be deployed before the IIS resources. Also, as you review the file notice that rules are defined that specify counts for the number of instances of each resource and metrics that trigger a new instance. For example, you can create a rule that starts a new instance when CPU runs greater than 80 percent. This is far more powerful than the scale capabilities in cloud services that require you to precreate all the VMs and direct Azure to simply stop or start them.

I hope in time to see a graphical tool to help create and manage the JSON files, but the Visual Studio environment can be picked up very quickly even for nondevelopers. The big news is this: JSON template notation will work for on-premises in addition to Azure in a future version of the Windows Azure Pack. This allows a real hybrid approach to deployment and enables a single template to be created and used wherever you wish to deploy it.

The Bottom Line

Understand why you should use availability sets.   Availability sets are used to ensure that multiple instances of a service—for example, IIS servers—are distributed over two fault domains (server racks). This achieves two things. If there is a hardware failure in a rack, not all instances of a service will be affected. The service remains operational. As an added bonus, when Microsoft performs maintenance, it will only perform maintenance on one of the fault domains at a time. Once again, this ensures that some instances of the service will stay available.

Master It   Why should workloads never be mixed in an availability set?

Enable PowerShell management of Azure.   The Azure PowerShell cmdlets can be downloaded here:

```
http://azure.microsoft.com/en-us/documentation/articles/install-configure-
powershell/
```

They are installed using the Microsoft Web Platform Installer. Once the Web Platform Installer is installed, the module can be installed using the `Install-Module Azure` command.

Master It   Why is it necessary to frequently check for new versions of the Azure PowerShell modules?

## Chapter 10

Managing Hybrid Environments with System Center

No matter how "into the public cloud" an organization is, on-premises infrastructure will likely be with us for a long time. Organizations will look to leverage both on-premises and the public cloud to maximize the strengths and efficiencies of each. This chapter looks at a Microsoft-centric private cloud capability for on-premises and how you can bring the on-premises infrastructure together with the Azure resources for a single management and end-user experience. The Microsoft management solution that provides these capabilities is System Center, and System Center will be the primary focus of this chapter.

In this chapter, you will learn to

◆ Understand why leveraging the Azure portal directly for users has limitations

◆ Explain the core components of System Center to deliver a private cloud

◆ Identify the value proposition for Windows Azure Pack

Looking Beyond the Azure Portal

Throughout this book I've shown you how to perform many actions with the Azure portal(s), but near the start of the book, I recommended that for the most part you don't want to use the portals. You especially don't want to use portals for your end users. Some of the reasons for this guidance have changed recently with the introduction of role-based access control (RBAC). RBAC now allows users to be delegated access to only certain resources in a subscription. You no longer have to make users coadministrators to allow them to perform any action within the subscription, but that was not the primary reason for not using the Azure portal for end-user interactions.

Remember that most environments will have a hybrid environment, with resources created both on-premises and in Azure. Ideally, you don't want users to have to use different interfaces depending on where resources are created. You don't want them to know whether they are accessing on-premises resources or those in Azure. You also don't want end users making decisions based on the location of the resources they access. Instead, as part of your provisioning process, you want the logic to decide where to deploy resources based on user requirements.

There are no workflow capabilities in the Azure portal, which means no ability to trigger other actions or even have approval activities as part of a resource provisioning request. This is a common requirement for many organizations that may also want to institute quotas that are more restrictive than those configured at the subscription level.

The Azure portal is becoming richer in terms of capabilities. However, it is still not designed for the mass deployments required in some scenarios.

For me, the biggest reason for not employing the portal for end-user interactions is simply this: what if there is a problem? It's highly unlikely Azure will ever have to fail over an entire region, but if that did happen and your resources were all provisioned via the Azure portals, you would have a hard time recreating them and attaching to the replicated storage via the Geo-redundant Storage (GRS) account. If you use a centralized provisioning process, it is possible to build into that process a logging system and the ability to recreate the environment in the event of a disaster.

If you decide to take the approach of not using the Azure portals for end-user interactions, you need to consider the types of service you must provide to the users, both for Azure and on-premises. What do they need? This list will vary, but the following is mandatory for most environments:

◆ The ability to provision and deprovision resources based on a defined set of templates that are made available to users

◆ The ability to modify the configuration of deployed resources within the capabilities of the fabric

◆ The ability to start, stop, and query the status of resources

◆ The ability to connect to resources and, for example, generate an RDP file

It is possible to create your own solution, and some companies have on various levels. Provisioning and deprovisioning is achievable with PowerShell, especially when integrated with System Center (as you'll see shortly). However, the greater the number of interactive elements, the more difficult it will be. Consider the rate of change in Azure. Creating a complete in-house system would be a full-time job for a team of developers. Consider also the lag between features in Azure and their availability in the Azure portal—and that is Microsoft; they know months before the features are even released to start development to implement them in the portal.

A better option is to use a third-party cloud management solution that will integrate with your on-premises and public cloud resources. Many solutions are available, but I am going to focus on System Center, the Microsoft solution. Keep in mind that this is not the only solution. If you currently use other cloud management solutions, you should look at their hybrid cloud capabilities and assess their ability to meet your requirements.

Introduction to System Center

System Center is the primary Microsoft product for all aspects of management of servers, clients, devices, and clouds, be they private or public. You may know System Center as a suite of products, but that changed with System Center 2012. All the different products that you could purchase separately or in various SKU combinations (there were over 30) were rolled in and became components of a single product. System Center 2012 is available as Standard Edition or Datacenter Edition. Both are licensed in two physical process (socket) increments. (If your server has four processors in it, you need two licenses for System Center.)

Just like Windows Server, System Center licensing differences between Standard and Datacenter relate to virtual instance rights. The Standard Edition includes two virtual instance rights. This means that a maximum of two VMs can be managed with Standard System Center. The Datacenter Edition includes an unlimited number of VMs. Standard is typically used for physical deployments or very light virtualization, such as in a branch office, whereas Datacenter is used for the virtualization environments.

It is possible to "stack" Standard licenses. For example, if you have four virtual machines, you can purchase two copies of Standard. Those two licenses will allow four virtual instances, but there are limitations. Note that you cannot move the licenses between hosts frequently. If you cluster hosts and wish to move the VMs, then each host has to be licensed for the high watermark of VMs that will ever run on the license. If you have eight VMs running on a host at any one time (maybe during maintenance), that one host will need four copies of Standard. Figure 10.1 shows the normal running of the environment, but also the possible requirement if VMs are moved. Additional licenses are required, since licenses cannot just follow the VMs. This is why in most environments Datacenter, with its unlimited number of virtual instances, is typically used.

FIGURE 10.1
Stacking Standard licenses in VM mobility scenarios

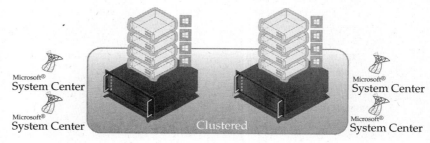

Normal running

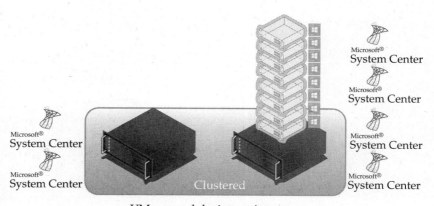

VMs moved during maintenance

Note that when managing OS instances in Azure, the Datacenter Edition works a little differently. It would not be financially viable for Microsoft to allow a single Datacenter license to allow an unlimited number of VMs running in Azure. There is no exposed concept of a host or physical sockets. Therefore, in Azure the two editions cover the following number of VMs:

◆ Standard: two VMs

◆ Datacenter: eight VMs

Another big difference from versions of System Center prior to 2012 is that there are no management server licenses now. You can deploy as many management servers as needed to provide service for the OS instances that are licensed to be managed by System Center. Additionally, SQL Server Standard rights are included. They can be used exclusively for System Center purposes.

Figure 10.2 shows the "donut" I always draw on the whiteboard when I talk about System Center. It shows the various components of System Center and their core focus areas. Note that this is current for System Center 2012 R2, but I expect this to change a little for the next version. The core components will still be mostly the same. Note how Windows Azure Pack looms over the top of System Center, just waiting to descend upon it. I like to start from the top right with Configuration Manager and work my way around the donut. Note that nearly all elements of System Center can run in Azure, and some even have specific functionality to take advantage of Azure. For example, Configuration Manager can use Azure as a distribution point where clients can download programs and updates. System Center Operations Manager can use Azure to help test whether public-facing resources are accessible from around the world by using the Azure resources. Data Protection Manager integrates with Azure Backup.

FIGURE 10.2
The System Center donut

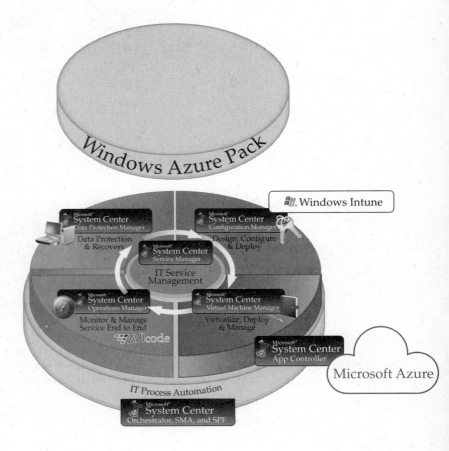

System Center Configuration Manager

System Center Configuration Manager (SCCM) provides capabilities to deploy operating systems, applications, and OS/software updates to servers and desktops. Detailed hardware and software inventory and asset intelligence features are a key aspect of SCCM. These enable great insight into the entire organization's IT infrastructure. SCCM 2012 introduced management of mobile devices, such as iOS and Android, through ActiveSync integration with Exchange and a user-focused management model. This was removed in the 2012 SP1 version, and instead a tight integration with Microsoft Intune is used for mobile device management, all through a single Configuration Manager console.

One key feature of SCCM for servers is settings management. You can now define desired configuration settings, such as OS and application settings, and then apply them to a group of servers (or desktops). This can be very useful for compliance requirements. The challenge I face in recommending SCCM for servers is that its focus seems to be shifting to mainly desktop management. The benefits SCCM can bring to servers—such as patching, host deployment, and desired configuration—are better handled through other mechanisms. For patch management, both SCVMM and Failover Clustering have one-click patching capabilities that leverage Windows Server Update Services (WSUS) and not SCCM. For host deployment, SCVMM has the ability to deploy physical servers for Hyper-V, to deploy physical servers for file servers, to automatically manage cluster membership, and more. Desired configuration is possible through PowerShell v4's Desired State Configuration feature. Therefore, if you are already using SCCM, you can take advantage of some of those capabilities in your environment. But I don't recommend implementing SCCM for the sole purpose of server management. In my opinion, there are better options in the other components and base operating system.

System Center Virtual Machine Manager and App Controller

I am covering the System Center Virtual Machine Manager and App Controller together, as they are symbiotic components. App Controller needs Virtual Machine Manager for any on-premises management. Virtual Machine Manager has no native web interface; it requires App Controller to offer web-based interactions.

Although Hyper-V ships with a native management tool (as does Failover Clustering), the expectation is that, if you are managing a production Hyper-V environment, you are using Virtual Machine Manager. Virtual Machine Manager is more than just a hypervisor manager and more than just Hyper-V. The 2012 R2 version supports Hyper-V, ESX, and XenServer. Virtual Machine Manager also integrates with both the networking and storage fabric of your on-premises environment. You can configure SCVMM to understand your networks—such as Production, DMC, and Backup—and then use SCVMM to configure the VLANs and IP space used for each network in each location. This approach enables a VM to be provisioned and configured to connect to, say, your Production network in London. SCVMM will then identify the hosts that have connectivity to that network, place the VM accordingly, and configure the correct VLAN and IP address. This is useful for administrators, but critical if you wish to enable end-user self-service. End users cannot be expected to create these advanced types of network configurations.

The storage integration enables SCVMM to integrate with both SANs via SMI-S and also Windows File Services to offer a similar capability to networking. Different aggregates on storage subsystems can be classified in each location. For example, you may have Gold, Silver, and Bronze tiers of storage based on the capabilities of the storage. Perhaps solid-state drive (SSD)-based storage in the SAN will be available on your Gold tier, whereas regular hard disk drive (HDD) may be the only option available to those with Bronze-tier privileges. When a VM is provisioned, it can be requested to be stored on the Silver tier of storage. SCVMM will identify the storage that can provide that tier of service in the desired location, allocate the logical unit numbers (LUNs) as needed, set permissions, and create the VM. Once again, this capability is critical if you want to enable flexible end-user self-service or just want to make your life simpler as an administrator.

SCVMM has other capabilities based on service templates, although they are being de-emphasized with the move to JavaScript Object Notation (JSON) with Windows Azure Pack. Later in the chapter, I will focus on other key capabilities that enable the grouping of compute, storage, and network resources together to form clouds. These clouds can also be assigned capabilities and limits to which groups of users, known as tenants, are then assigned access with their own tenant and user level quotas. This gets you one step closer to the private cloud. Note that SCVMM does not integrate with Azure in any way; it is focused on on-premises resources only.

The other half of the symbiotic relationship is App Controller, which is a Silverlight-based web interface that can connect to SCVMM clouds, which are clouds managed with Microsoft's Service Provider Foundation (SPF). Hosting organizations can leverage System Center for their operations. The App Controller also connects to Azure subscriptions showing resources in Azure. Figure 10.3 shows an example of App Controller. Notice that you can see resources running on Hyper-V, on ESX, and in Azure. The Hyper-V and ESX-based resources are surfaced through connectivity to SCVMM, whereas the Azure resources are accessed through a direct connection from App Controller to Azure.

FIGURE 10.3
A view of resources in App Controller

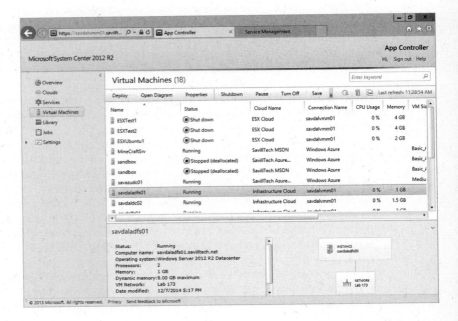

App Controller offers a rich ability to control resources in the various clouds but only a basic, nonworkflow-based provisioning and deprovisioning. It does not support the RBAC capabilities of Azure. The fact that App Controller is Silverlight based has hampered its adoption for users of browsers without Silverlight support. When you look at the next version of System Center, you will see App Controller is missing. Instead, Windows Azure Pack will be used as the web portal, but for today, you can use App Controller if you have not yet adopted Windows Azure Pack.

System Center Operations Manager

System Center Operations Manager (SCOM) provides a rich monitoring solution for Microsoft and non-Microsoft operating systems, applications, and hardware. Any monitoring solution can tell you when something is broken—and yes, SCOM does that—but its real power is in its proactive nature and best practice–adherence functionality. SCOM management packs are units of knowledge about a specific application or component. There is, for example, an Exchange management pack and a Domain Name System (DNS) for Windows Server management pack. Microsoft now mandates that any Microsoft product should have a management pack that is written by the product team responsible for the application or operating system component. The people who create best practice documents are creating management packs. You can then just deploy all the knowledge of those developers to your environment. SCOM will then raise alerts when it detects potential problems or when best practices are not being followed.

STOP THE ALERTS! I WANT TO GET OFF!

Often, customers raise objections that, when first implemented, SCOM floods them with alerts. The flood can happen for a number of reasons. Perhaps there are a lot of problems in the environment that should be fixed, but often SCOM will be tuned to ignore configurations that, though perhaps not best practice, are accepted by the organization.

Many third parties provide management packs for their applications and hardware devices. When I think about "all about the application" as a key tenet of the private cloud, the ability for SCOM to monitor the hardware, storage, network, and all the way through the OS to the application is huge, but it goes even further in SCOM 2012.

SCOM 2012 introduced a number of changes, but two huge ones relate to network monitoring and custom application monitoring. Microsoft licensed a technology from EMC called SMARTS, which enables a rich discovery and monitoring of network devices. With this functionality, SCOM can identify the relationship between network devices and services to understand that port 3 on this switch connects to server A. If there is a switch problem, SCOM will know the affected servers. Information such as CPU and memory information is available for supported network devices.

The other big change was the acquisition of AVIcode by Microsoft. AVIcode is now Application Platform Monitoring (APM) in SCOM 2012. APM provides monitoring for custom applications without requiring any changes to the application. APM currently supports .NET applications and Java Enterprise Edition (J2E). To understand this, let's look at a performance problem with a custom web application without APM.

The end user phones IT: "Application X is running slow and sucks."

IT phones the app developer: "Users say Application X is running really slow and really sucks."

The app developer talks to self: "I suck and have no clue how to start troubleshooting this. I will leave the industry in disgrace."

Now, see how the situation changes when SCOM APM has been configured to monitor the custom application.

The end user phones IT: "Application X is running slow and sucks."

IT phones the app developer: "Users say Application X is running really slow. I see in SCOM that the APM shows that, in function X of module Y, the SQL query `SELECT blah from blah blah` to SQL database Z is taking 3.5 seconds."

App developer talks to self: "It must be an indexing problem on the SQL server. The index needs to be rebuilt on database Z. I'll give the SQL DBA the details to fix."

App developer talks to SQL DBA: "Your SQL database sucks."

SCOM can be used in many aspects of the private cloud. It's great that it monitors the entire infrastructure to keep it healthy. Monitoring for health is critical to SCOM's ability to monitor resource usage. Trending helps you plan for growth and can trigger automatic scaling of services if a resource hits certain defined thresholds.

SCOM 2012 R2 also understands clouds and has a cloud view capability. Once the SCVMM management pack has been imported into SCOM and the SCVMM connector to SCOM has been configured, you will be able to navigate to Microsoft System Center Virtual Machine Manager ➢ Cloud Health Dashboard ➢ Cloud Health within the Monitoring workspace. Here you will find a list of all your clouds. After you select a cloud, you can select the Fabric Health Dashboard from the Tasks pane. That dashboard gives a nice insight into all the fabric elements that relate to the cloud. Also, a management pack for Azure helps expose basic health information about Azure services within SCOM.

System Center Data Protection Manager

I talked about Data Protection Manager (DPM) as it relates to disaster recovery and backup in Chapter 8, "Setting Up Replication, Backup, and Disaster Recovery." DPM is a best-of-breed backup, continuous protection, and recovery solution for Microsoft workloads. It presents a different approach from the rest of System Center, which is heterogeneous in nature and covers non-Microsoft hypervisors, operating systems, and services. DPM is aimed at being the best protection for Microsoft workloads, specifically Windows Server, Exchange, SQL Server, SharePoint, Hyper-V, and even Windows clients.

System Center Service Manager and System Center Orchestrator

System Center Service Manager and System Center Orchestrator are two separate components, but they are tied closely together and are most useful when used at the same time. This is especially true for issues related to provisioning of services with a rich workflow capability, which is desirable in your on-premises and Azure environments.

System Center Orchestrator provides two primary capabilities:

◆ The ability to communicate with many different systems

◆ The ability to automate defined series of activities that could span many different systems through runbooks

These two abilities can be highly beneficial to your hybrid cloud implementation.

At the most basic level, Orchestrator can be leveraged to create virtual machines, deploy services, and even create entire clouds through runbooks. I showed an example of a runbook back in Chapter 2, "When to Use IaaS: Cost and Options," in Figure 2.24. There I explained the idea behind a hybrid provisioning process. I will talk more about it later in this section.

Figure 10.4 shows a basic runbook. In the example, I've created a user and enabled that user using activities from the Active Directory Integration Pack. Numerous integration packs are included, and I've expanded the Active Directory Integration Pack in the figure to show some activities it contains. To create a runbook, you just drag activities from the Activities window and connect them to form sequences of actions. It is also possible to run PowerShell scripts to perform actions through Orchestrator via Run .NET Activity.

FIGURE 10.4

A basic Orchestrator runbook

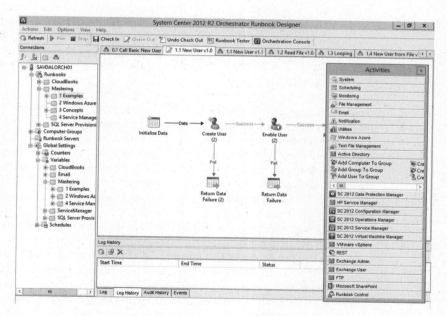

Each integration pack contains activities specific to the target. For vSphere, there are activities for virtual machine creation and management; the same type of activities are available for SCVMM. For Configuration Manager, the activities include deploying software. Using integration packs for systems, the built-in Orchestrator activities, and PowerShell, it is possible to automate any action related to the private cloud (and anything else). You can customize your runbooks to reflect exactly how your organization functions. Once you create the runbooks, they can then be called by the rest of System Center or triggered automatically. Here are scenarios where Orchestrator can be used:

◆ Creating a new cloud based on an IT request through a service catalog, which calls the Orchestrator runbook you created

◆ Deploying a new virtual machine or service instance

◆ Offering a runbook that automatically patches and reboots all virtual machines for a particular user or business group

◆ Automatically scaling deployed services up and down by triggering runbooks that perform scaling based on performance alerts from SCOM

◆ Deprovisioning virtual machines or services that have passed a given length of time or date in development purposes

Remember that the goal for the cloud is that the cloud is automated, and you can't automate by using graphic consoles. So, as you learn System Center and Azure management, look at the series of actions you perform, the PowerShell scripts you use, and the activities in integration packs. Start creating runbooks in Orchestrator that can be used. Once the runbooks are created, they can be manually triggered using the Silverlight web-based Orchestrator interface or triggered from other systems, such as an item in Service Manager's service catalog. Orchestrator is able to connect to almost any system. With a bit of work, any manual process you perform today should be able to be automated, and more important, orchestrated with System Center Orchestrator.

System Center Service Manager is the Configuration Management Database (CMDB) for your organization. It has feeds and connections to all the other System Center components and can offer various services, such as basic ticketing type activities like Incidents (things not doing what they should), Problems (something is broken), and Change Requests (somebody wants something). Because Service Manager connects to all the various systems, when there are problems in the environment, you can look at a computer in Service Manager and see information from all the systems. This gives you a single point of access and aids in your search for solutions. In Service Manager, you can see all of the hardware, software, and patch status that was gathered from Configuration Manager. You can see AD information that was pulled from AD. You can see any alerts that were generated by SCOM as well as complex service dependencies, such as all the systems that are responsible for providing messaging services to the organization.

So far I've talked about creating clouds, virtual machines, and services with the SCVMM console, App Controller, PowerShell, and Orchestrator. Problems arise when you begin to consider the end users for all these approaches. Their primary job is not IT, applications, data, hardware, and virtual environments. They don't want separate interfaces for requesting a virtual machine, for on-premises operations, or for accessing Azure resources. End users are not going to run PowerShell scripts, and giving them a list of runbooks through a web interface is likely to baffle them.

Service Manager 2012 introduced a new feature called a service catalog. A *service catalog* is a single source that can contain all the types of services offered by the organization. Your service catalog could include creating a new user, requesting the installation of a software package through SCCM, asking for a new keyboard—anything that Service Manager has some ability to enable through its connections to other systems. The service catalog is primarily available to end users through a SharePoint site that uses Service Manager Silverlight web parts. Users can browse the catalog as a single go-to place for all their needs, which makes it a perfect place to offer virtual services on the private cloud.

So, how do you offer the private cloud services in a service catalog? You just add runbooks from Orchestrator. When a user makes a request from the service catalog, your Service Manager workflows can be used. You can request authorization, and then, if granted, the workflow will call the runbook in Orchestrator to perform the actions. Service Manager and Orchestrator have great bidirectional communications in System Center; you can view the status of the runbook execution within Service Manager. Once the process is complete, the service request would be marked as completed, and the user can be sent an email.

I walk through creating this type of service using Service Manager in a video at http://youtu.be/T1jTX9xE66A. Service Manager has its own web interface that uses SharePoint, but it is fairly basic and is not easily extended—and it's kind of ugly.

Service Manager can also create chargeback price sheets that allow prices, such as the price per day for the VM; the price per core, memory, and storage per day; the price for a highly available VM or static IP address; and other items to be assigned to different aspects of the virtual environment. These price sheets can then be used within Service Manager to allow chargeback to business units based on their utilization.

All of these capabilities sound great, but there are some challenges. PowerShell is the de facto standard for automation with Microsoft, and other vendors have created PowerShell modules that enable PowerShell to interface with almost every technology that exists, but these vendors don't want to create Orchestrator integration packs. This has led to a lack of Orchestrator integration packs, and the ones that do exist are not being maintained. What this means is that the majority of the Orchestrator runbook logic is done using .NET activities, which in turn call the PowerShell scripts. Orchestrator is still useful as an engine to run the runbooks and to resume in the event of failure, and it offers features such as encrypted variables and a data bus to pass data between activities. But given the lack of integration packs, Orchestrator can't live up to the goal of being able to drag and drop activities onto a canvas without programming knowledge. As often as not, you will be writing PowerShell scripts.

To this end, Microsoft added Orchestrator Service Management Automation (SMA) in the 2012 R2 version of System Center. As you may expect, instead of using integration packs and activities, SMA is PowerShell workflow based. Still, it brings the benefit of a managed engine to organize and run those PowerShell workflows. SMA is the direction moving forward for the Orchestrator component.

Another challenge is that right now there are at least two interfaces. Rich, workflow-driven provisioning is available through Service Manager and Orchestrator, but to interact with VMs, you must use App Controller. This is not an ideal experience for you or your users.

Implementing a Private Cloud

Why am I talking about the private cloud in a book about Azure? After all, the private cloud is on-premises. However, when the goal is a hybrid solution, it is important that the on-premises environment share some architectural characteristics with the public cloud solution for the best experience.

"But I already have a private cloud—I run a virtualized environment," you say.

There is a big difference between virtualization and private cloud. The good news is that the difference is primarily in the management stack, and implementing a private cloud does not require changing the compute, network, or storage fabric.

What is the private cloud? One of my customers once said, "If you ask five people for a definition of the private cloud, you will get seven different answers." And that is 100 percent accurate. I like to think of the private cloud as having the following attributes:

◆ It is scalable and elastic; it can grow and shrink as the load on the application changes.

◆ It provides better utilization of resources.

◆ It is agnostic of the underlying fabric.

◆ It is accountable, which can also mean chargeable.

◆ It is self-service capable.

◆ It is all about the application.

Let's dive into these items, beginning with the last one, "all about the application."

If you consider the shift from physical to virtual, what really happened? In the physical world of yesterday, each physical server had a single operating system instance, which meant lots of wasted resources and money. The shift to virtualization has taken these OS instances and consolidated them in a smaller number of physical servers by running each OS instance in a virtual machine. Virtualization has saved hardware and money, but it hasn't changed the way IT is managed. You still log on to the OS instances at the console and still manage the same number of OS instances. In fact, you also have to manage the virtualization solution. Although you may not log on to the actual console of a server, you remotely access the OS to do management tasks. Basically, you still manage at the console level. The move to an application focus as part of the private cloud shifts the focus to the service being delivered and the applications used in that service offering. The private cloud infrastructure is responsible for creating the virtual machines and OS instances that are required to deploy a service, removing that burden from you as the administrator. The private cloud can also assist with the ongoing maintenance of the deployed service.

Now, think about scalable and elastic. Consider a multitiered service consisting of a web tier, middleware tier, and database tier. Focus on the web tier as an example. You could configure that tier to have a minimum of 2, a maximum of 20, and an initial of 4 instances. This means when the load increases, the user can just access the tool and scale out the tier to a higher number, such as 10. The backend infrastructure automatically takes care of creating the new virtual machines, setting up any configuration, adding the new instances to the load balancer, and any other associated actions. When the load dies down, the user can scale in that service, and once again, the backend infrastructure will automatically delete some virtual machines to reach the new target number and update the hardware load balancer.

That last example focused on an end user performing the scaling, but that same private cloud could have had monitoring in place, such as with SCOM. When a load hits a certain point, it would run some automated process using System Center Orchestrator that talks to System Center Virtual Machine Manager and performs the scaling. That's why, when I talk about the private cloud and focus on the application, it's not just about the System Center Virtual Machine Manager. The entire System Center product has its role for a complete private cloud solution. This scalability and elasticity—having access to resources when needed but not using them and allowing other services to leverage when not needed—is a key trait of the private cloud. Many organizations will charge business units for the amount of computer resource that is used by their applications, which is why this ability to scale out and in is important. By running many different services on a single infrastructure, you will see high utilization of available resources and get more bang for the infrastructure buck.

The concept of being agnostic of the underlying fabric can be confusing. Consider this: you want to offer services to your customers, which could be the IT department, business units in the organization, or individual users. You want to provide those customers with a menu of offerings; this is known as a service catalog. When those customers deploy a virtual machine or service, they should not need to know what IP address should be given to the virtual machine(s) or whether they are deploying a single or multitiered service. The customer should not have to specify which SAN to use or what part of the SAN they are allowed to access. Imagine that you have multiple datacenters, multiple types of networks, and multiple hypervisors. If you want to allow non-IT people to deploy virtual machines and services, you need to abstract all that underlying fabric infrastructure from them. The user must be able to say (or request through a self-service interface): "I want an instance of this service in Datacenters A and B, and it should connect to the development and backup networks on a Silver tier of storage." Behind the scenes, the private cloud infrastructure works out the details. It determines that for the development network in Datacenter A, the network adapter needs an IP address in a certain subnet connected to a specific VLAN and a different IP address for some other subnet and VLAN in Datacenter B. The infrastructure works out that Silver tier storage in Datacenter A means using the NetApp SAN and only specific LUNs, whereas in Datacenter B, the EMC SAN is used with other LUNs. The user gets the service and connectivity they need with zero knowledge of the actual infrastructure—which is exactly as it should be.

Self-service by the user for the provisioning of services is a great way to think of the difference between virtualization and the private cloud. Let me walk through the most basic case: creating a new virtual machine for a user. As I talk to clients about their current process for provisioning virtual machines in their virtual world, the process looks like this (see Figure 10.5):

1. The end user determines that they need a new VM.

2. The user makes a request to the IT department. This could be a phone call, an email, or a help-desk request.

3. The IT department gets the request and may do some validation, such as checking with management for approval.

4. IT launches their virtualization management tool and creates a virtual machine from a template.

5. IT contacts the user and gives them the IP address of the VM.

This sounds fast, but in reality, the process ranges from a few days to six weeks in some companies I've worked with. It's a manual process. IT teams are busy. They just don't like the particular business user. There could be "solar activity disrupting electronics" (which is the same as not liking the user). Because it's a manual process, it takes time and is often fairly low on the priority list.

Also, it can be hard to track the allocation of virtual machines and their usage. Often, there is no ability to charge business units for the requested virtual machines, which can lead to virtual machine sprawl as, to the business, the virtual machines are free.

FIGURE 10.5
Traditional process
for requesting virtual
machines, which
is hands on for the
administrator

In the private cloud, this changes to the process shown in Figure 10.6. Although the resources used are the same, the order of the steps and method has changed.

1. The IT team uses their management tool to carve out clouds of resources, which include compute, storage, and network resources, and assigns clouds to users or groups of users with certain quotas. This is all done before any users request resources and is the only time the IT team has to do any work. This frees them up to spend their time on more forward-looking endeavors.

2. The user accesses a self-service portal, fills out a basic request, and selects the type of VM or application and the cloud they wish to create it in based on their allocations and quotas.

3. The private cloud infrastructure takes the request and automatically provisions the VM. This could include workflows to request authorization from management, if required. The user would see the details of their new VM in the self-service portal and could even get an automated email giving them details.

4. The user is very happy, and if they had a red button, they would be pressing it.

FIGURE 10.6
Provisioning
process when using
private cloud

Now, self-service is the number-one fear of many IT departments I talk to. They are afraid that the ability for users and business units to serve themselves virtual machines will result in millions of virtual machines being created for no good reason. The IT infrastructure will be plunged into a dark age of misery, and VM sprawl beyond any previously envisioned nightmare scenario will ensue. Let me pull you back from that; it's simply not the case.

Remember what you are doing. First, you are creating clouds of resources. You define what these clouds can access in terms of which virtualization hosts. On those virtualization hosts, you specify how much memory, virtual CPU, and disk IOPS can be consumed. You set which tiers of storage that cloud can access and how much space is available. You set which networks that cloud can connect to. You set which VM templates can be used by the users to create the virtual machines. For each user or group of users, you set the quotas; you determine how many virtual machines they can create or how much memory and virtual CPUs they can use in each cloud. You can even set the type of virtual machines they can create and what those VMs can look like in terms of CPU and memory allocations. With a private cloud solution, you can set the chargeback and show-back (which shows users how much of a service they use) capabilities. If a business unit creates a large amount of virtual resources, they get charged accordingly, so the solution is fully accountable. You can set an expiry for virtual machines, so they are automatically deleted after a period of time. Users can only create VMs on the resources you have defined and within the limits you configured. If they have a limit of five virtual machines and want to create a sixth, they would have to either delete a virtual machine, export a virtual machine to a library that you have granted them, or request an extension of their quota, which triggers an approval process.

Read that last paragraph again. I think you will find that the private cloud's automated, self-service processes are more controlled and enforceable than any manual processes you may have today. When users request a VM today, you give it to them—it just takes you weeks. This might discourage business units from asking for virtual resources unless they really need them, but making the process painful is a terrible way to control resources. Business users will just go elsewhere for their services. Do you really want them setting up their own infrastructures or using public cloud services? I've seen that happen at a lot of organizations. It's far better to get good processes in place. Enable the business so they get functionality in the most optimal way and use internal services where it makes sense. Remember, with the private cloud you can configure costs for virtual resources and charge the business. If more virtual resources are required, because the business units can now provision resources more easily, the IT department can use those chargebacks to fund procurement of more IT infrastructure as needed.

I started this section by telling you that having virtualization does not mean that you have a private cloud. By now, hopefully you see a clear difference between virtualization and the private cloud. It is simply the management infrastructure. The same compute, network, and storage resources used for a virtualization infrastructure can all be used for a private cloud. To turn virtualization into a private cloud solution, the right management stack is added. For a Microsoft private cloud, that means adding System Center 2012 R2 to the virtualization foundation provided by Hyper-V 2012 R2. It is also possible to use other hypervisors, but some native capabilities will be lost. I provided a brief overview of System Center at the start of this chapter, but I want to go back to the components that are critical for a private cloud and explain why they are critical.

CAPABILITIES OF HYPER-V

When I talk at conferences, I ask the attendees about their current environment and their current hypervisor. Nearly every hand goes up for ESX. I won't say a bad word about ESX—it's a great hypervisor. (I'm VMware VCP 4 and VCP 5 certified.) However, you are paying a lot of money for that great job, and its management story is not so great, especially when compared to System Center, and especially if you are looking for a hybrid management solution. In the past, there was no serious alternative to ESX. With the Windows Server 2012 version of Hyper-V, you get a hypervisor that is enterprise ready. It just got better with Windows Server 2012 R2 and is getting even better in the next version of Windows Server. We now live in a world where ESX is playing catch-up with Hyper-V in some areas, and there are very few organizations that could not use Hyper-V instead of ESX. Hyper-V and ESX are the only hypervisors in the Gartner magic quadrant for x86 virtualization. (I'll be talking about this more in Chapter 12, "What to Do Next.") Remember, Azure runs on Hyper-V!

Some key features of Hyper-V are

◆ Virtual machines can have up to 64 virtual CPUs that are Non-Uniform Memory Access (NUMA) aware and can have up to 1 TB of memory that can be dynamically managed.

◆ The 64 TB VHDX virtual hard disk format can be hot-added to VMs and even shared between VMs.

◆ VMs have full mobility between nodes in a cluster using Live Migration and migration between nodes outside of a cluster using Shared Nothing Live Migration.

◆ Full storage migration is available with no downtime to VMs.

◆ Virtual Fibre Channel and SR-IOV (Single Root I/O Virtualization) support is available for highest levels of performance.

◆ QoS is available for storage and networking.

◆ Fully extensible virtual switching can be employed.

◆ Replication of VMs can be accomplished using Hyper-V Replica.

◆ Full support for Linux is available; Hyper-V integration services are built into modern Linux distributions.

◆ Network virtualization is possible.

◆ Microsoft RemoteFX enables rich graphical capabilities for VMs, including the virtualization for graphics processing units.

There is so much more. (If you would like more details, check out my book, *Mastering Hyper-V 2012 R2 with System Center and Windows Azure* [Wiley, 2014]). My key point here is to take a look at Hyper-V to see if it can be a good fit for your organization. It will help you with integration to Azure. Don't change to Hyper-V just for the sake of change, but if it saves you money, enables simpler management, and facilitates integration with Azure, then you should take time to evaluate it.

A large number of the benefits of virtualization relate to the abstraction of resources, scalability, and controlled self-service. All of these benefits primarily come through SCVMM, and I want to look at some of them.

Consider a typical virtualization administrator who has full administrative rights over the virtualization hosts and the compute resource, but who has no insight into the storage and network. This leads to many problems and challenges for the virtualization administrators, such as:

"I have no visibility into what is going on at a storage level. I would like to have insight into the storage area networks that store my virtual machines from SCVMM."

"Deploying server applications requires following a 100+ page procedure, which has human area possibilities and differences in implementation between development, test, and production. I want to be able to install the server application once and then just move it between environments, modifying changes only in configuration."

"My organization has many datacenters with different network details, but I don't want to have to change the way I deploy virtual machines based on where it's being deployed to. The management tool should understand my different networks, such as production, backup, and DMZ, and set the correct IP details and use the right NICs in the hosts as needed,"

"I need to save power, so in quiet times I want to consolidate my virtual machines on a fewer number of hosts and power down unnecessary servers."

Although you may think that SCVMM is focused on virtual machine management only, some of its most powerful features relate not to virtualization but to the storage and network fabric. SCVMM integrates with the storage in your environment and allows the network to be designed in SCVMM. This provides easy network assignment for the virtual workloads, including providing network virtualization with connectivity to nonvirtualized networks with 2012 R2. All the resources are exposed and managed centrally, which leads to a greater utilization of resources, a key goal of the private cloud.

A key piece of the private cloud is creating the clouds that can be consumed by different groups within an organization. As you know, these could be business units, teams of developers, or different sections of IT. In other instances, the clouds might be used by the same group of administrators for provisioning. Having separate clouds for different uses or groups makes tracking of resources simpler. A cloud typically consists of a number of key resources and configurations, which include:

- The capacity of the cloud—for example, which hosts and how much memory, processor, and storage resource can be used by the cloud

- The classifications of storage exposed to the cloud

- The networks that can be used by the cloud

- The capabilities exposed to the cloud, such as the maximum number of vCPUs per VM

- The library assets, such as templates, available to the cloud

- The writable libraries for the purposing of storing virtual machines by cloud users

Notice that the cloud has specific capacity assigned rather than exposing the full capacity of the underlying resources. This allows a single set of hosts and storage to be used by many different clouds. Once clouds are created, the cloud is assigned to different groups of users or tenants. The tenants have their own quotas within the capacity of the cloud, and individual users in the tenant group have their own subset of quotas, if required. Very high levels of granularity and control over the consumption of resources can be achieved in the cloud. As with clouds and underlying resources, many different tenants can be created for a single cloud. The concept of clouds and tenants are defined and enabled through SCVMM. SCVMM also enables visibility into the use of current cloud capacity and features RBAC, which means that end users could be given the SCVMM console to use for the creation of virtual machines. They would see only options related to their assigned actions. You should understand that this is not a good interface for end users to consume.

To provide the self-service management and basic provisioning capability commonly associated with the private cloud, the System Center App Controller component is used. For a richer, workflow-driven provisioning capability, Orchestrator and Service Manager are used. These enable capabilities such as show-back (what am I using?) and chargeback (billing for what is being used).

What does all this mean? For the key features of the private cloud, such as scalability, utilization of resources, abstraction of the fabric, and self-service, the key components required for a Microsoft solution are Hyper-V, SCVMM, and App Controller. Other components such as Orchestrator and Service Manager bring additional functionality, such as workflow, approval, and chargeback, but are not required for a core private cloud solution. SCOM and DPM provide the insight and protection for the workloads.

You can start slow. Maybe use the private cloud for development and test environments first—get used to the idea and get your users used to working within quotas. The private cloud infrastructure can be used in production, but perhaps it's the IT department using the private cloud and maybe even the self-service portal initially. Then, over time, you can turn capabilities over to your end users. You can deploy SCVMM with App Controller, and then integrate with SCOM, and then enable rich provisioning with Orchestrator and Service Manager.

Enabling a Single Pane of Glass

When IT people talk about *panes of glass*, they are referring to interfaces to systems. First, people always talk about a single pane of glass. In reality, I don't think many people want a single pane of glass for every aspect of their operations, both for administrators and users. It does not make sense. Think of your house. Would you want the same type of glass in your front room as in your bathroom? No. In your front room, you want large panes of clear glass so you can see out, whereas in your bathroom, you want small panes of frosted or textured glass so people can't see in. The same is true in an organization. The IT monitoring team needs a certain type of view, whereas end users want a completely different view with different capabilities. The key point is that, for each category of user, there should be only a single pane of glass for their tasks and not one pane of glass for looking at on-premises and another for the public cloud.

Earlier, I talked about App Controller being discontinued and also how the Service Manager web interface was not the best experience. Windows Azure Pack (WAP) addresses these items and, going forward, is a core component for your management solution deployment with System Center.

WAP is an open platform designed to deliver cloud resources and services—it is not a management UI. It is a REST-based system intended to deliver other REST-based systems. It acts as an aggregator that sits above the resources that are provided by Microsoft and other vendors. This is key for WAP; it provides an open platform with functionality added by resource providers. The resources can come from anyone.

WAP brings the Microsoft Azure portal experience to your on-premises infrastructure and enables several services through the aforementioned resource providers, including IaaS (creating virtual machines on Hyper-V), websites, databases, and more.

Depending on the components of the WAP you want to use, there are different requirements. The minimum requirement is to have a single virtual machine (plus a SQL Server database deployment) that hosts the actual WAP deployment and provides the Service Management portal and the Tenant portal in addition to the Service Manager API. (Yes, there are two portals: one for administration purposes and one for tenants. Each has different methods of authentication that can be changed.) In production, you would split the roles (seven roles for WAP and additional roles for the database) over multiple servers. The Microsoft TechNet Windows Azure Pack architecture web page shows this:

```
http://technet.microsoft.com/en-us/library/dn296433.aspx
```

Splitting services is a best practice for scaling resource utilization, as well as for different placement of services, because some services are Internet facing and some should be kept on the internal network. The seven roles include the following:

◆ WAP Tenant Management portal

◆ WAP Tenant authentication site

◆ WAP Tenant public API server

◆ WAP Tenant API server (internal to WAP)

◆ WAP Admin Management portal for administrators

◆ WAP Admin authentication site

◆ WAP Admin API server (internal to WAP)

There are additional OS instances for the various services offered. If you choose to deploy the Web Sites (PaaS) feature of WAP, you need a minimum of an additional seven virtual machines for the various Management Server, Controller, Publisher, Web Worker, DB, and file server components. These can't be colocated but are automatically deployed through the Web Platform installer. If you use Database as a Service (DBaaS), you need database hosts. To deploy IaaS (virtual machines), you need System Center Virtual Machine Manager (VMM) and the Service Provider Foundation (which is used to connect to VMM from WAP) as previously discussed. You also need Orchestrator Service Management Automation (SMA) deployment for the full life cycle management of the environment. For full reporting and monitoring, you most likely want SCOM and System Center Service Manager deployed.

I mentioned earlier that a SQL Server database deployment and a large number of databases are required based on the different services enabled. Table 10.1 lists typical databases for various workloads. You would also see databases for SMA, VMM, SCOM, Service Manager, and so on, which aren't WAP specific.

TABLE 10.1:   Databases used for core WAP services

WORKLOAD	TYPICAL DATABASES REQUIRED
IaaS (VMs)	Microsoft.MgmtSvc.PortalConfigStore
	Microsoft.MgmtSvc.Store
	Microsoft.MgmtSvc.Usage
	SPF
PaaS	Web Sites Hosting
	ResourceMetering
	WebAppGallery
DBaaS (database)	Microsoft.MgmtSvc.MySQL
	Microsoft.MgmtSvc.SQLServer
	Usage Reporting
	UsageDatawarehouseDB
	UsageETLRepositoryDB
	UsageStagingDB

The actual Windows Azure Pack hosts require:

◆   Internet Explorer Enhanced Security Configuration (ESC) for Administrators disabled via Server Manager

◆   .NET Framework 3.5 and 4.5 installed and patched to the latest level (enabled through Server Manager)

◆   Web Server (IIS) and ASP.NET 4.5 (under Application Development within the Web Server role services)

After all the prerequisites are in place, install and run the Microsoft Web Platform Installer from here:

www.microsoft.com/web/downloads/platform.aspx

In the Web Platform Installer, select Products and then Windows Azure, as shown in Figure 10.7. This allows different components to be installed on different servers, as documented in this Microsoft TechNet article:

http://technet.microsoft.com/en-us/library/dn457767.aspx

If you want to install all the core Windows Azure Pack portals and APIs on a single server, run the Windows Azure Pack Single Machine Installation Tutorial available here:

http://go.microsoft.com/?linkid=9832690

This is also available via the Web Application Platform Installer as Windows Azure Pack: Portal and API Express. Full install instructions are provided in this Microsoft TechNet article:

http://technet.microsoft.com/en-us/library/dn296439.aspx

FIGURE 10.7

Installing components of Windows Azure Pack

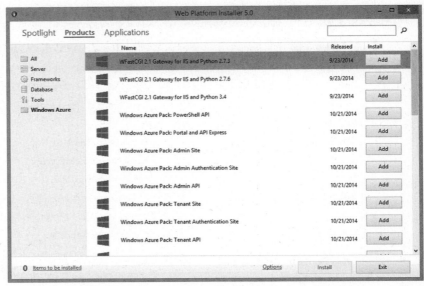

Note that even with the express installation, you can still specify an external SQL Server database. You don't need to run it on the Windows Azure Pack server. Your SQL Server machine must have SQL Authentication enabled. You can enable authentication through the Security node of the SQL Server properties in SQL Server Management Studio.

After the components are installed, you must perform the basic configuration, such as configuring the SQL Server database. The Microsoft guides walk through this in detail. After the core services are in place, you can add other services, such as virtual machines, websites, and so on. When you run the configuration, be sure to do so with full administrator rights elevated in Internet Explorer or the configuration will fail.

After installation is complete, I typically replace the automatically created self-signed HTTPS certificate with a trusted certificate. (This can be from an enterprise certificate authority.) The public-facing sites should be updated. To change the certificate, simply change the binding for each of the key sites in IIS Manager (MgmtSvc-AdminSite, MgmtSvc-AuthSite [tenant authentication using ASP.NET Membership Provider], MgmtSvc-TenantSite and MgmtSvc-WindowsAuthSite [admin authentication using Windows Authentication]). If you installed each of the components on different servers, you can also change the ports from the special ports to standard 443 ports, as documented here:

```
http://blogs.technet.com/b/privatecloud/archive/2013/12/10/windows-azure-pack-
reconfigure-portal-names-ports-and-use-trusted-certificates.aspx
```

If you're using a third-party firewall, you need to ensure that all required firewall exceptions are enabled for the various ports used. This is done automatically for Windows Firewall.

If you have trouble during installation, try the following:

1. Check the Web Platform Installer log files, which are located at `C:\Users\`*<user who ran the installation>*`\AppData\Local\Microsoft\Web Platform Installer\logs\install\`*<date and time of installation, e.g.2014-06-16T14.47.42>*. The exact logs present will depend on which components were installed on that server.

2. Check the event logs for each component, located in Event Viewer under Applications and Services Logs, Microsoft, WindowsAzurePack, *<component name>*.

3. If you still need more information, you can enable trace logging. Trace logging is useful if you're having trouble performing a certain configuration. It can be enabled and disabled via IIS Manager and by adding Failed Request Tracing rules under the IIS section of a site. However, you need to have the Web Server, Health and Diagnostics, and Tracing feature installed.

4. If all else fails, check out this troubleshooting article:

`http://blogs.technet.com/b/privatecloud/archive/2013/11/06/troubleshooting-installation-and-configuration-of-windows-azure-pack.aspx`

The installation of WAP is a big job that uses a lot of resources, but it delivers a huge amount of open and customizable functionality. One item I hope to see improved in the next version is a simpler installation experience. Even the most skilled WAP person will take many days to deploy WAP.

The steps and tutorials I just described install the WAP open platform. You must add the resource providers to enable functionality. This becomes your single pane of glass. Through this open platform, it is possible to expose resources on-premises across many technologies, as well as those in the public cloud. Here are some key resource providers:

Infrastructure as a Service (IaaS) Using Hyper-V Microsoft makes this resource provider available in the form of the Orchestrator Service Provider Foundation that integrates with SCVMM to enable access to cloud resources. See the setup instructions here:

`http://windowsitpro.com/private-cloud/enable-iaas-windows-azure-pack`

In that article, I also walk through downloading gallery items that you want to make available through Windows Azure Pack to enable various types of services. Note that even though SCVMM supports hypervisors such as ESX, the only hypervisor natively supported for WAP through SPF is Hyper-V. Also note that, though SCVMM is used for fabric management, WAP has its own service model that is not based on SCVMM Service Templates. This new service model will align more tightly with Azure models going forward.

Infrastructure as a Service (IaaS) Using ESX Using ESX for IaaS is supported through a third-party resource provider called VConnect from Cloud Assert. Information on this is available here:

`www.cloudassert.com/Solutions/VConnect/tag/4135/VMWare`

Integration with Azure (and Other Clouds) Integration with Azure is supported through third-party resource providers, including Konube Integrator from Schakra. Information is available here:

`www.konube.com/home`

Integration with Service Manager's Service Catalog   GridPro provides a connector for WAP to Service Manager to expose its service catalog content in WAP. GridPro also has connectors that enable Service Manager to connect to Orchestrator SMA. Learn more here:

www.gridprosoftware.com/en/

GridPro also provides functionality that natively connects SCSM to Orchestrator SMA and enables PowerShell workflows to be executed.

There are many more, but the resource providers I just mentioned enable WAP to be the single pane of glass across on-premises and Azure. Figure 10.8 and Figure 10.9 show examples of the WAP interface via the Tenant portal. You can see the service offerings that are enabled through Service Manager via GridPro. I also show creating a VM based on a gallery item facilitated through SPF and SCVMM.

FIGURE 10.8
Request offerings exposed through WAP

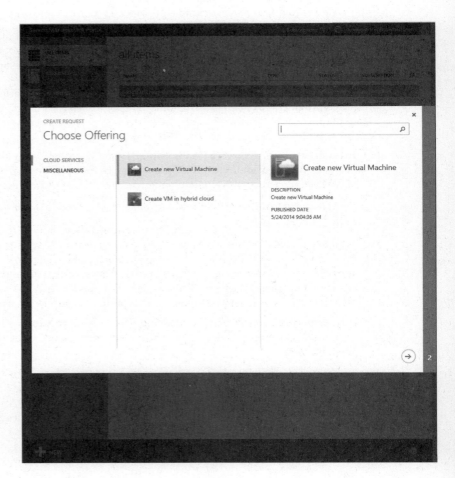

FIGURE 10.9
Creating VMs
through WAP

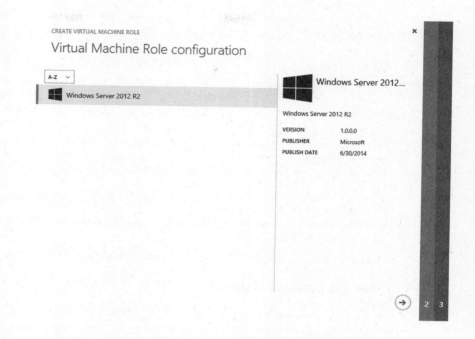

Note that currently, WAP looks like the legacy Azure portal, but it will be updated to match the preview Azure portal over time. In addition to its look, there will be tighter correlation between capabilities, allowing even more of an Azure experience to be enabled on-premises. Although WAP is optional in System Center 2012 R2, it is a critical component in the next version of System Center and will replace the separate interfaces in 2012 R2 related to App Controller and Service Manager. Windows Azure Pack is the single pane of glass.

Buying the Cloud Platform System

I've talked about the challenge of deploying WAP, and that did not include the deployment of technologies it leverages, such as System Center, Hyper-V, and the configuration of the various hardware components. Wouldn't it be nice to purchase "Azure in a box" for your environment? Such a solution would consist of the physical hardware, Hyper-V deployed, System Center deployed, and WAP all designed and deployed by Microsoft to the absolute best practices. Additionally, wouldn't it be nice for it to be sold and supported by Microsoft, directly enabling one source in the event of problems? This is a reality with the Cloud Platform System (CPS).

CPS provides a solution that consists of hardware that was designed by Microsoft and manufactured by Dell that currently leverages Windows Server 2012 R2, System Center 2012 R2, Windows Azure Pack, Dell PowerEdge servers, as well as Dell storage and networking. Note that CPS does not leverage a SAN, but instead uses the storage technologies found in Windows Server, such as Storage Spaces. The solution is purchased in racks, with up to four racks able to operate as a single unit that provides 128 compute nodes and support for 8,000 VMs. (These numbers apply for four racks.) See Table 10.2.

TABLE 10.2: Cloud Platform System scalability

CAPABILITY	PER RACK	WITH 4 RACKS
Compute nodes	32	128
Cores	512	2,048
Memory	8 TB	32 TB
Usable storage capacity	282 TB	1.1 PB
Maximum VMs	2,000	8,000

*Source:*http://download.microsoft.com/download/1/4/C/14CE6FE8-E5EA-4979-8278-8156A5CDAE2B/
Cloud_Platform_System_Datasheet.pdf

In addition to being purchased and supported by Microsoft as part of the offering, the CPS will be configured on-premises and integrated with your existing environment for you. For more information on CPS, see

www.microsoft.com/en-us/server-cloud/products/cloud-platform-system/

The Bottom Line

Understand why leveraging the Azure portal directly for users has limitations. Although the Azure portal exposes many capabilities of Azure, it lacks customizable workflows for provisioning, such as authorization stages, and does not integrate with other on-premises systems. Another major challenge comes into play when considering disaster recovery in the event of an Azure region fail and the need to reprovision services that use replicated storage accounts. To enable these capabilities, you must leverage another method of provisioning that can be used across services.

Master It What is a major limitation of using App Controller today?

Explain the core components of System Center to deliver a private cloud. The most critical component is Virtual Machine Manager, which provides the compute, storage, and network fabric management capabilities and also allows the definition of clouds that can be assigned to tenants. App Controller provides a web-based interface that allows end users to interact with those defined clouds. Other components that are not required but that add functionality are SCOM, which can monitor the utilization of resources and the fabric health to enable actions to be triggered; DPM, for protecting workloads; and Service Manager and Orchestrator, which provide customized provisioning and other services.

Master It Which hypervisors does SCVMM support?

Identify the value proposition for Windows Azure Pack. Windows Azure Pack provides an open platform into which resource providers are integrated. This enables access to almost any type of service as long as a resource provider is available. Microsoft offers resource providers for certain types of service, such as IaaS, websites, and more. Third parties provide resource providers for other scenarios, such as Service Manager integration, ESX integration, and even Azure. Windows Azure Pack brings the Azure experience to your on-premises environment and can also be used by hosting organizations to help provide their own services to customers.

Master It Which hypervisors are natively supported when providing IaaS using Orchestrator SPF and SCVMM?

Chapter 11

Completing Your Azure Environment

If you have been reading this book from the start, you have seen the capabilities available to you using Azure Infrastructure as a Service (IaaS). Likely, you now know nearly any workload you could run in Azure, but think back to Chapter 1, "The Cloud and Microsoft Azure 101." Where possible, you don't want to use IaaS. IaaS requires the most work in terms of maintaining the OS in the VM, maintaining applications in the VM, backing up the VM, and so on. Where possible, it is better to use PaaS (Platform as a Service), Database as a Service (DBaaS), or even Software as a Service (SaaS). Even without those capabilities, there are many other capabilities in Azure that can complement Azure IaaS and enable you to offer richer solutions. This chapter looks at those complementary technologies and how they can improve your overall architecture and solution. The goal of this chapter is not to dive into detail on any of the technologies covered but rather to make you aware of them. If they are a fit, you will have been introduced to their capabilities and can investigate further.

In this chapter, you will learn to

◆ Execute PowerShell workflows in Azure

◆ Use Azure to deliver desktop applications to users

◆ Publish internal applications to clients on the Internet

Azure Websites

When running web applications on-premises, application developers have traditionally turned to Windows Server and Internet Information Services (IIS). IIS is a set of services that allow Windows Server to host web applications and serve web content. IIS can accommodate applications written in many popular application frameworks, such as .NET, PHP, and Java, among others. This model can be applied to Azure by using a virtual machine instance configured with IIS. Although this model works very well in Azure, developers still have the same responsibilities for supporting the application in the cloud as they did when it ran on-premises. These responsibilities include configuring the operating system, installing and configuring IIS, and deploying and configuring the web application. In addition to these initial responsibilities, the developer has to provide ongoing maintenance of the virtual machine, which includes patching and monitoring. Azure provides automation capabilities, such as VM Agents with configuration technologies such as PowerShell DSC, Puppet, or Chef, that can make these responsibilities easier. However, these responsibilities still exist, and it is up to the developer to find a way to service them.

Because web applications are such a common workload, Azure provides a highly optimized compute environment for web workloads that builds on the knowledge Microsoft has gained from running large websites at scale. The Azure Websites service provides an application hosting environment, which allows you to scale from low-cost, shared multitenant servers to dedicated servers on demand. Azure Websites are designed under the PaaS model and allow you to focus on maintaining the application, while letting the platform take ownership of the operation of the application. The application developer can focus on the application and data and let the Azure Websites platform control the rest of the infrastructure. Azure websites are available in a number of different service levels.

Microsoft makes getting started with Azure Websites both quick and easy, because you leverage your existing knowledge and skills for application development. Azure Websites supports many popular application runtimes, and moving your app to the cloud can be as simple as redeploying the application code to Azure Websites. As part of the service tiers, Microsoft provides you with 10 free Azure websites in your subscription. As your performance needs grow, you can scale these websites to higher-performance tiers on demand.

Azure Websites works with almost any web technology, including classic ASP, ASP.NET, PHP, Java, Python, and Node.JS. Your developers can continue to develop on any platform, including Windows and Linux. Additionally, many types of data storage, such as SQL Database, MySQL, DocumentDB, MongoDB, Search, and popular extensions and content management systems such as WordPress, Umbraco, Joomla, and Drupal, are supported. Although it is possible to upload content using protocols such as FTP, Azure Websites also integrates with source control and collaboration tools, such as Visual Studio, Git, and Visual Studio Team Foundation Server (TFS), as well as online solutions such as Visual Studio Online and GitHub.

Many of the practices of traditional development can be applied to Azure Websites, but the cloud provides developers with opportunities to change their mind-set on how to operate and deploy applications. One such opportunity is thinking about how developers manage and propagate code across environments. In a traditional on-premises environment, developers have to maintain several physical or virtual environments for server development, testing, staging, or production. As code is moved from environment to environment, there are dependencies. Each environment is carefully configured to ensure that the application code will run properly on it. To accomplish this, developers and IT administrators have created complex build documents and scripts that must be applied to each environment before the code is applied. But even with careful planning, documentation, and scripting, it is difficult to ensure that the environments are consistent and identical.

When moving to the cloud, developers could provision separate Azure websites to mimic each of their on-premises environments. However, the responsibilities I noted earlier still apply. Developers have to figure out how to move code from each environment in a consistent manner. Azure Websites provides a means to make this experience easier. Each Azure website provides a feature called *deployment slots* that allows developers to install multiple versions of their web application in the Azure website. Deployment slots can be created to represent anything; many developers use them to mimic their on-premises environments, such as development, testing, or staging. Developers can deploy their application code into any one of the slots they have provisioned.

The power of deployment slots shines when developers need to move code from one slot to the next. In a scenario, think of developers who deployed code into the Dev deployment slot and need to move that code to the Test deployment slot. Azure Websites supports the capability to swap deployment sites. From the portal, or using PowerShell, the administrator can initiate a swap between two slots. Swapping slots is very fast; the process lasts only seconds. During a swap, the contents of each slot are switched. For example, when a developer swaps the Dev slot with the Test slot, Windows Azure updates the Test slot with the Dev slot application code. Additionally, the code that was in the Test slot is moved back to the Dev slot.

The power of the swapping approach can be seen when swapping code into production. In a traditional environment, moving code into production is a highly visible event. There is a responsibility to ensure that the code is properly installed and configured into the production environment. Additionally, the application teams must have mitigation plans in the event that the code cannot be properly installed. These mitigation plans typically involve building complex documentation, rollback scripts, or troubleshooting guidance. Using the swapping model, Azure Websites can make mitigation extremely easy. In this new model, code from a Staging deployment slot will be swapped into the Production slot. The production code will then be swapped back into the Staging slot. While the new application code is running in Production, the prior version of Production is available in the Staging slot. If at any point the application team feels that Production is not performing as intended, they can roll back to the prior production code in a matter of seconds. This is a powerful capability that improves the agility of the application team and increases the integrity of deploying production application versions.

Creating and using Azure websites can literally be done in seconds. Let me walk you through the process:

1. Azure websites can be managed using either Azure portal, but the richest experience comes from using the preview Azure portal. Go to https://portal.azure.com.

2. Select the New command and select Website from the list that is displayed.

3. Enter a name for the new site. That name with a suffix of azurewebsites.net will be the site's URL. For example, if I enter the name savillsite, my full URL will be savillsite.azurewebsites.net. Also select a subscription and location. Optionally, you can select a specific resource group or leave the default.

4. Select the Web Hosting Plan part to open the Web Hosting Plan blade. The blade displays the various types of Azure website plans that are available to you. Instead of directly selecting a tier for an Azure website, Azure Websites uses a web hosting plan (WHP) that uses a certain tier of service. The WHP maps to the infrastructure that will host the deployed websites. Many websites can be placed in the same plan, thus simplifying the management operations. WHPs further allow the sites to share the same backend VMs and scale together as the WHP is scaled. For example, if I create a WHP on the Standard tier and then deploy two Azure websites to the WHP, those two websites will use the same backend VMs. If that WHP is scaled to five instances, then both Azure websites run on the five VMs. Any existing plans in the subscription will be shown on the Web Hosting Plan blade. You can create a new plan by giving a name for the new plan and selecting the price tier. Select the Browse All Pricing Tiers option, as shown in Figure 11.1, to see all the pricing options. (These will be explained in more detail later in this section.) Select an existing plan that matches the price and capability required or create a new plan to meet your requirements.

5. Once you finish configuring the settings, click the Create button.

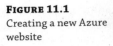

FIGURE 11.1
Creating a new Azure
website

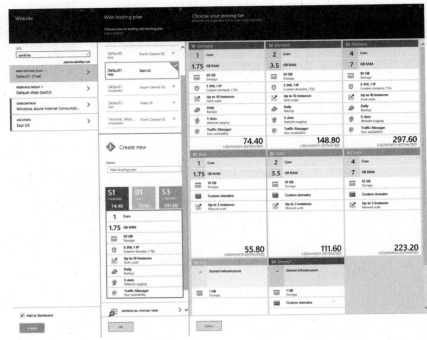

In these steps, the one major decision was selecting the pricing tier. As I previously mentioned, you can have up to 10 free Azure websites per subscription, but as the saying goes, "You get what you pay for." Free Azure websites have the lowest level of functionality, but they're fine for trying out Azure Websites and running a basic, single-instance website. As you start to use the service more, you will want to use the higher pricing tiers and gain access to the major features outlined in Table 11.1. Note that all tiers support the various languages and platforms.

TABLE 11.1:   Azure Websites pricing tiers

TIER	FEATURES
Free	1 GB of storage
	Uses a shared infrastructure; your site is on the same OS instance as other sites.
Shared	1 GB of storage
	Uses a shared infrastructure; your site is on the same OS instance as other sites.
	Can use a custom domain name

TABLE 11.1:   Azure Websites pricing tiers   *(continued)*

TIER	FEATURES
Basic	10 GB of storage
	Dedicated OS instance; the exact specifications of the VM depend on the size selected.
	Supports multiple instances, which are manually scaled; you need to manually stop and start instances.
	Custom domain names
Standard	50 GB of storage
	Dedicated OS instance; the exact specifications of the VM depend on the size selected.
	Supports up to 10 instances, which are autoscaled; Azure fabric starts and stops as required based on load.
	Custom domain names and SSL support with multiple names supported via Server Name Indication (SNI); allows a single IP address to be used for different sites using different SSL certificates.
	Daily backup of content
	5 slots (Development, Test, Staging, Production)
	Traffic Manager support

As can be seen from the tiers, Free and Shared have limited features and run in a shared infrastructure, but are the cheapest. The Basic and Standard tiers use dedicated VM instances for your websites, but you still are not responsible for the OS. Even though the instances are dedicated, they are managed for you, and your only responsibility is the deployment of your application and data to the Azure website. Once the website is deployed, you can use the Azure portal to view detailed information related to configuration, usage, deployment status, and more. The features depend on the tier selected. It is possible to change the tier of a deployed Azure website by clicking the three dots in the Actions bar and selecting the Change Web Hosting Plan action, as shown in Figure 11.2. This opens the Web Hosting Plan blade, where you can choose another plan of a different tier or create a new plan that meets your tier requirements.

FIGURE 11.2
Changing the tier of
an Azure website

Once you create the Azure website, it is ready to have applications deployed. For infrastructure-focused people rather than developers, the preferred way to upload content may be via FTP, which requires the creation of a deployment credential. Follow these steps:

1. Open the Azure website in the preview Azure portal (Browse ➤ Websites ➤ *<website name>*.

2. In the Azure Websites blade, scroll down to the Deployment lens.

3. Select the Set Deployment Credentials part.

4. Enter a new username and password, as shown in Figure 11.3. The username must be globally unique across Azure.

5. Click the Save action.

FIGURE 11.3
Changing the tier of an Azure website

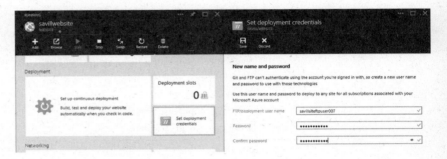

To find the FTP server name that the new credential will be used with, select the Settings part in the Azure Websites blade in the Summary lens. When the Settings blade opens, click the Properties link. When the Properties blade (shown in Figure 11.4) opens, the FTP hostname is displayed. The FTP hostname in combination with the deployment user can be used in any standard FTP client.

FIGURE 11.4
Finding the FTP hostname for an Azure website

Initially, you may start out using IIS running in Azure IaaS VMs, but look for opportunities to leverage Azure websites. Azure Websites is not just a means of simplifying management. If you look at the capabilities of Azure Websites, Standard tier in particular, the multiple deployment slots and automatic backup offer a level of functionality beyond that available by installing IIS in a Windows Server Azure IaaS VM. For more information on Azure Websites, see

```
http://azure.microsoft.com/en-us/documentation/services/websites/
```

Azure Traffic Manager

When examining cloud service VIP endpoints, you can use load balancing while allowing a single endpoint to resolve to multiple targets inside the cloud service. This enables high availability and load balancing for clients accessing the endpoint. The load-balancing capabilities, however, are provided only for services residing within the cloud service. Azure Traffic Manager takes the concept of high availability and load balancing globally across both Azure services and your own on-premises services.

Azure Traffic Manager provides globally aware DNS resolution to Azure services and non-Azure services located in different regions. An intelligent set of processes based on specified configurations and the geographical location of the user's local DNS server (LDNS) are employed. It's easiest to understand this by looking at an example like the one shown in Figure 11.5.

FIGURE 11.5
Example Traffic
Manager usage
scenario

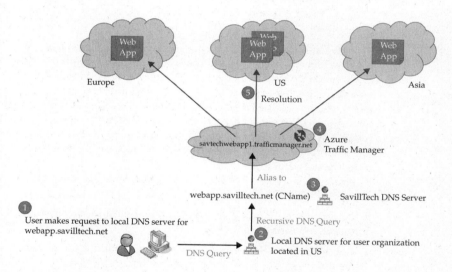

In this example, a Traffic Manager profile (a specific set of configurations for an address) was created for `savtechwebapp1.trafficmanager.net`. The site is configured with three endpoints that are separate deployments of the application hosted in Europe, the United States, and Asia Azure regions. An endpoint is a possible target that traffic can be directed to.

The Traffic Manager profile name always has `trafficmanager.net` as the DNS suffix, but you set the prefix part of the name. That prefix must be unique within the Traffic Manager service. However, this prefix will not actually be seen by end users.

The organization's actual DNS server has a CName (alias) record created for the public DNS name in the organization's own DNS zone. (That DNS zone is known as a *vanity domain* in this case; it's the public name used to make it look nice for end users.) The alias record points to the

Traffic Manager profile name record. Here, `webapp.savilltech.net` is an alias that resolves to `savtechwebapp1.trafficmanager.net`.

There are several load-balancing options for Traffic Manager profiles. These control how requests are distributed. The most common is Performance, which attempts to resolve requests to the Azure service that's closest to the requesting user's local DNS server. Here's how it works:

1. A user in the requesting organization enters `webapp.savilltech.net` in a web browser.

2. The user's local computer has a DNS configuration, which connects to their organization's DNS server, which in turn sends the DNS request for `webapp.savilltech.net`. The local DNS server performs a recursive lookup to resolve the name.

3. The authoritative DNS servers for the target DNS domain (`savilltech.net`) has an alias record that was created for `webapp`. That record points to the Traffic Manager profile named `savtechwebapp1.trafficmanager.net`.

4. The local DNS server now resolves the record returned by the Traffic Manager. This resolves via the Traffic Manager service. Traffic Manager attempts to ascertain the geographically closest Azure service based on a network ICMP latency map between DNS servers and Azure regions. The closest endpoint that is available is returned to the client.

Note the ICMP latency; whichever Azure region is considered closest is always based on the user's local DNS server and not where the users are physically located. This means if users are located in Asia but are using a DNS server located in the United States, then those users would be directed to services in the U.S.—even if there is a service physically located in Asia. Users who use global DNS servers will not be redirected to the closest Azure service with a high degree of confidence. Also, the network latency maps are generated based on ICMP echo requests (pings) to DNS servers. This means if the local DNS server blocks ICMP, then the latency information is not ascertainable. (This isn't common since this ICMP approach is an industry standard.)

I previously mentioned different types of load-balancing options. What follows is a description of the three options:

Performance Requests are directed to the Azure service that is closest to the local DNS server and is online.

Round-Robin Requests are directed in a round-robin fashion between all endpoints that are online. It is possible to set weights that enable certain endpoints to receive more traffic than others. Weights can only be configured using PowerShell using the `-Weight` parameter (which accepts values between 1 and 1,000) with the `Add-AzureTrafficManagerEndpoint` cmdlet.

Failover All requests are directed to the first endpoint, and if that endpoint is not available, the requests go to the next endpoint. This is completely independent of the local DNS server physical location.

To ascertain if an endpoint is online, every 30 seconds the Traffic Manager service performs a request using HTTP or HTTPS. The request can use a custom port to a specific URL—for example, the URL of a specific application on the web service. Specifying a path (as opposed to the base DNS name) is useful to ensure that the service is responding rather than just the base web hosting infrastructure. The configuration screen is shown in Figure 11.6. If four requests go unanswered or if it takes longer than 10 seconds for each request, then the endpoint is considered unavailable and requests will not be directed there. The requests will continue every 30 seconds, and when the endpoint responds again, it will be considered online and requests will once again be directed to the endpoint as appropriate.

FIGURE 11.6
Configuration screen for an Azure Traffic Manager profile

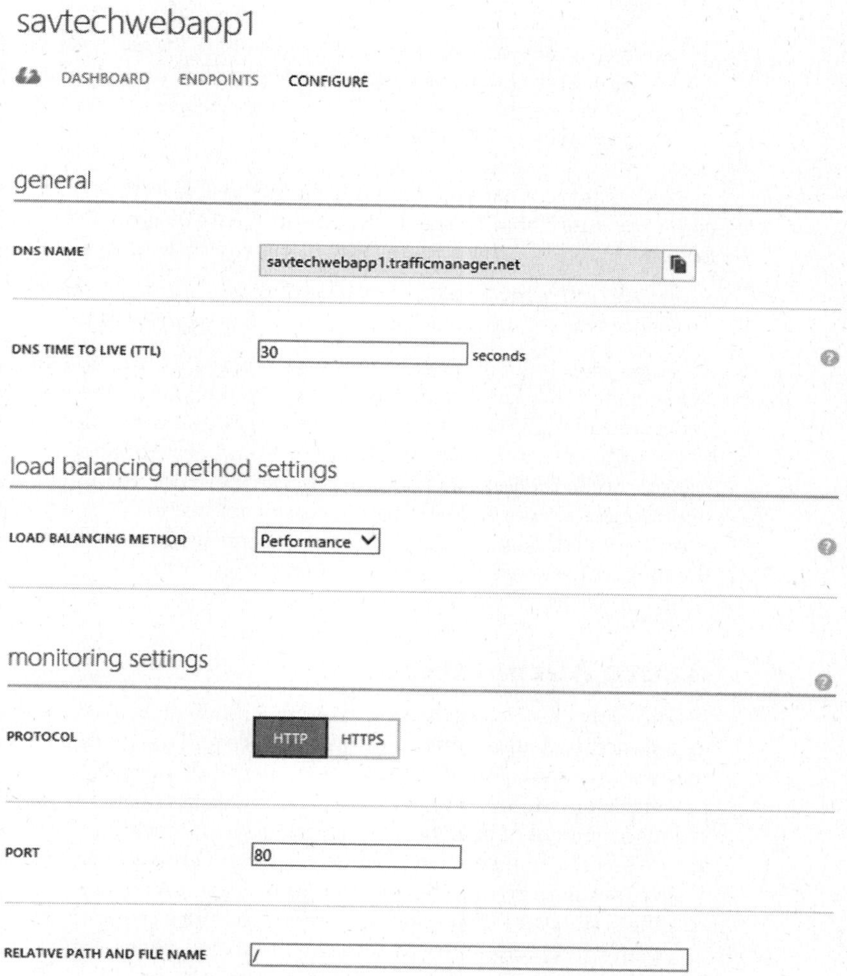

savtechwebapp1

DASHBOARD   ENDPOINTS   **CONFIGURE**

general

DNS NAME

savtechwebapp1.trafficmanager.net

DNS TIME TO LIVE (TTL)

30   seconds

load balancing method settings

LOAD BALANCING METHOD

Performance ∨

monitoring settings

PROTOCOL

HTTP   HTTPS

PORT

80

RELATIVE PATH AND FILE NAME

/

Note that a TTL (the time-to-live of the record in the DNS cache) can be configured as part of the profile. TTL is set to 5 minutes by default. The smaller the TTL, the faster clients will be directed to another endpoint if an endpoint is not available. You should be aware that lowering the TTL setting increases the number of requests to Traffic Manager, which might increase your cost.

Traffic Manager endpoints can be Azure cloud services, which means the cloud services used need an endpoint for port 80 or 443 or whatever custom port you are using for the monitoring settings to be defined. The endpoints could point to a single VM in each cloud service or to a load-balanced set in each cloud service. Traffic Manager endpoints can also be Azure websites, Azure web roles, and even a non-Azure resource, such as a website hosted with another service provider or even on-premises. To add an external endpoint, you have to use PowerShell. Here's an example:

```
profile = Get-AzureTrafficManagerProfile -Name "JohnProfile"
Add-AzureTrafficManagerEndpoint -TrafficManagerProfile $profile `
    -DomainName "www.savilltech.com" -Status "Enabled" -Type "Any" |
    Set-AzureTrafficManagerProfile
```

Note that these external endpoints aren't visible in the Azure portal. For more information about this functionality, see the Microsoft Azure blog post "Azure Traffic Manager External Endpoints and Weighted Round-Robin via PowerShell" available here:

```
http://azure.microsoft.com/blog/2014/06/26/azure-traffic-manager-external-
endpoints-and-weighted-round-robin-via-powershell/
```

There are a large number of scenarios where this functionality is very useful. Consider an organization that has operations all over the world. Services could be deployed in each major geographical region and then Traffic Manager used in the Performance load-balancing mode as the initial point of entry. Clients then would be redirected to the service closest to them offering them the lowest latency and best experience. Imagine a customer who wants to use his on-premises for normal hosting of his web applications but uses Azure for disaster recovery. With Traffic Manager in Failover mode, clients would only be directed to the Azure hosting if the on-premises web presence was unavailable.

Azure Automation

It's probably clear to you by now that PowerShell is the technology that provides the best experience, both as a command-line interface and a scripting environment, to achieve all manner of automation. Azure can be managed through its various REST APIs. The Azure PowerShell module leverages these capabilities to enable full Azure management, along with the management of most other environments and technologies. Although it is possible to run Azure scripts from your on-premises environment and perform actions in Azure or even within VMs running in Azure, this places the emphasis on ensuring the particular host is available to run the scripts and managing the various modules required.

Azure Automation provides the ability to run PowerShell workflows within the Azure fabric. The experience is very similar to Orchestrator SMA with Windows Azure Pack when used on-premises. The PowerShell workflows created in Azure are called *runbooks*. PowerShell cmdlets are contained in modules; by default, the Azure module is available within Azure Automation—however, you can also upload additional modules to make additional cmdlets available to your PowerShell workflows. Any service that has an endpoint that can be connected to from the Internet can be accessed via Azure Automation. Runbooks in Azure can be executed manually, or schedules can be defined that automatically run them at your desired times.

Why use PowerShell workflows rather than just regular PowerShell? Consider a long-running PowerShell script that might perform numerous actions over many systems. If a problem occurs, the script execution might fail and would need to be restarted. In a regular PowerShell script, this would mean writing the script with the assumption that some of the actions might have already been performed—which means for every action in your script that isn't idempotent (after being performed once, it can be performed multiple times without affecting the subject), you need to insert logic to check values, check whether the action has been performed, and so on. This is a huge amount of work. PowerShell workflows feature checkpoints that save the current state of any variables and the current point in the workflow to disk. If a problem occurs, the workflow can be resumed from the last checkpoint. Checkpoints are typically inserted in the workflow after any major action. While using PowerShell workflows with Azure Automation, if any kind of interruption or failure occurs, the runbook can be resumed automatically from the last checkpoint.

The code that follows creates the most basic PowerShell workflow possible. It does not achieve anything useful (it simply writes text), but it shows the basic structure for creating a new PowerShell workflow. In this example, MyWorkflow and its content is contained in the curly brackets. The workflow is executed by calling the name of the created workflow, as shown in the final line.

```
Workflow MyWorkflow {Write-Output -InputObject "Hello from Workflow!"}
Get-Command –Name MyWorkflow –Syntax
MyWorkflow
```

Next is a workflow that contains a number of checkpoints. These are the points in the workflow from which execution can be resumed.

```
Workflow LongWorkflow
{
Write-Output -InputObject "Loading some information..."
  Start-Sleep -Seconds 10
  CheckPoint-Workflow
  Write-Output -InputObject "Performing some action..."
  Start-Sleep -Seconds 10
  CheckPoint-Workflow
  Write-Output -InputObject "Cleaning up..."
  Start-Sleep -Seconds 10
}
```

Azure Automation features a basic scripting environment; however, I recommend that you use the PowerShell Integrated Scripting Environment (ISE) locally. When you've finished creating PowerShell workflows locally, paste those workflows into the Azure Automation runbook editor. Remember that the goal of Azure Automation is to run PowerShell workflows without any interaction; therefore, you can't use any type of command that requires interaction or that is based on formatted output.

You can run almost any logic within Azure Automation. Some key use cases include stopping and starting VMs running in Azure at certain times to help optimize the Azure spend. Create new VMs based on certain scenarios or patch VMs without any downtime to services.

Here are the key steps to get started with Azure Automation. Currently Azure Automation processes are performed through the legacy Azure portal.

1. Access the Automation area in the portal.

2. A new Automation account is required and must be created in a specific region. Click the Create action and select a name for the new account and a region to create it in. I typically include the name of the region in the automation account name, as shown in Figure 11.7.

FIGURE 11.7
Creating a new
Automation account

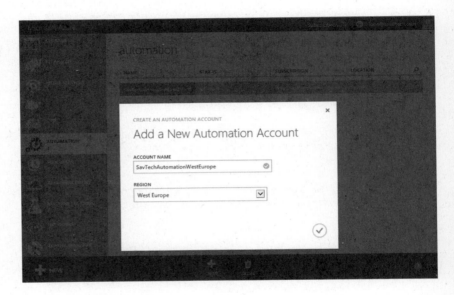

3. There are two methods to authenticate from the runbooks you create to the Azure subscriptions they will perform actions on: either a certificate is used or an Azure AD account that is associated with an Azure subscription is supported. I recommend using the Azure AD account approach; it is easier to use and enables support for Azure Resource Manager. To add an Azure AD credential, select the Assets tab of the Azure Automation account and select the Add Setting action. For the type, select Add Credential. For the credential type, select Windows PowerShell Credential, specify a name for this credential, and provide an optional description. Click the Next arrow, enter the credential username and password, and then click the check mark to save the change.

4. A new runbook can be created and the credential used to authenticate from the runbook to an Azure subscription. Select the Runbooks tab and select the New ➢ App

Services ➤ Automation ➤ Runbook option. For a new empty runbook, select Quick Create to enter only a name and description. As an alternative, you can select the From Gallery option, which features over 100 PowerShell workflows that already have been created for many common tasks. Figure 11.8 shows the From Gallery option. Even if a precreated script does not perform exactly what you need, it can still be a very good starting point.

FIGURE 11.8
Azure Automation runbooks available in the gallery

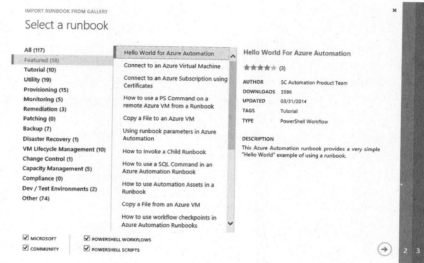

5. Once the new runbook is created, select the runbook and then select the Author tab. Here you can set the actual PowerShell workflow that makes up the runbook. At this point, there is no published version of the new runbook, only a draft. In the Draft area, enter your code and select the Save action, and to make it available to be used, click the Publish action. Notice there is also a Test action, as shown in Figure 11.9. If you choose Test, the current draft runbook content will execute. The following is a sample runbook using a PowerShell credential:

```
workflow QuickTest
{
  $Cred = Get-AutomationPSCredential -Name 'JohnSavillTechNet'
  Add-AzureAccount -Credential $Cred
  Select-AzureSubscription -SubscriptionName 'Windows Azure Internal Consumption'
  Get-AzureVM
}
```

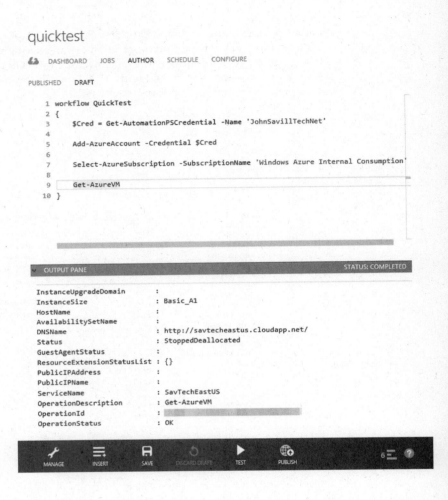

FIGURE 11.9
Modifying an Azure
Automation runbook

Note that, if you decided to use a certificate to authenticate to Azure, you should download the Connect-Azure.ps1 script from this site:

http://gallery.technet.microsoft.com/scriptcenter/Connect-to-an-Azure-f27a81bb

In the Azure Automation account, select the Runbooks tab, and then import the downloaded script. The script enables the use of connections added as an *asset*, which can use certificates that were also added as assets. To add a certificate, select the Automation account, select Assets, and choose Add Setting ➢ Add Credential ➢ Credential Type Of Certificate. When prompted, give a name (and remember it; you'll need it when using the certificate as part of a connection). On the next screen, select the PFX file and enter its password. To create a connection to Azure using a certificate under the same Automation account, select Add Setting ➢ Add Connection ➢ Connection Type Of Azure and assign a name. On the next screen, specify the name of the certificate that you uploaded previously and the Azure subscription ID; then click the check mark, as shown in Figure 11.10.

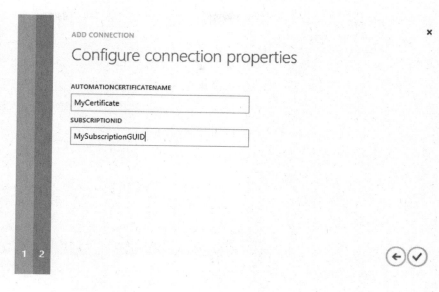

FIGURE 11.10
Adding a connection to an Azure Automation account

You can use the connection in your runbooks by using the `Connect-Azure.ps1` script that you imported as a runbook. In the runbook that follows, I use the `Connect-Azure` runbook to connect to the subscription. Note that the `$subName` must match exactly the name of the connection created in the Automation account:

```
workflow GetVM
{
    $subName = 'SavillTech Internal Consumption'
    Connect-Azure -AzureConnectionName $subName
    Select-AzureSubscription -SubscriptionName $subName
    Get-AzureVM
}
```

Once an Azure Automation runbook is published, it can be called from other runbooks and triggered manually via the Start action or through a schedule, which you can define using the Schedule tab of the runbook. The schedule will be useful if you create runbooks to stop and start VMs. The stop VM runbook can be scheduled to run each weeknight at 6 p.m., whereas the start runbook can be scheduled to run each weekday morning at 8 a.m.

A full history of the runbook execution can be seen through the Dashboard and Jobs tabs. A basic source control is available. Through the detail of a job execution, you can select a View Source action, which will show the source as it was when that job was executed. You can adjust various settings, such as level of logging, on the Configure tab. You can also configure tags on this tab, which is very useful when you wish to search for specific runbooks by using the tags you define. On the main start page of an Azure Automation account is an overview of all runbooks, and if you click the search magnifying glass, you can search by the tags, as shown in Figure 11.11. I recommend always populating your runbooks with tags to make them easy to find.

FIGURE 11.11
Searching for a
runbook using tags

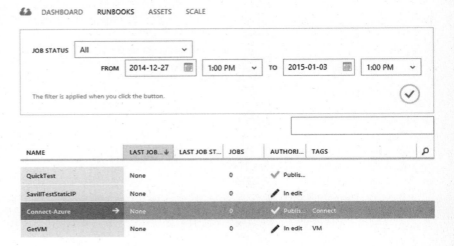

Azure Scheduler

As the name implies, the Azure Scheduler allows you to schedule actions. You create scheduled actions using JSON definitions; the Azure portal is able to create these JSON definitions. The JSON-based definitions are submitted to the Azure Scheduler, which is responsible for invoking the services based on the defined schedule and records a history of the execution.

The Azure Scheduler is geo-redundant; any scheduled jobs are replicated to the paired region. Scheduled jobs are assured to run, even if there is a problem in the primary region where the job is scheduled.

Actions for an Azure Scheduler job can be:

◆ HTTP/HTTPS put/get/post/delete

◆ Storage queue message posting

Remember that systems that leverage REST expose HTTP/HTTPS endpoints and enable the Azure Scheduler to interact easily with those REST services. If you need to schedule the triggering of any service that leverages HTTP/HTTPS or creates storage queue messages on a schedule, the Azure Scheduler is a good choice.

Azure Scheduler features a configurable retry for each job in addition to error handlers and logging. One previous downside was that the Azure Scheduler could not trigger Azure Automations. This was because Azure Scheduler supported only basic authentication, whereas Azure Automation uses certificate-based authentication and Azure AD credentials. This has now changed with the addition of certificate and Azure AD support, with Azure Scheduler enabling the triggering of Azure Automations. This is documented at http://azure.microsoft.com/blog/2015/01/27/ scheduling-azure-automation-runbooks-with-azure-scheduler/.

Azure RemoteApp

Many organizations leverage the Windows Server Remote Desktop Services (RDS) role to enable the publishing of applications to devices that support Remote Desktop Protocol (RDP). It is possible to enable this functionality in Azure by deploying Windows Server Azure IaaS VMs, enabling the RDS role, installing the applications you wish to publish, and then publishing them using the RDP protocol. Microsoft has a set of documents to help you deploy RDS to an Azure environment:

```
http://msdn.microsoft.com/en-us/library/azure/dn451351.aspx
```

Note that the method for delivering applications from Azure always uses server operating systems as the hosts, and not client operating systems, which is common with virtual desktop interface (VDI) environments that are based on client OS deployments. There is no way to license Windows Client in a public cloud, which is why there are no public cloud Windows–based desktop or application publishing solutions available.

Azure RemoteApp is a managed service in Azure that provides either:

◆ A standard image (as shown in Figure 11.12) containing the Office applications and enables publishing Office applications to any device with an Azure RemoteApp client

◆ A custom image that contains any applications you wish to publish, which can be uploaded to Azure RemoteApp

The Azure RemoteApp enables specific users to be given access to applications and the service autoscales based on the number of users connected.

FIGURE 11.12
Selecting the template used during an Azure RemoteApp Quick Create

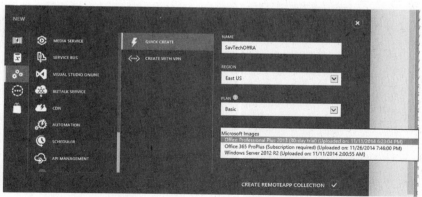

The Azure RemoteApp client is used to access the applications published using Azure RemoteApp. As of this writing, the client is available for all major platforms and devices, including the following:

◆ Windows 7 SP1

◆ Windows 8.1, Windows 8

◆ Windows 10

- Windows Phone

- Windows RT

- iOS

- Mac OS X

- Android devices

- Windows Embedded Standard 7 SP1

- POSReady 7 (based on Windows Embedded Standard 7 SP1)

- Windows Embedded Thin PC (based on Windows Embedded Standard 7 SP1)

- Windows Embedded for Industry 8.1

The client can be downloaded here:

```
https://www.remoteapp.windowsazure.com/
```

Once it's installed, users must authenticate, and the list of applications published to them is displayed, as shown in Figure 11.13. Note that specific applications are published and not complete desktop sessions. Publishing just the application window is the best option when dealing with devices with different form factors where a complete desktop environment is not used.

FIGURE 11.13
Using the Azure
RemoteApp client

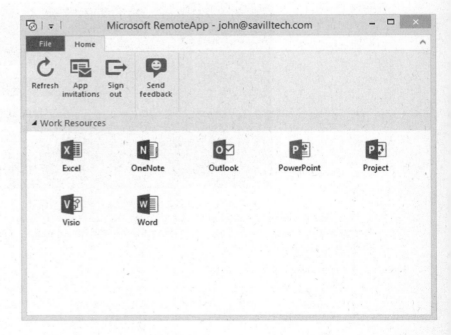

If you want to use your own image instead of using a Microsoft-provided image, you need to ensure that the following criteria are met:

- Use a Generation 1 virtual machine.

- Use VHD rather than VHDX.

- Use MBR rather than GPT disk partitioning.

- Use Windows Server 2012 R2 that's fully patched.

- Install the Remote Desktop Session Host role and the Desktop Experience feature (part of User Interfaces and Infrastructure).

- Install and publish the applications you want to make available.

- Run Sysprep to generalize the image (`sysprep /oobe /generalize /shutdown`).

You can then upload the custom image by selecting the Upload action from the RemoteApp workspace. This process provides you with the PowerShell code to make the image usable. Note that if you use your own custom image, you are responsible for keeping the image patched. Patching is done automatically when using the Microsoft-provided images.

You can use this service whenever you need to publish Windows applications to devices. This is common in Bring Your Own Device (BYOD) environments where users utilize many different types of devices that cannot natively run Windows applications. It's also useful for making corporate applications available to noncorporate assets, such as a user's home machine or a contractor's laptop. In a disaster scenario where users cannot access their normal work computer, the Azure RemoteApp solution can be provisioned quickly to grant remote access to applications.

Azure AD Application Proxy

Windows Server 2012 R2 introduced a new feature, Web Application Proxy. Primarily, it is a reverse proxy. A regular proxy acts as an intermediary between your web browser in the office and services, like websites, that are accessed on the Internet. When a website or web-based application is selected, your browser communicates to the proxy. The proxy communicates with the target, receives data, and then relays it back to you. The proxy provides security as a single point that communicates with the Internet and prevents individual users from directly communicating with Internet entities. Using the proxy allows checks of the returned data to protect against malware and can limit access only to white-listed sites. The proxy further enhances optimal usage of the Internet connection, since it can cache content. If someone accesses a site, that returned data is cached on the proxy. Then, if a second person accesses the same site, the proxy can return the data from its cache without having to download data from the Internet again. If you have a 10,000-person company and every morning people check CNN.com, caching saves a huge amount of bandwidth.

A reverse proxy, as the name suggests, works in the opposite direction. It is designed to make services hosted internally for your organization (on your Intranet) available to the Internet without directly exposing those servers offering the service to Internet-based clients. As shown in Figure 11.14, services hosted internally, for example IIS, SharePoint, ADFS, and Exchange, are made available to the Internet via the reverse proxy, in this case Web Application Proxy.

Any SSL connections are terminated at Web Application Proxy, which enables even encrypted communications to be checked for malware and attacks. The use of a reverse proxy allows the servers hosting the service to stay on the Intranet while the reverse proxy is placed in the DMZ, accessible to the Internet.

FIGURE 11.14
Reverse proxy with
Web Application
Proxy

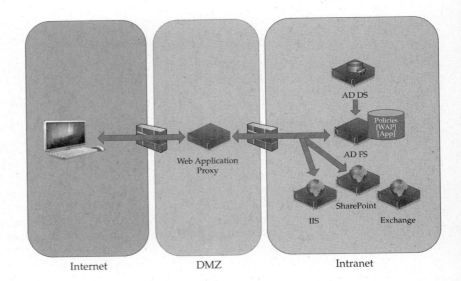

Web Application Proxy offers benefits beyond reverse proxy services. As Figure 11.14 shows, Web Application Proxy integrates with AD FS, which provides federation services between organizations, which can include identity federation between on-premises Active Directory and Azure AD. Through the integration with AD FS, Web Application Proxy also enables single sign-on across different applications, even when the application does not natively support claims. This enables users accessing services to sign on once and then access multiple applications that are published through Web Application Proxy. Web Application Proxy can also perform preauthentication. Users can be authenticated before any communication is forwarded to the backend servers.

Web Application Proxy in Windows Server 2012 R2 provides huge functionality, but its deployment can be intimidating because it requires the deployment of AD FS and various policies to function. Azure AD Application Proxy provides Web Application Proxy services hosted in Azure and integrated with Azure AD for the services you host in your network, as shown in Figure 11.15. It is made possible through the deployment of the Azure AD Application Proxy Connector in your environment. That enables the secure communication between the Azure AD Application Proxy services in Azure and the services in your network. This enables services hosted on your internal network to be published to the Internet via Azure.

The Azure AD Application Proxy is disabled by default, but you can enable it by accessing the Configure tab of an Azure AD instance and setting the Enable Application Proxy Services for this directory to Enabled. Then, install the Azure AD Application Proxy Connector on a Windows Server 2012 R2 server in your network. The connector is available from the Configure

FIGURE 11.15
Azure AD Application
Proxy architecture

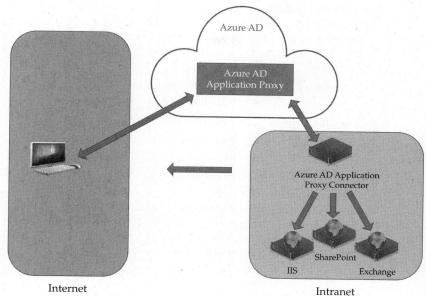

page of your Azure AD instance once the Azure AD Application Proxy has been enabled. A full step-by-step guide to installing the connector is available here:

`http://msdn.microsoft.com/en-us/library/azure/dn768214.aspx`

Once the connector is in place, applications from the internal network that will be accessible from outside your network can be published through the Applications tab of the Azure AD instance by selecting the Publish An Application option. Once the option is selected, an external URL will be generated with an `msappproxy.net` suffix. You then will configure the internal URL that hosts the application on your internal network, which will be accessed via the connector and published to the Internet, leveraging Azure AD for the authentication. Single sign-on is enabled for users, and the same preauthentication capability available with Web Application Proxy is available with Azure AD Application Proxy.

If you need to make internal applications available from the Internet and enable a single sign-on experience but don't want to make your internal resources directly accessible from the Internet, then leveraging Azure AD Application Proxy provides a simple solution.

Azure Operational Insights

Azure Operational Insights started life as System Center Advisor, a cloud-based aid that connected to your on-premises servers via an agent that was integrated with the Microsoft Knowledge Base and best practices. It was intended to advise when deployments were not configured to best practices or simply misconfigured. Initially, System Center Advisor was focused on Windows Server and key workloads, such as SharePoint, Exchange, and Lync, but the list of workloads expanded over time.

These capabilities increased with the metamorphosis to Azure Operational Insights and the introduction of Intelligence Packs, which provide specific units of functionality. In addition to the features already available in System Center Advisor that focused on configuration and best practices, key areas of functionality now available with Azure Operational Insights include the following:

Capacity Planning   Provides information on the utilization of resources, identifies overallocated resources, and projects future needs

Update Status   Identifies missing system updates on deployed servers

Change Tracking   Identifies changes to an environment, which can help identify the source of problems by examining what recently changed

Searching Logs   Provides an easy-to-use search of event and IIS logs

You can enable additional functionality by downloading more packs from the Intelligence Packs Gallery, as shown in Figure 11.16. Note that Azure Operational Insights can monitor servers that are running on-premises and in public cloud environments such as Azure. Azure Operational Insights can also coexist with System Center Operations Manager, provided the requirements are met. Information about the requirements is maintained here:

```
http://msdn.microsoft.com/en-us/library/azure/dn884656.aspx
```

FIGURE 11.16
Enhancing capabilities via the Intelligence Packs Gallery

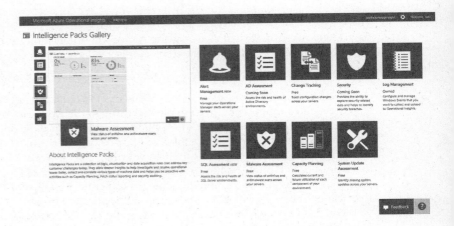

Operational Insights features an easy-to-use dashboard that provides access to all the various data gathered. A mobile application version for Windows Phone is available here:

```
www.windowsphone.com/en-us/store/app/operational-insights/4823b935-83ce-466c-
82bb-bd0a3f58d865
```

As of this writing, Microsoft was requesting customer feedback on other platforms for the mobile application. At that time they were focused on iOS, Android, and Blackberry. For more information on Azure Operational Insights, visit this site:

```
http://azure.microsoft.com/en-us/services/operational-insights/
```

The Bottom Line

Execute PowerShell Workflows in Azure.   Every aspect of Azure (and almost any other system) can be managed with PowerShell. PowerShell workflows provide a method for running scripts. Azure Automation provides a service through which PowerShell workflows can be executed. Both certificate- and credential-based authentication is possible within Azure Automation runbooks.

> **Master It**   Why are PowerShell workflows a better fit for long-running scripts than regular PowerShell scripts?

Use Azure to deliver desktop applications to users.   Azure RemoteApp provides a simple means of using RDP to publish applications to users who have the Azure RemoteApp client installed. Microsoft provides standard images that include the Office suite. Custom images containing the applications you wish to publish also can be used.

> **Master It**   How is Azure RemoteApp licensed?

Publish internal applications to clients on the Internet.   Azure AD Application Proxy enables the reverse proxy publication of applications that are hosted on-premises to the Internet via the Azure service. Authentication is performed using Azure AD. Single sign-on and preauthentication are enabled.

> **Master It**   How does communication from the Internet through Azure AD Application Proxy to on-premises resources work?

## Chapter 12

What to Do Next

The technical capabilities of Azure Infrastructure services have been described in detail throughout this book, and the key point that Azure becomes an extension of your datacenter is hopefully clear. Those services in Azure can be used in many different ways: to offer complete solutions, to supplement on-premises environments, as test/development environments, and even for disaster recovery. Often the adoption of a public cloud technology such as Azure is not solely based on technical capability, but also on learning to trust a solution and overcome barriers—both real and imagined. This chapter focuses on overcoming both types of barriers and starting your journey to Azure services.

In this chapter, you will learn to

◆ Address the common concerns related to using the public cloud specific to Azure

◆ Use encryption in Azure

◆ Understand the first steps when adopting Azure

Understanding and Addressing Azure Barriers

Most concerns related to the utilization of public cloud services, including Azure, relate to perceived security risks. For systems running in your own datacenter, you have full control. You can see the physical servers, you can see if someone enters the server room, you know the other administrators who have access, and you know all the various users of the infrastructure. You are the master of the environment and all things are known to you. It's similar to having kids. When the kids are at home, you know you have the doors locked; you know who else is in the house; if they have friends visit, you know those friends and know they will not steal your kids' lunch money. Compare this to sending your kids to a summer camp. Do the people at the summer camp remember to lock the cabin doors? What if one of the counselors is a mass murderer? Some of the other kids on the bus looked mean and were looking very intently at the goodie bag you packed for your little Timmy. The reality is the kids are safe at camp, the counselors are probably better trained to handle a problem if there is one, and the kids have a great time. But there is a perceived risk because you don't have control. This is the same for public cloud. The majority of the fear is because you must trust others rather than have direct control. The reality is Microsoft operates some of the most secure datacenters in the world—probably more secure than yours. They operate with processes that adhere to the highest standards, but I will expand on this later in the chapter.

The one aspect that I do think is very real is access and awareness of access to your data. It has been the focus of a lot of media attention and legal actions. In your datacenter, if someone wants access to your data (outside of hacking), you are aware of it. If the government wants your data, you are handed a warrant and you hand over the data. The data was acquired, but you are aware of the fact. If your data is in the public cloud, that vendor may be handed a warrant to hand over the data, but it could also say that any notification to the affected parties is prohibited, which means that you (the customer) are not aware your data was handed over. This is a big difference. You might not be aware of access or the focus of the ongoing legal proceedings between public cloud vendors, including Microsoft, and many government bodies. The solution to this, as you'll see later in this chapter, is for customers to encrypt their data in such a way that the public cloud vendor cannot decrypt it. Therefore, if asked for the data, all they can provide is encrypted data—which is of no use.

Building Trust

The ultimate barrier to adopting public cloud is a lack of trust, and so trust in your public cloud vendor—that is, Microsoft—needs to be established. Microsoft needs to earn that trust through actions, sharing information, and proving capability. This trust will come. Any change initially is resisted until the trust is established. Look at how many organizations are leveraging Office 365, a public cloud Software as a Service (SaaS) solution hosted by Microsoft that hosts several of a company's most critical assets: its email, its communication, and its document storage. The trust in this service was earned, and the same datacenters that host Office 365 host Azure. I heard a great analogy once about trust from David Chappell and Associates, which is roughly paraphrased in the following:

> If you would have told me 30 years ago most of our goods would be manufactured in communist China, I would have laughed at you. But here we are today; most items are manufactured in China. That trust in the goods has been built, and we accept it.

Of course once trust is earned, it has to be maintained with constant investment in the technology and constant vigilance for security. If you look at Azure, it has some of the brightest minds in the industry focused on its security. Security expert Mark Russinovich, who is CTO of Microsoft Azure, is focused primarily on the core security of Azure. However, there is still a perception that the public cloud is less secure than on-premises solutions, which is what I will look at in detail next.

Understanding Risks for Azure

Of all concerns organizations have related to the public cloud, the number-one concern is security. The loss of control, compliance, and complexity are also big concerns. To a lesser degree, concerns such as maturity of technology, lack of expertise, and cost exist, but security is the big one. Every public cloud vendor knows this. A major security vulnerability in any of the major public cloud vendors could set back the public cloud many years. But why is security such a major concern? This is best answered by examining the various elements and potential vulnerabilities of Azure (or any public cloud service), shown in Figure 12.1. You will notice many of the perceived possible vulnerabilities are the same ones that are concerns for your on-premises datacenters.

1. Azure is a service offered in the public cloud.

2. Azure runs on Hyper-V, which is a known hypervisor in the industry.

3. Each customer has its own services.

4. Customers also have their own datacenters.

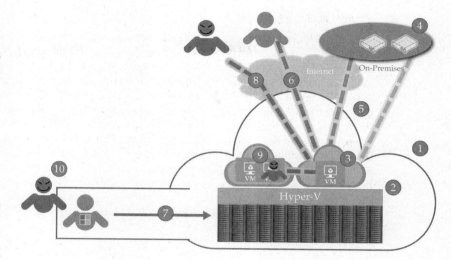

FIGURE 12.1
Elements and perceived possible vulnerabilities for a public cloud service

5. Azure customer resources are linked to their on-premises resources using links such as S2S VPN or ExpressRoute.

6. Services can also be accessed from the Internet using endpoints to a VM via the cloud service VIP or via an instance-level IP that provides direct access to a VM. You may want these endpoints to offer services out to the Internet but want protection also.

7. Microsoft people in various roles touch your data and/or services. Developers write the code, and DevOps people may need to connect to the fabric. Some people just do datacenter operations tasks on the servers but don't have access to service information; they have a separate private network to access the fabric via a private backbone.

8. Then, you have the primary concerns. People accessing your information or services via the Internet who attempt attacks may be trying to steal data; they may be attempting to prevent access through denial of service, or DoS; or they may be trying to redirect your traffic.

9. Someone in another tenant may try to attack you. Another enterprise or some guy in a basement could set up a tenant next to you. They could try to inject a virus into the Azure infrastructure/Hyper-V. They could attempt to hurt your performance by using more than a fair share of resources.

10. Microsoft operations people could be bad or could be ordered to do something by someone more powerful, such as the government or in response to an issued warrant.

As it turns out, there are nine common concerns related to the public cloud. The Cloud Security Alliance calls them the Notorious Nine. Their report is available here:

```
https://cloudsecurityalliance.org/download/the-notorious-nine-cloud-computing-
top-threats-in-2013/
```

I will walk through each of these, in reverse order, and discuss specifically how they relate to Azure.

EXPOSED SOFTWARE

Azure has its own specification for fabric elements such as compute and storage. However, commodity components, such as off-the-shelf processors rather than some Azure-specific CPU, are used. This means that common CPU firmware is used. Azure also uses a common hypervisor, Hyper-V, the same way other major public cloud operators do. (Amazon Web Services [AWS] uses Xen, and Google uses Kernel-based Virtual Machine [KVM].) Common web components—for example, IIS in Azure—and common API support are used. If there is a vulnerability in one of these, it exposes the risk in a huge way when in public cloud at the mega-scale of Azure where the resources are shared between organizations. If, and I'm stressing the *if* here, there was a hypervisor boundary exploit in Hyper-V (one VM could access resources in another VM through nonstandard means) within your company, it's not a huge pain point; all of the users of the Hyper-V servers are within your organization and trusted. In a public cloud, where your VM is next to some other entity who could have malicious intentions, it is a huge concern.

Cloud organizations have to constantly balance security and stability. You can be secure and out of business. As author Mark Minasi explains, you can be so supersecure that no one can get to your business, so you are out of business anyway. You have to assess the vulnerability and act accordingly. When a vulnerability exists within your company, you assume a certain level of trust for the tenants. There are consequences if someone acts irresponsibly or with malicious intent—they get fired. There is not a huge rush to patch vulnerabilities unless the vulnerability is exposed to the public. For example, if a vulnerability exists on your public Internet website, then you would want to patch quickly.

This balance of security and stability is more complex in public cloud environments, especially when international boundaries are involved and fewer consequences may be possible. (If someone outside the United States attacks American resources, it's likely difficult to pursue legal recourse.) The exposure for vulnerabilities may be greater. Consider the implications of a vulnerability that punctured the hypervisor to enable access to other tenants. This would be a disaster in the public cloud and is a great concern for all public clouds, so there is a huge engineering effort, and procedures are in place to protect against these types of attack. For Azure, Microsoft is constantly evaluating all possible attacks and vulnerabilities and then patching accordingly. Microsoft has a new bug classification, Cloud Critical, that is specific to the impact of a bug on its public cloud services. If a Cloud Critical bug is found, a patch is rolled out as quickly as possible since the bug represents a vulnerability to the cloud and the risk outweighs stability.

INSUFFICIENT DUE DILIGENCE

This area has a number of different concerns, but the principal one is Shadow IT, or Bring Your Own IT (BYoIT). This occurs when a business group sidesteps the IT department and uses cloud services because the IT department does not offer the service they want or cannot respond with the speed required. I see this a lot in organizations. A certain business unit believes the IT department responds too slowly, so the business unit takes out a credit card and directly procures services in the public cloud. Now they are in control and can provision very quickly. In reality, the IT department with its private cloud infrastructure *can* be faster but may need to change how they offer services and the like. The big problem with business groups directly using services in the public cloud is that the IT, compliance, and security departments are not involved and may not even be aware that business units are directly using public cloud services. This represents a liability for the organization in a number of ways. If corporate intellectual property (IP) is being stored in the public cloud, is it properly secured? Does the service meet corporate policies and regulatory requirements in terms of the manner in which data is stored and the processes that are used? Is the data being backed up? These things are typically details that business units will not concern themselves with, but if something goes wrong, those same business groups will come to IT for a fix. IT will also get the blame if there is a data breach, which causes a "Resume Generating Event" for the IT department.

The solution is to make using services provided by the IT department, whether on-premises or as part of an IT managed public cloud, preferable and less painful for business users than directly purchasing their own public cloud services. This means the IT department needs to embrace the public cloud, embrace the private cloud, and enable use in a way that the corporate governance can be enforced, data secured, and all other requirements met. To find out if, how, and by whom public cloud services are being used in your organization, Azure provides the Azure API Discovery. After pushing an agent onto local machines, Azure API Discovery tracks Internet access and presents the data on a portal.

ABUSE OF CLOUD SERVICES

Consider the scalability of the cloud and how relatively easy it is to set up infrastructure. (For IaaS, this means a VM in the cloud.) Obtain a stolen credit card, set up a cloud service, and then start attacking whomever you choose using botmasters, distributed DoS (DDoS) platforms, and so on—all hosted in a public cloud service. Because most companies trust the IP addresses of public cloud services such as Azure or AWS, use of public cloud services becomes even more appealing to parties with malicious intentions. If you look at the top 10 ISPs hosting malware, Amazon is number 1 with AWS, then GoDaddy, and so on. This is because it's so easy to spin up VMs in the public cloud and run pretty much anything you want. Think of storing bad data in the public cloud. Think about governments blocking access to services. Users can just set up a VM in Azure and access services from there.

It's not even users with malicious intentions that cause problems. Look at modern crypto-currencies such as BitCoin. Want to mine BitCoins or more specifically crypto-currency, which then converts to BitCoins? (Azure is not good for mining BitCoins since there are no GPU services.) Set up some VMs in Azure and get mining. To give an idea of the scale of this problem, Azure shuts down between 50,000 and 75,000 VMs a month that are performing illegal activities of some kind. Microsoft worked out that with an Azure trial account with $200 of free usage, you could mine about $40 worth of Quark crypto-currency. You may wonder what is the harm in this type of activity—who is being hurt? These activities use large amounts of resources that then cannot be used by other parties. Although Azure has mechanisms in place to avoid "noisy neighbor" issues that allow these activities to steal your CPU or memory, they still use resources that aren't being paid for, increase the cost of Microsoft doing business, and affect Microsoft's bottom line—thus affecting the price of Azure services. The impact is the same as credit card crime. The top offenders are people from Russia, then Nigeria, and then Vietnam. Not what I expected! Microsoft uses machine learning to try to detect the fraudulent use of Azure services and close them down quickly using various heuristics, such as the use of the same credit card or the same email address in addition to the actual resource usage characteristics of the VMs.

Note that this is not unique to the public cloud; it happens on-premises as well. There was an interesting story about Harvard being hacked and someone using their supercomputer (that was supposed to be turned off) to mine crypto-currency. The hack was discovered when the electric bill was received.

MALICIOUS INSIDERS

The idea here is that a DevOps person puts something bad into code or processes that are deployed to the fabric or uploads something directly into the cloud service that does something bad. Maybe the datacenter operations personnel try to do something malicious such as stealing information.

To mitigate this risk, Microsoft employs a number of processes and procedures. Most obviously, Microsoft performs background checks on all personnel who interact with the Azure service. The best way to stop people performing activities they shouldn't is to remove their ability to do so by minimizing their privileges. But then, how can people perform their jobs without privileges? The key is just-in-time (JIT) administration or, more specifically, JIT granular access—grant privileges only as the need requires. When some action in the Azure environment is required, a request is made through the service system in the form of a ticket. The ticket then interacts with a JIT access control system. Each ticket specifies the system that needs to be accessed and the permissions needed. After the ticket is reviewed and approved, granular permissions are assigned to the systems required for a limited amount of time. This enables the support person to perform the actions required. All of the actions performed are logged and reviewed, and once the actions are performed, the permissions are revoked. This ensures that people do not have any standing permissions and cannot perform actions that are not approved and reviewed. In addition, there is constant monitoring for any signs of unauthorized activity.

To help you have trust in their processes, Microsoft goes through a number of industry standard certifications and audits. These certifications are published and can be viewed here:

```
http://azure.microsoft.com/en-us/support/trust-center/security/
```

Also available through the Trust Center are compliance details, which are important. When people are new to the cloud, they tend to focus on security. Once the use of the cloud is better understood and the usage more mature, the main focus becomes compliance.

DENIAL OF SERVICE

This covers any scenario where your services are not available. On the malicious side, this could be parties attacking the Azure Internet endpoints of your specific services or generic Azure service endpoints with a DoS attack. Azure has DDoS appliances that are placed on datacenter routers and other applicable elements of the Azure infrastructure. If these appliances detect a DoS attack, the traffic is redirected to a black hole to limit its effect. This is done for the Azure fabric and for customer endpoints, but note that this protects against large-scale attacks only and not small-scale attacks. It's important to practice defense-in-depth and have your own protection in the VMs. Remember, if you don't need a service on the Internet, remove the endpoints from the VM.

On the flip side, there could simply be an outage of an Azure service due to a hardware failure in a datacenter, a software bug, human error, and so on. One well-publicized example of this was reported here:

```
www.huffingtonpost.com/2011/08/08/amazon-microsoft-dublin-lightening_n_920875.html
```

This outage was basically the result of the electrical design of the datacenter. A brownout (a minor interruption of power to the servers) occurred, just for a second. That minor interruption caused the entire Azure fabric to reboot. Every server had to reboot; the outage lasted hours. Obviously, Microsoft learns from these types of events and rearchitects accordingly. Efforts are also focused on additional levels of resiliency through hardware and software.

INSECURE INTERFACES AND APIs

Consider how quickly new services are being added to Azure. Those services typically involve new APIs and interfaces to enable interaction with the service. In other cases, an existing API or interface is being used in new ways. Perhaps it is just a matter of services offered in the public cloud instead of on-premises. The concern in any of these scenarios is that a vulnerability may exist. Perhaps it's poor encryption or even simple mistakes made when implementing the service in production.

For those who have used Azure, the concept of features being released in a preview mode first enables customers to help test new features and validate all functionality. Additionally, Microsoft follows strict development practices, security life cycle, and validations throughout the entire process to minimize risks associated with the concerns mentioned.

ACCOUNT OR SERVICE TRAFFIC HIJACKING

When someone gets unauthorized access to your account, it could be for a number of reasons:

◆ Weak passwords can be attacked through brute force. I read an interesting study from Deliotte, which found that 10,000 passwords account for 98 percent of all the passwords that exist. In a matter of seconds, 98 percent of passwords can be found by brute force trying those 10,000 passwords.

◆ Passwords can be stolen through weaknesses in services that expose data, through malware, and even through social engineering attacks.

◆ Passwords are reused. When one service is compromised and people used the same password on multiple systems—Facebook, the "I love puppies" website, and their corporate network—all of those systems could be compromised.

This is where using multifactor authentication (MFA) is so important. The industry direction is to move away from passwords because they are inherently weak. It is far better to leverage something a person "is" (biometric data, like a fingerprint), something a person "has" (a secure ID device or even application on their phone), instead of just something a person "knows" (their password). MFA leverages two of these types to maximize security. I've seen some organizations attempt to solve this by setting very complex password requirements, such as 25-character minimum lengths. This can work if people focus on a passphrase, `ImUsingAComplexPasswordWhichIsGreatAndIllRememberThisEasily`, instead of a password, such as `Qy684jfhy&4#thckp70dF`. Unfortunately, setting very complex password requirements typically fails, as people either write them down or keep forgetting them. The resulting help desk calls cause lost productivity. Focus on leveraging MFA to mitigate risks related to passwords.

Note that this is not a cloud-specific risk, but potentially it can be more prominent in the cloud since the services are accessible through public interfaces. Microsoft also considers this; if a Microsoft person gets attacked and their access is used, that could expose services. However, remember that Azure uses JIT access with no standing permissions, so even if an account was compromised, that account would not be able to do anything without a ticket.

In addition to leveraging strong passwords and MFA, remember to minimize your attack surface. For example, delete unnecessary endpoints and ensure you use antimalware in your services. If you do require endpoints to the Internet, use network control lists where possible to control who can access those endpoints. Where possible, use private connections, such as S2S VPN or ExpressRoute, for communications between on-premises and Azure.

DATA LOSS

Data loss is a concern that's simple to understand. People don't want to lose their data—this is really the most important asset of almost every organization today. This category covers data loss through the following:

◆ Customers accidentally deleting data

◆ Attackers intentionally deleting or encrypting data

◆ Microsoft deleting the data

◆ Datacenter blows up and the data is lost

The mitigation here is simple. If you care about data, you need to back it up. Microsoft does not back up IaaS disks in Azure storage. Also, remember that you should never store data on the nonpersistent temporary disk. Although Microsoft replicates all data in Azure storage three times at a minimum, if there is a deletion of data, that deletion would replicate three times. Multiple copies of the data protect from hardware failure and not from deletions. To provide some level of protection from data loss due to a Microsoft datacenter failure, use Geo-redundant Storage or Zone Redundant Storage.

There is one area where Microsoft can help with lost data. Microsoft now tombstones accounts for 90 days when they are deleted in case you delete an account by mistake. If you delete your Microsoft account and then realize you left important data in it, you can contact Microsoft support and they can help get you access to it again.

DATA BREACH

Nearly all these threats end up with this as the concern: someone gets access to your all-important data. How could this happen?

I'm sure one of the most common concerns related to this in the public cloud, and Azure specifically in this case, is some kind of physical attack on the media. Maybe a disk taken from the datacenter. Realistically, I don't consider this a very likely scenario for the following reasons:

◆ The Azure datacenters are highly secure. They employ huge amounts of security and have outer gates that can literally stop a tank.

◆ For an internal person to remove a disk, a work order must exist. Every disk has a bar code that must match the bar code on the work order, which is checked by a separate person prior to leaving the particular co-lo the disk was in. Additionally, any disk leaving a datacenter is either wiped to military specifications or destroyed by machines that reduce the disk to parts that must be able to pass through a sieve. Remember that Azure goes through many industry-standard audits and compliance exercises to ensure this happens.

◆ Even if someone got a disk, I doubt it would be useful. Remember that Azure distributes content across a storage stamp, which consists of thousands of disks. Any single file has parts spread over many disks. One disk would be of limited value.

Even with these security measures in place, people often ask why data in Azure is not encrypted *at rest* (that is, on disk). If you step back and look at Azure encrypting at rest, you quickly see it would not offer much. Encryption relies on a key to encrypt and decrypt. In a public cloud, either the cloud provider has the key or you do. If the cloud provider, Azure, has the key and encrypts the data at rest, what benefit does it achieve? If the cloud provider encrypts and decrypts automatically and someone finds some vulnerability in the APIs or interfaces of Azure, the encrypted data would be decrypted automatically. Imagine what would happen if a malicious Microsoft employee wanted to access your data. (They can't because of the JIT access.) They would have the key. If an external party, like the government, asked Azure for your data, then Microsoft has the key and would have to decrypt and hand it over.

The better solution is for you to encrypt the data and hold the key. This way, Microsoft cannot access the data if they want to and have no ability to hand your data over to anyone. It is this ability for users to encrypt their own data that Microsoft is focused on. They have added and continue to add features to enable this. (I will cover more later in this chapter.) Also, remember that you can leverage application features such as SQL encryption.

Another form of data breach is a man-in-the-middle attack. In this scenario, your data is sniffed on the network. This attack has gained a lot of attention after the 2013 Edward Snowden document leaks that highlighted all the ways the National Security Agency (NSA) sniffs the data on the Internet and from public cloud providers. Note that the flip side of the Snowden case is that if the NSA practiced no standing privileges and JIT access, it may have been much harder for Snowden to take all those documents in the first place. An interesting article on this topic is available here:

    www.washingtonpost.com/world/national-security/nsa-infiltrates-links-to-yahoo-
    google-data-centers-worldwide-snowden-documents-say/2013/10/30/e51d661e-4166-
    11e3-8b74-d89d714ca4dd_story.html

One solution to this problem is to make sure data is encrypted as it travels between Azure and your computers. The Azure APIs support Transport Layer Security (TLS) for encryption using strong ciphers with Federal Information Processing Standard (FIPS) Publication 140-2 (FIPS PUB 140-2) support. The Azure S2S VPN uses Internet Protocol Security (IPsec) to encrypt all data sent over it. Do not use unencrypted communications to Azure.

Side attacks, where a VM on the same host as your VM can try to look at processor side effects to get keys, are yet another concern. Realistically the chances of this happening are almost nil. To accomplish this kind of attack, even in the most controlled lab environment:

◆ You would need to know who to attack and find a way to colocate on the same physical server; there is no way to do that in Azure.

◆ You would need to be using the same processor core, which does not happen for many types of Azure VMs and is even harder to make happen.

◆ You would need to know which key and cryptographic type are being used.

Another concern is access to the data via your account or a breach of Microsoft protection. I have already discussed these concerns and shown the mitigations in place. Although I would never say something is impossible, I consider the Azure fabric like Fort Knox. If someone gets access to your data, it would likely be because your credentials were compromised and used, rather than some weakness in Azure.

SKYNET

Microsoft Azure CTO Mark Russinovich has jokingly expressed another concern: Azure becomes self-aware and tries to take over. If you look at some of the new capabilities, such as Azure machine learning, it's getting closer. The best course of action here is to adopt Azure early and use it well, so you will be a favored human pet when it does take over.

There are new risks in adopting the public cloud, but teams of very smart people are working on them, mitigating the concerns and taking steps to ensure that those concerns are not as bad as they initially seem. The end goal is for you to place your data in Azure and give Microsoft no way to access it.

Data Encryption in Azure

As I have mentioned throughout this chapter, Azure is highly secure. However, security is not everything. There can be legal means to compel Microsoft and other cloud providers to provide a tenant's data. You may want data protected from other parties within your own company or simply need to encrypt data to meet policies or regulatory requirements. Some applications have their own native encryption capabilities. For example, SQL Server has Transparent Data Encryption (TDE), which encrypts the entire database and any backups; can be managed by the database administrator; and has column-level encryption. There are also other ways to encrypt data using third-party utilities and native Windows features. In this section I'll focus on using the Windows built-in encryption capabilities in Azure.

Three primary types of encryption are native to Windows:

Encrypted File System (EFS) This has been in Windows for a long time and enables specific files or folders to be encrypted using a key that is stored in a certificate in the user's profile. It is possible for organizations to configure recovery keys to enable encrypted data to be decrypted in the event the user certificate is lost or the person holding the certificate leaves the company. Although EFS encrypted data is encrypted at rest, it is sent over the wire unencrypted, and its encryption status on the target depends on whether or not the target supports EFS. EFS can be used to encrypt enterprise data like SQL databases, but it is typically used only as a last resort when other features like SQL TDE or BitLocker cannot be used.

Rights Management Services (RMS) Like EFS, the data is encrypted, but it also has policies attached that control how the data can be used. For example, a Word document may be configured to prohibit printing and for access to expire at a certain time. Unlike EFS, RMS data stays encrypted, even when sent over the wire to any targets. Typically RMS is used for user data because of its focus on policies that control how data is used.

BitLocker BitLocker is a volume-level encryption technology; the entire volume is encrypted using a full-volume encryption key (FVEK) that is typically stored in a Trusted Platform Module (TPM) within the computer hosting the volume being encrypted. Different options for unlocking the FVEK from the TPM exist, such as requiring a PIN, a password, the insertion of a USB device, or being connected to the corporate network. The data is always encrypted on the disk and is automatically decrypted to memory as needed.

It is the last option, BitLocker, I want to focus on. It is the one used by most IT people where possible. Historically, TPM introduces some complexities in Azure, because Azure does not expose a TPM to VMs in the same way that Hyper-V does not expose a TPM to VM. On-premises and using Hyper-V, you would use BitLocker on the Hyper-V host to encrypt the volumes containing the VHDs. That is not an option in Azure; the encryption needs to be done within the VM.

USING BITLOCKER WITHIN AN AZURE VM

The use of a TPM to store the FVEK for Azure is not a requirement—it just provides great security for the key. Remember that there are essentially two types of disk in Azure for IaaS VMs: the OS boot disk that contains Windows and then additional data disks. If you wish to protect the OS disk without a TPM, a change can be made to Windows via Group Policy as outlined here:

```
http://technet.microsoft.com/en-us/library/ee424319(v=WS.10).aspx
```

This approach leverages a USB stick containing the key that needs to be inserted at boot time. However, Azure provides no way to insert a USB device, real or virtual. What can be protected in Azure with BitLocker without any additional services are data disks.

The first step to using BitLocker in Windows is to enable the feature. (It is not enabled by default.) Enabling BitLocker can be performed using Server Manager via the Add Roles And Features wizard and then enabling the BitLocker Drive Encryption option on the Features page of the wizard. BitLocker can also be installed using PowerShell:

```
Install-WindowsFeature BitLocker
```

Once BitLocker is installed, it can be used to encrypt a data drive. You select the type of protector, which is used to unlock the drive. Examples include a password, USB drive, or a very useful new type of protector that was introduced in Windows 2012/Windows 8—a user security ID (SID). By using the SID as a protector, it is possible to provide a seamless experience by using the SID of the account you logged in with to unlock a drive. If a service needs to unlock a BitLocker drive, the service account for the service can be added as a protector for the BitLocker volume. When encrypting an Azure drive with BitLocker, it is critical to use the -usedspaceonly parameter. Remember that Azure Storage uses sparse storage, which means only space written to actually consumes space in Azure and therefore results in charges. By default, when BitLocker encrypts a drive, it encrypts all space, even empty space. This ensures the most secure encryption, as remnants of deleted data may still exist on a regular disk. In an on-premises scenario, encrypting even empty space provides the most security. In Azure Storage, this is not necessary and would actually cause all blocks of your disk to be written to, therefore causing you to pay for the total size of the data disk instead of just paying for the data you have written to the disk. To encrypt a drive with BitLocker using an SID protector for a user, use the following command:

```
manage-bde –on e: -sid DOMAIN\user –usedspaceonly
```

If an additional user SID needs to be added as a protector allowing that account to unlock, you can use:

```
manage-bde –protectors –add e: -sid DOMAIN\user2
```

To check the encryption status and state of a disk, to lock a drive, and to unlock a drive using the account SID, use the following commands:

```
manage-bde -status e:
manage-bde -lock e:
manage-bde -unlock e: -sid
```

These steps provide a fairly simple way to BitLocker-protect data drives in Azure, but they cannot be used to protect the boot volume because it would be necessary to unlock the drive during the boot process. The absence of a TPM in the Azure VM and the lack of an option to use a virtual USB drive or virtual floppy drive would prevent the boot. Some third-party solutions integrate with Azure and provide encryption for the boot and data drives for both Windows and Linux VMs:

Instant-On Cloud Security for Microsoft Azure Instant-On Cloud Security for Microsoft Azure from Trend Micro is one of these third-party solutions, and additional information can be found at

www.trendmicro.com/us/business/saas/deep-security-as-a-service/microsoft-azure-security

This solution leverages an agent that is placed between the disk driver and the file system driver and enables a transparent encryption that is completely transparent to the operating system. It uses FIPS 140-2 certified AES encryption, and the keys used for the encryption can be hosted by Trend Micro in their key store or in your own on-premises key store. When an OS that is leveraging this technology starts, it detects a key is needed, requests the key from the configured key store, and releases the key based on a policy enabling decryption of the drive.

CloudLink CloudLink (www.cloudlinktech.com/) leverages the native encryption technologies of the OS, such as BitLocker for Windows and dm-crypt for Linux. CloudLink has its own small agent that is deployed in the VM and that manages the keys required for the encryption native to the OS to function. Various options are supported for the key storage, including on-premises and the Azure Key Vault service.

Azure Key Vault The Azure Key Vault service was released in 2015, and information on the service can be found here:

http://azure.microsoft.com/en-us/services/key-vault/

As the name suggests, it provides a service in Azure where keys can be stored in a manner such that Microsoft cannot access them, which provides maximum protection for your data. Microsoft hosts host security modules (HSMs) that meet FIPS 140-2 Level 2 and Common Criteria EAL4+ standards to store the keys. The introduction of this service provides Azure with a place to securely store keys. I expect that this capability will be natively available shortly to BitLocker running in Azure VMs, thus enabling BitLocker to encrypt the boot drive without requiring third-party software.

Why You Should Use Azure and Getting Started

This is probably the most important part of the book. Now that the technical capabilities are understood, why should you choose to use Azure and how do you get started? There are many providers of public cloud services, and deciding which one is right for your organization can be challenging. Remember that there are many types of public cloud service (IaaS, PaaS, and SaaS), and providers offer one or more of those types. At the start, you likely will have on-premises services, so you need to consider not only the capabilities of the provider but how it can integrate with your on-premises services and management.

Understanding Azure's Place in the Market

A good place to start to understand the capabilities of providers and their positioning against their competition is to look at the Gartner quadrants. Gartner quadrants are maintained for many types of service, such as on-premises x86 virtualization, cloud IaaS, enterprise application PaaS, and more. Figure 12.2 shows the structure of Gartner quadrants. Notice that the quadrants focus on the ability to deliver the service and the completeness of what they deliver. You'd want a service that appears in the leader quadrant.

FIGURE 12.2
Gartner
Methodologies and
Magic Quadrant
Source: www.gartner.
com/technology/research/
methodologies/research_mq.jsp

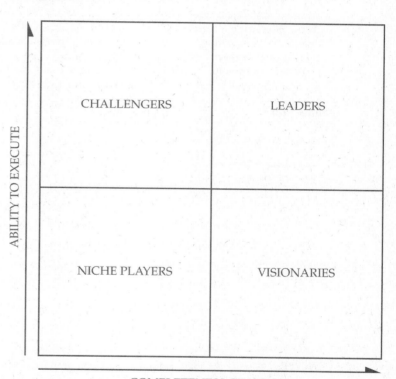

CHALLENGERS   LEADERS

NICHE PLAYERS   VISIONARIES

ABILITY TO EXECUTE

COMPLETENESS OF VISION

NOTE Gartner does not endorse any vendor, product, or service depicted in its research publications, and does not advise technology users to select only those vendors with the highest ratings or other designation. Gartner research publications consist of the opinions of Gartner's research organization and should not be construed as statements of fact. Gartner disclaims all warranties, expressed or implied, with respect to this research, including any warranties of merchantability or fitness for a particular purpose.

Microsoft Azure IaaS is one of only two (as of this writing) leaders in the Magic Quadrant for Cloud Infrastructure as a Service, published 28 May 2014 by Lydia Leong et al. for Azure IaaS, its cloud IaaS solution. Microsoft is one of only two leaders in the Magic Quadrant for x86 virtualization with Hyper-V. Azure PaaS is in the leader quadrant for the Magic Quadrant for Enterprise Application PaaS, as is Azure Storage for the Public Cloud Storage Services. Microsoft is the only company to have solutions in all those leader quadrants, which I believe shows their leading position in delivering true hybrid solutions. I should point out that there are many other Microsoft services in the Magic Quadrant for other services, but those mentioned here are the critical ones when thinking of leveraging Azure and integrating with on-premises. Azure is one of the leaders in the public cloud.

But what about feature x provided by service y? That's a common concern for customers just starting to evaluate services. You may have heard that a certain service has a specific feature that Azure does not. Frequently, you will be prompted to ask about that feature while evaluating Azure or another vendor. Consider the rate that new features are being introduced to Azure; if Azure is missing a feature that a competitor has, it's a safe bet that that feature is being worked on and will be coming to Azure in time. Many times when a feature is missing, it is because there are other ways to meet your needs. I suggest that you focus on your requirements and see if those requirements can be met with the capabilities available from the vendor. The second evaluation tool is the Hype Cycle, as shown in Figure 12.3.

FIGURE 12.3
Gartner
Methodologies and
Hype Cycle
Source: www.gartner
.com/technology/research/
methodologies/hype-cycle.jsp

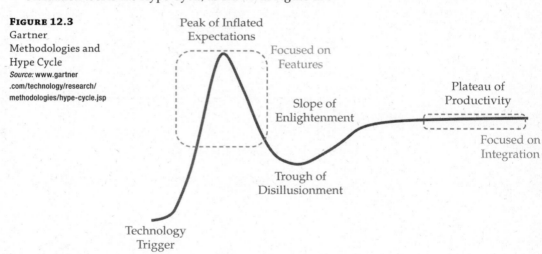

NOTE   Gartner does not endorse any vendor, product, or service depicted in its research publications, and does not advise technology users to select only those vendors with the highest ratings or other designation. Gartner research publications consist of the opinions of Gartner's research organization and should not be construed as statements of fact. Gartner disclaims all warranties, expressed or implied, with respect to this research, including any warranties of merchantability or fitness for a particular purpose.

What is interesting about the Hype Cycle is that, although in this case I am using it specifically to address adopting public cloud services, it applies to anything, including non-IT acquisition scenarios.

Initially, you obtain a technology, the technology trigger, and as you research and use that technology, you rapidly build excitement. It appears to solve all your problems. This is the peak of inflated expectations. Once you pass the peak, you start to find things it cannot do. Maybe it's slower than you thought. Maybe it only works with a subset of systems. Maybe a certain feature costs more than you thought. The excitement drops until you hit a low, the trough of disillusionment.

Once you have hit rock bottom, you grudgingly try to make the best of the technology and gradually discover what the technology can offer (the slope of enlightenment) and that, though it's not as great as those inflated expectations, it does provide benefits. You achieve the plateau of productivity where you get real value from the technology.

The reason I use this squiggle with the customers who are fixated on feature x and feature y is that, when a technology is initially being evaluated, the parties are in the "peak of inflated expectations" phase. They are focused on features because, at this point, they don't understand what technologies will work with other technologies, so they can only focus on individual features. For example, they are focused purely on features in the public cloud with no consideration of how it will integrate with other systems for a hybrid solution. The thinking is simply "best-of-breed," without any thought to integration with the rest of your environment. Once technologies reach the plateau of productivity, organizations care more about integration with their other technologies and the holistic solution rather than specific features.

Don't get me wrong—I want features. But don't make a decision today based on "a" feature. That feature will come, and looking at the history of innovation in things like Azure and even Hyper-V, it will come very soon. Focus on how the solution will integrate with your environment and your management. Hybrid is a key consideration that sets Azure apart.

Azure is a safe horse to bet on. Realistically it's one of the three main players that will be leaders in the IaaS public cloud. (The others are Amazon and Google.) There will be other providers of IaaS in the public cloud, but they will struggle to really compete against the big three, given the billions of dollars needed to be geographically available and commit to the scale required for hyperscale. In fiscal year 2015, Microsoft spent $4.5 billion on capital investment in datacenter build-out. Other providers will likely carve out niche markets. Some major providers have already exited the public cloud IaaS market because they cannot compete.

Remember what I said earlier in this chapter. If Azure does become self-aware and takes over, by being an early adopter, you will be treated well.

First Steps with Azure IaaS

The first steps to start leveraging Azure will vary based on the needs of each organization: its existing environment, its goals, and its knowledge of the cloud. In this section I want to call out some key considerations to think about as you start your Azure IaaS journey. These will help you to maximize efficiency and long-term manageability.

Plan how your organization will use Azure. Specific project details are not required, but you do need to think about what subscriptions you require, and if you have a Microsoft Enterprise Agreement (EA), you will need to decide who owns the agreement, who will be the enterprise administrator, and who will be account owners with the ability to create subscriptions. (This was discussed in Chapter 1, "The Cloud and Microsoft Azure 101.") It's important to get this right; it can be difficult to reorganize services later on. Implement your Azure model early on, or business units may start to buy their own Azure subscriptions or use MSDN subscriptions, which will be harder to consolidate later on.

Your on-premises datacenter likely has a naming standard, and your Azure resources should follow this naming standard, even if it means updating the standard to enable the correct identification of resources in Azure. Ideally, the naming standard should include location (which in Azure would be the region) along with a way to identify the project or business unit that owns the VM and use of the VM. If your Azure subscriptions are project or business unit specific, identifying the project in the name may not be required—although you should consider that including the project or business unit in the name does provide benefit when running reports that may be broader than just a specific subscription and can help identify where VMs are used.

Once you have an Azure subscription, the first thing you create should be a virtual network. Even if you have no plans to connect to your on-premises environment today—even if you will only have a single cloud service—create a virtual network and use an IP space that is unique that does not overlap with your on-premises environment. Additional virtual subnets can be added to that virtual network in the future should your needs change. The important point is to create the virtual network and create services on that virtual network. There is no harm in using the virtual network; it does not add any complexity. It safeguards your deployment if requirements change in the future. Consider whether you have a requirement to connect to on-premises, communicate with services in different cloud services, need custom DNS configuration, or need static IP addresses. These require your services to be on a virtual network. There are so many benefits to using a virtual network, and few if any negatives, so you should always use one. Trying to move existing services to a virtual network postcreation is difficult and very time consuming.

Connect the virtual network to your on-premises environment using the site-to-site VPN gateway or ExpressRoute. This will make Azure an extension of your datacenter and is the first step to enabling the hybrid cloud. Once the site-to-Azure connectivity is in place, configure the virtual network to use on-premises DNS servers. This will enable Azure resources to resolve on-premises names and join the on-premises Active Directory (AD) environment.

Decide on the type of storage replication and create storage accounts with the required redundancy configuration. Name the storage accounts with meaningful names, such as the region, type of redundancy, and their intended purpose. This will make it easy when creating services to quickly identify which storage account should be used. Remember that each storage account has a certain input/output operations per second (IOPS) limit based on its type. As services are deployed, ensure you do not deploy more VHDs to a storage account than can be supported by that storage account's IOPS limit, or performance will be impacted.

If Azure resources will integrate with the on-premises AD, consider deploying domain controllers (DCs) as VMs in Azure. Remember that Azure should be configured as a separate AD site, and be sure to define an AD site link between Azure and the location that has the connectivity to Azure. This will ensure efficient replication of AD content and also that AD clients will use the DC closest to them. DCs in Azure should use a reserved IP address, and once that is done, the DNS configuration of the virtual network is changed to point to the Azure DCs first, which ensures Azure clients will use Azure DCs for name resolution first.

Decide how VMs will be created in Azure for infrastructure purposes. Will Azure gallery images be used, or will your organization's customized image be uploaded to Azure for use? Ideally, you will not use the Azure portal for large-scale VM deployment. Instead, use a repeatable process, such as a provisioning engine, or maybe just a PowerShell script. This is necessary not just to simplify the deployment of resources, but also so that the VMs can be recreated when necessary. For example, in the event of an Azure disaster, VMs must be recreated using the replicated storage.

Deploy services to Azure using the virtual network and create storage accounts using the planned method and templates. Remember to remove unnecessary endpoints as services are deployed to limit their accessibility from the Internet. Most communication should be via the on-premises to Azure secure links. Add endpoints as services need to be available to the Internet, such as an endpoint for HTTP on port 80.

Ensure that Azure is part of your change control, disaster recovery, and other processes. It's important that the same procedures and checks be performed for services deployed to Azure as would apply to on-premises. Ensure that services deployed to Azure are managed. These services will require patching, backup, antimalware, and monitoring. The Azure fabric does not perform those actions on IaaS VMs.

Once core infrastructure services are available in Azure, if end users will be deploying to Azure, you need to enable a controlled process through a deployment service/service catalog that your users can use. Ideally, the end-user experience for deploying services to Azure should be the same as the experience for deploying to on-premises.

Take time to reevaluate how you deliver solutions. Initially, you will most likely move OS instances into Azure IaaS VMs, as this matches how the services were deployed on-premises. Remember that there are other types of services in Azure, such as Azure Web Site, Azure SQL Database, PaaS, and more, that require less maintenance than a traditional VM. Over time as your knowledge and experience in Azure grows, look to rearchitect how services are delivered and take advantage of the broader Azure service options. Move your websites from an Azure IaaS VM running IIS to Azure Web Sites, move the database from an Azure IaaS VM running SQL Server to Azure SQL Database—you get the idea.

Finally, stay current with the changes to Azure. New features are constantly being added, and it's important to be informed about these features. Evaluate how you could use them in your organization and determine whether a rearchitecture of a service is required to use the new capabilities. I recommend frequently reviewing the following resources to stay current:

- Azure blog: `http://azure.microsoft.com/blog/`

- IaaS Azure blog entries: `http://azure.microsoft.com/blog/tag/iaas/`

- Azure VM blog: `http://azure.microsoft.com/blog/topics/virtual-machines/`

- Azure storage team blog: `http://blogs.msdn.com/b/windowsazurestorage/`

- Channel 9 (videos and TechEd content, which will include Azure topics): `http://channel9.msdn.com/`

- Azure VM documentation: `http://azure.microsoft.com/en-us/documentation/services/virtual-machines/`

- Dear Azure: `www.dearazure.com`

- My blog (information about new videos I create and other resources): `www.savilltech.com/blog`

- The Master Azure Infrastructure application that accompanies this book. (In addition to updating the digital version of this book, I will update the app frequently with information on changes.)

I hope this book has put you on the right path to maximizing the benefits of Azure in your organization.

The Bottom Line

Address the common concerns related to using the public cloud specific to Azure.
A number of key concerns are shared among most organizations, and many of them are
based on someone gaining access to an organization's data. For each of the concerns there are
safeguards and processes in place in Azure to mitigate the risk and provide a safe, functional
environment for services.

Master It Why are no standing privileges so important?

Use encryption in Azure. Various levels of encryption can be used in Azure, including
application encryption, OS encryption, and third-party encryption. For Windows it is
possible to use BitLocker to protect data volumes, and with third-party solutions, the boot
volume can also be encrypted.

Master It Why is it important that the customer have the encryption keys and not the
cloud vendor?

Understand the first steps when adopting Azure. Follow the process outlined in the
last section of this chapter. Have a clear design for how accounts and subscriptions will be
deployed. Deploy a virtual network before deploying any service and then use an intuitive
naming scheme for resources. If desired, integrate Azure with the on-premises environment,
including Active Directory. Deploy storage accounts and resources in the most secure
manner and constantly reevaluate the architecture of services, especially as the capabilities of
Azure change.

Master It If you were to pick one way to stay current, what would it be?

Appendix

The Bottom Line

Each of The Bottom Line sections in the chapters suggest exercises to deepen skills and understanding. Sometimes there is only one possible solution, but often you are encouraged to use your skills and creativity to create something that builds on what you know and lets you explore one of many possible solutions.

Chapter 1: The Cloud and Microsoft Azure 101

Articulate the different types of "as-a-Service."   Three core types of service are offered within clouds. Infrastructure as a Service (IaaS) provides a virtual machine with all the underlying compute, network, and storage fabric provided by the service vendor. The customer has full control of the operating system and services running within the virtual machine. Platform as a Service (PaaS) provides an environment where applications can be deployed without the customer having to consider the management or maintenance of operating systems or middleware services. Applications may be required to follow certain guidelines to run in a PaaS environment. Finally, Software as a Service (SaaS) provides a complete solution that requires customers to perform only basic administration. Good examples of SaaS are services such as Office 365.

Master It   Why do many organizations initially use IaaS but ultimately move to PaaS and SaaS?

Solution   IaaS provides a virtual machine that allows the customer full manageability and flexibility, which is most like their on-premises environment and so provides the greatest level of familiarity. It also provides an environment where services can easily be moved to without modification, but at the expense of the customer having to perform all management (such as patching and backing up) within the VM. Ultimately, customers do not want to perform this type of management, and PaaS and SaaS provide great levels of capabilities without the ongoing management effort.

Identify key scenarios where the public cloud provides the most optimal service.   A key attribute of the public cloud is that customers pay only for what they consume. This means any type of scenario where the usage is not flat over time is a great fit for the public cloud; when there is a lull in activity, the customer can scale back the service and pay less. The public cloud can also be useful for start-ups that wish to avoid the initial outlay for hardware and software. Again, in the public cloud you pay only for what is needed.

Master It   How is the public cloud used in hybrid scenarios while still gaining the benefits of public cloud pay for consumption only?

Solution   It is very common in hybrid scenarios to run the "steady state" level of service on-premises and then, in the burst scenarios where additional capacity is required, leverage the public cloud. The example used earlier in this book would be the pizza chain that runs the normal ordering service website on-premises but, on Friday nights and for the Super Bowl, scales out to supplement using public cloud resources.

Understand how to get started consuming Microsoft Azure services.   For individuals who want to try Azure, the best way to gain access is to sign up for a free one-month trial. If you have an MSDN subscription, you can activate the Azure benefits for monthly Azure credits to be used for test and development purposes. For organizations wishing to leverage Azure for production purposes, numerous options exist, including Pay-as-You-Go via credit card or invoice, Open Licensing, or adding Azure services to your Enterprise Agreement. A key point is to have a clear project that you wish to implement in Azure that will help you start leveraging Azure quickly.

Master It   How can I avoid going over my MSDN monthly quota each month?

Solution   By default, a spending limit is enabled on the MSDN Azure subscription, which stops services automatically once the MSDN included Azure quota is reached to avoid any charges being incurred. This spending limit can be removed with the understanding you will incur charges.

Chapter 2: When to Use IaaS: Cost and Options

Understand all the cost elements related to hosting services.   When trying to compare costs between on-premises and the public cloud, it's easy to consider only the price of the VM in the public cloud, the cost of a license, and some server space on-premises. But the real costs are completely different; you need to factor in the entire datacenter, power, cooling, and labor. Take time to look at all the aspects to perform a true cost comparison.

Master It   Why does the amount a service that is used heavily change when comparing on-premises to Azure?

Solution   In Azure, you only pay for a service while it is running. This means if you have a service that has to run only for a limited time, it will be more cost efficient to run in the public cloud than to make the resources permanently available on-premises.

Identify workloads that can run in Azure IaaS.   Azure IaaS VMs can cater to a large number of workloads. The most successful are based on the capability profiles that, when exposed, are focused on VM series and sizes, network speeds, types of traffic, storage size, and performance. If your workload fits within the Azure capabilities, uses an Azure-supported OS, and runs an application that is supported by the vendor for Azure, then it can be evaluated more closely as a potential workload to run in Azure.

Master It   What operating systems are supported in Azure?

Solution   Although Azure is built on Hyper-V (which supports both 32-bit and 64-bit operating systems), Azure only supports 64-bit operating systems. For Windows, this is specifically Windows 2008 R2 SP1 and above.

Describe how Microsoft Azure infrastructure provides services.   Azure consists of geographically distributed regions. Each region contains one or more datacenters. Within the datacenters are multiple Azure scale-units, or stamps, which consist of about 1,000 servers that are split among multiple racks. A central Red Dog Front End accepts service requests and distributes to fabric controllers running in each stamp for the actual deployment and life-cycle management.

Master It Do all Azure regions provide the same Azure services?

Solution No. While the core Azure services are available in most regions, not every service is offered from every Azure region. Instead, the focus is on making services available throughout the major markets, which may mean a service is offered from one region in each geography. Additionally, as new services are rolled out, this does not typically happen instantly in all regions but rather is staged over a period of time.

Chapter 3: Customizing VM Storage

Understand the types of storage exposed to a virtual machine. By default, an IaaS VM will have a C: drive containing the operating system, which is 127 GB in size, and a D: drive, whose size will vary based on the VM size. By default for Windows VMs, the D: drive contains the paging file. The C: drive is stored on the durable, persistent Azure Storage service. The D: drive is stored on disks local to the host and should be considered nonpersistent. Any operation that results in the VM being moved to another host—which could include maintenance, resizing of VMs, or failures—will result in loss of the D: drive content. Additionally, data drives can be added to a VM; they are also stored on Azure Storage, which means their content is durable and persistent even in the event of failures.

Master It Why should data that you care about not be stored on the D: drive?

Solution The D: drive uses local storage on the host and should be considered nonpersistent. Only use the D: drive for scratch purposes and for application data that is considered temporary. A good example is storing the SQL Server TempDB on the D: drive.

Know when to use Azure Files. Azure Files enables Azure Storage to be accessed via the SMB protocol. Any scenario that needs a shared or central storage location is a good candidate for leveraging Azure Files, which includes centralized storage of data, configuration, logs, and performance information.

Master It What version of SMB is supported by Azure Files?

Solution As of this writing, Azure Files supports SMB 2.1. Refer to the Azure website for updates on Azure Files SMB protocol-level support.

Understand how StorSimple uses Azure Storage. StorSimple is an on-premises storage appliance that supports different tiers of storage based on its internal SSD and HDD storage. StorSimple can use Azure Storage as an infinite cloud tier. The least used data is moved to Azure Storage, but thumbprints are maintained on-premises. To the users connecting via iSCSI, the data appears to still be stored locally. In the event data that has been moved to Azure is accessed, it is pulled down from Azure at a block level. Additionally, all data on the StorSimple appliance is saved to Azure to provide protection in the event of a StorSimple appliance failure or loss. The StorSimple 8000 series tightly integrates with Azure for management and access to the data. In the event of a disaster, a virtual StorSimple appliance, which essentially is an Azure VM, runs the StorSimple software and can access the data stored in Azure through the shared encryption key.

Master It   What are good use cases for StorSimple?

Solution   Because StorSimple provides "infinite" storage by moving the least used data to Azure, the best use cases are those where large amounts of data need to be retained but only a portion is frequently used, the "working set." Therefore, any type of file server or archive is a perfect workload for StorSimple. Additionally, because all data on StorSimple is also saved to Azure, it provides a good option for workloads that need to be protected to the public cloud—provided that workload fits within the IO capabilities of StorSimple. StorSimple is not designed to be a backup target because of the nature of how data is saved to Azure once the StorSimple reaches a certain threshold of utilization, which would mean any future data written would need to be written directly to Azure, which would result in poor backup performance.

Chapter 4: Enabling External Connectivity

Understand how communication to services running in a VM from the Internet works.   VMs are housed in a cloud service, and that cloud service has an Internet-addressable IP, the virtual IP (VIP). Endpoints map ports on the VIP to ports on specific VMs. This enables inbound communication from the Internet to be sent to specific VMs, thereby offering services out to the Internet.

Master It   Can a VM have its own Internet-addressable IP to accept all traffic sent to it?

Solution   Instance-level public IP addresses can be assigned to VMs, which results in all traffic sent to the IP address being sent to the VM. It is important to have adequate security on the VM to provide protection when using an instance-level IP.

Use load-balancing capabilities.   You can create a load-balanced set, which consists of one or more members that will have traffic sent to them based on the distribution mode configured. A probe is configured to enable the load-balancer component to detect whether a member is not responding and therefore is not eligible to receive traffic. An internal load balancer works in a similar fashion but does not use the cloud service VIP. Rather, it has its own internal IP address and enables load balancing within a cloud service or virtual network.

Master It   What are the available distribution modes for a load-balanced set?

Solution   By default, a load distribution set uses 5 tuples: source IP, source port, destination IP, destination port, and protocol. Alternatively, 2 tuple (source IP and destination IP) or 3 tuple (source IP, destination IP, and protocol) can be used.

Differentiate between a stopped and a deprovisioned VM.   A stopped VM is one that, while not running, is still provisioned on the Azure compute fabric. It is deployed to a cluster and has resources reserved for it. A stopped VM still incurs cost, the same as if it were running. It also maintains items such as the VM's DIPs. A deprovisioned VM is not deployed to the Azure fabric. No costs are incurred, other than the storage cost for its virtual hard disks. When a deprovisioned VM is restarted, it is provisioned to the Azure fabric and gets new resources, including a new virtual NIC and a new DIP.

Master It   Is there any way to help automatically deprovision and then restart at different times of the day?

Solution   Use Azure Automation, which will be explored in Chapter 11. Azure Automation enables the execution of PowerShell workflows (runbooks) in Azure. This means that a runbook could be created to deprovision and restart VMs at different times of day.

Chapter 5: Using Virtual Networks

Articulate virtual network and virtual subnet basic concepts.   A virtual network is an administrator-defined IP space that is divided into virtual subnets. Virtual machines are joined to virtual networks at time of creation, and their IP addresses will be allocated from the virtual subnet specified in the provisioning configuration. All VMs in a cloud service must be part of the same virtual network.

Master It   Why must the IP space used in the virtual network not conflict with the space used on-premises?

Solution   To enable connectivity and eventual communication between Azure and on-premises networks, there must be no overlap in IP address space. If an overlap exists, it is not possible for traffic to correctly route between Azure and on-premises locations.

Use multi-NIC VMs.   Azure enables certain VMs to be configured with multiple virtual network adapters. Each network adapter must be connected to a different virtual subnet within the same virtual network. Additional network adapters can be configured only during the creation of a virtual machine.

Master It   What VMs can use multiple NICs?

Solution   As of this writing, the number of network adapters depends on the size of the VM. A3, A6, A9, and D3 VMs support up to two network adapters, whereas A4, A7, D4, and D13 support up to four network adapters.

Chapter 6: Enabling On-Premises Connectivity

Explain the connectivity enabled with a site-to-site VPN.   An S2S VPN connects a virtual network to another network, which could be an on-premises location or another virtual network. Once connected, Layer 3 routing is provided between the networks. When a virtual network is connected to on-premises resources via the S2S VPN, Azure essentially becomes an extension of your datacenter.

Master It   What is the difference between a standard S2S gateway and a high-performance gateway?

Solution   There are two key differences. First, the expected speed for the standard S2S VPN is around 80 Mbps, which contrasts with 200 Mbps for the high-performance gateway. Second, the standard VPN gateway supports 10 connections, whereas the high-performance supports 30.

Understand the key benefits of Azure ExpressRoute over standard site-to-site VPNs.   Although an Azure S2S VPN provides IP connectivity between an on-premises location and Azure, it operates over the public Internet and uses CPU-heavy cryptography to ensure security. These factors result in high latencies, limited maximum speeds, and no dedicated path. ExpressRoute operates over dedicated connections that result in low single-digit latencies and higher speeds. ExpressRoute also provides connectivity to other Azure services, not just VMs in a virtual network. When deciding between S2S VPN and ExpressRoute, you should take time to fully understand the requirements, how workloads between Azure and on-premises will interact, and the tolerance of each workload to latency.

Master It   What is the difference between using a Network Service Provider and an Exchange Provider?

Solution   An Exchange Provider works by hosting the customer's servers in the Exchange Providers location or by having a dedicated fiber connection from the customer's location to the Exchange Provider. The Exchange Provider then has connectivity to Azure, and the virtual circuit is modified to connect the customer to their Azure resources. A Network Service Provider works by extending the customer's MPLS into their Azure resources. Higher speeds are available using an Exchange Provider, whereas a Network Service Provider typically provides easier onboarding. Network Service Providers include unlimited egress data; a limited amount of egress is included with Exchange Providers—additional egress incurs charges.

Chapter 7: Extending AD to Azure and Azure AD

Build an Active Directory architecture that integrates with Azure resources.   For Azure resources to integrate with Active Directory, it is necessary for the resources using AD to be able to resolve AD DNS records and communicate via a number of ports to domain controllers. Virtual networks can be configured to use specific DNS servers. For VMs in the virtual network, that is configured via DHCP. Also, you can place domain controllers in Azure to enable local connectivity to domain controllers.

Master It   Why is it important to define a separate AD site for Azure and a site link?

Solution   Many services—and Active Directory itself—use AD sites to understand where services are physically located. Site links are used to identify the locations that have connectivity and the speed of that connectivity. By correctly defining sites and site links for Azure locations, the AD replication topology will be optimal, and services will use the closest domain controllers.

Understand the difference between Active Directory Domain Services and Azure AD.   Active Directory provides a rich directory service set of capabilities with an X.500-based hierarchical structure. AD can be communicated with using protocols such as LDAP and primarily uses Kerberos for authentication. It allows machines to be joined to the directory and can enable rich policy deployment. Azure AD is primarily an identity system aimed at enabling identity across cloud-based systems. Therefore, it uses protocols designed for the Internet over HTTP and HTTPS. Azure AD's number-one feature is its ability to enable SSO for thousands of applications for an organization's users. Other key features include multifactor authentication and reporting.

Master It   How does on-premises Active Directory link to Azure AD?

Solution   To populate Azure AD with identities from Active Directory, Azure AD Connect is used to create the synchronization connection. This enables the initial population of Azure AD, along with ongoing synchronization for changes, to source in either the Active Directory or Azure AD. Federation between Active Directory and Azure AD can be established. This enables authentications to Azure AD to be performed by on-premises Active Directory domain controllers. Federation is not required. As an alternative, you can synchronize a hash of the hashed account passwords. An end user then uses the same password in AD and in Azure AD, thus enabling a single sign-on experience.

Chapter 8: Setting Up Replication, Backup, and Disaster Recovery

Plan your disaster recovery strategy.   Discovery of the environment, understanding how businesses use systems, ascertaining the dependencies between systems, planning how the DR plan will be activated, drawing up communications plans, and so on are all critical. However, the single most important part of DR planning is to have a good test routine. The number-one cause of DR failover problems is because organizations never tested the failover process. They only discover in the event of an actual failure that some replication was not working or that a dependent system had been missed. Create a good testing routine to ensure your DR plan works, but ensure the test does not impact or interfere with the ongoing production systems.

Master It   Why is it important that DR be part of the change control plan of an organization?

Solution   No IT system stays the same. New systems are added and capabilities change. As any modification to the IT department is implemented, it should go through a change control process. This is the perfect point at which to assess whether the change impacts the DR process. If it does, now is the time to determine what is needed to ensure it is protected.

Understand the sources that can be protected with Azure Site Recovery.   Azure Site Recovery uses a number of channels to provide protection. This includes Hyper-V Replica for Hyper-V to Hyper-V on-premises and Hyper-V to Azure. Another channel uses InMage Scout, which provides protection from VMware to VMware on-premises, VMware to Azure, physical to Azure, and more. SQL Server AlwaysOn is also integrated and allows ASR to manage SQL Server failover, as is SAN management through SMI-S integration via SCVMM. Finally, ASR also integrates with Azure Automation and enables any action possible through PowerShell workflows to be part of a recovery plan.

Master It   Why is it recommended that you map networks between on-premises and Azure?

Solution   The IP space used on-premises will be different from that used in Azure virtual networks. By mapping the logical networks defined in SCVMM to virtual networks defined in Azure, you ensure that VMs in Azure can automatically be assigned IP addresses from the correct corresponding network without requiring any action from you.

Chapter 9: Customizing Azure Templates and PowerShell Management

Understand why you should use availability sets. Availability sets are used to ensure that multiple instances of a service—for example, IIS servers—are distributed over two fault domains (server racks). This achieves two things. If there is a hardware failure in a rack, not all instances of a service will be affected. The service remains operational. As an added bonus, when Microsoft performs maintenance, it will only perform maintenance on one of the fault domains at a time. Once again, this ensures that some instances of the service will stay available.

Master It Why should workloads never be mixed in an availability set?

Solution An availability set only guarantees workloads will be split over two fault domains. If workloads are mixed—for example, IIS and SQL services placed in the same availability set—then it is quite possible all of the IIS servers would be placed on one fault domain and all the SQL servers placed on the other fault domain. This means that during a failure or routine maintenance, all instances of one of the services would be unavailable. Create separate availability sets for each workload to ensure that the instances specific for each workload are distributed between fault domains.

Enable PowerShell management of Azure. The Azure PowerShell cmdlets can be downloaded here:

```
http://azure.microsoft.com/en-us/documentation/articles/install-configure-
powershell/
```

They are installed using the Microsoft Web Platform Installer. Once the Web Platform Installer is installed, the module can be installed using the `Install-Module Azure` command.

Master It Why is it necessary to frequently check for new versions of the Azure PowerShell modules?

Solution Azure is constantly updated with the new capabilities, and these are quickly enabled through PowerShell. I recommend that you check for new versions of the Azure cmdlets monthly. You can check the current version of the module installed on your systems by using the `(Get-Module Azure).Version` cmdlet.

Chapter 10: Managing Hybrid Environments with System Center

Understand why leveraging the Azure portal directly for users has limitations. Although the Azure portal exposes many capabilities of Azure, it lacks customizable workflows for provisioning, such as authorization stages, and does not integrate with other on-premises systems. Another major challenge comes into play when considering disaster recovery in the event of an Azure region fail and the need to reprovision services that use replicated storage accounts. To enable these capabilities, you must leverage another method of provisioning that can be used across services.

Master It   What is a major limitation of using App Controller today?

Solution   There are a number of limitations with App Controller. It is Silverlight based, which limits its compatibility with certain browsers and platforms. It also has very basic provisioning capabilities. The major limitation many organizations face is that App Controller does not support the RBAC capabilities of the Azure Resource Manager, which minimizes its usability.

Explain the core components of System Center to deliver a private cloud.   The most critical component is Virtual Machine Manager, which provides the compute, storage, and network fabric management capabilities and also allows the definition of clouds that can be assigned to tenants. App Controller provides a web-based interface that allows end users to interact with those defined clouds. Other components that are not required but that add functionality are SCOM, which can monitor the utilization of resources and the fabric health to enable actions to be triggered; DPM, for protecting workloads; and Service Manager and Orchestrator, which provide customized provisioning and other services.

Master It   Which hypervisors does SCVMM support?

Solution   SCVMM supports Hyper-V, ESX, and XenServer in the 2012 R2 version of System Center.

Identify the value proposition for Windows Azure Pack.   Windows Azure Pack provides an open platform into which resource providers are integrated. This enables access to almost any type of service as long as a resource provider is available. Microsoft offers resource providers for certain types of service, such as IaaS, websites, and more. Third parties provide resource providers for other scenarios, such as Service Manager integration, ESX integration, and even Azure. Windows Azure Pack brings the Azure experience to your on-premises environment and can also be used by hosting organizations to help provide their own services to customers.

Master It   Which hypervisors are natively supported when providing IaaS using Orchestrator SPF and SCVMM?

Solution   Only Hyper-V is supported natively. To use other hypervisors, third-party resource providers would need to be leveraged.

Chapter 11: Completing Your Azure Environment

Execute PowerShell Workflows in Azure.   Every aspect of Azure (and almost any other system) can be managed with PowerShell. PowerShell workflows provide a method for running scripts. Azure Automation provides a service through which PowerShell workflows can be executed. Both certificate- and credential-based authentication is possible within Azure Automation runbooks.

Master It   Why are PowerShell workflows a better fit for long-running scripts than regular PowerShell scripts?

Solution   In a regular PowerShell script, the onus is on the script developer to ensure that the script handles being restarted in the event of a failure mid-execution. The developer is responsible for handling the error and checking if actions have been performed. PowerShell workflows enable checkpoints to be implemented. Checkpoints store the current state of the environment and can be resumed in the event of a failure. This burden is removed from the script developer.

Use Azure to deliver desktop applications to users.   Azure RemoteApp provides a simple means of using RDP to publish applications to users who have the Azure RemoteApp client installed. Microsoft provides standard images that include the Office suite. Custom images containing the applications you wish to publish also can be used.

Master It   How is Azure RemoteApp licensed?

Solution   Basic and Standard licenses are available. Basic is designed for users who will run their own line-of-business applications only, and the Standard license is for users who need access to productivity applications such as Office. The license cost includes the rights to use Office.

Publish internal applications to clients on the Internet.   Azure AD Application Proxy enables the reverse proxy publication of applications that are hosted on-premises to the Internet via the Azure service. Authentication is performed using Azure AD. Single sign-on and preauthentication are enabled.

Master It   How does communication from the Internet through Azure AD Application Proxy to on-premises resources work?

Solution   An Azure AD Application Proxy Connector is deployed to one or more Windows Server 2012 R2 (or Windows 8.1) machines on the internal network. These machines securely communicate to the Azure AD Application Proxy service. Requests from the Internet terminate at the Azure AD Application Proxy service. The proxy service then communicates to on-premises resources via the connector that runs on-premises and passes responses back to the requesting Internet client.

Chapter 12: What to Do Next

Address the common concerns related to using the public cloud specific to Azure.   A number of key concerns are shared among most organizations, and many of them are based on someone gaining access to an organization's data. For each of the concerns there are safeguards and processes in place in Azure to mitigate the risk and provide a safe, functional environment for services.

Master It   Why are no standing privileges so important?

Solution   In a typical system, an administrator has a certain set of permanent permissions that make it hard to truly secure environments. With a no standing privilege environment, no one has administrator privileges, and privileges are granted as required to perform actions in a granular fashion. Minimum privileges and access required to perform actions are enabled for a limited amount of time. This helps to provide protection for resources and avoids accidental damage by service staff with high privileges.

Use encryption in Azure.   Various levels of encryption can be used in Azure, including application encryption, OS encryption, and third-party encryption. For Windows it is possible to use BitLocker to protect data volumes, and with third-party solutions, the boot volume can also be encrypted.

Master It   Why is it important that the customer have the encryption keys and not the cloud vendor?

Solution   You need to trust your cloud vendor, but where possible, only your organization should be able to access your data. This maximizes your security and also provides protection for your data in the event your cloud provider is compelled to hand over your data to an external party. If your data is encrypted and the cloud provider does not have the key, the provider would be able to share only the encrypted form of your data. The Azure Key Vault provides a secure location for key storage that is accessible only to you.

Understand the first steps when adopting Azure.   Follow the process outlined in the last section of this chapter. Have a clear design for how accounts and subscriptions will be deployed. Deploy a virtual network before deploying any service and then use an intuitive naming scheme for resources. If desired, integrate Azure with the on-premises environment, including Active Directory. Deploy storage accounts and resources in the most secure manner and constantly reevaluate the architecture of services, especially as the capabilities of Azure change.

Master It   If you were to pick one way to stay current, what would it be?

Solution   Ensure you have downloaded the companion application for this book, which I will keep updated along with the digital version of this book.

Index

Note to the Reader: Throughout this index **boldfaced** page numbers indicate primary discussions of a topic. *Italicized* page numbers indicate illustrations.